HERBERT BAKER

ARCHITECTURE AND IDEALISM
1892 – 1913
THE SOUTH AFRICAN YEARS

MICHAEL KEATH

ASHANTI
PUBLISHING LIMITED
GIBRALTAR
A DIVISION OF ASHANTI INTERNATIONAL FILMS

Published by Ashanti Publishing Limited, Gibraltar,
a division of Ashanti International Films Limited,
Suite C, Regal House, Queensway, Gibraltar.

ISBN 1874800 37 5

Book and Cover Design: Nicholas W Combrinck
Cover Photograph: Peter van Niekerk Photography (Pty) Ltd
Cover: The Penrose Press
Typesetting and Reproduction: RT·Sparhams
Printed and bound by CTP Book Printers, Cape Town

First edition © Michael Keath
Index © Naomi Musiker
Additional photographs © Peter van Niekerk, AIP Hon FIP

TO MY FATHER AND THE

MEMORY OF MY MOTHER

Charles H Thompson's portrait of Sir Herbert Baker.

CONTENTS

Union Buildings, Pretoria, construction scaffolding on dome.

PREFACE

This book has a dual origin. It is based partly on a series of lectures and articles I prepared in 1987-9 on aspects of Baker's work. Other parts of it go back to my research in England prior to 1985, when I began seriously to gather material for a large book on Baker which would embrace his complete life and works, worldwide. The task set, and to which I have most willingly subscribed, was to write a much shorter book which dealt only with Baker's South African architecture. I have however, also included, by way of an epilogue, some brief discussion on those buildings of his in other countries which, in an artistic and in an emotional sense, have a particular South African interest. Such buildings include South Africa House, London; Rhodes House, Oxford and the Delville Wood Memorial in France.

But perhaps this book has a deeper origin, more remote in time, than these researches. Since my childhood I have had a fascination for Herbert Baker's architecture and his career, split as it was between England and South Africa. In this sense only has there been any similarity between Baker's life and my own. It is, nevertheless, something which at moments has led me to believe I might have some special insights into his unique experience. My curiosity has been sustained ever since reading the prospectus for the Natal school I was shortly to be sent to. With dreamy anticipation I viewed pictures of the most beautiful school I had ever seen, and first saw the name of Sir Herbert Baker.

Returning to England, no matter where I lived I always seemed to be in close proximity to some Baker building; sometimes just a village War Memorial Cross, sometimes a major English work of his. I seem to have been pursued, if not haunted, by his presence all my life. It was a great disappointment to discover much later that only the school chapel,

alas now largely destroyed, was his! Despite persistent claims to the contrary, all else was either there before he came on the scene or was the much later work of his successors. For me, this revelation stands as a paradigm for the central problem in all Herbert Baker studies: attribution, a subject I shall return to frequently.

It was in South Africa, between his thirtieth and fifty-first years, that Herbert Baker made himself master of his profession and learned to organize a vast practice, operating eventually from offices in Cape Town, Johannesburg and Bloemfontein. It was in this country that he produced not just his own finest work but a distinctive style, emulated by many, which has left its mark on almost every town in southern Africa, and in many further north. When Baker left South Africa in 1913 to join Sir Edwin Lutyens at New Delhi he left behind partnerships which bore his name until they were finally dissolved in the 1920s. During those years, when he was London based, a great number of buildings were erected by his remaining partners in the style which he earlier had evolved with them. Though most of these show his influence they could not have been by his own hand. These 'Baker' buildings have caused, and no doubt will continue to cause, widespread confusion as to the question of attribution.

Equally difficult to unravel is Baker's architectural philosophy, the motives and objectives which stand behind his ever evolving approach to design. Baker was no theorist. He left little record of what he thought about the majority of his buildings, so we have to deduce much of his intentions from the works themselves. In the few writings of a philosophical nature he did leave us, he tends to rationalize his eclecticism rather than to speculate or pioneer. But then that was more characteristic of his times. At best his ideas concerned the adaptation of European precedents to climatic and topographical environment and to national sentiment; at worst they were stoically defensive of historicist and imperialistic quirks. It is hard to think that Baker was a near contemporary of the great modernist pioneer, Frank Lloyd Wright (1867-1959), and yet it seems unfair to expect him to have espoused modernism simply for that reason.

Most South African readers will readily identify the source of some of his architecture as being Cape Dutch, the colonial vernacular style he fell in love with on his arrival in 1892. In other buildings the English Arts and Crafts movement will be evident. But, his work as a whole, and in particular the Cape architecture, may perhaps more accurately be seen as a regional variant of the Queen Anne movement. As Mark Girouard has observed, 'Queen Anne' has comparatively little to do with Queen Anne: 'It was the nickname applied to a style which became enormously popular in the 1870s and survived into the early years of this century.' The style rejoiced in 'red brick and white-painted sash windows, with curly pedimented gables and delicate brick panels of sunflowers, swags, or cherubs, with small window panes, steep roofs, and curving bay windows, with wooden balconies and fancy little oriels jutting out where one would least expect them...a little Dutch, a little Flemish, a squeeze of Robert Adam, a generous dash of Wren...a mixture that had a strong character of its own...'[1] This description closely matches Baker's architecture in most of its aspects.

It should be borne in mind that he practised at a time when the 'battle of the styles' had already been waged and younger architects were exploiting both the classical and Gothic traditions in an attempt to create a new manner of architecture appropriate to the times and to a building's place and function. And it is this aspect that underscores the unique quality of his work. An attribute which was well beyond mere stylistic invention pervades Herbert Baker's architecture: a sense of rightness, of appropriateness to climate, materials and, above all, to the expression of high ideals. First, at the Cape, it was Rhodes's Empire idealism that inspired him. Later, in the hinterland, it was the Imperial ideals of Lord Milner in the aftermath of the South African War, that gave him a sense of destiny shared by few architects in history.

Both statesmen saw that architecture could help them attain their political ideals, and both put their faith in Baker as the architect who could give substance to those ideals. That he should be responsible for the two most significant Imperial buildings of his time, the Union Buildings in Pretoria and, with Sir Edwin Lutyens, the government buildings at New Delhi, seems entirely appropriate. But these prestigious commissions were the result of years of idealistic development and a working towards the destiny which he had no way of knowing was to be his. Baker's idealism spread to everything he did, whether it was Empire building or the proper training of craftsmen to meet his own exacting requirements. It was the hallmark of his character and his art.

If Baker's personal contribution to the design of his buildings is sometimes hard to pinpoint, his personality and private life are even more obscure. Anecdotes and reminiscences abound but documentary evidence is scant. I have found Baker's personality elusive and his private life almost impenetrable; and a full biographical picture of Baker, the man, almost impossible to depict from available documentary sources. Compared with the masses of material available on his work, the amount concerning his private life is disproportionately small. Considering that he is considered by many to be the most important architect in South African history, a man who was something of a world figure, and considering that he belongs to comparatively recent history, it is strange that so little has come to light.

As Herbert Baker was a very plain speaking and direct man, I have tried to make my account of him as an architect match his character. Wherever possible I have allowed him to speak for himself. Throughout I have tried to set him in the context of the political stage of his time, which he was able to view so closely through his friendship with so many of the players. In 1925 Professor Pearse of the University of the Witwatersrand was contemplating writing a book on Baker, a book which unfortunately never came to fruition. In reply to a letter from Pearse concerning his proposal, Baker himself said he would like to see it written 'with a political thread binding it together. First the Rhodes revival and then the Milner...reconstruction and homebuilding – and then the Union.'[2] I have followed this advice, but the political history of his times is beyond my competence and must be read elsewhere; I have given it only the most cursory of treatment, recording no more than the milestones.

And so, I hope, a composite picture, although much of it in shadow, does emerge. It is not always an attractive one. In his business dealings Herbert

Baker was shrewd, at times bordering on the ruth-less. When he set out to get work he would elbow out the opposition, sometimes in ways which now-adays might seem unacceptable by our codes of professionalism. Having secured a foothold he was relentless in getting his own way – aesthetically, economically and professionally. He would leave his imprint on everything he touched. Restoration, as we know it today, was rarely his objective; he would wish to improve on what had been there before, and in so doing make it his own.

And yet Dougal Malcolm, a member of Milner's Kindergarten, the nickname given to the group of gifted young men brought out to set up a new post-war administration in the Transvaal, said he was 'the gentlest, kindest, and most modest of men.'[3] In a memoir to Pearse, Franklin Kendall described his senior partner as 'tactful and thoughtful for others – at all events in all important matters.' But, adds Kendall, he did not worry himself much about appearances, generally speaking, and was 'careless in the matter of dress.'[4]

Baker was likely to be less straight-laced in the company he preferred most. According to Kendall, Baker's friends were always drawn from the 'intel-lectuals' and he never had time for 'gossip or small talk, or the side of life which merely concerns itself with amusements, sheeplike orthodoxy, or slack-ness.'[5] Baker himself admitted that he was never a good mixer, preferring the company of a few cul-tured individuals.[6] His interests naturally embraced architecture and the allied arts, but 'while certain branches of literature and poetry – including clas-sic and Shakespearean drama' attracted him, 'mod-ern drama, flippant plays or literature, or even music' did not.[7] The latter remark is confirmed by Vernon Rees-Poole's story of his falling asleep at concerts he was compelled to attend for social reasons in Cape Town.[8]

Edwin Lutyens, Baker's friend from their days with Ernest George and Harold Peto in London, found him 'beneath his reserved and serious man-ner, prone to be moody and introspective, and pos-sessing little sense of humour.' In his celebrated biography of Lutyens, Christopher Hussey quotes his saying in a letter to Baker: '...directly you intro-spect you may be sure you are wrong, – morally.' And again: '...if want of faith is shown, – convinced faith in the eventual success of the attempt, then a battle may be counted half lost, as you begin by run-ning away.' Lutyens added: 'This is not meant to be ungracious or in any way critical of your really wonderful broadminded and gentle character which I appreciate so very greatly...'[9] But, 'I never know which are your grumpy letters and which are not! Your language is never bleached with pas-sion!'[10]

It does seem there was a certain austerity about his dealings with his underlings and associates. Vernon Rees-Poole's anecdote illustrates this mar-vellously: 'I was called into HB's private room, as he required some alteration to a drawing. Above his desk he kept a small antique pot that had a circular top, in which he placed rubbers that had worn to the size of marbles. Whilst he was explaining, still keeping his eye on the drawing, he put his hand into this pot and grasped a rubber; having secured the rubber he was not able to withdraw his hand. Not thinking, I immediately informed him, "that's the way they catch monkeys!" There was perfect silence for a moment or two. He then said, in his quiet way, "It is not usual for a pupil to pass a witti-cism with his Chief." I think he was inwardly amused at my cheek.'[11] Kendall was probably right when he said Baker had 'quite a fine sense of humour, but preferred to keep it rather in subjec-tion.'[12]

Sir Charles Wheeler remembered Baker and Mon-tague Rendall, headmaster of Winchester College, 'meeting first when they were over fifty-six, seemed to enjoy a second boyhood together. One day when they were eighty...they linked arms and did a two-step on my studio floor while they chanted "We are the octogints".'[13] Other than his relations with the members of the Kindergarten there is little record of Baker's social life in South Africa, particularly where female company is concerned. Indeed Ken-dall declared him to have been 'a martyr to his pro-fession; his work was never ending. If he slept for seven hours out of twenty-four, it was that the remaining seventeen might be the more profitably spent in the most strenuous application to some branch of his art. He set himself to save every min-ute he possibly could, so that on a long railway journey, for instance, he would be well provided with books and writing materials, and would be almost as busily occupied as when in his office.' Kendall regarded it as delightfully characteristic that a letter from England should have the posts-cript: 'Excuse scribble, I'm being massaged as I write!'[14]

Baker was a natural athlete. He was tall and had a fine physique. From the schoolboy cricketer and footballer to the mature horseman who, after the age of fifty, ran three miles each morning to the site at New Delhi, he had extraordinary physical and mental stamina.[15] 'But', concluded Kendall, 'his rigid determination to place his work before everything else induced him to throw over anything that could be regarded as a mere pastime – anything that encroached upon his sacred mission. For purely health reasons he permitted himself early morning rides, and even these he often combined with visits to buildings. He contrived to distribute his attentions over a wide field, and trained himself to absorb the very essence of each problem that presented itself, with the minimum expenditure of time.'[16]

So little has come to light about Baker's relationships with women that inevitably questions are raised about his sexuality that few would have dared to pose in his own day. In our more inquisitive, sensation-seeking times, when solitary lives are examined, innuendo frequently takes the place of real evidence, as is the case with Cecil Rhodes's suggested homosexuality. Even to raise the subject is, in a way, to invite doubts. Certainly Baker was not known for his fondness of female company; but, equally certain, his closer friends were not limited to single men, whatever their proclivities may have been. Baker did marry, perhaps late in life by our standards but not excessively so by those of his own time.

A word about method. My concern has been to trace Baker's artistic and professional development, year by year, during his twenty-one years in South Africa. It follows that establishing the order in which his buildings were completed is of lesser importance than the sequence of their conception. In the main I have tried to follow a chronological or narrative approach, rather than to discuss the works thematically. Inevitably this means that buildings which had long gestation periods make their appearances and reappearances according to the stage they had reached during the years under discussion. Some, such as St George's Cathedral, took many years to reach completion. The year in which the Cathedral was conceived was 1897; the year in which it began to enter the public imagination was 1906. Between these dates Baker had not only acquired new partners and considerably more experience, but had moved from Cape Town to Johannesburg. The circumstances of his most important commissions, the ambient influences of style, topography and climate, which play such a vital role in Baker's architectural design, are discussed in the narrative.

Inevitably this book will be compared with the late Dr Doreen Greig's *Herbert Baker in South Africa*, published in 1970. Her pioneering work will stand as a most valuable contribution to Baker literature, owing to her fine descriptions and analysis, and her more widely drawn contexts. To draw attention to its few errors and omissions would seem churlish, for without her path-finding work my own would be immeasurably poorer. I have had the benefit of much new research and access to documents which she did not have.

I have incurred many debts in the preparation of this book. My gratitude and thanks are due to such a large number of people that it seems invidious to single out but a few. I owe my greatest debt to Mrs Jo Walker of the Human Sciences Research Council, for providing me with endless pieces of information about Baker and his associates, and for listening to me talk about Baker, equally endlessly. I have profited from discussions with Mira Kamstra-Fassler and Marcus Holmes. For their generosity and helpfulness I am indebted to the Education Committee of the Transvaal Institute of Architects for funding and arranging the lecture tour of South African Universities and Provincial Institutes in 1987.

I must record my gratitude to all the owners, public and private, both in England and South Africa, who welcomed me into their houses and other buildings and gave me free access to their knowledge and their papers. I am immeasurably indebted to all the librarians and archivists who patiently dealt with my enquiries, especially the exemplary Leonie Twentyman-Jones and her staff at the Jagger Library, University of Cape Town, and the staff of The Strange Collection of the Africana Library, Johannesburg Public Library. To the staff of the British Architectural Library at the Royal Institute of British Architects, London, I owe a similar debt.

I also thank the numerous private individuals who gave me their time and special knowledge; to Michael Munnik for showing me Noordhoek; to John Oxlee for giving me a valuable collection of Baker documents; to the late Desirée Picton-Seymour, for her wisdom and her time in driving me around the Cape Peninsular; I am grateful, too, to John Rennie of the University of Cape Town and to R R Langham-Carter for kindly letting me use the unpublished manuscript of their book on the Rhodes Memorial. To Dr André de Villiers and other members of staff, and my own fourth-year design students at the University of Pretoria, for stimulating discussion and enlightenment on arcane matters of style in architecture. Likewise to Professor Brian Kearney and the staff of the University of Natal, Durban, for the stimulating opportunities and encouragement they have given me. My sometime tutor at Thames Polytechnic in London, Dr Anthony Quiney, is remembered for the initial encouragement and advice he gave me, and the late Professor Barrie Biermann for first awakening me to the fascinating history of architecture, as an undergraduate.

To Jonathan Stone and Professor Kirby of the Department of Architecture, University of the Witwatersrand, for so readily making available invaluable Baker material, and for their keen insight, I am greatly indebted.

To my wife Judi for putting up with my absence, both mental and physical, and, after reading my cumbersome first drafts, for encouraging me to continue; to my colleagues at the Council for Scientific and Industrial Research for their kindness and understanding, and for stretching their patience at having a Bakermaniac in their midst.

In the course of researching and writing this book I have received numerous queries concerning Baker's architecture, especially where authorship of a building has been in doubt. It is my fervent wish that such queries will continue; by no means has the last Baker design been uncovered, nor the last word said on the topic of attribution.

PART ONE
ENGLISH UPBRINGING

CHAPTER ONE

1862-1886

KENTISH BACKGROUND

OWLETTS

The village of Cobham, in Kent, lies on the ancient path that led from London to Canterbury, on to the English Channel and the wider world beyond. Even before the Romans built their Watling Street through Cobham, the earlier British had followed a ridgeway here. Nowadays the M2 motorway flows close to the old Roman route, a mile or so north of the village centre.

On the outskirts of Cobham, alongside the road running west to Sole Street, stands Owletts, a modest late-Stuart house. It is the house in which Sir Herbert Baker was born and in which he died nearly eighty-four years later. The house has a solid-looking shape resulting from its square plan, each side being four rooms long. The warm red-brick walls and vast, reassuring pair of chimneys spell the comfortable, and practical, home of a small squire or a prosperous yeoman. A carved inscription on one of the panelled brick chimneys which dominate the roof-line reveals that the house was built in 1683. Its builder was Bonham Hayes who owned the adjoining six-hundred acre farms of Owletts and Jeskyns. The small red bricks with which it is built were probably baked from earth two fields away; the lime was likewise burned from a nearby chalk hole. Owletts has an exceptionally fine staircase with twisted balusters characteristic of its period, and a richly moulded plaster ceiling bearing the date, 1684, which accurately confirms the date of building. Above the staircase windows are three small circular windows, 'bull's eyes', two filled with armorial glass. In one the Baker crest — with the Castle of Rochester which the family once owned — can be seen, whilst in the other is that of the Edmeades family, who lived nearby at Nurstead Court and 'who were twice united with the Bakers in the ownership of Owletts.'[1]

Several minor alterations have been made to the house over the years. The original lead window casements were probably replaced with wooden sashes during the eighteenth century and, in 1754, George Hayes trimmed the roof eaves to raise the walls and form a parapet. No doubt the purpose of this simple remodelling was to keep abreast of Georgian fashion. In 1877, whilst Herbert was a boy of fifteen, his father added a north wing to the original house. In 1917, after an absence of twenty-five years, the middle-aged Baker returned to live at his birthplace. He too was to leave his mark on the house, most notably in the addition of the two Ionic columns at the top of the staircase in place of a supporting side wall, and in the addition of a bay to the library.[2]

Owletts and its farmlands first came into the ownership of Herbert Baker's forebears when it was bought by an Edmeades from the Hayes family in 1790. Henry Edmeades, of Nurstead Court, who acquired the property for his eldest son, was one of Herbert's great-great-grandfathers; another, whose name was Baker, was a clockmaker and the father of Samuel Baker of Satis House, on Bodley Hill, Rochester. Samuel Baker was a builder whose extensive business stretched beyond the Medway Towns. He built the British Museum, 1823-47, and was related to its architects, Sir Robert Smirk (1781-1867) and his son Sydney (1798-1877). A monument on the wall of Rochester Cathedral proclaims Samuel's virtues — 'enough to divide amongst his own thirteen children and the eleven children of his grandson'! Samuel Baker's thirteen included Herbert's grandfather, a sea captain in the service of the East India Company. Captain Thomas Baker, commander of the *Lowther Castle*, married Maria Edmeades and, as the monument says, had eleven children — one of whom was Thomas Henry Baker, Herbert's father. On his mother's side, Herbert's

Owletts, Cobham, Kent. Watercolour sketch by Baker.

great-grandmother was a Nicholson, 'a family of soldiers and sailors', whilst his Edmeades grandmother 'came from a long race of Kentish Yeomen...' His mother's father, he records, was Irish 'with the blood of tribal chieftains in his veins.'[3]

COUNTRY BOYHOOD

Herbert Baker was born at Owletts on 9 June 1862, the fourth son of Thomas Henry Baker. He had eight brothers and two sisters; a third sister had died in early childhood a short time before his birth. As he wrote in his autobiography, he was 'born in sorrow.' His family recorded that Herbert could not talk until he was four years old – 'I have always consoled myself', he wrote, 'that good fruit ripens slowly.' But his apparent backwardness was shortlived. His boyhood interests and imagination were amply stimulated by the beauty and variety of his rural surroundings. Walking and exploring were among his favourite pastimes. He and his younger brother Alfred were inseparable; they roamed the neighbouring countryside searching out the ancient remains of previous civilizations in an area rich with historical associations. 'Our favourite walks as boys were on the old yew-marked [Pilgrims] Way and on the Downs above; and we loved to explore the old tumuli or cromlechs...and Kits Coty House across the Medway along the way of the reputed crossing of the Saxons under Hengist and Horsa.' The Downs they roamed had a thin covering of springy turf, deliciously sympathetic to walk on. The fresh breezes and breath-taking views made it sheer delight. And all around was the romance of history to nurture and enliven his youthful imagination. The old architecture of the locality impressed him too.

Vividly and lovingly recalled in later life were 'two beautifully proportioned Kentish church towers...Wrotham, with its archway under, built of many-coloured flints and stone; and the picturesque little gem of a tower, Birling.' They searched for treasures beside the old Roman road, Watling Street, which ran for half a mile through their land, but found none. 'I, as a boy...liked to fancy the Chaucer Pilgrims, and many another cavalcade, ambling through our woods; the eight black horses that carried the Black Prince on his last journey to his tomb in the choir of Canterbury Cathedral...'[4]

Inside the early thirteenth-century chancel of Cobham Church the complete floor of brasses, richly inlaid with the heraldry of the early Lords of Cobham 'made an early and deep impression on my architectural affections.' Cobham Hall, too, the nearby Elizabethan home of the descendants of these Lords, with its long wings like Hatfield House and its romantic heraldic decorations, 'made an early appeal to my imagination.' One of Herbert's fondest memories of childhood was his delight in the poetry which his father read to him – chiefly from Pope's *Iliad* – 'many Homeric combats I then knew by heart.'[5]

Herbert's love of adventure and exploration was unbounded; his often lone pursuit of them taught him self-reliance and toughness. As one of a family of eleven children it is probable that he found relief in solitude and independent action; and solitude would have encouraged his boyish romantic imagination to dwell on the stories of history and to dream of myths and legends.

SCHOOLING

It was not easy to acquire a sound elementary education in rural England in the 1860s and 70s; and Thomas Baker could not afford to send his nine sons to good preparatory schools, of which there were few in those times.[6]

Herbert was sent for some terms to a dame's school in the old Elizabethan Restoration House in Rochester, where his mother had been a pupil. He then had 'some teaching' at a vicarage two miles away – 'I remember the rides there on my pony, but nothing of my schooling.' But it was a poor substitute for a preparatory school education. The lack of proper preparation, especially in the classics, was to cost him an ignominious rebuff when he went up to the public school his father had chosen, Haileybury College at Hertford Heath, Hertfordshire, in 1875. Without warning or time for preparation he was set an examination, which he failed, and was ruthlessly sent home. He later wrote – 'Of that illfated expedition I remember only a grim blackbearded headmaster, and sitting all forlorn on my school box, which smelt of meat pies, at the station on my retreat homeward.' Baker's recollection of the event is touched with a revealing irony – '...but I was able to retrieve my disgrace, joyfully but silently, when I caused a Greek inscription to be cut into the stone of the war memorial [hall] which I designed for the College.'[7]

But the headmaster of Tonbridge School, nearer home in Kent, was to offer the forlorn youth a more welcoming face. Herbert entered Tonbridge at the beginning of the Christmas term, 1875. His years there were not crowned with academic glory – he won no important prizes. Teamwork and leadership opportunities, however, came to him early, for he gained his cricket colours in 1878 and was captain in 1880 and 1881. His football career was almost as illustrious, with his colours won in 1879 and the captaincy in 1880, to which his brother Alfred succeeded in the winter of 1881 after Herbert's departure at mid-year.[8]

Baker later wrote that he owed most to the influence of the headmaster, The Reverend T B Rowe, MA. Baker's remark that Rowe cared less for gaining scholarships than for '...drawing out the thinking powers of even the lower boys of his form' was probably a grateful tribute to a sympathetic head, and one who, above all, had 'infected me with a love of Wordsworth.' He remembered also 'with gratitude the Science master, Whitmell, who took me each summer for walking tours to Cornwall, the Welsh and Westmorland mountains, and the Yorkshire fells.' At all events Whitmell also encouraged Baker's interest in poetry. Much of it he learned by heart and never forgot. In the way that poetry learned by heart does, it became part of him, part of the mental furniture which gave character and quality to his mind. By having his poetic sensibilities roused at Tonbridge the seal was put on what has been called his literary and narrative, rather than abstract turn of mind.

It is a remarkable fact that of the twenty-nine boys who, with Baker, entered Tonbridge School in the Christmas term of 1875, seventeen were to spend significant portions of their lives as soldiers, administrators or farmers in overseas territories.[9] There can be little doubt that the public school ethos, with its assumptions of leadership and fair play, loyalty and piety, found in the captain of cricket and football a willing adherent. For a class bred, if not born, to rule an empire, the rules for the conduct of life were substantially those of the cricket field, and if one could lead a cricket team to victory, one could lead anyone, anywhere.

In his last year at Tonbridge, Baker's belated study of classics was abandoned in favour of mathematics and mechanics; he had decided to become an architect. In his memoirs Baker gives no more reason for this than that his parents thought he was good at drawing, adding that he was not, but was

fond of it. 'I was vilely taught at school', he wrote, '...to copy and stipple, not to visualize, represent, and design.' His headmaster's final report observed that he could have done better but for his 'many avocations', his absorption in athletics and games. His own summary was that he had 'learned perhaps enough to get a glimpse of the beauty of the old poets; a sense of the priceless gems of poetry that could be discovered in them...'[10]

PUPILAGE

There was to be no university education for Herbert. His family could not afford it for one thing; two of his younger brothers were already at Tonbridge School when he left, and a further three were to follow in due course. But having decided to become an architect, a thorough training for the profession could, in those days, follow only one direction: articled pupilage, coupled with evening classes and private study. The problem of placing Herbert in a suitable office was made easy for Thomas Baker, whose nephew, Arthur, was an established architect and an obvious choice.

Arthur Baker (1841-96) had an office in Kensington, at 14 Warwick Gardens, within walking distance of the South Kensington museums. It was a small but growing practice dealing mainly in ecclesiastical restoration work. Thomas saw no reason to doubt the wisdom of placing his son with a minor architect; competent, but of little distinction. Besides, one could not easily dismiss the comfort and confidence brought by family ties and familiarity. Last, but by no means least for Thomas Baker, there were financial advantages in keeping it in the family; the usual fee of three hundred guineas could be negotiated for a more affordable sum.[11]

So, in about September of the year in which he left Tonbridge, 1881, Herbert Baker entered his cousin's office to begin the customary three-year pupilage – at the age of nineteen. Arthur was twenty-one years older than Herbert and a Fellow of the Royal Institute of British Architects (RIBA). He had begun his own career in 1864 as an articled pupil in the office of the great Gothic Revivalist, Sir George Gilbert Scott (1811-78) remaining there as an assistant until Scott's death fourteen years later.[12]

Unlike G F Bodley (1827-1907) who had left Scott's practice in 1856, and by the 1860s was beginning to turn his back on the Gothic Revival and was looking towards the Queen Anne style,

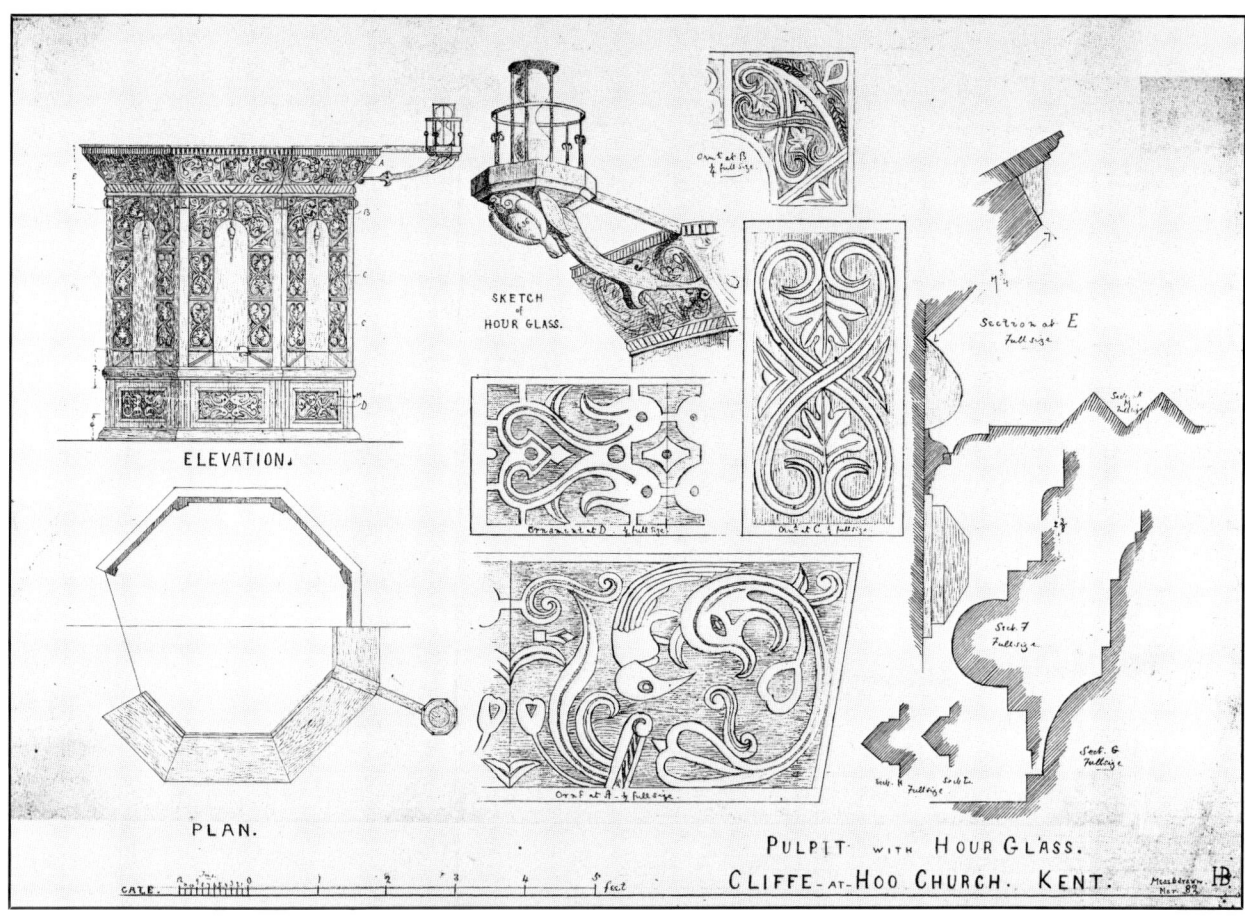

Pulpit and details. Drawings by Baker.

Arthur Baker continued in his own small practice to follow the Scott tradition, working alone until he took on a Mr Hughes as partner in 1891. Not only did he persevere with his Scott-influenced Gothic Revival, albeit somewhat watered down, but he seemed also to inherit the master's propensity for destructive renewal. His restoration of the church at Gyffylliog in the Vale of Clwyd was described as 'wanton and senseless destruction...to all purposes a new church on an old foundation.'[13]

Of Arthur Baker's new churches three are notable: that of St Laurence, Northampton; St Paul in Kensington and St Padarn at Llanberis in Caernarvonshire – the latter designed and built, under Herbert Baker's supervision as Clerk-of-Works, following on from his pupilage.[14]

For some years Arthur Baker served on the Science Standing Committee of the RIBA. His only known publication is an article entitled 'Model drainage and plumbing specifications' written for

Building News. He died relatively young at the age of fifty-five. For Herbert Baker, young and ambitious, Arthur Baker's small office was not the most inspiring atmosphere in which to develop and train as an architect. By way of compensation for an office routine which seems to have lacked excitement and stimulation, every opportunity was taken to get out into the countryside and study buildings. Sketches made during his pupilage show how widely he travelled around England and Wales, recording details of church furniture, roofs and gables, and ruined abbeys.[15] Among surviving studies which he took to South Africa, are painstakingly detailed drawings of a pulpit in Kent and a church roof in Wales, both dating from the first year of his pupilage. Another, of a staircase in the Old Restoration House at Rochester, dated 1883, undoubtedly served as an inspiration and as a reminder in his future work.

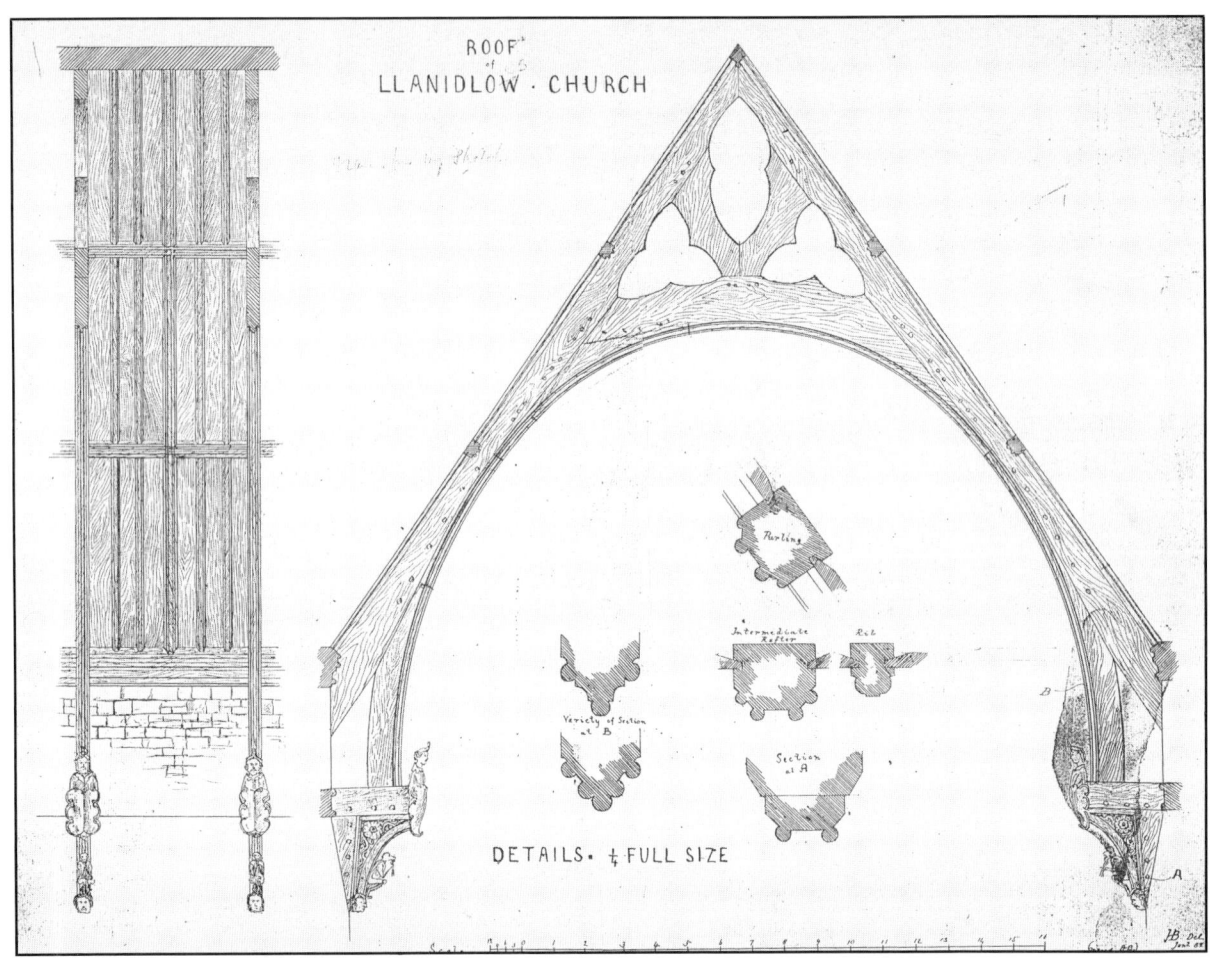

Llanidlow church. Drawing of roof details by Baker.

On completion of his three-year pupilage, in June 1884, he crossed the Channel, returning with sketches of gables in Haarlem and Antwerp, which, like the intricately carved Flemish fanlight he drew, seem now to presage his work in South Africa.[16]

In London Herbert Baker's evenings were invariably spent in study; it seems he had little or no social life. In later years he bemoaned having made few 'valuable' friends after leaving school, except among architectural students, until he lived in South Africa. He wrote: 'I have realized more fully ...what I missed by not going to a university, in the making of friends and in the communion of youthful intelligence.' But the 'absence of the attractions of society', so he rationalized, bore him compensations in the 'early close apprenticeship to my profession and classes at the Royal Academy Schools...' Such was the pattern of Baker's life dur-

ing his pupilage, and it continued into the years when he was an assistant to Ernest George and Peto, the firm he joined after completing his pupilage — and the ensuing year and a half spent at Llanberis.[17]

It was in these years when he began his probationary period, prior to entering for the examinations of the RIBA, that he enrolled at the Royal Academy. His visits to the museums were greatly facilitated by the proximity of Arthur Baker's office to South Kensington. Walking along the Cromwell Road he would have passed the newly completed Natural History Museum, the vast Romanesque pile designed by Waterhouse and built between 1873 and 1880. Alfred Waterhouse (1830-1905), who was one of the most significant Victorian architects, had designed the museum without the contrived picturesque asymmetry which was so prevalent at the time. Baker must have noticed the elaborate way in which naturalistic animal figures, modelled in ter-

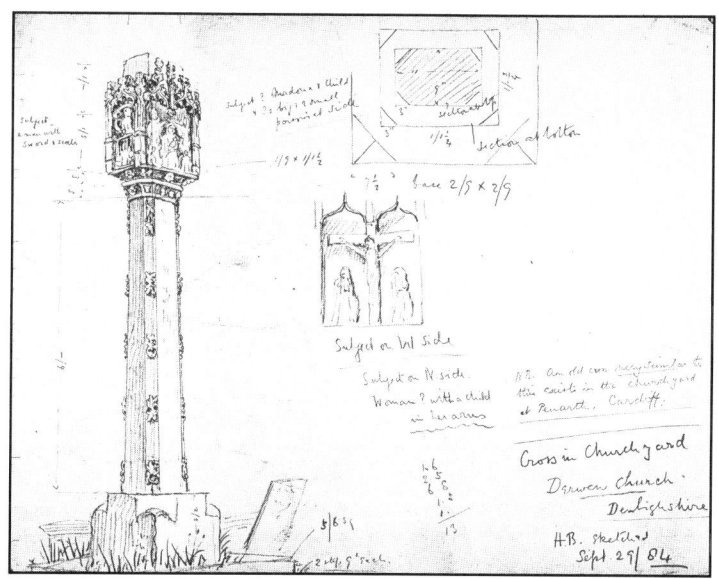

Top.
Cross in Derwen churchyard, Denbighshire,
North Wales. Pencil drawing by
Herbert Baker, 1884.
Bottom.
Staircase in Restoration House, Rochester.
Drawing by Baker. Right. Chimney piece,
Plas Mawr, Conway, North Wales, by
Robert Wynne, 1588. Ink drawing by
Herbert Baker, 1887.

Church of St Padarn, Llanberis, Caernarvonshire, North Wales.
Ink drawing by Herbert Baker, circa 1886.

racotta, were used to decorate the façade and symbolize the departmental functions within the museum. The South Kensington Museum, which he knew intimately, was the nucleus of the vast 'cultural centre' which now stretches from Kensington Gore to Cromwell Road. But it was still to have its south range added by Sir Aston Webb (1849-1930), begun in 1899 and not completed until 1909, when its name was changed to the Victoria and Albert Museum.[18]

Towards the completion of his office pupilage Baker was offered a new opportunity and adventure. He later wrote: '...from the dullness of it I was sent as clerk-of-works to the building of a church at Llanberis...an invaluable practical training.' Characteristically, he adds: '...and a delightful experience among the mountains and lakes which I loved.' Whilst enjoying the natural beauties of North Wales, Baker found further opportunities to explore old buildings in the surrounding country and continued to fill his sketchbooks with their details. He drew a delicate pencil sketch of the cross in the churchyard at Derwen in Denbighshire, dated 29 September 1884, to which he added

The young Herbert Baker.

dimensions and details. Again with hindsight, this particular form of cross seems to have remained in his memory to emerge many years later as a prototype for his many memorials following the Great War.[19]

The drawing he made of St Padarn's Church during, or soon after, its construction – which he was supervising – shows the extent to which his draughtsmanship had developed. Its rather intense technique also indicates his early love of richly textured surfaces.[20]

St Padarn's Church, planned to hold a congregation of about five hundred worshippers, was built in local stone; grey with red dressings. Designed in a simpler, sturdy mode of Gothic, quite unlike anything of Scott's, it testifies to Arthur Baker's independent spirit; an attribute his pupil would develop in full measure. But for the aspirant the most valuable experience of all was watching country tradesmen employing the traditional crafts; skills which were quite impossible to learn from the observation of finished work. Still less could one learn from books their implications for design.[21]

Baker was to spend a year and a half on the supervision of the Llanberis church, time which in this remote place might have been put to more productive use had he been in London. But, making the most of it, he found another project on which he could gain further knowledge and experience of historical architecture. In their spare time, when Arthur came up to Wales, the cousins measured and drew Plas Mawr, a large Elizabethan manor house built by Robert Wynne in 1588. The house contained many features which were later incor-

porated into vernacular buildings of the neighbouring countryside. Inside, the house was enriched with the armorial motifs of the Wynne family, a form of decoration which had fascinated Baker since his childhood in Cobham and which he himself would use again and again particularly in his later years. The plans and perspectives they drew, together with the comprehensive description they wrote, were eventually published in 1888 in what is now an extremely rare book.[22]

Whether at Llanberis or in Kensington, Herbert Baker's years of pupilage were spent working somewhat mundanely by day, gaining that vital practical experience which was, and still is, the foundation of a profession in architecture. Surprisingly, Baker gives scant mention in his memoirs to the time he spent in Arthur Baker's office. He is non-commital on Arthur's qualities as an architect or as a mentor; no mention is made of the value he gained from the training he received, only the 'dullness' of it. His spare time, holidays and weekends, were usually devoted to walking and sketching, observing and noting, furnishing his mind with a stock of historical details gleaned from villages and churches in the English and Welsh countryside. On completion of his duties at Llanberis, Baker went abroad again, this time to Italy where he travelled for six weeks before commencing work with the firm of Ernest George and Peto.[23] A study he made of the canopy over the entrance to Campo Santo, at Pisa, gives the exact date of his visit: 8 May 1886.

In the years 1885-86 Baker first experienced the satisfaction of seeing his work in print. Drawings he made of the monuments and rood screen in

Lullingstone Church in Kent, and of Cobham Hall near his home, were published by the journal of the Kent Archaeological Society, *Archaeologia Cantiana*. Another, of the Elizabethan Restoration House in Rochester, where he had attended school as a boy, was printed in *The Builder* in August 1885.[24]

Considering the nature of his cousin's earlier experience and the work of his practice, it is more than likely that Baker worked solely on Gothic Revival schemes throughout his pupilage. By doing his pupilage with his cousin, Baker seems to have barred himself from any direct feel for the pulse of architectural ideas, ideas which were throbbing and fermenting in the early 1880s. It tended, too, to isolate him from the society of close friends, fostering what was already a potential weakness in his nature: the desire to retreat from the real world into the nature-inspired, idealistic world of poetry and romance. In contrast, it must have given him first-hand experience of the workings of a small architectural practice, increasing his self-reliance and forcing him to face the practicalities of building and office management head on.

CHAPTER TWO

1886-1892

ENGLISH PRACTICE

THE LEADING ASSISTANT

In October 1886 Herbert Baker joined the firm of Ernest George and Peto having completed his articled pupilage and the building of St Padarn's Church. Their office was on the top floor of 14 Maddox Street, Mayfair, just a block away from the headquarters of the Royal Institute of British Architects, at that time 9 Conduit Street; and a short walk away to the south was the Royal Academy. Ernest George (1869-1944) — Sir Ernest from 1907 — was the son of a Southwark iron dealer and had been a brilliant student, winning the Royal Academy Gold Medal in 1859. His partner Harold Peto (1828-97) was the ·brother of the building contractors, Peto Brothers, the sons of Sir Samuel Morton Peto. Sir Samuel had built numerous buildings of importance including several London clubs and theatres, and railway works in many parts of the world. As a partnership, their respective skills and contacts were conveniently complementary. Ernest George did all the design work himself, leaving his pupils and assistants to trace and develop his sketches into working drawings. Unlike his partner, Harold Peto was rarely seen, spending most of his time with his clients or in seeking new ones.[1]

Apart from the drawing office, the Maddox Street office consisted of a waiting room, a manager's office and two private rooms for the partners. The drawing office staff comprised, on average, six articled pupils and one or two paid assistants; the office manager dealt with the accounts and general administration and a number of clerks-of-works handled site supervision. Herbert Baker began his duties as an 'improver' but by 1887 he was in the position of 'a leading assistant.'[2]

The office of Ernest George and Harold Peto was one of three London firms which predominated in the training of architects in the 1880s. That of the church architect J D Sedding (1838-91) was another; the third was the office of Richard Norman Shaw (1831-1912) the best-known architect of the three, if not of his time, and a rival of Ernest George in the domestic field from the 1870s onwards. Each of these large practices — and there were many others which trained articled pupils — tended to produce its own kind of architect. George, himself a modest and unassuming man, was immensely proud of the fame so many of his able assistants acquired in future years.[3]

Guy Dawber (1861-1938) remembered the George and Peto office with great affection. In the obituary he wrote on Sir Ernest's death he recalled: 'When I first came into his office just forty years ago, he was perhaps one of the busiest architects in England, large country houses and other buildings filling his office with work.' Dawber, who entered the office two years before Baker, was one of the numerous architects who passed through the office and later achieved eminence. Another was Robert Weir Schultz (1860-1951) who was there from 1886 to 1888. Both Dawber and Schultz (or Weir, as he later called himself) were contemporaries of Baker. But the best known of all George's men was Edwin Lutyens (1869-1944). Lutyens began his pupilage under George late in 1887 at the age of eighteen, after spending two years at the South Kensington School of Art, now the Royal College of Art.[4]

George has been described as 'the most frankly romantic and picturesque of the successful London architects of the later nineteenth century; he had never had the hard, moral Gothic training which Shaw, Stevenson or E W Godwin had to shake off.'[5] The contrast between Arthur Baker and Ernest George could hardly have been greater.

It was John Ruskin (1819-1900) who had given

the Gothic Revival its high moral tone, propagated through his romantically vague but immensely popular books, *The Seven Lamps of Architecture* (1849) and *The Stones of Venice* (1851-53). During the three decades up to mid-century the principal prophet and propagandist of the style had been A W N Pugin (1812-52), succeeded by Sir George Gilbert Scott after Pugin's premature death at the age of forty. Whereas Pugin, trained as an architect, had stressed the importance of construction and honest utilitarian planning, Ruskin, an art historian, had emphasized the importance of ornament. Both these aspects of the Gothic Revival became fused in the High Victorian style, which reigned supreme from 1850 to 1870. The style was characterized by vigorous structural emphasis, ornamented with surface texture and pattern in polychromatic brickwork. But long before 1870, by which time its passion was spent, Ruskin himself had grown disillusioned with the style and Gothicism was on the wane. From the 1870s it was the Queen Anne style, ushered in by W E Nesfield, J J Stevenson and Richard Norman Shaw, which predominated. Based on the early seventeenth-century English domestic style, Queen Anne abounded with Dutch and Flemish features – gables and strapwork in comfortable warm brickwork and white-painted sash windows.

The style was, at least in part, a reaction to the gloom and inconvenience of Gothic houses, with their stone walls and mullioned windows. It was seen as a less earnest revival of older traditions of English building, rather than an historically-based style. Queen Anne, if it was a style at all, as opposed to an 'approach' to building, was in fact part of a wider movement towards a new vernacular. The search was now on for a style rooted in local or national traditions, set free from the dictates and rigours of historical styles.[6]

The history of late Victorian and Edwardian architecture in Britain has been described as being 'of great complexity, with waves of fashion and many cross-currents confusing the sequence of developments.'[7] Through it all flowed the consistent search for this elusive, free 'modern vernacular', emerging as what was aptly named the Free Style. Although the term was meant to be applied to architecture in a new style appropriate to its time, it was also used to describe any building which used a free treatment of an historical style or combination of styles – even a free vernacular style. As Hermann Muthesius, author of *Das englische Haus* (1904-5) found when he tried to characterize 'the

exemplary qualities of the English house', the qualities he admired most were not based on style but arose from the restraint and 'honesty' derived from simple vernacular buildings.

Most of the architects aligned themselves with one or another of the new societies and guilds that were springing up to foster this new progressive approach. In 1882 the architect Arthur Mackmurdo (1851-1942) formed the Century Guild, concerned particularly with proto-Art Nouveau design; in 1884 the Art Workers' Guild was founded by five pupils of Richard Norman Shaw: Gerald Horsley, W R Lethaby, Ernest Newton, Mervyn Macartney and Edward Prior, with the aim of bringing together all the visual arts. Then C R Ashbee (1863-1942) formed the Guild and School of Handicraft in 1888 and, in the same year, The Arts and Crafts Exhibition Society was formed, to provide a platform for the various sections of the movement. From the latter the collective name, 'Arts and Crafts Movement' was adopted. The Art Workers' Guild became the architectural centre – almost a club – for the architects of the Arts and Crafts Movement.[8]

Ernest George was a perfect example of a Free-Style architect, able to turn his hand to any style, singly or in eclectic combination. He is best known for his houses at 20-26 and 35-45 Harrington Gardens and 1-18 Collingham Gardens, Kensington. These elegant houses broadly reflect the Queen Anne approach but also lean heavily towards an authentic Dutch style. Both of the Harrington Gardens schemes were built between 1881 and 1884. The Collingham Gardens houses were built between 1883 and 1888, and would have been well known to Baker who may well have worked on their drawings. Waterside, the house Ernest George designed at Westgate-on-Sea for W H Peto, Harold Peto's brother, has a gable dated 1880, six years before Baker joined the firm. With its triple-gabled roof, patterned tile-hanging and a variety of bay windows, it is as delightful, and as typical, an example of Queen Anne and free vernacular as one might find.[9]

In total contrast is Batsford Park at Moreton-in-the-Marsh, Gloucestershire (1888-93) described by Mark Girouard as a 'clever working up of the Dorset Tudor-Gothic style into a country house on the grand scale which at first sight...might be genuine sixteenth-century work.' The house was designed to 'avoid prettiness and fanciful features' as Girouard suggests 'in reaction against Norman Shaw, and indeed against George and Peto's earlier

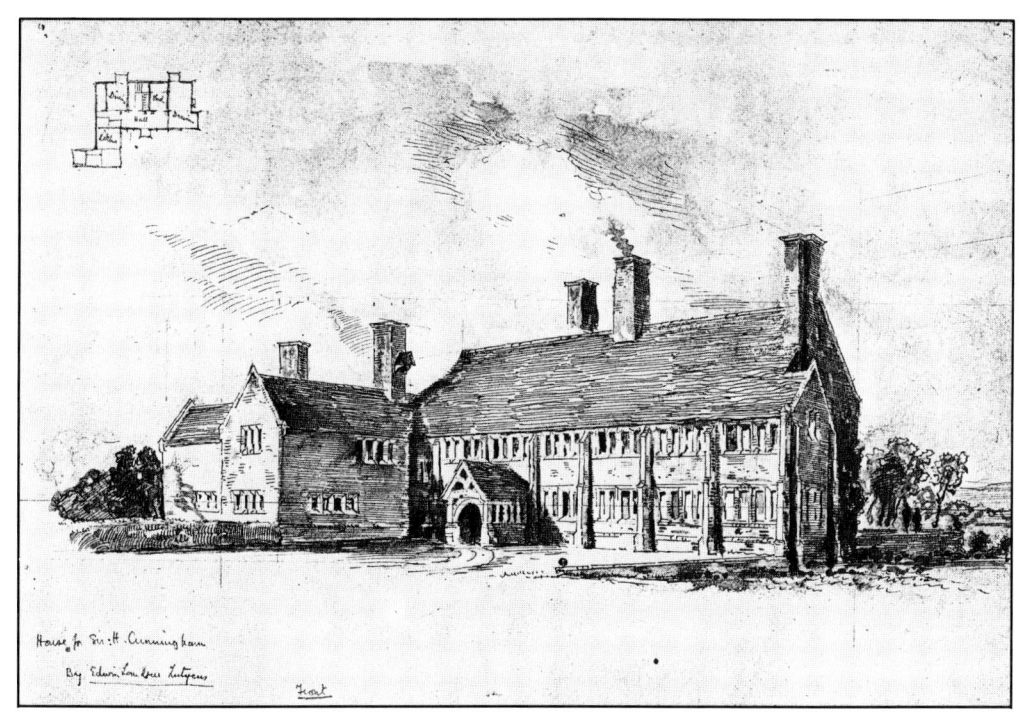

Top. *House for Sir Henry Cunningham by Edwin Lutyens, sepia ink and wash drawing by Herbert Baker. Bottom left. Cross at Rochester. Drawing by Baker. Bottom right. Design for a house at Southend, Herbert Baker, circa 1890.*

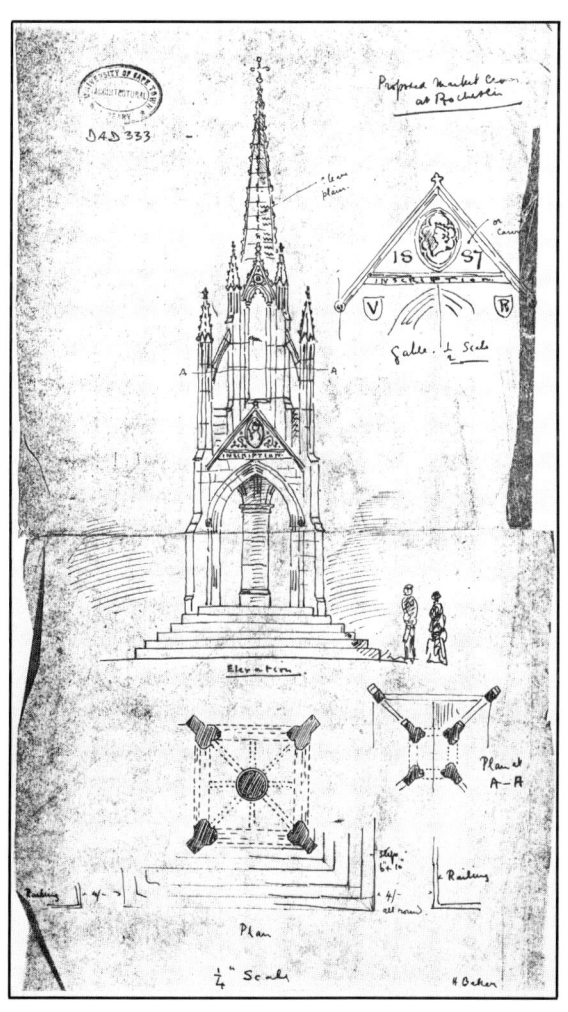

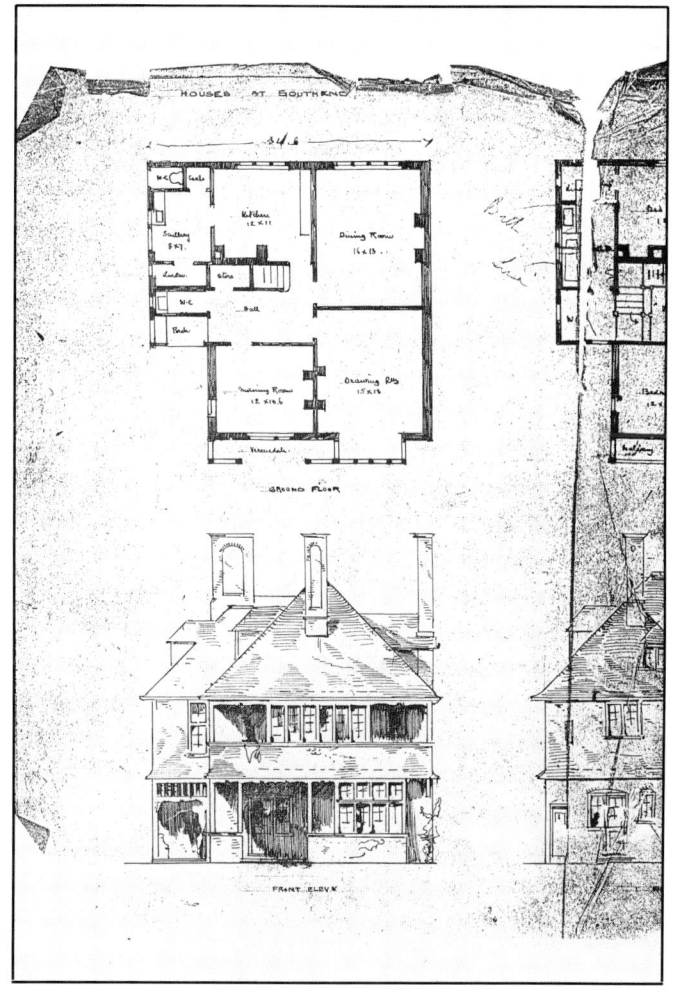

manner.'[10] Other houses which were designed by George, or were under construction, between 1886 and 1889 include Glencot in Somerset, Dunley House in Surrey, Shiplake Court in Oxfordshire and Motcomb in Dorset.

George was among the finest exponents of water-colour rendering and architectural drawing of his day. Margaret Richardson has described his approach as a '...largely pictorial one. He did not start by working on a plan or section – but with a brilliant sepia perspective. He also angled his buildings from a low viewpoint...'[11] His skill in representing his buildings as objects which grew from the landscape, and looked as if they had been there for centuries, probably accounted for much of his success with his clients and popularity with his pupils. One of his pupils, Edwin Lutyens, adopted George's 'Worm's-eye view' approach, and with charming effect. Edwin Lutyens, however, was not so flattering with regard to Ernest George's drawing ability when, as his former pupil saw it, it influenced his approach to design. With only the mildest attempt to disguise the victim of his derision he recalled in later years '...a distinguished architect who took each year, a three weeks holiday abroad and returned with overflowing sketchbooks. When called on for a project he would look through these and choose some picturesque turret or gable from Holland, France, or Spain, and round it weave his new design. Location mattered little, and no provincial formation influenced him...'[12]

Baker's own contribution to design while in Ernest George's office is obscure, but since George appears to have done all the design work himself it is unlikely that he, or any of his assistants, did little more than 'improving' and the preparation of working drawings and specifications.

During his pupilage with his cousin, Herbert Baker's training had been of the most informal kind: practical work by day, study in the museums at evenings and constant exploration, noting and sketching of buildings. By now he had travelled on the continent of Europe too. From George's Maddox Street office, the School of Design at the Royal Academy was easily reached on foot; lessons there were usually from 6-9 p.m., three evenings a week. Although by no means a school of architecture in the present-day sense, the Academy nevertheless offered a formal and disciplined method of tuition. The system was for designs to be set by the architect Royal Academicians in rotation; the masters would then perform criticism sessions with entire classes, enabling students to learn from each other's 'mistakes' as well as from the remarks of the famous. Although they all held somewhat divergent views, it was a wonderful opportunity to come face to face with some of the great names of the day. George Edmund Street had died before Baker enrolled at the Academy but his advice 'sketch, sketch, sketch' was legend. At the other extreme G F Bodley, recalled Baker, would say in answer to a question whether he knew some French cathedral: 'I smoked three cigars over it.' The problem for the student was to find a path of one's own between them all, 'to take hints and discriminate.' That way, observed Baker, 'much could be learned from them...'[13]

Competition for the Gold Medal Travelling Studentship of the Royal Academy, with the prize of a year's travel and study in Italy, proved to be a disappointment to Baker, though probably less so at the time than in retrospect. The subject set was a town mansion. Baker's design was in the manner of 'a severe Italian palace' after the Palazzo Sparda in Rome, but without its 'superabundance of ornament.' He had attempted what he called a break-away from the fashionable Free Renaissance then prevailing – only to find a Free Renaissance design was to win.[14]

By way of compensation he gained some satisfaction in an ambitious publishing project. The measured drawings he and his cousin Arthur had done earlier in Wales were made ready and were published later in the year by Farmer and Sons in a limited edition of 200 copies. Only a few were for sale, at 25s each; the rest went to the twenty-five or so relatives and friends who, with the authors, had borne the cost of publication by subscription. With the production of *Plas Mawr* complete, and encouraged by its forthcoming appearance as a book, Baker turned to more spare-time drawing for publication.

EDWIN LUTYENS

Late in 1887 a fresh young eighteen-year old joined Ernest George and Peto. His name was Edwin Landseer Lutyens and his meeting with Herbert Baker was to prove one of the most fateful events of both men's lives. Seven years older, Baker was the Leading Assistant in the firm. Despite the age gap, which one might think considerable at that stage in life, they soon became friends. But there were even more fundamental differences between them; differences of temperament, attitudes to life and art, and social background – perhaps accentuated by the fact that Baker had been to a public school where he had excelled at games, and Lutyens had done neither. Whereas Baker has written with frankness of their early relations saying that he 'greatly enjoyed [Lutyens's] company', there is no such record from Lutyens. The likelihood is that Lutyens was slightly overawed by the senior man's confidence and position in the firm, although Baker himself had yet to qualify for membership of the RIBA. And yet Lutyens had his own kind of confidence, a cocksureness that had caused him to leave the South Kensington School of Art without completing the course, believing that he could fill his time better elsewhere.

Baker recognized that Lutyens, '...though joking through his short pupilage, quickly absorbed all that was best learning: he puzzled us at first, but we soon found that he seemed to know by intuition some great truths of our art which were not to be learned there.' In the early days of their friendship Baker appreciated too the younger man's 'wit and good stories; his jokes, which were pleasing in his freshness and innocence of youth' – though in old age, and with hindsight, he would write: 'I found out afterwards were apt to be wearisome in repetition and less becoming to his mature manhood.'[15]

Together they went to meetings of the Art Workers' Guild. Founded in 1884, the Guild's object was to provide a forum for artist-craftsmen to meet to get to know each other's work, to hear lectures and present demonstrations on every aspect of their art and work. In the first decade of its existence three-quarters of its 250 members were non-architects. Members were elected in recognition of their actual artistic achievements, and Baker did not himself become a member until many years later. The meetings and discussions were regarded by Baker as a rare treat. Apart from Lutyens, Guy Dawber, Herbert Read, R Weir Schultz, C E Mallows, Owen Fleming and Reginald Blomfield were among the friends and acquaintances he would meet there. Blomfield remembered their fortnightly gatherings at Barnard's Inn in Holborn: 'Everyone smoked who wished to. The paper was read after which we adjourned for an interval in an adjoining room, for whiskies and sodas and other drinks, and then returned to the hall for discussion. These sometimes became vivacious. Most of the discussions were extremely practical dealing with the technical processes of various arts.' Although it had been

founded by five architects, in its first two years only one architectural subject was discussed – 'Architecture, from the different craftsmen's point of view.'[16]

In September 1888 Baker visited France; among his surviving sketches are a drawing of the Tower of Catherine de Medici at Blois and another tower, that of Agnes Sorrel at Amboise. Then in the autumn of the same year he set out on a few days' walking tour with Edwin Lutyens through Wales and Shropshire. They visited the ruins of Wenlock Abbey, designed mainly in the Early English style, near the famous view sites of Wenlock Edge. Nearby, at Craven Arms, they delighted in the moated fortified manor house, Stokesay Castle, where the simple carpentry and great thirteenth-century cruck-construction made an indelible impression on them both. Lutyens said in later life that its timber framing had inspired the best of his subsequent designs for carpentry work. Further east near Llangollen, the church at Rug caused Lutyens to recall in a letter to Baker fifty years later, that its 'delicious old chandelier, all made of wood painted green' and its ceiling, 'painted by some Jacobean – red and blue – even the timbers of the roof painted with blue, white and red roses' had inspired some of his later work.[17]

Lutyens never sketched, wrote Baker, but 'after a quick glance relied on retentive memory.'[18] But this was a pose, part of his amused contempt for professionalism and the development of his own architectural persona, as Margaret Richardson suggests. His scornful rejection of sketchbooks, particularly those of Ernest George, is somewhat contradicted by the existence of a set of fifty-four topographical sketches, datable to 1886-87.

Lutyens was steadily acquiring a practice in the small private commissions which he undertook all through his pupilage. Early in 1889, soon after his twentieth birthday, he was commissioned to build a small country house, Crooksbury, near Farnum in Surrey, whereupon he left George and Peto's office to open his own at 6 Grays Inn Square.[19]

Perhaps some of Lutyens's eager desire for success rubbed off on Herbert Baker for he grew restless and, not long after Lutyens's departure, he too resigned with the object of starting a practice of his own. But he had no large commission with which to establish himself and was, at that time, apparently without his friend's capacity to attract any clients of importance. He expected that he might go abroad; whether or not he felt at that time such a move would improve his prospects is unclear but he was probably influenced by the fact that his younger brother, Lionel, was at the time preparing to leave for the Cape. With this idea taking shape in his mind he turned to the more serious business of preparing to write the November 1889 Examination in Architecture of the Royal Institute of British Architects. It was, he modestly recalled, '...a hurried decision which left little time for preparation; yet to the surprise of myself and my friends I passed at the top of the list and thus gained the Asphital Prize for the year.'[20] He was elected an Associate on 31 January 1890.

A LITTLE PRACTICE

The years 1890 and 1891 were a period of doubt and reassessment in Baker's life; now on his own he began to seek a new direction to follow, perhaps build a small country practice; maybe seek adventure and fulfilment in some distant corner of Britain's vast overseas empire. By the end of 1889 he had completed his drawn-out architectural training and education; it had taken him eight and a half years since leaving school to qualify for Associate Membership of the RIBA. But in the light of the times this was not by any means an exceptionally long period. More importantly it had been a wide ranging experience and particularly thorough in the practicalities of building; it had involved leadership and responsibility in a thriving London practice, extensive foreign travel – a liberal education in itself – in all the countries of Europe which were, at the time, of significance in relation to the British architectural scene with the exception, perhaps, of Greece. And he had crowned it all with a noteworthy success in his examination and gained a coveted prize. He was probably at least as well trained, in what was important to architectural practice then, as any young architect of equivalent age would be today, despite the now customary five full-time years of university or polytechnic education.[21]

All seemed set for a highly successful career. In May 1891 he opened a small office in Gravesend, not far from Cobham. But work was slow in coming. Life in the country had a more leisurely pace than in London; the summers were good and there was time to concentrate on cricket, time to sketch and do the odd watercolour and enjoy county life. But Herbert Baker grew restless. Deep down, he wanted to strike out a path of his own in life; to do 'something individual, to vindicate my nature.' Of the

work he did in these first two years of independence all Baker wrote was that '...I was acquiring a little practice of my own in reporting on and restoring some Tudor timber houses in my neighbourhood...'[22] One such restoration he did was at Nurstead Court, the home of his Edmeades cousins; another project was drawings for the restoration of the Cross at Rochester.

Whilst Baker's practice languished, Lutyens's went from strength to strength. Their friendship continued and Lutyens would sometimes take Baker to visit his buildings under construction. It was when working on Crooksbury that Lutyens first met his 'fairy godmother' in the form of the great landscape gardener, Gertrude Jekyll, who was to have such a remarkable and fortuitous influence on his career. Gertrude Jekyll lived at Munstead House near Godalming in Surrey, and it was here that Lutyens took his friend to meet her. Baker was as enthralled with her as Lutyens was, later writing: 'She had a great personality and rare gifts; she was a skilled craftswoman and not only an expert gardener, a planter of flowers, but she had the painter's sense for their arrangement in colour harmonies. But her outstanding possession was the power to see, as a poet, the art and creation of home-making as a whole in relation to Life; the best simple English country life of her day, frugal yet rich in beauty and comfort; in the building and its furnishing and their homely craftsmanship; its garden uniting the house with surrounding nature; all in harmony and breathing the spirit of its creator.'[23]

Baker recalls that when he first met her, a controversy was raging between the Formal garden, on which Reginald Blomfield had written a book, and the Wild garden, of which William Robinson was the champion. When Baker asked her opinion on the rival combatants she replied, 'You can judge best by this: Blomfield has a good wild garden, and Robinson a formal one.'[24]

The drawings which Baker made for two small houses at Southend, with differing elevational design treatments, give some indication of the direction of his architecture in these years.[25] Whether or not the houses were built is uncertain and they may even have been designed as 'samples', or for speculative building, as they seem to lack the conviction that real clients bring to design and were no more than typical of much of the minor English domestic architecture of the period.

With little work of his own Baker assisted Edwin Lutyens by drawing perspectives for him. One, that of Lutyens's pair of lodges at Park Hatch at Hascombe in Surrey (1890) for Mr Joseph Goodman, was published in *The Builder* (15 November 1890). Those he drew of Lutyens's design for Sir Henry Cunningham, rendered in sepia wash, in the manner of Ernest George, are pleasing sketches but not of especially high quality. Interestingly, they seem unlike the general run of Lutyens's architecture at that time, or subsequently for that matter. Baker's undated drawings illustrate a country house in the Gothic Revival manner, complete with stepped buttresses, mullioned windows and a rather church porch-like entrance. The design, which appears not to have been built, in fact looks more like Baker's work than that of Lutyens.

NEWS FROM THE CAPE

Lionel Baker was eight years younger than his brother Herbert. He was the seventh son of Thomas Baker and the third in a succession of six to enter Tonbridge School. For twenty years, from 1875 when Herbert began the tradition, until 1895 when the youngest left, Thomas Baker had at least one son at the school, and sometimes three. In 1890 Lionel, then aged twenty, went to the Cape in search of adventure. The family was fortunate to have a highly placed relative in the colony, for another cousin, Admiral Nicholson, was in command of the Royal Navy at Simonstown.

Lionel was staying at the Admiral's house and sending back all the exciting news. Of particular interest in a family who lived surrounded by orchards were Lionel's enthusiastic remarks about the prospects for fruit farming at the Cape: '...the price of oranges was so much, we were told; a tree grows so many; a few thousand will make your fortune!' Lionel was requesting the financial assistance of his family to start a fruit farm in the Cape. The development of a fruit exporting industry was talked about excitedly in Cape Town as the possibilities for ships with refrigerated chambers were turning into reality.[26]

Herbert Baker was still in England when the first fruit to be imported from the Cape arrived in London. The trial consignment was shipped in the newly refrigerated *Drummond Castle* in early February 1892. The fruit were table peaches, delicate for long-distance travel and everything depended on their condition on arrival. Percy Molteno, son-in-law of the Chairman of the Castle Shipping Company, Sir Donald Currie, had persuaded the com-

pany to equip some of its mailships which plied between Britain and the Cape with cool chambers. Molteno was present when the first cases were opened at Covent Garden; he recalled: '...with great delight we saw case upon case opened up in splendid condition...' The fruit caused a sensation and sold for the staggering price (in 1892) of 2s 3d per peach. If there had been any doubt about Lionel's assessment it was dispelled by this historic event.[27]

Thomas Baker must have thought very hard about the request; he could ill-afford it. It had rained continuously throughout the summer of 1879; the harvest blackened everywhere. Indeed for four successive summers the rain and cold persisted, forcing more and more landowners and tenants into ruin. The census of 1881 showed how, in the previous ten years, a hundred thousand labourers had left the land. As it happened, the failure of agriculture went hand in hand with a slump in industry. Britain was in a great economic depression and unemployment was rife. But whereas industry could and did revive, for agriculture it was no passing phase; it never recovered. Thomas Baker had been no more immune to these events than other landowners and had suffered heavy losses; and the worst years occurred at a time when he had massive school fees to pay. 'My generous father', wrote Baker, 'having already mortgaged his estate to the limit in order to send his nine sons to school, had nothing to spare.' But squeeze out some money he did and Lionel's request for assistance was granted. However, that last straw when added to his losses brought about by those awful summers ten years earlier 'compelled him to sell his estate with the exception of 25 acres of the homestead. It was an anxious decision for my parents to take.'[28]

Herbert Baker's father had made great sacrifices for his family already and he was aware of what risks were involved; and after all, Lionel was only twenty. Herbert was considered to be serious-minded and responsible and it must have seemed a blessing that his practice was small enough to be abandoned at short notice, or suspended for a while. When his father suggested that Herbert go out to the Cape to keep an eye on Lionel's enterprise, he leapt at the chance. 'And could there be', he thought, 'a career for an architect also in this land of promise?[29] In March 1892, just one month after the first Cape peaches arrived fresh and juicy in London, Herbert Baker sailed in the opposite direction in the *Norham Castle*. He was three months short of his thirtieth birthday.

PART TWO
CAPE COLONY

Top. Groote Schuur, Rondebosch. Watercolour by unknown
artist as it looked in 1838. Bottom. Groote Schuur today,
view of rear.

CHAPTER THREE

1892-1896

CAPE HOPES

FIRST IMPRESSIONS

The beauty and grandeur of Table Mountain, the vast flat-topped rock that is the scenic backdrop to every Cape Town vista, are staggering. Alas, one seldom now approaches it by sea as, in the past, all travellers did. To first see the mountain after seemingly endless days at sea is awe-inspiring; to see it by the first glow of the rising sun would be good fortune indeed. It is one of the world's most unforgettable sights. Herbert Baker was to recollect his own first impressions, some fifty years after, with these words: 'I myself did not fully feel the magic of the mountain until I walked up its slopes from Rondebosch, first through a pinewood carpeted with pale-purple lachenalias, on through a jungle of tall heathery and aromatic plants, cup- and cone-shaped flowering protea bushes and the taller silver-trees. The silvery-white down of the under-leaves of these trees in the mass when stirred by the wind brings out the rich colouring of the vegetation on the mountain slopes, in the same way that the silver-greens of the umbrella-shaped stone-pines frame a view of the turquoise surf-fringed Table Bay and False Bay, and the dimmed blue distant headlands of the mountains of the hinterland; and hanging overhead the precipices of the Devil's Peak. Then in my delight I said to myself, "This is the land for me."'[1]

Baker's dearest memories of Table Mountain were of going out early to walk, and later on to ride, on the lower slopes below Devil's Peak, not far from Groote Schuur; he then realized what Rhodes saw and held in such deep reverence. The majesty of the scene could hardly be believed. 'From the mountain side you could see the Flats covered by a sea of white mist, which the tops of the umbrella-shaped stone pines studded with islands of emeralds; and

beyond, the ring of the mainland mountains appeared pure cobalt and clear-cut in the serenity of the Cape air against the rising sun, which above us made the cedar tops and hills seem burnished gold.'[2]

On his arrival he went first with his brother Lionel to Simonstown to stay with Rear-Admiral Henry and Lady Nicholson at Admiralty House. In the bay the flagship *Raleigh* lay at anchor; it was one of the last full-rigged ships of the Royal Navy. The Admiral was his cousin and, being Commander-in-Chief, Cape of Good Hope, was perfectly placed to immediately introduce Herbert to the high society of the Cape. They then moved on to a farmhouse at Franschhoek in the valley where the Huguenots had settled, and the brothers spent a week there. This was Herbert's first chance to explore this exciting new country on foot, ranging widely over 'the heathery veld and fells with my gun, expectant like a newcomer of a great sport, but soon disappointed at the lack of game.'[3]

But he was thrilled to discover the dignity and beauty of the old Dutch and Huguenot homesteads, 'dignified in the ordered layout of the house, out-buildings, avenues, orchards, and vineyards; beautiful in the simplicity of the architecture, white walls, solid teak or green-painted shuttered windows and doors, gracefully curved gables with softly modelled enrichments and quiet moleskin thatch...' No doubt it brought back memories of architecture he had seen and sketched in Holland and Belgium, even of Ernest George's 'Dutch' houses in Cadogan Square, Chelsea. But above all, here was a real working vernacular; not so much a style but a way of building, rooted in the soil and, though it was little appreciated by the colonists themselves, beautiful.[4]

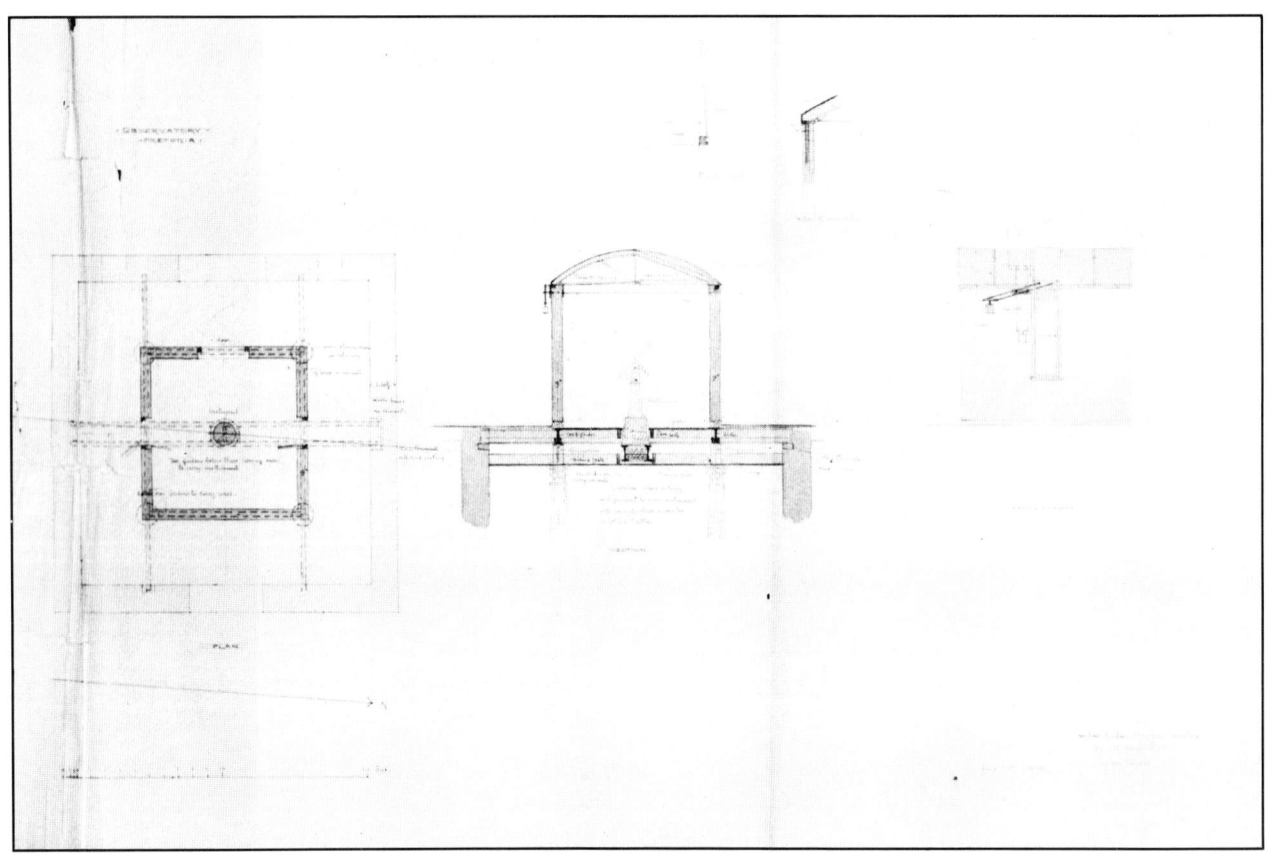

Observatory to be erected on the Government Building, Pretoria.
Herbert Baker, June 1892. The earliest known drawing by Baker in
South Africa.

And there was much more to learn besides. From 'having many talks with wise and helpful people, who were anxious to promote our adventure...', he got to know the Western Province farmers and their farms, the country and the difficulties they would be faced with in starting to farm in a strange land.[5]

Baker had been in the Cape two weeks when a young Englishman, H E V Pickstone, arrived in the Colony. Harry Pickstone was twenty when he first came to Africa in 1885, and served in the colonial mounted troop, Methuen's Horse, in Cecil Rhodes's Bechuanaland expedition. He later worked his way through Canada and, after some eighteen months, found himself in California on an orange nursery. A few years later he was on his way back to the Cape again, via London, where he had seen the first refrigerated Cape peaches and where Rhodes's business partner, C D Rudd, gave him a letter of introduction to Rhodes in Cape Town. Two months after his arrival in 1892, Pickstone published an article in the *Agricultural Journal* on the commercial prospects of growing deciduous fruit for export. Rhodes was impressed by Pickstone's vision and confidence; here was the man who could fulfil Rhodes's ambitions for the fruit industry.[6]

Herbert and Lionel were invited to Groote Schuur, the old house, which for the previous two decades had been rented by a succession of prominent Cape politicians and was now the home of Rhodes, to discuss fruit farming. Several talks with Pickstone and 'the enthusiastic J X Merriman' took place and things were looking up. It seemed that Fate, in the form of this dynamic young man who glowed with energy, and who enjoyed the trust and generosity of Rhodes, had come to their rescue.[7]

Later in the year the Pioneer Fruit Growing Company was formed with Harry Pickstone, backed by Rhodes, at its head. His partners were a local farmer named Sebastian van Reenen and Lionel Baker.

They would immediately establish a nursery of 50 000 imported deciduous fruit trees on the farm Nooitgedacht, near Stellenbosch. Alas it was a false start. Herbert Baker saw the reasons thus: 'The local farmer, excitable by nature, could not understand Pickstone's Californian methods, nor sympathize with his generous nature...' It must have come as a blow to the Baker family, who had sacrificed so much to give Lionel his chance, but the partnership was dissolved and the nursery abandoned. Rhodes helped Pickstone to start again, this time in the Constantia district, whilst Lionel Baker found work as a government forester. Before long Cecil Rhodes was employing Pickstone to buy and establish his fruit farms, particularly in the Groot Drakenstein Valley where, by 1904, he had more than a million trees growing. Lionel Baker became the manager of one of these farms – land 'with vineyards and orchards beside the clear and swift Berg River' and on which stood the picturesque thatch-roofed house, Weltevreden.[8]

MEETING RHODES

Baker recorded that he first met Cecil Rhodes shortly after his arrival at the Cape in March 1892. The occasion was a dinner party at the home of Lewis Vintcent, a Member of the Cape House of Assembly and brother-in-law of John X Merriman, also a Cape Parliamentarian. The seating arrangement seems to have been a strange one, for the unknown young architect found himself sitting directly opposite the Prime Minister. 'I sat entranced at their talk on South Africa and world affairs, but I said little or nothing, and went away much discomforted at having proved myself so unable to make the most of this golden opportunity.' Agnes Merriman, Vintcent's sister, had sat next to Baker that evening and the following day gave him the consoling news that Rhodes had asked her to tell him more about 'that silent young man.' It was probably Mrs Merriman who put the word in Rhodes's ear that Baker was making an enthusiastic study of the old Cape architecture.

He was making drawings of the old farms and houses he saw on his visits to the neighbouring districts; but he was astonished by the lack of interest his new friends and acquaintances showed when he talked to them about these wonderful, simple buildings. He really felt that he had made a discovery, and in a sense he had. Such information could

not have reached Rhodes at a better time, for he was contemplating the restoration of his house, Groote Schuur, which he had first rented and was now buying. He knew, as if by instinct, that these early Cape houses had harmonious qualities which were worth preserving. In an unusual way for his time, he sensed too that there was a political value in doing something to make the public more aware of their own heritage; that a well-loved national architecture has a potent symbolic value. Perhaps by his example he could make the general neglect turn into love and respect.[9]

FIRST WORK

Baker was an habitual early riser, and frequently began the day with a walk on the lower slopes of the mountain. One such morning, not long after the dinner meeting, he met Rhodes and Sauer, 'another member of the Ministry', returning from their morning ride on the Cape Flats. Rhodes stopped and asked him to breakfast the next morning; he wanted Baker, he said, to restore his house.[10]

'This happy meeting and invitation determined my fortunes. Having done what I came out for and settled my brother on a farm, I decided that I would stay and try my luck as an architect.' So wrote Baker of the key event of his career and his life. Work on Groote Schuur did not really get going for a year or two but, having decided to stay at the Cape, he now needed an office and the only one he could find – or afford – was a roof-top turret over an old house at 43 St George's Street.

This eight-foot-square room, glazed all round with small panes of old glass, was called an *uitkyk*, literally a 'lookout' from which one could see ships approaching and departing Table Bay and, of course, the ever-present mountain. The first client to climb up to his studio was another member of Rhodes's cabinet, James Rose Innes, then Minister of Justice. He had brought with him Baker's 'first job, a small addition to the reformatory at Tokai.'[11]

Alas, no positive record has been found to show what Baker built at Tokai. It might have been a whole wing of accommodation, which was hardly a 'small job.' More likely it was the bell-tower with bull's-eye features similar to Karatara, the house he was to build for Rose Innes in Kenilworth three years later.[12]

The earliest drawings found thus far done by Baker in South Africa are for an 'Observatory to be erected on the Government Buildings, Pretoria.'

House for J B Moffat, Kenilworth, 1892. Demolished.

These two drawings are clearly dated, in Baker's hand, June and July 1892 respectively. This roof-top structure is devoid of any architectural style, the structure being simply a utilitarian housing for a moving telescope. Whether the ingenious counter-weighted mechanism for opening and closing the roof aperture is of Baker's own devising is open to conjecture. But perhaps the most remarkable aspect of this project is that it should have been in Pretoria and commissioned within two to three months of Baker's arrival in Cape Town.[13]

Possibly even before he designed the observatory Baker was engaged in the design of the first buildings to be built on the present site of the Wynberg Boys' High School. The plan was composed of a large assembly hall surrounded by teaching rooms in the manner of the School Board buildings of England in the nineteenth century.[14]

In October that year Baker designed what appears to be the first house he built in South Africa. The exact address of this house – for J B Moffat – at Kenilworth, is unknown and it has almost certainly been demolished. However, a surviving photograph shows a homely, double-storey house with rendered walls and strong brick quoins on the corners and on the chimney which towers over a tiled or slated hipped roof. The window facing on to the stair has side-hung casements; others appear to be of the vertical sliding sash type. The distinct entrance porch and the shallow arched, brick lintels unite with the brick quoins to produce a pleasing, but quite unremarkable, 'Englishness'. A drawing dated 6 October 1892, entitled 'House at Kenilworth' has been linked to the photograph and it seems likely to represent a plan of the Moffat house. However, the elevation accompanying the

24

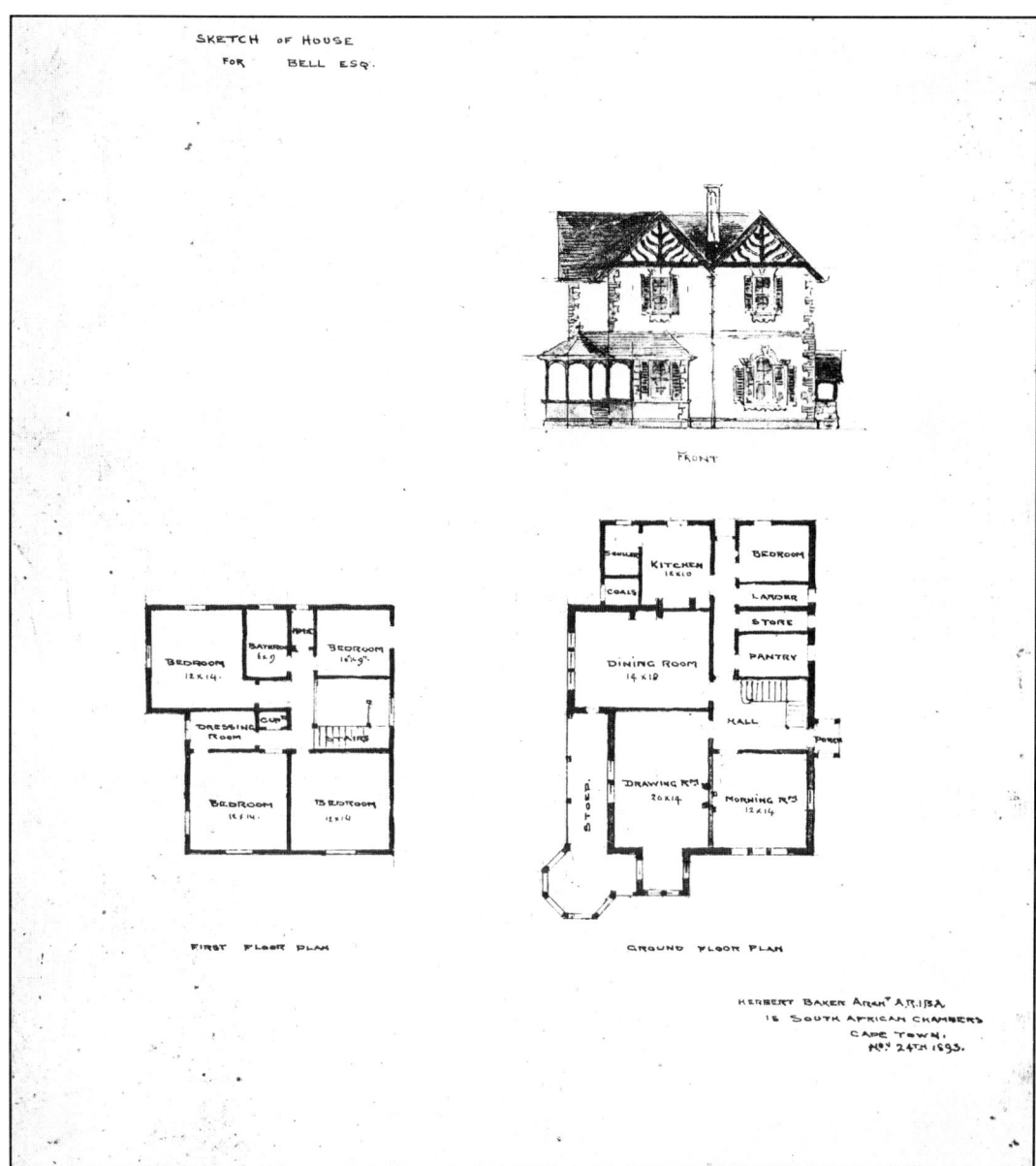

Hopetown House for Alex Bell.

plan shows a Flemish gable, and a veranda on the northern side, that do not appear in the photograph.[15] But this drawing should not be discounted for that reason: it is, of course, quite customary for designs to be altered during their development on the drawing board, or even, as occurs in some cases, during construction.

Still standing in Burg Road, Rondebosch, is the house called Linköping which Baker designed during the following month for a Dr Smuts. Its survival makes it the oldest known, extant Baker house in South Africa. Although much larger than the Moffat house, Linköping has several features in common with its lost predecessor, including the arched heads of the four-pane sash windows, a veranda with a projecting bay and the chimney with its arched recessed panel. It is possible that it had brick quoins too, which, like the string course at first-floor level, may have been obliterated with plaster.

By April 1893, Baker had moved from his *uitkyk* to a larger office, but he was still without an assistant. He was to remain single-handed until the following year, when he took on one G G Milne.

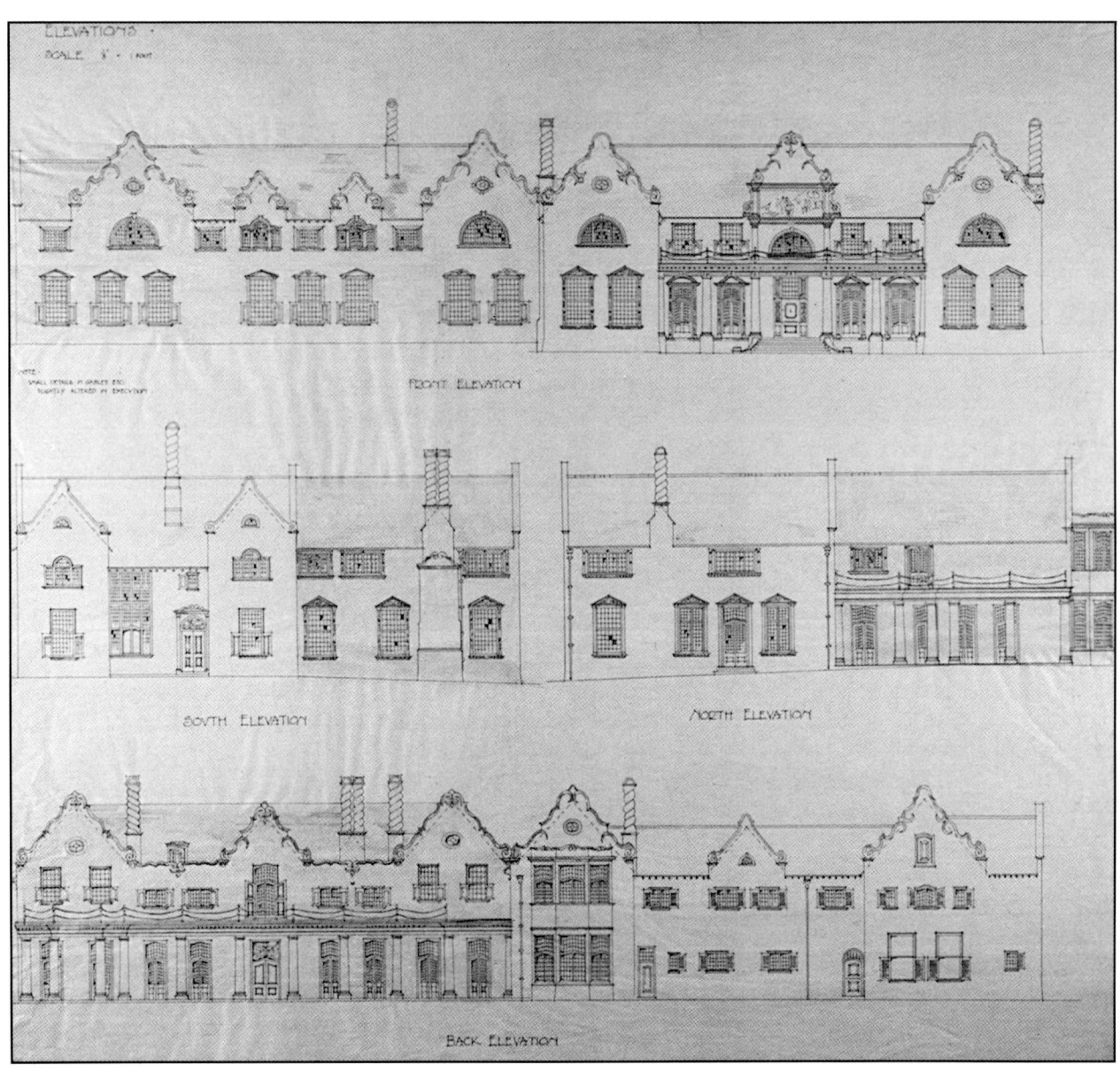

Groote Schuur, Rondebosch, for the Rt Hon C J Rhodes. Elevations,
circa 1897.

In his second year at the Cape, 1893, Baker was involved with a number of minor projects; alterations and additions to existing houses. These include a double-storey wing to Glion – now called Sunningdale – in Tennant Road, Kenilworth, for W T Buissine and which may not have been built; alterations to Roodebloem for A van der Byl at Woodstock; and to Hopetown House for Alexander Bell in November.

During 1893 Baker was also invited to design conversions for new premises for the City Club in the Colonial Insurance Company's building and also in The Colonnade, both of which were on the lower side of Greenmarket Square. However, for the time being it was undecided about where this prestigious club was to be located and they continued to examine other offers of sites. Although nothing came of his proposals Baker was making useful contact with members of the club, and it was not until August 1896 that he became involved again. But the most important work to begin in 1893 was Groote Schuur for Cecil Rhodes.[16]

GROOTE SCHUUR: FROM BARN TO VILLA

The original Groote Schuur had been erected as a granary by the Dutch East India Company, and was originally known as *de Schuur*, which means 'the granary.' It was built in 1657, just five years after Jan van Riebeeck had landed at the Cape to establish the first white settlement in southern Africa. The building and its surrounding estate has changed hands, and names, many times over the years. But it was in 1791 that its most important change took place when the 'great barn' was sold by the Company as part of an economy drive; it was then converted into a two-storey dwelling.[17]

The earliest known representation of Groote Schuur dates from 1830, two years before the house was bought by Abraham de Smidt. This water-colour, made by Lady Helen Walker, shows a flat-roofed 'stoepkamer' house, similar to Leeuenhof and typical of many others in the area. The roof was altered twice by de Smidt; the first change, from flat to pitched, was made in the 1830s, and is illustrated in a drawing of 1838 which shows the addition of a stepped and pedimented central gable and the thatched roof. Neither of the drawings mentioned was seen by Herbert Baker when he was considering restoration of the house.

Following a mountain blaze which destroyed the thatch and the unusual gables, in 1842 de Smidt rebuilt the roof in slate and gave it hipped ends where the gables had been. Also in existence are two drawings attributed to an artist known to have stayed on the estate in 1838; these illustrate some details corresponding to the earlier drawings and others relating to the changes made by de Smidt. But depicted in these later drawings is the strangely uncharacteristic colonial Dutch appearance which the building had acquired, especially in the form of its new gables. The house retained this look for no more than ten years; but, ironically, it was to these drawings, or a painting copied from one of them, that Baker was referred and on which he based his designs. One can but speculate on the form his restoration might have taken had he seen the slightly earlier drawings.[18]

When Cecil Rhodes bought the house in 1893, after having rented it for two years, it was called 'The Grange'. Ten years earlier it had been bought by the Public Works Department for leasing to the British Governor of the Colony and had been badly restored and remodelled into a sort of Victorian villa and given the strangest sunflower-like window surrounds. Rhodes cared neither for its name nor its appearance and raised some colonial eyebrows when he changed the name of his new home to the decidedly Dutch-sounding Groote Schuur.[19]

By now there was little trace of the original barn, or even much of de Smidt's work; but Rhodes had the ambition to re-create the original estate, with the house authentically restored to its historical appearance, and all the suburban home-building plots reconsolidated into an estate which he would preserve in his Will for the Nation. When they met for breakfast Rhodes told Baker he had heard that he had been studying with interest the old colonial architecture and, '...so hoped that he would be able to restore Groote Schuur to its original architectural character.' According to Baker, a descendant of Abraham de Smidt had given Rhodes a drawing showing, '...the original high-pitched roof, and the windows of the gable.' Baker, whilst recognizing that the evidence was scanty, believed that the drawing was representative and that, together with the knowledge he had acquired of other old Cape houses, it had 'made it possible to rebuild the front with some degree of faithfulness to its original form and type.'[20]

Baker cannot be blamed for accepting the only documentary evidence that appears to have been available at the time. Nevertheless one does wonder why he fails to remark, even forty years after, on the atypical Cape character of the de Smidt drawing. As Barrie Biermann has commented: 'It is ironical that this particularly shortlived and eccentric phase in the history of one building should have been singled out as typical of two centuries of the colony's architectural development, for the progeny of this ephemeral structure...ultimately multiplied and migrated further over the sub-continent than its contemporaries, the wagons of the Great Trek.'[21]

BIG, SIMPLE AND BARBARIC

It was a surprise to Baker that Rhodes, 'the chairman of great business corporations', should give him no details of his requirements. 'He just gave me in a few words his idea...and trusted me to do the rest.' By early September 1893, Baker had completed his design and working drawings, and received tenders from six contractors. Later that month, having given his architect his 'thoughts', Rhodes sailed for Beira on his way to sort out prob-

Groote Schuur, Rondebosch, kitchen gable details. November 1897.

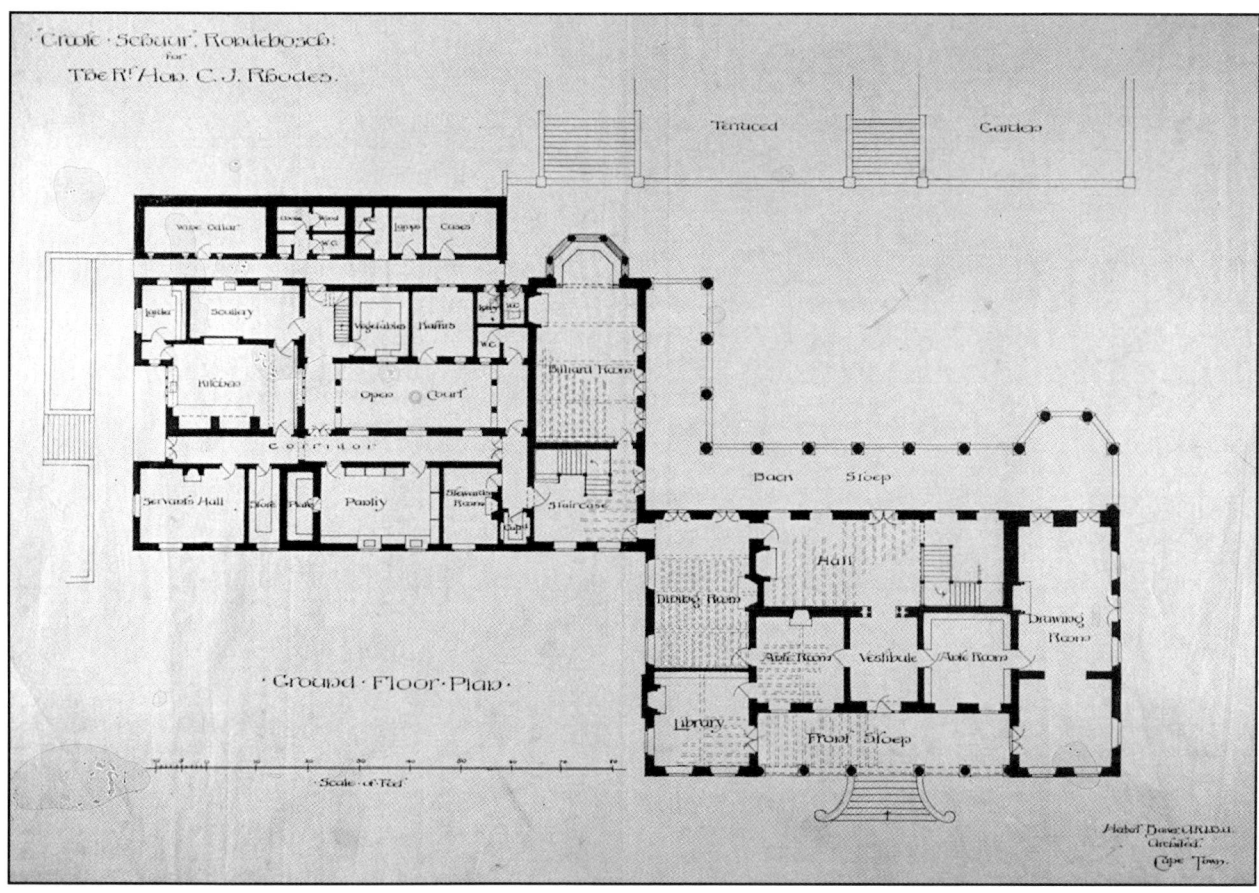

Groote Schuur, Rondebosch, ground floor plan.

lems in Mashonaland. He returned early in January 1894, after the conquest of Matabeleland, to find the new front part of the house completed, despite the problems Baker was having in recruiting a 'scratch labour' force. Rhodes was characteristically silent but Baker inferred Rhodes's approval from his enthusiasm to proceed with the extension block and to restore the rest of the old house. The extensions were to comprise the kitchens and billiard room, with his bedroom over it and a new loggia, or columned stoep, at the back of the house, facing his beloved Table Mountain.[22]

Throughout the restoration and rebuilding, Baker lived in a cottage close to the gardens of Groote Schuur. It was called The Grotto and stood at the head of a kloof, its garden watered by a small stream. He had restored it himself and furnished it with old blue Dutch china and beautiful oak furniture; watercolours hung on the walls. Lionel Curtis confessed to being 'astonished' by it when he visi-

ted the house in May 1901. For keeping an eye on the progress of the house, it could hardly have been more convenient; indeed it was so close that when – after late discussions with Rhodes – Baker was asked to dine, he would 'scramble through the dark pine trees, dress, and rush back as the last of the mixed assembly of guests arrived.'[23]

For Rhodes, the problems of home-making and furnishing – so new to a man who, since his days at the Bishops Stortford vicarage where he had been brought up, had known little else but the rough life of mining camp, veld and farm – suddenly began to interest him. Baker recalls him saying he wanted: 'The big and simple, barbaric if you like', and, 'I like teak and whitewash.' And he was prepared to pay for it. He told Baker to tear out from work already completed all deal joinery, which needed painting, and replace it with teak, the timber widely used by the old colonists. Baker also had to replace all imported ironmongery; 'the things he hated, such as hinges and metal work for doors and windows – even screws in those places where they could be seen...' Craftsmen had to be found and 'taught to hammer in iron or cast in brass and bronze, as in the golden days of the crafts before the hostile influences of machinery.'[24]

But the architecture, and its detail design, was a matter for Baker to interpret according to his own judgement and the de Smidt drawing. Where would he start? Should he attempt to build a direct copy of the drawing – or simply take from it what he felt to be its best features?

CAPE DUTCH STYLE

In recent years Baker has frequently been accused of 'misusing' the Cape Dutch style at Groote Schuur. But it should be remembered that there was no 'Cape Dutch' style until he came on the scene – it became a style when its self-conscious revival began. Barrie Biermann has written: 'In the past there has been a tendency to consider the buildings at the Cape in isolation as a style in its own right, the so-called "Cape Dutch Style", on the assumption that every country is entitled to its own architectural tradition and that every such tradition is the product of indigenous evolution.' Biermann regards this view as largely a child of its time, when historical-revival styles were the architect's stock in trade, and when 'research into the sources of the [Cape Dutch] designs had not progressed beyond informed conjecture.' It would be more accurate to see the old Cape architecture as a 'regional variant of a world-wide European colonial vernacular'. And, as such, utterly dependent upon European prototypes.[25]

By adopting the local vernacular and freely translating some of its elements, adding others borrowed from other sources, or of his own invention, Baker was designing exactly as his comtemporaries in London and elsewhere were doing. If the semi-circular windows in the gables of de Smidt were unusual when they were built, that was a matter of chance. Baker, in retaining them with such apparent relish in his revivalist architecture was not at fault. They, together with his twisted chimneys, became part of the new revival style – which could rightly be called the 'Cape Dutch style'. His only misjudgement, for he surely cannot have been persuaded by Rhodes, was to think – and later write – that the prototype he used was typical of the genre.

As a former assistant of the great pictorialist, Ernest George, and an Arts and Crafts man to the core, Baker could so easily have drawn on the latest trends back home. Instead, he evolved a brilliantly original design that employed the principles of Free Style vernacular and was, for that reason, rather than mimicry, completely in step with his English contemporaries.

DIOCESAN ARCHITECT

In September 1893, the month in which work on the restoration of Groote Schuur began, a site on the north side of Kildare Road in Newlands was bought from J C Nesser in order to build a new church of St Andrew. Events moved fast and a foundation stone for the St Andrew Church was laid on 6 May 1894.[26]

The Diocesan appointment was a watershed for Baker. He was now in his thirty-second year and had not designed a church of his own before, either in England or South Africa. His Llanberis experience as clerk-of-works a decade before must have been almost forgotten. Although square-ended chancels had been a commonplace feature of English church architecture since Anglo-Saxon times, his cousin's design for Llanberis may have influenced him. Like Llanberis, St Andrew has three lancet windows in the east-end chancel wall, behind the altar. But that is all. With its broken roof-line it more resembles some of A W Pugin's later parish churches, such as St Mary, Brewood, Staffordshire, 1842-4, or St Lawrence, Tubney, Berkshire, 1845-7. He may also have been influenced by the local work of the amateur architect, Sophie Gray whose settler churches proliferated in the Cape. In particular he would have seen her St Saviour, the fashionable church at nearby Claremont, which he was himself largely to rebuild and extend some six years later.[27] But the style of the Newlands church was uniquely Baker's, and the most positive attempt to adapt English Arts and Crafts design to local conditions he had made so far. The character of the west gable wall, with the projecting timber bell-housing, the small rose-window and the rough stonework and heavy timber door, affirm his Arts and Crafts intentions, but the small windows and rugged stone walls, inside and out, make it a child of the Cape sunlight, and of its mountain setting.

St Andrew was built of Table Mountain sandstone, dressed and coursed, with stubby buttresses

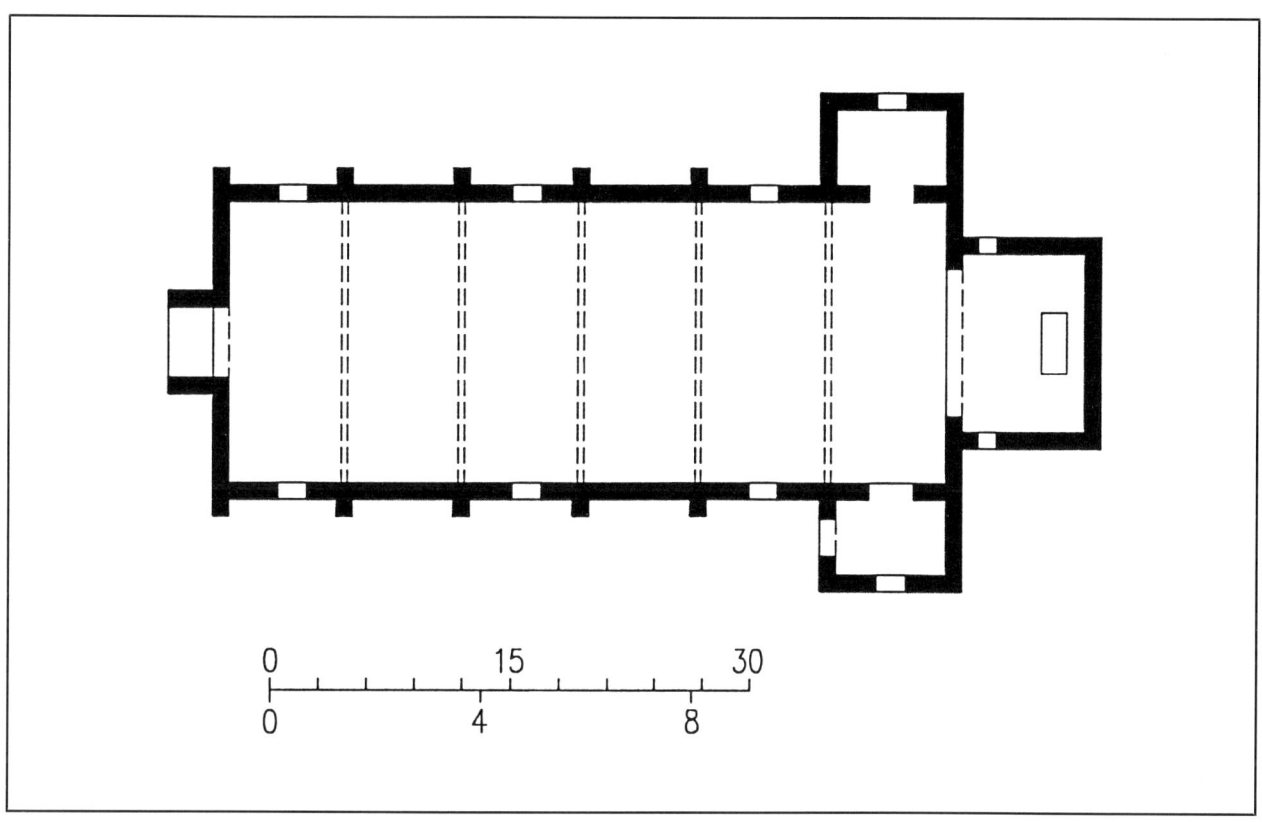

Church of St Andrew, Newlands (St Andrew's in the Oaks). Plan.

dividing each bay where the simple king-post timber trusses were supported. The six nave windows; one to each alternate bay have trefoil heads, mullions and transoms carved in grey sandstone by J Dollidge of Wynberg.[28]

The serene hall-like nave, without aisles or transepts, is divided from the low-roofed chancel by a simple, emphatic arch. Over the nave dark, stained-boarding follows the line of the roof which was originally covered with thatch, subsequently in wooden shingles (1949) and, most recently, in Mazista slate in 1967. The slate is less evocative on its mountain setting, tending towards suburban ordinariness: imagine it once more in thatch! In 1971 the floor was renewed in the same material and the original wooden chairs replaced by oak pews. Often thought to be the work of Baker is the lych gate, designed by W Boyce in 1908. The white stone octagonal font, with its oak top was the 1897 work of London church furnishers, Jones and Willis.[29]

Of all the furnishings and embellishments, the most interesting comprise the glass in the three lancet windows over the altar. They were designed by the English Pre-Raphaelite artist, Sir Edward Burne Jones and are the sole examples of the artist's work in South Africa.

In the church of St Andrew, Baker had created a near-perfect Arts and Crafts building, adapted to Cape conditions. In a sense Groote Schuur too was born of the same thinking, tempered with a more obvious Dutch influence. But Baker did not restrict his design or his interests to the development of such a style: compared with Groote Schuur, his early Cape houses betray more distinctly English origins. Perhaps out of general interest, perhaps out of his talks with Cecil Rhodes – but whatever the reason – it is interesting to note that in August 1894 he ordered from Batsfords, the London bookshop, a volume of an expensive German work on Renaissance architecture. A Schutz's *Die Renaissance in Italien* was a four-volume work which had been appearing volume by volume since 1891.

An eventful year ended fittingly for Baker when, on 30 November 1894, 'St Andrew's in the Oaks' was consecrated.[30]

Church of St Andrew, Newlands, 1894. East-end gables.

Church of St Andrew, Newlands. West gable.

Church of St Andrew, Newlands. Nave interior.

Karatara. House for J Rose Innes, Kenilworth, 1894.

In January 1895 Baker began work on a series of 'villas' for H W Struben, the brother and sometime partner of Frederick Struben, founder of the first successful gold mining company on the now booming Witwatersrand. After the discovery of gold Hendrik Struben withdrew, and settled in Rosebank in 1890. Of the projects built for Struben only Burnage, in Woolsack Road, exists today.[31]

It is difficult to determine exactly when James Rose Innes, the client for Tokai, Baker's first job in South Africa, commissioned him to design the house, Karatara, in Kenilworth, but actual construction did not start before 1895.[32] Karatara shows more English Arts and Crafts influence than the surviving photograph of the Moffat house indicates, despite having been taken three years later. The Rose Innes house has vaguely English gables pierced with circular apertures over a pair of oriel windows. The walls are rendered in white with incongruously rough, stone quoins at the corners.

For the most part, 1895 was a quiet year for Baker who spent much of his time on the Groote Schuur restoration and in his continued struggle to raise standards of workmanship. As he later wrote, it was a time when 'the building crafts of the Colony were not of a high order. Cheap sea freights and scarcity of skilled labour encouraged the importation of everything ready-made from Europe. The building industry was under the influence of the merchants and retailers.' But in all these matters he found Rhodes's example and encouragement an inspiration. In his search for skilled men, he found the remarkable George Ness in an engineering workshop, and was able to give an 'enterprising young builder', A B Reid, his opportunity. 1895 now saw Baker with two assistants, B Bowley and J C Tully. The latter acted as clerk-of-works for Groote Schuur. Rhodes himself was frequently away on business, leaving his architect to get on with it, though Baker did not have it all his own

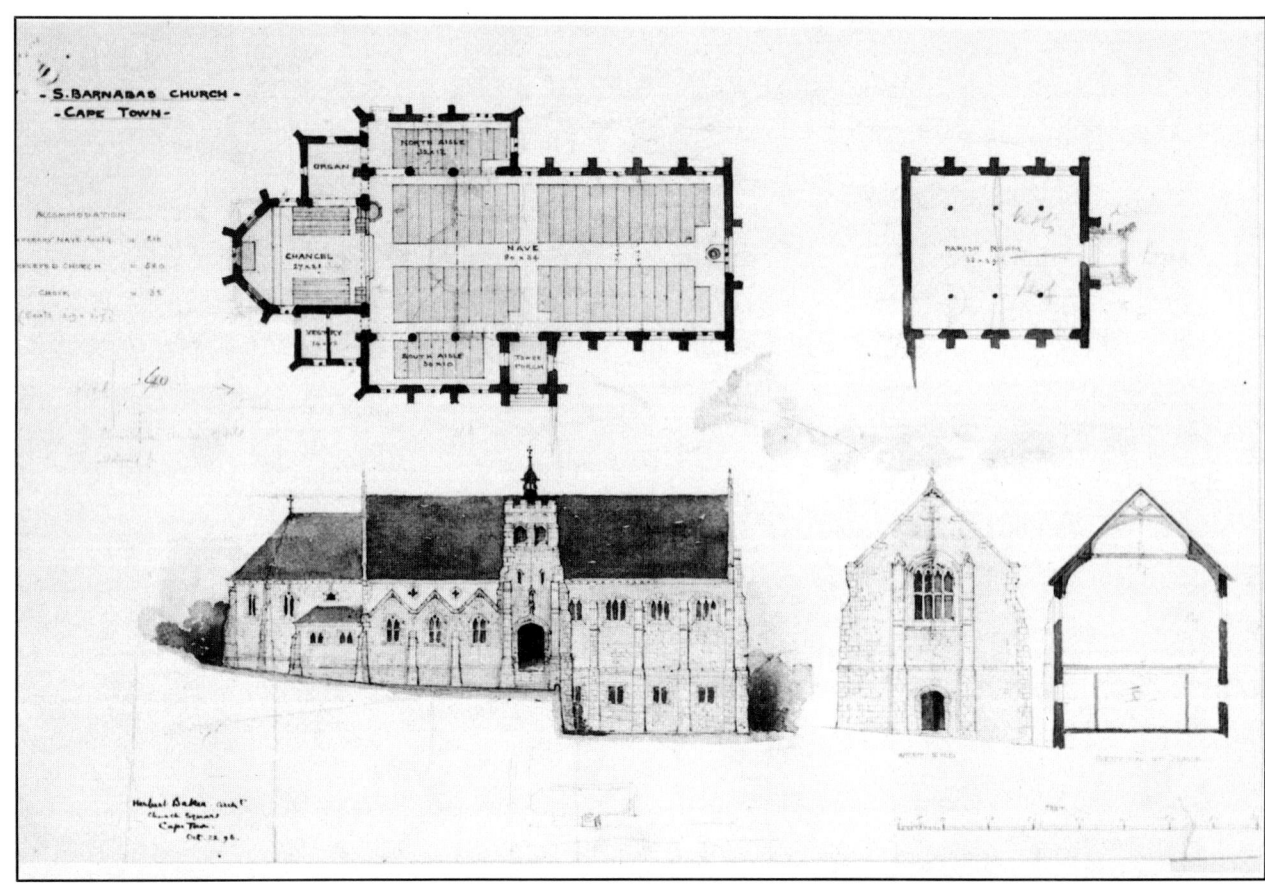

Church of St Barnabas, Tamboerskloof. Drawing of first design, 22 October 1896.

way, however. Rhodes 'had an instinct and the right feeling for personal craftsmanship and good honest material' – teak and whitewash.[33]

Early in 1896 Cecil Rhodes made a trip to England to face a meeting of the shareholders of his Chartered Company and to discuss with the British Government the aftermath of the Jameson Raid. The year had begun with political disaster: Dr Jameson's ill-judged invasion of Paul Kruger's tiny, independent Transvaal Republic ended abruptly with his force's surrender at Doornkop on 2 January. The long-term effects of that event were to be profound and change the course of history in southern Africa. More immediately it led to Rhodes's resignation from the Cape premiership. Then, on 24 March, the Matabele Rebellion began in the land his name had been given to, the year before. On 26 June he resigned from the board of the British South Africa Company – which he himself had founded by Charter from Queen Victoria in 1889.

For Rhodes's architect, 1896 had begun quietly with little new work coming in. There was a house, Kolaro – in Goldbourne Road, Kenilworth – built for E Hutchins, for which drawings dated June 1896 exist. In Kenilworth Road, he also designed some semi-detached villas for Dr C F K Murray.[34] But apart from progressing with Groote Schuur, for the Diocesan architect the greatest plum of all was ripening – a new Anglican Cathedral for Cape Town. He was well on the way to doing 'something individual, to vindicate my nature'. But there were to be some interesting twists in that path.

By May 1896, the City Club had finally decided to buy a property in New Street (now Queen Victoria Street) for their new premises. Baker had advised the club three years earlier and was by now well known to many of its members. Among them were several Cape Parliamentarians, including Cecil Rhodes himself. There was also Edmund Garrett, the influential editor of the *Cape Times*,

Church of St Barnabas, Tamboerskloof. Entrance elevation facing Kloof Road.

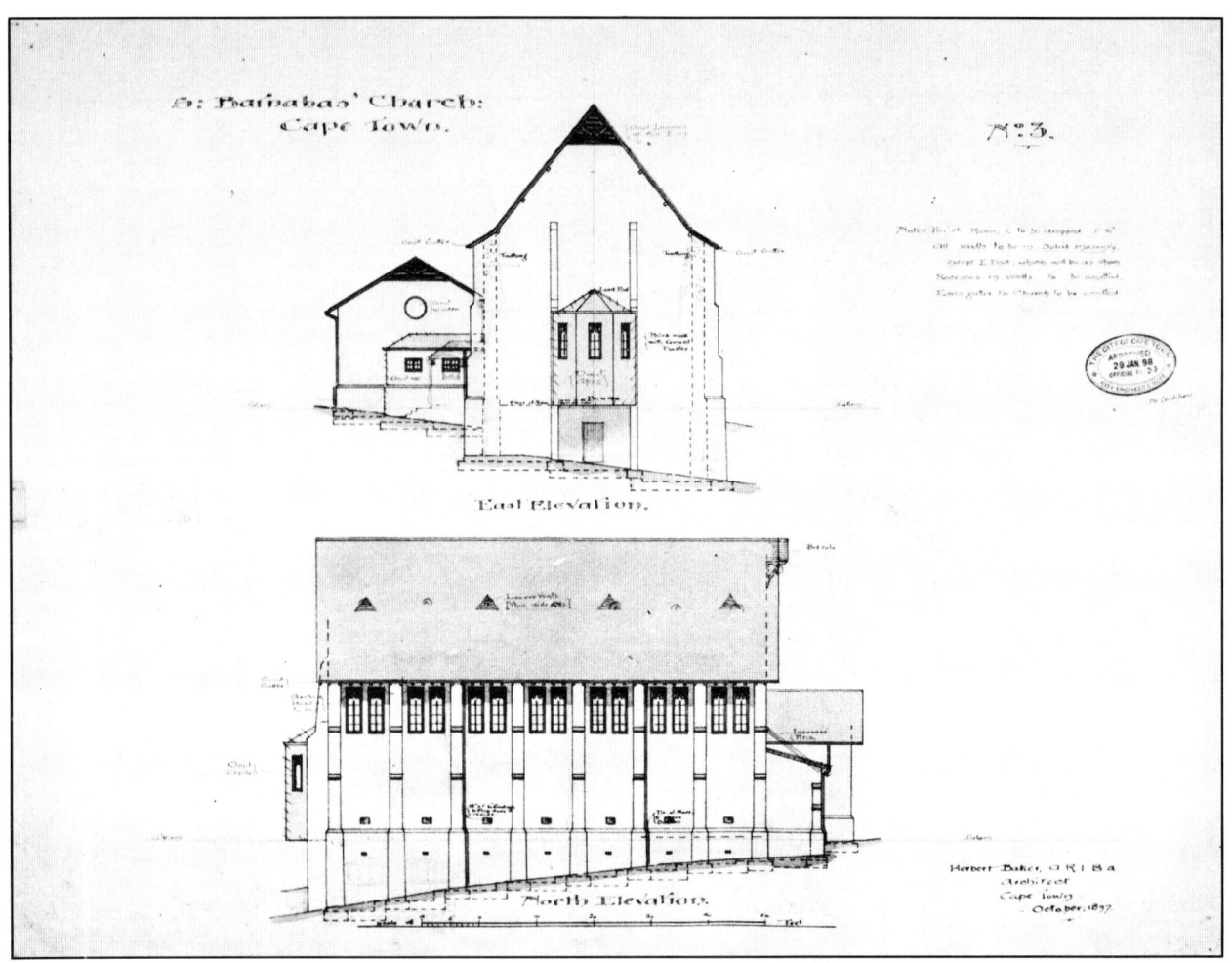

Church of St Barnabas, Tamboerskloof. Elevations, October 1897.

and an up-and-coming Cape Town architect named John Parker (1866-1921).[35]

Baker was asked to 'confer with the committee with reference to plans for the new Club' and, on 25 August, 'it was then decided to award two prizes for architects' plans for the club and that the competition should be limited to architects of Cape Town, the first prize to be £100 and the second £50.' It seems unlikely that Baker – or any architect – would recommend a competition of his own volition, especially when already favourably placed to receive the commission. More plausibly, had someone or some group objected to Baker's appointment, possibly favouring their own man? And, if so, could John Parker, who had become a Club member the year before, have been involved? The competition seems to have been a compromise, a solution to which Baker did not disagree. At all events he now had to take the matter of competition seriously and much was at stake, as it doubtlessly was for Parker too.[36]

ST BARNABAS

Whilst the Club competition drawings were being prepared Baker received his second church commission: for the Church of St Barnabas in Kloof Road, Tamboerskloof. It came three years after the construction of St Andrew and, following the confident pioneering adaptation of Arts and Crafts to local conditions at St Andrew, it may come as a surprise to learn that the earliest scheme he produced for St Barnabas was in the Gothic Revival style. It was, indeed, in a very thorough and workmanlike English parish church Gothic manner. The design

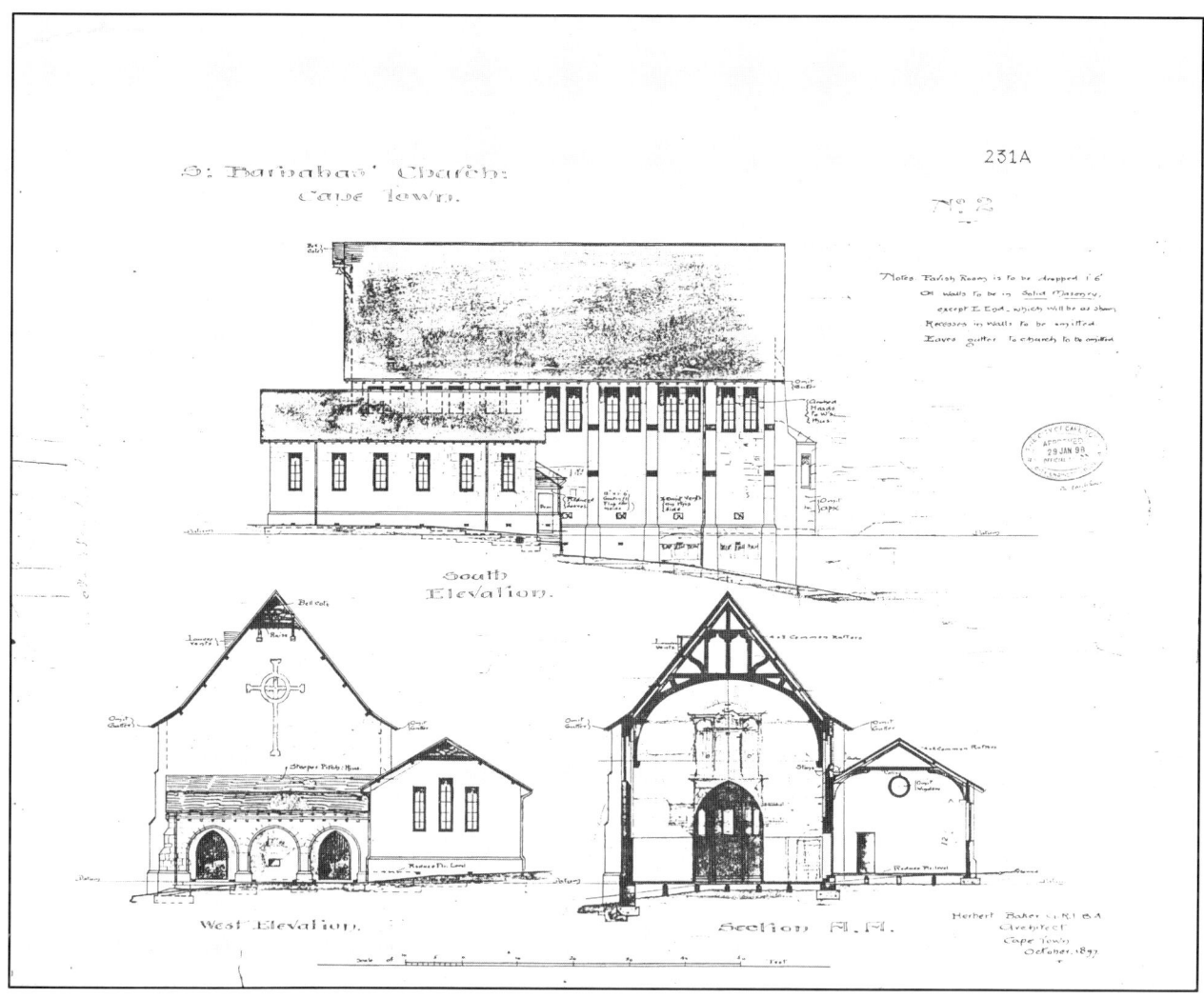

St Barnabas, drawing of church as built, October 1897, stamped 'approved' by the City Engineer of Cape Town, 29 January 1898.

is dated 22 October 1896 and a drawing also exists which shows a variation of this design, but its date is unclear, as is the reason for its preparation.[37] Both versions show the chancel facing north-west into Kloof Road and include a battlemented tower over the entrance porch, similar in compositional placing to his design for St George's Cathedral, as shall be seen later.

The drawings of the church as it was finally built were not completed until October 1897. They show the church facing in the opposite direction, with the parish room ranging alongside the main body of the church, a position less favourable for the church's corner of site position, but clearly a more economical solution than its previous siting under the nave.

In the meantime, Baker had taken on a new assistant, a twenty-six year old Australian-born architect named Franklin Kendall, who was a nephew of the Rector of the Newlands church that Baker had built earlier. After an English schooling and architectural training, and some four years of experience in England, Kendall arrived in Cape Town in March 1896. He then worked for a short while in Cape Town, first for John Parker and then with Sydney Stent, before joining Baker as a junior partner later that year.[38] It is just possible that Kendall might have had some influence on the earlier Gothic versions of St Barnabas.

Baker was developing the design for St Barnabas, and was busy with Groote Schuur and the Club competition, when he fell ill with typhoid fever.

Top. *Languedoc, rectory.* Bottom. *Languedoc village,*
workers' housing, recently restored.

Languedoc, church-cum-schoolhouse, circa 1898.

Whilst in hospital Baker was visited by a past fellow student of the Royal Academy, a Soane Medalist for the year 1885, who had also won the Tite Prize in 1888 and the Owen Jones Student Medal in 1889. His name was Francis Edward Masey and had recently come to the Cape on a three-year agreement to work for the Public Works Department. Francis Masey was finding the work 'uncongenial' and, hearing of 'an English architect in hospital' paid Baker a visit. Masey offered to look after Baker's work for him during his illness and, before long, he had broken his contract and was working, with Kendall, for Baker from his office in The Grotto.

Thus the design story of St Barnabas is complicated still further by the fact that Francis Masey joined the firm during 1896, possibly in time to influence the final design, and in whose hand the as-built plan appears to have been drawn. This latter drawing was not in fact approved by the local authority until 29 January 1898.

But whatever the true history of this design, in many ways it has some stylistic resemblance to the Newlands church. Like St Andrew it was faced in stone with Table Mountain for its backdrop but, unlike its predecessor, the interior is in brick. The entrance elevation to Kloof Road is a charming asymmetrical Arts and Crafts composition, with a bracketed bell over the apex of the gable. There is some uncertainty as to which of the identical pairs of doors is the main entrance. Again the nave is a simple rectangle, not only without side aisles but without a separately defined chancel. The flat, unpierced east wall was built as a temporary structure but is still there today. At the west end is a gallery over a narthex, supported on the coupled Tuscan columns that were to become one of Baker's trademarks. With its lower half panelled, the interior effect is almost classical and in striking contrast to the rough stone of St Andrew. The impressive timber roof spans thirty-four feet, with eight queen-post trusses springing from corbelled pad-stones. Complementing the panelled dado, the roof is ceiled with dark boarding beneath clay tiles.

GROOT DRAKENSTEIN

Beginning in 1896 and continuing until about 1901, Baker did a series of projects for the Rhodes Fruit Farms in the famed Groot Drakenstein Valley.

There was a simple cottage for Cecil Rhodes and some staff cottages at Boschendal, where the homestead dated from the eighteenth century. At Languedoc he built a large scheme of 110 cottages for farm workers in a charming rustic Arts and Crafts style. Even more rustic was the simple but utterly delightful church-cum-school he built to serve the community. The accompanying rectory is a larger house in a less remarkable, simple, white-gabled Cape Dutch idiom. The Languedoc scheme amounted to an orderly planned village but, as it turned out, the buildings were too far from the canning factory for convenience. This made it difficult to let them, and an imaginative but unsuccessful attempt was made in 1904 to get Dr Barnado's Homes in London to make use of them for British orphans. Today, in their reconditioned state they stand in an oak-lined avenue, the 'village' having been expanded with new Cape-Modern cottages; the few kilometres distance from the cannery being no longer of any account. Other homesteads renovated, restored or altered by Baker included Weltervreden, where his brother Lionel was the farm manager; Lekkerwyn; Nieuwedorp; Champagne and Nooitgedacht, where Harry Pickstone had established the first fruit tree nursery for Rhodes.[39]

For Cecil Rhodes 1896 ended as dramatically as it had begun. Almost a year after the Jameson Raid, which so drastically altered his fortunes, his virtually completed Groote Schuur burnt down. The fire broke out in the early hours of 15 December 1896. Its cause was never properly established. When the disaster occurred, Baker was not long out of hospital after his typhoid attack and was convalescing at The Grotto. Rhodes had been in Matabeleland again and, reaching Umtali on his way back, found Lord Grey there who gave him the news that Groote Schuur had been burned to the ground and nothing saved. As several of Rhodes's biographers have lamented, the fire destroyed the bulk of his papers up to the end of 1896. Rhodes later ruefully remarked to Lord Grey, 'What with the Raid, rebellion, famine, rinderpest, and now my house burnt, I feel like Job, all but the boils.'[40]

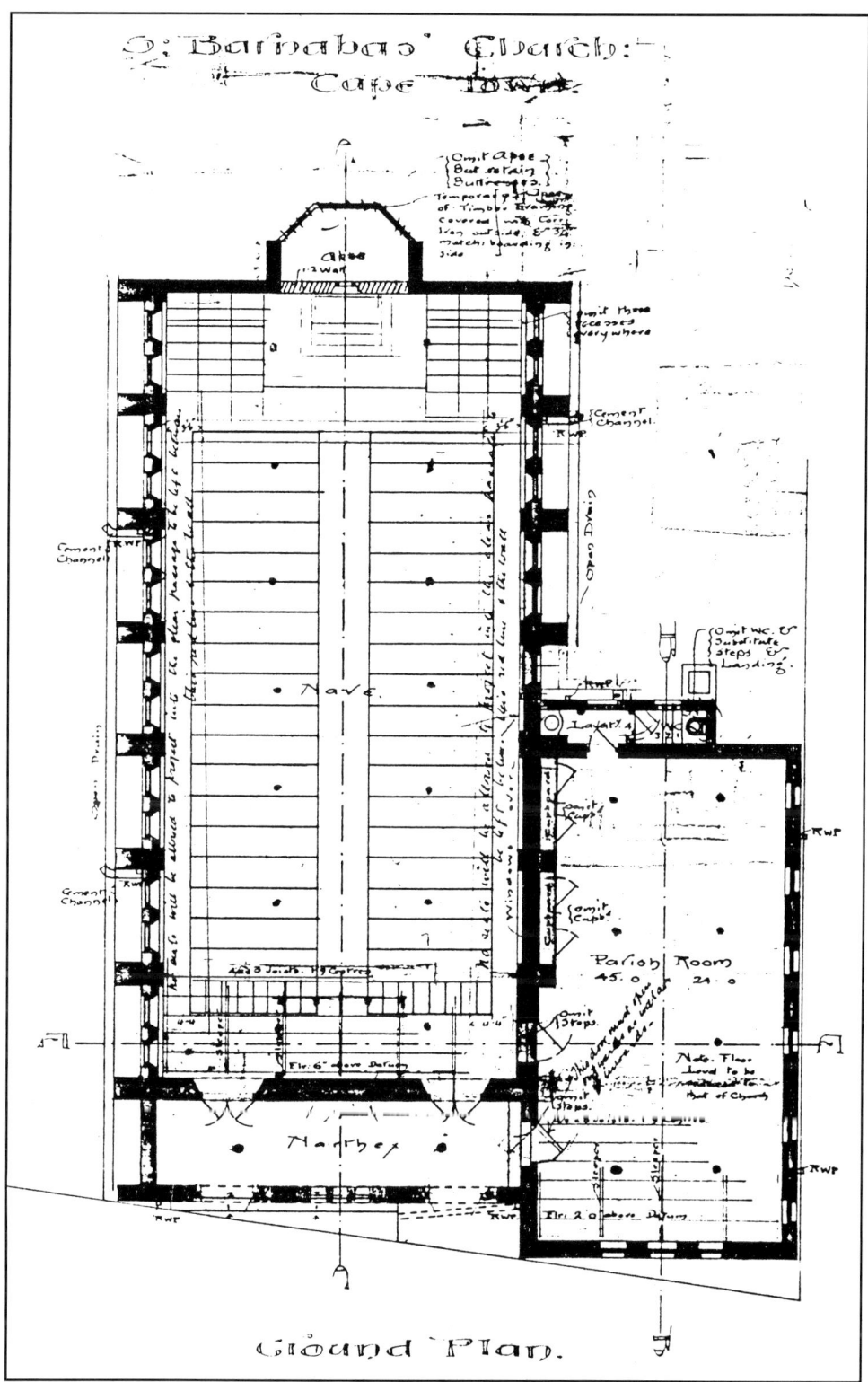

Church of St Barnabas, Tamboerskloof, ground plan, working drawing. Approved 29 January 1898.

Overleaf. Languedoc, church-cum-schoolhouse, gable end,
circa 1898.

City Club, facing Queen Victoria Street, Cape Town.

CHAPTER FOUR

1897-1899

RISING TO FAME

CAPE DUTCH PHOENIX

On New Year's Day, 1897, one year but a day after Jameson had surrendered his private army to the Boers at Doornkop, Rhodes arrived at the ruins of the home he had not even seen completed. It had been a disastrous year. For a few days he lived in the servants' outside quarters whilst arranging for the rebuilding of the house. Baker was immediately asked to carry out the task, so, he wrote: 'I did not go home [to England] as I had intended, but stayed and gave my whole time to rebuild and furnish the house anew.' All was ready to start rebuilding by 10 September 1897. According to the contractor, Arthur Reid, of A B Reid & Co, there seemed to be 'acres of drawings' to work from. But on the site things went quicker the second time round, and fifteen months later the final account would be signed.[1]

Now that Baker had the help of Masey and Kendall, the task of preparing detailed drawings could be more fully addressed. It also meant he could divide his time and devote more to building up his practice. Together, he and Masey produced fifty-seven reports on the work, running until 31 December 1898, when the contract was completed and the final account submitted.[2]

Architecturally, there was little difference between the 'restoration' and the 'rebuilding'. One difference, however, is hard to understand: the Doric columns of the front stoep, which were retained in the restoration, and appear to have survived the fire, were now changed to Ionic, but without altering their overall proportion.[3] The result is a column which now looks squat in Ionic, whereas its dumpiness had looked apposite in Doric. Could this change have been the result of Masey's influence? There is no way of knowing, and conjecture can only be based on matching a slight change of style with a change of circumstances. However, a trend towards a greater 'ornateness' gradually becomes apparent in the evolution of certain of Baker's buildings from about this time onwards.

To some purists the house is most wanting for not being 'typically' Cape Dutch; the gables in particular are criticized for their oval and semi-circular openings – which Baker did copy – or for their floridness; but this is no more so than with the main gable of Nooitgedacht (1774) with which they have some features in common, and which has been described as 'a very fine example of the early florid type.'[4] Certainly there are numerous Cape gables which are at least as florid as Baker's. But perhaps the most contentious point of all was Baker's incorporation of a large bas-relief panel in the main, central gable.[5] This bronze, which was fortunate to survive the fire, is a depiction of the 'Landing of van Riebeeck in Table Bay' by the Scottish sculptor, John Tweed (1869-1933). It was Tweed's first important commission, the model for which was exhibited at the Royal Academy in 1894, and which he did not see in its intended situation until his first visit to South Africa in 1928. Tweed later completed the full-length statue of Jan van Riebeeck in Cape Town in 1899 and of Cecil Rhodes in Bulawayo in 1902.[6] The panel is framed between Ionic columns and deep classical mouldings, the whole being supported in turn on a pair of Tuscan columns which flank a semi-circular 'fanlight', separated from the front door by the roof of the stoep.

Within Groote Schuur, Baker's development of Cape Dutch motifs reaches unexpected heights of imagination in the archway separating the hall from the vestibule. Here the columned Palladian 'venetian window' motif, usually capped with a central semi-circular arch, has, instead, been given a sweeping curved top, rather like the top of an armoire cabinet.

In order to help Rhodes carry out a 'much wider search' for old furniture and artefacts with which to

Overleaf. Groote Schuur, Rondebosch, end gable.

Top. Groote Schuur, Rondebosch, gargoyle detail.
Bottom. *Kelvin Grove, Newlands, main entrance.*

City Club, Queen Victoria Street, Cape Town. Gable detail.

furnish the rebuilt house, Baker recommended that he employ Arthur Collie of Old Bond Street, London, whom he regarded as an 'expert of sure taste and instinct.' Baker reports that Collie actually came to South Africa and lived in the house whilst searching for old things, '...priceless things often unknown and unprized in the lofts and outhouses of farms, or hidden in paint in labourers' shanties.' It was Collie who persuaded Rhodes 'that the drawing-room should be in the style of a Dutch house of Holland of the earlier period, rather than a Cape *voor-huis*.' It was thus that a young English architect, whose name has not been traced, was employed by Collie to design the panelling of the drawing-room in what Baker rightly observed was '...a style smaller in scale and more elaborate in detail than the rest of the house.' But Baker generously acknowledged Collie's contribution to Groote

Schuur before it was burned down. However, in the rebuilding, '...ambition prompted him to interfere and control beyond the scope of his professional appointment.' Baker recalled that Collie lost Rhodes's confidence and '...to his great grief and my [Baker's] regret' was dispensed with.[7]

The house Baker built for Cecil Rhodes is today recognized as one of South Africa's seminal buildings; a symbol of the country's past and its faith in the future. Unlike many other buildings which have had such roles thrust upon them by chance, Rhodes intended it to be so from the beginning.

CITY CLUB

Soon after the Groote Schuur fire, the competition for the design of the new City Club building — which had been held in August 1896 — reached a strange conclusion. On 15 January 1897 the assessor's award was announced, '...the first place being taken by Mr Herbert Baker and the second by Mr John Parker; and in recognition of the excellence of the plan submitted by Mr E Austin Cooke the committee decided to present him with a bonus of £20.' The minutes of the meeting do not disclose the name of the assessor and it has been suggested that it was Baker himself. When asked about the matter many years later, in 1938, Baker recalled somewhat vaguely that '...my impression was that there was no professional assessor, and the only person coming prominently to mind in connection with it is Mr Fuller, the worthy Member of the House of Assembly at that time...'

The Mr Fuller was in fact T E Fuller, Chairman of the Club from its foundation in 1878 to 1898. Thomas Fuller (later Sir) was a highly influential Cape liberal politician and an early friend of Cecil Rhodes. From the ethical point of view it does seem odd that the architect who proposed the competition, or at least advised on its conduct, should himself be a competitor, and possibly the assessor too. But however questionable may have been Baker's role in the matter, his design was a worthy one and in June 1897 a contract was signed with R H Morris to build it for the sum of £22 066.[8]

Franklin Kendall, still relatively new to the firm at the time recalled how Masey, who had only just joined the firm, burned the midnight oil in completing the competition drawings. Kendall later wrote: 'Masey did two excellent perspectives and most of the sketches, while I did the final plans...' Referring to the relationship between them, Kendall adds: 'I think it is right to say that this was the turning point of the situation and the partnership between the three of us followed.'[9]

Baker's City Club, now known as the City and Civil Service Club, has a distinctly colonial air about it, making it difficult to imagine the building in a London street, even though it represents street architecture at its best. Its colonial character is mainly derived from the façade-plus-lean-to genre to which it belongs. Here, four pairs of slender Roman-Doric columns, with linking capitals, support a deep first-floor balcony which provides shade and cover to the pavement below. The paired columns are repeated at balcony level where they become square in shape and support a tiled lean-to roof. Above this applied structure, run nine bays of Italianate shuttered windows beneath a deeply projecting, dentilled cornice. The main roof rises

steeply from the cornice, broken by three dormer windows which have a hint of the Cape about them, but could have appeared anywhere in England at that time and would probably have been considered 'Flemish baroque'. This explains why the roof is perhaps less at home in the Cape sunlight than the projecting balcony structure below it, which casts such magnificent shadows. The panelled interiors complete this typically English colonial club, today looking much as it did when it opened in December 1898.

Whilst the new City Club building was under construction, out in the suburbs in Campground Road, Newlands, Baker was remodelling Kelvin Grove for J C Rimer, who had bought the early nineteenth-century house in 1896. It is possible that Rimer had been influenced by what he knew of Groote Schuur, which had received much publicity after the fire. There is indeed a great deal of resemblance between the houses in their form and in the number, positioning and florid character of the gables. Likewise, details such as the mouldings above windows, and the semi-circular air vents, are similar to Groote Schuur. Inside the building, the entrance hall has a fine wooden staircase with chubby wooden Doric columns supporting the landing, as they do in so many of Baker's interiors. The resulting effect is somewhat redolent of his birthplace, Owletts, and entirely appropriate to its future purpose as a colonial country club.[10]

Contemporary with these works, in which a degree of Italianate detailing is evident, was the largest of all the houses associated with Baker in the Cape, Trovato. Although he later declined to acknowledge his authorship of this house, built for Carl Jeppe in Herschell Walk, Wynberg, numerous drawings exist that establish his involvement in its design. The matter is confused by the existence of two undated floor plans signed by Herbert Baker 'for' Sydney Stent, a local architect. One of these was stamped as approved by the Wynberg Municipality in July 1897, giving an approximate date for the design. It would be interesting to know just how this commission came into Baker's hands but only the plans have come to light. Possibly Stent was simply unable to cope with this large commission owing to his failing health. Sydney Stent died the following year at the age of fifty-two.[11]

In many ways the design is atypical of Baker's work either before or after that date. In particular, the projecting steps of the symmetrically rising columned stoep in the grand manner of classicism,

Trovato, Wynberg, side front.

and the dentilled treatment of the triangular gables, reinforce the feeling that a new influence is at work here. This may be explained as resulting from Stent's original ideas, however far they may have been developed, or by the arrival of Francis Masey in the firm.

Another possible explanation lies in Baker's own growing interest in classicism, confirmed by his purchase of two more books on English Renaissance architecture earlier that year. It would indeed be fascinating and instructive to know the full extent of his book purchases and the contents of his library at that time. It is known that on 21 January 1898 he bought in Cape Town, Reginald Blomfield's two-volume *History of Renaissance Architecture in England*, published in 1897. Blomfield (1856-1942) was known for his Arts and Crafts sympathies. However, Blomfield was apt to interpret everything he admired about English architecture as being the expression of permanent national characteristics. This racial interpretation of style was close to the long established, but now firmly discredited German tradition. Then, just a week later, Baker bought the just-arrived first volume of a two-volume set of *Later Renaissance Architecture in England*, giving examples of the domestic buildings erected subsequent to the Elizabethan period, by John Belcher (1841-1913) and Sir Mervyn Macartney (1853-1932).

Both authors had a similar outlook to Blomfield. All three were eminently successful architects associated with the return to classicism around 1900. Their books were sumptuously illustrated folio volumes; frankly presented as pattern books for other architects. Avoiding theory and concentrating on visual history, Belcher and Macartney admitted of the buildings in their book that 'no attempt has been made to classify them or to arrange them in chronological order, or to trace by examples the growth of development of Renaissance architecture.' Instead they emphasize what they saw as the essentially English qualities of 'modesty and restraint, purity and dignity.' They believed that English architecture, especially that of the seventeenth and eighteenth centuries reflected 'a grace and sober demeanour...a quiet dignified charm...a sturdy masculine feeling.' Of later Renaissance architecture they observed that it 'appears to adjust itself to the English character; there is no need of any extravagant display or extreme severity.' In retrospect their remarks would seem appropriate to any discussion of Baker's own work.[12]

Both Blomfield and Macartney belonged to the editorial panel of *The Architectural Review* which had been founded in the previous year, the first issue having made its appearance in November 1896, reaching Cape Town by Christmas. From the start this had been a stylish and influential journal, concentrating on the artistic rather than the technical aspects of architecture. One cannot help wondering to what extent Baker was influenced by the books these leaders of taste and fashion had written, and by the monthly issues of this exciting new journal.

In the early part of 1898 Baker built a house, St Cyrus, in Tennant Road, Wynberg, for Sir Charles Abercromby Smith. It has been suggested that, like its near contemporary, Trovato, it was possibly taken over from another architect such as Stent. Again, Baker himself later declined the attribution, though there is sufficient documentation to establish some kind of involvement on his part.[13] Also around the same time in May, he designed a house for W A Budler, which was to have been built next to Hutchins's Kolaro in Kenilworth. Although the Budler house does not appear to have been built, plans reached an advanced stage. It would have been the first house of Baker's to include a Gothic turret, which Johnson describes as a popular feature on houses built on the Peninsular at that time. In most other respects the design is similar to his other houses of the period.[14] Other minor works of that year included alterations and additions to a house in Harfield Road, Kenilworth, for S R French; another for G Pauling in Belmont Road, Rondebosch, and for Dr Murray in Kenilworth Road.[15]

Baker's status as the architect to the social elite of Cape Town was greatly consolidated by his club commissions, and an ever-growing circle of influential friends were finding his energy and sincerity convincing. Even more important was the fact that, although his work still had to compete with the status quo in cheapness and acceptability he nevertheless managed to strike a distinctive note. 'Here', wrote Kendall, 'was real design – buildings plain and simple enough – but always with a hint of the master touch.' No frills, but fitness and common sense, and a 'determined striving for better materials and workmanship.'[16]

CASTLE LINE

Sir Donald Currie, Chairman of the Castle Line and

famous in South African sporting life for his donation of the Currie Cup, acquired the Mount Nelson property in 1897 to build a new Mount Nelson Hotel. Competition between the Castle and the Union shipping lines had intensified after the discovery of gold in the Transvaal. This rivalry led to a merger in March 1900 and the founding of the Union Castle Steamship Company. Currie's line felt the need for a first-class hotel to meet the requirements of English passenger traffic equal to the standard of comfort of the best hotels in Europe and, indeed, of the passenger liners themselves. The design of the Mount Nelson was the work of London architects, Dunn and Watson of Lincoln's Inn Fields. The responsibility for supervising the hotel's construction, vitally important in such a contract, was entrusted to Baker.

Concurrent with the new hotel was the Castle Line's new office building in Adderley Street, also designed by Dunn and Watson. Baker's appointment as resident architect for both these projects gave him a splendid opportunity to indulge in high-quality building with all the best in materials, workmanship and imported fittings. The hotel in particular was equipped with up-to-date engineering services which provided the last word in comfort and safety for its patrons. Baker's experience of building would be extended still further by working with the large London contracting firm of Cubitt and Co. on a cost-plus-percentage basis. Cubitt's site management expertise, blended with Baker's local knowledge, formed a formidable and mutually advantageous combination.

But Baker still appears to have put a lot of himself into the hotel's detailing. The plaster reliefs in the dome of the dining-room, composed of heraldic shields and emblems representing Great Britain, the South African colonies and the City of Cape Town, and a relief showing Vasco da Gama's ships in Table Bay, are particularly Bakerish features. Such devices were to become increasingly appealing to Baker as he grew older. The Mount Nelson probably provided him with his first real opportunity to express deep-seated aesthetic sympathies, which perhaps began with the weeks he spent drawing Plas Mawr with his cousin Arthur, or exploring Cobham Hall as a boy.

The use of as much local labour and material as possible on this building of such unusually high quality must have given something of a fillip to Cape industry. For Baker the whole experience must have assisted greatly in his struggle to raise

standards by acquainting local industry with the best materials and the most technically advanced methods. Not only did it deepen his pool of local skills and resources, but by working closely with London architects and contractors he went through an invaluable refresher course, gaining experience which could only be bettered by going overseas for a year or so himself.[17]

Getting work to design was one thing; quite another matter was getting the hotel built to the standards Baker had set for himself. The quality of workmanship and the availability of materials which prevailed at that time made for endless frustrations. 'When Herbert Baker began to practise in Cape Town...he did not find a smoothly paved path awaiting him – indeed, it was quite the reverse', wrote Franklin Kendall, '...the local building traditions were about as unedifying as they well could be. The oak-grainer, the tuck-pointer and the corrugated iron fiend held undisputed sway in all directions and, to make matters worse, the public were entirely satisfied with what was being given them.' Kendall recalls the overriding commercialism and the ways in which architects took the line of least resistance whilst Baker 'had to fight tooth and nail all the way in the interests of his Art.' It was a scene of complacency in which 'some of the older hands regarded it as rather a good joke to watch this newcomer – this youngster – setting out to teach his elders...how to do things!'[18]

A CATHEDRAL DESIGN TAKES SHAPE

As the year 1897 closed, Baker's thoughts on the design for the new Anglican Cathedral were crystallizing. He had been in poor health again but managed to complete his revised design by the date required, the end of December. We are fortunate to have a document which tells us much about his thoughts on the design. In his report to the Archbishop of Cape Town, Dr William West Jones, he explained: 'Although these drawings have been prepared at greater leisure, and under more favourable circumstances than my former hastily considered sketches, I must even now ask for your indulgent consideration of them.'[19] Referring to his recent 'very indifferent health', and, 'without sacrificing my existing obligations, I have found it difficult to bestow on the design and drawings the time and care which such important work demands. For the

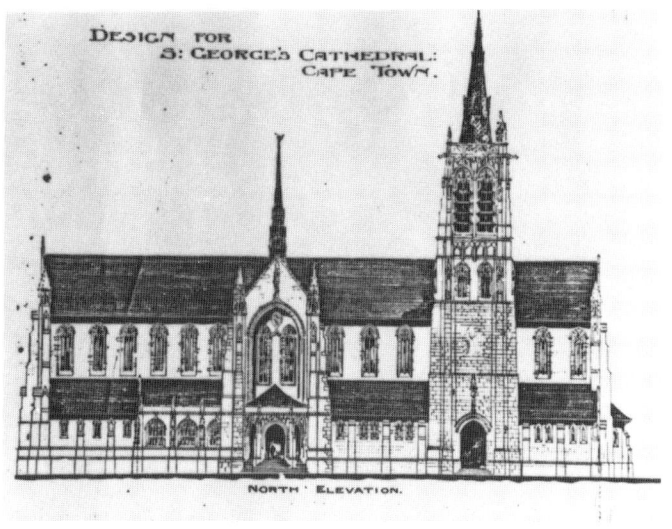

Top left. *Cathedral of St George, Cape Town, the apse as built.* Top right. *St George, first design, north elevation.* Right. *St George, perspective view from the north-east.*

last ten days I have been completely incapacitated ...and...therefore been unable to finish the geometrical drawings or to colour the perspective as I intended...'

But, apart from the drawings, he seems to have been remarkably diffident about the design itself, apologizing too for the 'many instances of want of thought and care in the minor details of the design.' He goes on to stress 'the necessity that I should complete my design only after careful study amongst the best examples in England and France, and consultation with some leading Architect at home', and, he added curiously, 'of my willingness to devote time for the purpose.' His use of the word

'home', meaning England, strikes one as somewhat contradictory in view of his following remark: 'It has been said that there can be no good architecture which is not indigenous, and I trust you will allow the fact that I have made South Africa my home and have spent some of the best years of my life in developing the architectural resources of the country to weigh with you in considering my design.'

Baker acknowledged that he had had no 'outside opinion' to guide him, except the few suggestions 'contained in your letters from time to time, and to these I have given the fullest consideration.' Although the cathedral as built has the apsed chancel originally conceived by Baker, it had been aban-

Cathedral of St George, Cape Town, the nave.

Cathedral of St George, Cape Town, foundation stone, 22 August 1901.

doned in the design that accompanied this report '...with some regret, I must confess, as I consider the "chevet" in French Gothic the most beautiful and poetic creation in all architecture, expressing as it does internally and externally a distinctive crowning glory to the Sanctuary.' The reason he gave for this change – and for other aspects of design contained in his report – provides one of the few contemporary statements he made on his architectural philosophy.

With particular regard to the use of materials, he wrote: 'It requires for perfect treatment a groined roof inside, the expense of which would be excessive if truly executed in stone, whilst wood groining...is inconsistent in my opinion with truthful construction. The gabled east end, on the other hand, besides its economic advantages, is more in accordance with English tradition.' Baker's response to the Archbishop's preference for a central tower is equally interesting for his rationalizations; he argues: '...whilst not overlooking the extreme beauty and essentially English character of this position...[however] unless the Tower be of very large dimensions it would be necessary to have a comparatively narrow Nave and very large obstructive central piers. Both of these would be inconsistent with your expressed desire that the Altar should be visible as far as possible from all parts of the building. In addition...the great expense of strengthening the piers and arches must be incurred at the commencement of the building, [and] there is always a risk of vibration in hanging a large peal of bells in a central Tower, and that the true value of the height of a tower is only realized when it rises direct from the ground.'

Paramount in Baker's mind was the position of the tower at the head of St George's Street where it was to replace that of the old St George, and which he appears to have had no compunction about destroying. 'Those to whom I have shown my plan, agree with me that this position as a semi-detached Campanile is the right one, and that we should not destroy an old and well known landmark of Cape Town without putting a nobler substitute in its place.'

If Baker, in his role of Diocesan Architect, had by now given any special thought to the question of a consistent and appropriate style for the design of his Cape churches, it was certainly not apparent. Indeed his report at this point again seems to contradict his earlier remark that 'there can be no good architecture which is not indigenous...' Instead, on

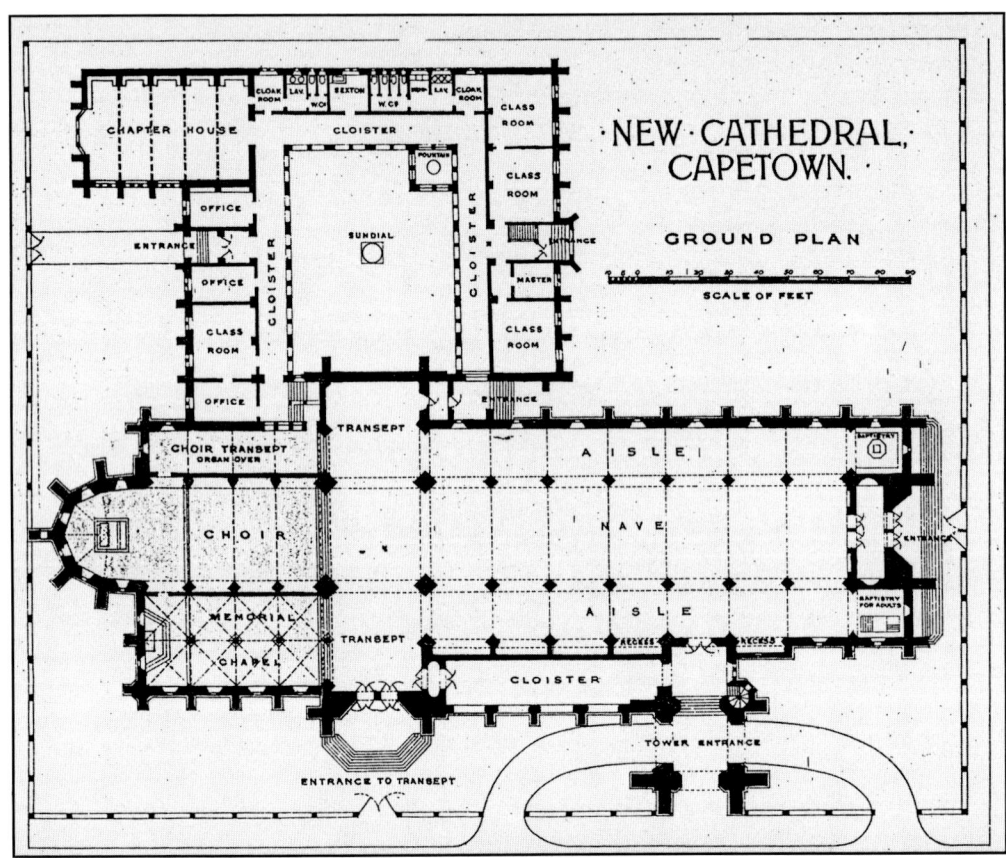

Cathedral of St George, Cape Town, final ground plan.

the style of his cathedral design, he openly declares his arbitrary, eclectic approach. He writes: 'While not slavishly adhering to any particular period, I have endeavoured to work on the lines of the severer and nobler forms of late English Gothic, incorporating some characteristics of French architecture of the same period.' To that end Baker had 'attempted by deeply shaded eaves unbroken by pinnacles, long straight lines of roofing, and a generally simple treatment – to give effective contrast and to prevent the great height of the buttress-pinnacles, of the gables, and the flèche and spire from clashing with the surroundings and the mountain.'

To the question of window design and the dangers of overlighting caused by the size and height of openings exposed to the brighter African skies, his answer was to overcome such problems 'by recessing the clerestory windows in very thick walls carried by arches and buttresses below. The effect produced will be that of a strong contrast of light and shade, brightening the arcade against the

less strongly lighted aisles behind. The deep arches over the windows will throw the roof into mystery and gloom.' In the application of these principles, which despite their aesthetic consequences have nothing to do with style, Baker was undoubtedly correct and amply demonstrated in all his churches an understanding of the climate in a way that was well ahead of his time in South Africa.

Baker concluded his report with the sadly prophetic suggestion that 'part of the existing Church should be temporarily devoted to a Chapter House, and that the Vestry and what other parts may not be consecrated, as well as part of the new school buildings be used, until the whole scheme can be completed, as a Library and Church Offices.' As is well known, Baker completed neither the nave nor the tower and, in the end, the old church was needlessly destroyed amid much enlightened protest. Neither was this extreme act of vandalism remedied by building the present chapterhouse, which fails to make Baker's 'nobler substitute' and simply

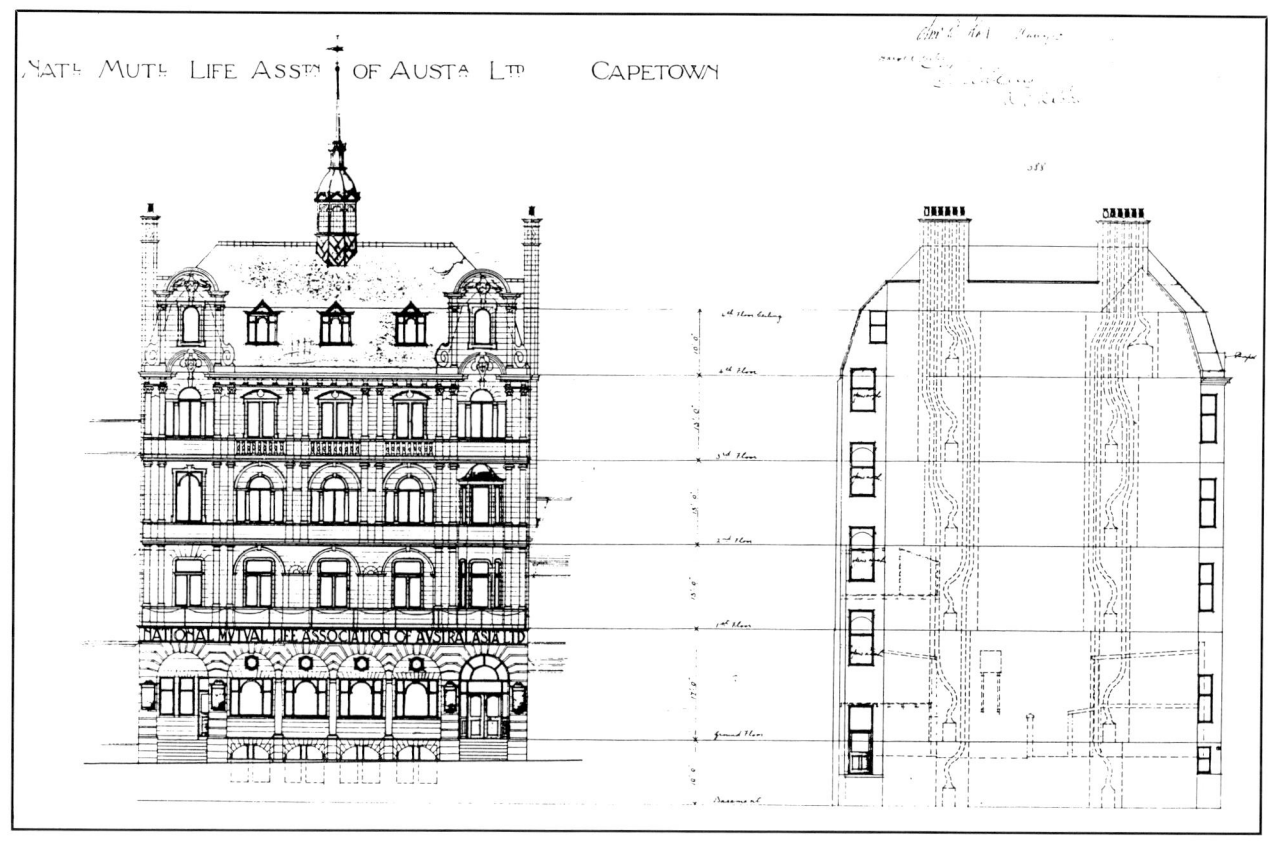

NAT^ MUT^ LIFE ASS^ OF AUST^ L^ CAPETOWN

National Mutual Life of Australasia, Church Square, Cape Town,
elevation.

provides what the old church might have done with some sensitive internal conversion. But in the words of R R Langham-Carter, whose history of the old church describes in understated detail the whole sorry episode: 'South Africa does not possess a wealth of old buildings and there must always be differing views on the wisdom of destroying old St George's.'[20]

The new Cathedral will be discussed in greater detail further on in this book. Although a foundation stone was laid in August 1901, it would not be until 1904 that the foundations of the choir were laid, and a further two years before any real progress was to be made on the superstructure.

FIRST CITY OFFICE BUILDINGS

By January 1898, plans were well advanced for Baker's first block of offices, the new Guardian Assurance building at the top end of Adderley

Street, a building which was destroyed in the mid 1950s. The job had come at an opportune time as he was still supervising the construction of the Castle Line's offices for Dunn and Watson at 44 Adderley Street, gaining valuable experience in the problems of building on urban sites. By the following April (1899) Baker had moved his offices into the new building. Such is the overlapping nature of architectural commissions, that he was still engaged in the construction of the Mount Nelson Hotel and the rebuilding of Groote Schuur, following the dramatic fire of two years before.

Ironically, the fire had undoubtedly brought Baker's work and his ideas to the public's eye, focusing particular attention on his manner of weaving Cape Dutch elements into his architecture. Although this approach was a typical aspect of the Queen Anne style, with its common use of Dutch gables, the general perception was that he had drawn his inspiration solely from Cape sources. It is known that Baker did make considerable use of

Church of St Philip, Chapel Street, Woodstock, apse end.

Church of St Philip, Chapel Street, Woodstock, interior.

these sources but in precisely what proportions can only be guessed, for he has left little to go on apart from the buildings themselves. Such a perception may have gone a long way towards making the new Guardian Assurance building so acceptable to Cape Town.

The building was constructed by Mitchell and Mackie in 'granite concrete' supplied by the Salt River Cement Works. It was an innovative blend of bow-windowed Arts and Crafts, and triple-gabled Cape Dutch which owed nothing in style to the Castle Line offices. The building had four storeys and an attic roofed with tiles and fronted with gables each containing a miniature venetian window. The style was well-received and the Guardian Assurance was considered 'one of Cape Town's handsomest buildings, the first in the City where the offensive cast-iron verandah was dispensed with and its place taken by a substantial one supported by polished granite pillars – an excellent example subsequently followed by others.'[21]

During the same year Baker was to design two more churches. The first was St Michael and All Angels, Observatory, which is cruciform in plan, with a six-bay nave – again without aisles – leading to the crossing where a fine timber construction supports a flèche and where there might have been a central tower in earlier times. St Michael has more of a French feeling than Baker's two previous churches, St Andrew and St Barnabas, perhaps indicating the influence of Francis Masey. On the whole St Michael lacks charm and is not helped by its poor siting.

In complete architectural contrast is the second church of that year: St Philip, in Chapel Street, Woodstock; on the edge of the now shamefully destroyed District Six. Here Baker and Masey designed another quasi-cruciform plan, but now with low lean-to, windowless aisles and transepts. The roof is of dark boarding over six king-post trusses, with bearing posts resting on brackets. The high brick walls have narrow round-headed windows above the aisles and in the semi-circular apse. Above the lean-to roofs of the aisles are small round windows beneath the eaves. All in all, the effect is gloomy; more Romanesque than Gothic. This mission church was constructed cheaply for the Coloured community at a cost of £5 000 including £215 for the land.[22] The original temporary corrugated-iron narthex through which one entered the church has since been replaced with a permanent brick structure. Its partly rendered external walls today look shabby, but could be improved with regular painting. This would set off the brick window surrounds, the pilaster-like flat buttresses and the tiled roof, as presumably Baker intended.

1898 ended with the final account for Groote Schuur being signed on 31 December for the sum of £39 759.[23] It had taken over five years, from conception to completion, and undergone the fire, but if it had not 'established a nation' it had certainly established an architect! Then, early in the new year, another city office building came Baker's way. The National Mutual Life of Australasia, which stands today in Church Square, Cape Town, is radically different to the building Baker and Masey first began to design in January 1899. Nevertheless, some of the character of their work still persists despite the total remodelling carried out by architects J Perry and W J Delbridge in the late 1920s. Baker's first design, which had a five-bay façade, was superseded by another of six bays – and today there are thirteen. Not only that, the building has been increased in height by the addition of one storey and all the floor elements have been shunted upwards to make compositional sense of their vast additions. Furthermore, the building has been extended backwards into Plein Street where it emerges wearing a rather half-hearted Art Deco grin. Baker's original had a high-pitched Flemish roof capped with a magnificent flèche, and a row of four dormers, flanked by Cape Dutch gables, and giving light to the attic floor. Each floor was treated differently, each with four central arcaded bays flanked by tall round or square-headed windows, one level of which has the projecting balcony motif which was to become a hallmark of the Baker style. However, as will be seen, the final design was not completed until 1904.

In the meantime, to the right of the Castle Line's building in Adderley Street, which he was still supervising for Dunn and Watson – and in which he had taken offices for himself in April 1899 – Baker designed a new block of offices for Wilson and Miller, with a department store on the ground floor. Baker's somewhat florid design is in total contrast to the neighbouring building which looks austere by comparison. The Wilson and Miller building has a steeply pitched, hipped roof from which only a pair of finicky, Flemish-Cape Dutch, gabled dormers protrude. Below that the plastered spandrels and pilasters, which separate identical windows vertically and horizontally in the three main floors, are decorated with various heraldic

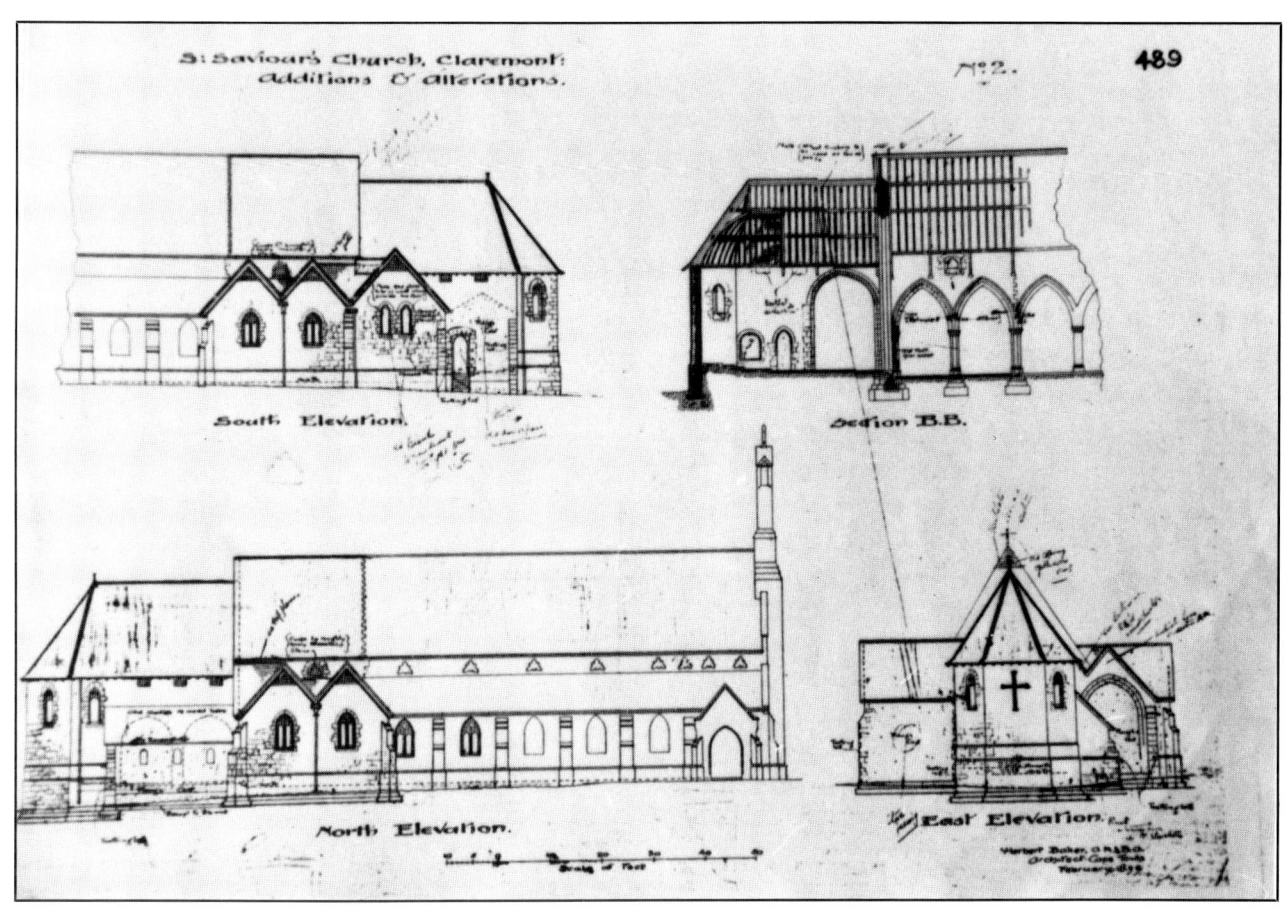

*Church of St Saviour, Claremont, first design. Shown are the
elevations, roof plan, ground plan and cross-sections.*

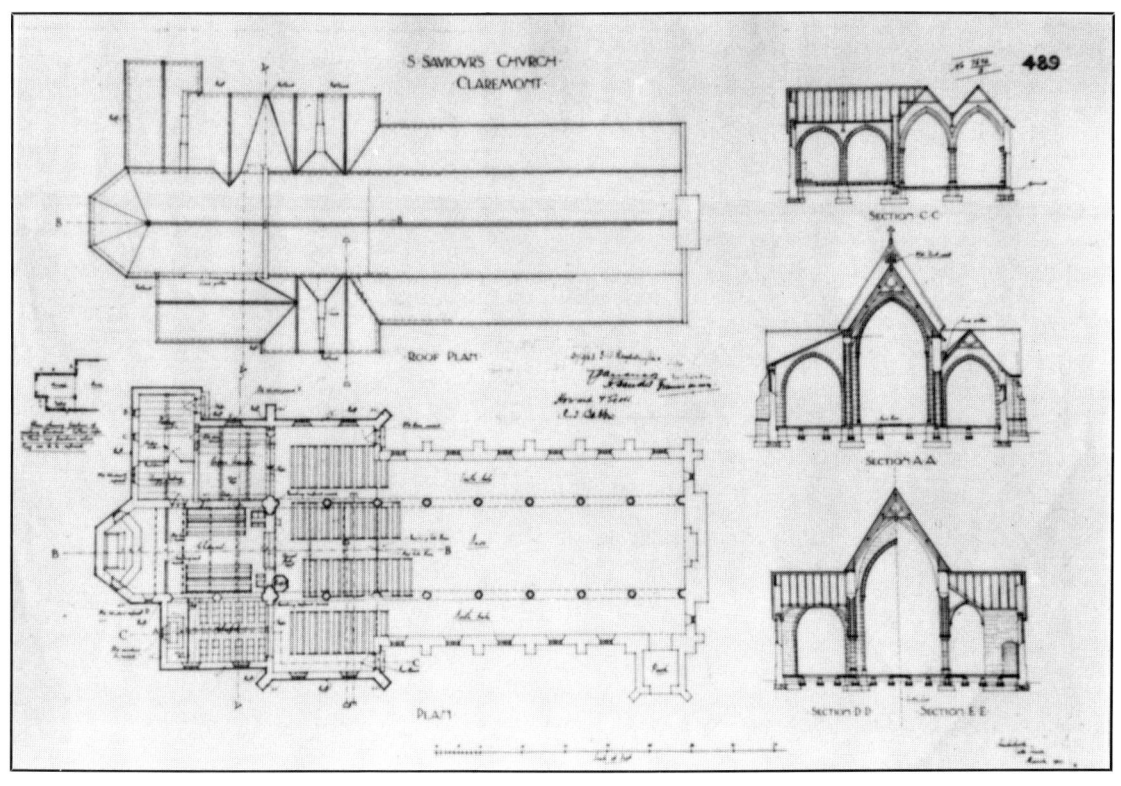

National Mutual Life of Australasia, Church Square, Cape Town,
drawings by Baker and Masey.

Church of St Saviour, Claremont, interior of Baker's side chapel.

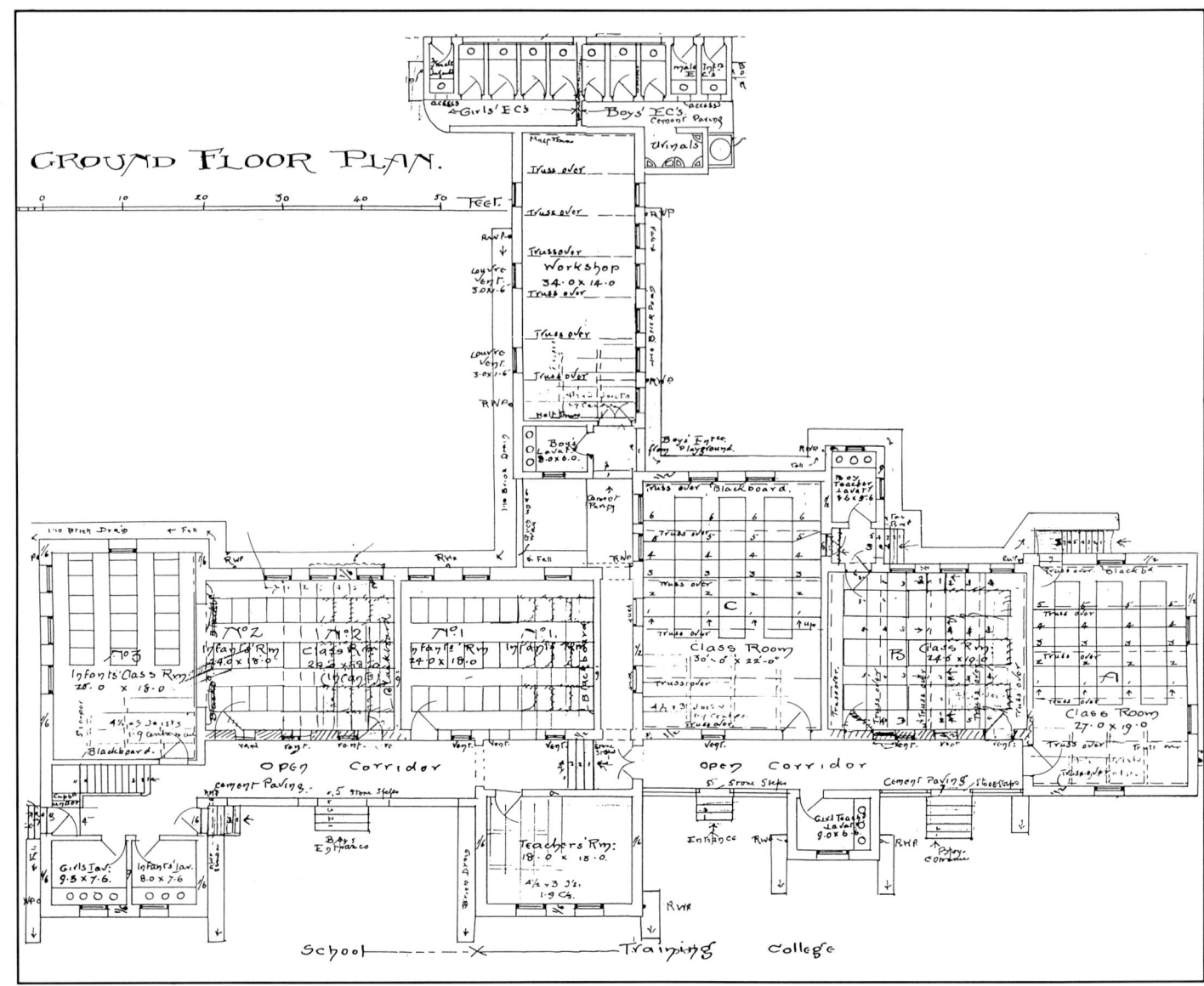

GROUND FLOOR PLAN.

Non-denominational school at Burghersdorp, ground floor plan.

and miscellaneous designs. Overall, because of the regular sizing and spacing of windows, the building has a rather modern, or functionalist look. Francis Masey – whose name had still not appeared on the firm's drawings – seems to have contributed to the Flemish-inspired decorations.

In February Baker did his first drawings for the enlargement of the Church of St Saviour, Claremont. This church was originally the work of Sophie Gray, but was first enlarged to plans 'sent out by Butterfield' in 1880.[24] An ever-growing congregation, an inevitable result of the suburban railway which had reached Claremont in 1864, meant

further enlargement was necessary. In the words of Langham-Carter's church history: 'It was decided to demolish Sophie Gray's chancel, to build two eastern bays of the nave on its site with a new chancel beyond and to add two transepts, a side chapel, two vestries and an organ chamber. Three architects submitted plans and those of Herbert Baker...were accepted.'[25] One wonders whether all three worked to a standard brief or whether each made his own recommendations; for the proposals would mean the virtual effacement of Mrs Gray's original work. As for the execution of the new extensions, which Baker later evolved in stages, that would have to

66

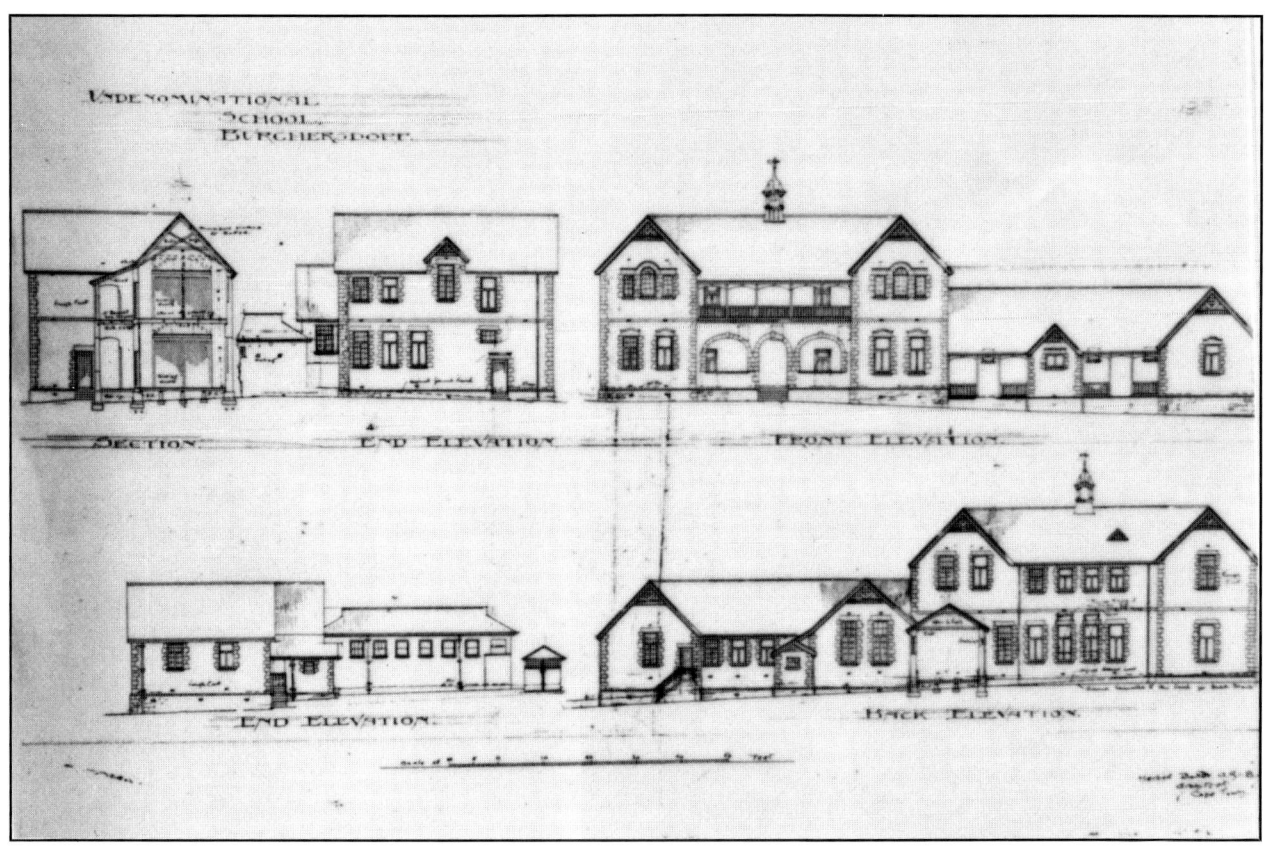

Non-denominational school at Burghersdorp, elevations.

wait until the end of the South African War before a start could be made.

Meanwhile Baker had a great deal of other work to do, and much of it for Cecil Rhodes. By June he had completed plans for his largest domestic project to date, a speculative scheme of some nineteen villas in Strubens Road, Mowbray. The client was H W Struben, for whom he had previously designed villas in Rosebank. Today only a much altered and varied group of houses remains, totally lacking in cohesion. But what does remain of Baker's design seems to indicate that they were built on the cheap. And such efforts as were made to decorate these basic structures, with 'English' half-timbered motifs and brackets were doomed to fail on account of their flimsiness. As Johnson says: 'This project is a salutary reminder that even the architect with the highest personal standards and ideals is capable of producing work that is cheap and almost nasty.'[26]

The question arises whether Baker was driven to these uncharacteristic depths by Struben's economic demands and, if so, whether he could realistically have turned them down. Despite Baker's current workload, Struben was a valuable client; a client who returned to his architect. Or was Baker now too busy to be personally involved in every project on his drawing boards? Perhaps a further clue to this possibility lies in the drawings for an non-denominational school at Burghersdorp.

Although undated, the style of drawing and lettering clearly marks them as a product of this period. Here it may prove surprising to see a somewhat crude reinterpretation of his domestic planning in the H-plan, modified by extension, but with projecting gable walls on the front elevation.

CHAPTER FIVE

1899-1901

TRIUMPHS AND DISASTERS

AFTER GROOTE SCHUUR

Ever since Jameson's raid into the Transvaal in the last days of 1895 many had thought the country was drifting towards war. Rhodes, however, to within weeks of its eventuality did not think it was inevitable, and if it came, believed it would be a short-lived affair of a few days. Despite his deep involvement in the politics of the moment he was still able to find space in his thoughts for matters of the most unwarlike kind. With his architectural ambitions for Groote Schuur now fulfilled, Cecil Rhodes turned his thoughts to other buildings on his various estates.

Not far from Groote Schuur itself was Welgelegen, a dilapidated but seemingly restorable farmhouse – judging from a watercolour made by Baker.[1] The original house was a Mostert family homestead built in 1818 and its successor is today part of the University of Cape Town campus. Rhodes wished to make the property a gift for life to the Currey family in gratitude for the kindness they had shown him during his younger days in Kimberley. Whose decision it was to destroy it and rebuild is unclear, but destroyed it was, and totally.

Unlike Groote Schuur, Baker's design, which he started soon after Rhodes's return from the Continent, Egypt and England on 18 July 1899, bears no relation to the original house.[2] But, like its neighbour, Welgelegen has considerable charm, owing to, at least in part, its curious and unexpected inconsistencies. The house is approached through an avenue of oaks from the north. Flanking the doorway are two small windows which relate awkwardly to the gable, which is itself unusual on account of the central portion being projected slightly to align with the width of the door. On the west the two gable walls differ in shape, and in the arrangement of openings. The left-hand gable is on the end of a short projecting wing which terminates the veranda. Adding to this informal effect, which arises from the practicalities of the plan, are two dormer windows set asymmetrically in the main roof. Fronting the north and east sides of the house is a delightful L-shaped terrace, over which is a pergola supported on Tuscan columns. Taking advantage of the slope of the ground, the south end of the house is double-storied, again enhancing the informality of the plan.

Baker relates that he provided the house with 'but few mirrors' and how Mrs Currey and her 'brood of daughters' forced him to promise '...ere I could escape, all the mirrors they wanted.' That, as Doreen Greig observes, was before he was married, and provides a sidelight to his 'essentially masculine approach.'[3]

A further project begun for Cecil Rhodes as the war clouds threatened, was the restoration and alteration work Baker did at Nooitgedacht, near Stellenbosch, and where Rhodes had first established Lionel Baker with Pickstone in 1892. Baker's drawings show the work to have included removing some extraneous lean-to rooms, some new doors, a chimneypiece and a screen. Most significant however, was the new bow-topped window he inserted in the main gable; quite unlike the square-headed window which was there before. As Johnson has pointed out, Baker actually illustrated the original window in the introductory chapter he wrote for Alys Fane Trotter's book, *Old Colonial Houses of the Cape of Good Hope,* published in 1900.[4] Johnson writes: '...while this was not a major restoration, what he had done indicates something of Baker's attitude. Baker did not confine himself to replacement, but added his own stamp to even the smallest feature.'

Johnson also suggests that this gable strongly influenced Baker's two larger front gables at Groote Schuur, where similar inwardly curving scrolls were used.[5] In the centre of the Nooitgedacht gable is an inverted fleur-de-lis, not unlike a fuschia flower, which Baker used both at Groote Schuur, and Welgelegen and a little later, in 1900, at The Woolsack.

SANDHILLS

In September 1899 Baker was preparing his application for Fellowship of the Royal Institute of British Architects, of which he had been an Associate since 1890. He was required to enlist the support of two Fellows who would, from their 'personal knowledge of him, propose and recommend him for election.' The two who signed his supporting statement were H S Greaves of the Cape Public Works Department, and his former London employer Ernest George. Apart from having to submit a statement listing one's achievements the main qualifications for this distinction were that an applicant should have been engaged as a principal for at least seven years and have attained the age of thirty. Baker was thirty-seven.[6]

In the same month Baker bought from H W Struben some land on the sands at Muizenberg, not far from the cottage where Rhodes was spending much of his time owing to his declining health. There, during the opening months of the war – which began on 11 October – Baker built his first house for himself, a modest seaside cottage, remote and windswept, which he named Sandhills. It was built around a tiny atrium which regularly filled with wind-blown sand and which, not surprisingly, today is glazed over. Although a simple Cape Arts and Crafts dwelling, Sandhills displays many of Baker's characteristic design principles, such as the twin gabled walls enclosing a shadowed, recessed, stoep or veranda. Similarly the gables are pierced with half-round roof vents as at Groote Schuur. The house stands on a stone plinth, high at the front to take account of the slope of the site.[7]

Baker described his house as having a long, low, hall-cum-living room, 'beam-ceiled with red-brown Jarrah-wood,' which had 'a continuous mullioned window which gave us a wide view through the white-columned stoep of the breaking surf. It was paved with large deep-red tiles from an old Dutch farmhouse; and on the dresser we had a collection of pewter, which was apt to crash on the tiles when the doors were opened. The salt sea-air, breathing ozone, came in everywhere; too much for some of our friends or tenants, when the sand was "spun before the gale".' Sandhills was for some time the only house on the Muizenberg sands. Here Baker could entertain his friends and relax, and here they could run 'straight into the sea out of bed which was on the deep Roman Stoep with white pillars in front.'[8]

Also at about this time, office premises were designed for Geo Findlay and Co, still standing in Adderley Street, but now known as Musikland. The narrow-fronted Findlay building was to be a precursor to the Isaacs building, designed about a year later and which, as will be seen, had many similarities of detail and character.

Likewise, as war drew near, Baker produced his elegant design for the now demolished South African Association building, which was built on a wider site, and was in many ways a forerunner to the Rhodes Building.

The week before war began in October, J C Molteno acknowledged plans for a house called Sandown in Weltervreden Road, Rondebosch, and that work was completed by the contractors Small and Morgan in April 1901. However, neither an adequate set of Baker's drawings nor the house itself is extant. The most interesting surviving document is a letter from Baker to Mrs Molteno on the subject of colour schemes in which he suggests they visit Isaacs's shop together to select curtains and carpets. They are 'beginning to understand our taste', wrote Baker of his future client.[9]

WAR

On 9 October Rhodes, now realizing that war was inevitable, left Cape Town by train for Kimberley, arriving late the following day. The day after his arrival the South African War began. One of the first actions of the war was the Boer investment of Kimberley; Rhodes was to remain there for the duration of the siege.[10]

The war was in full swing when, during November, Baker and Masey began to design a series of buildings for the Cape Explosive Works, the dynamite factory at Somerset West. The first was the Entrance Block, having offices on the ground floor, six bedrooms upstairs and a two-storey roofed veranda. The three gables on the entrance façade are

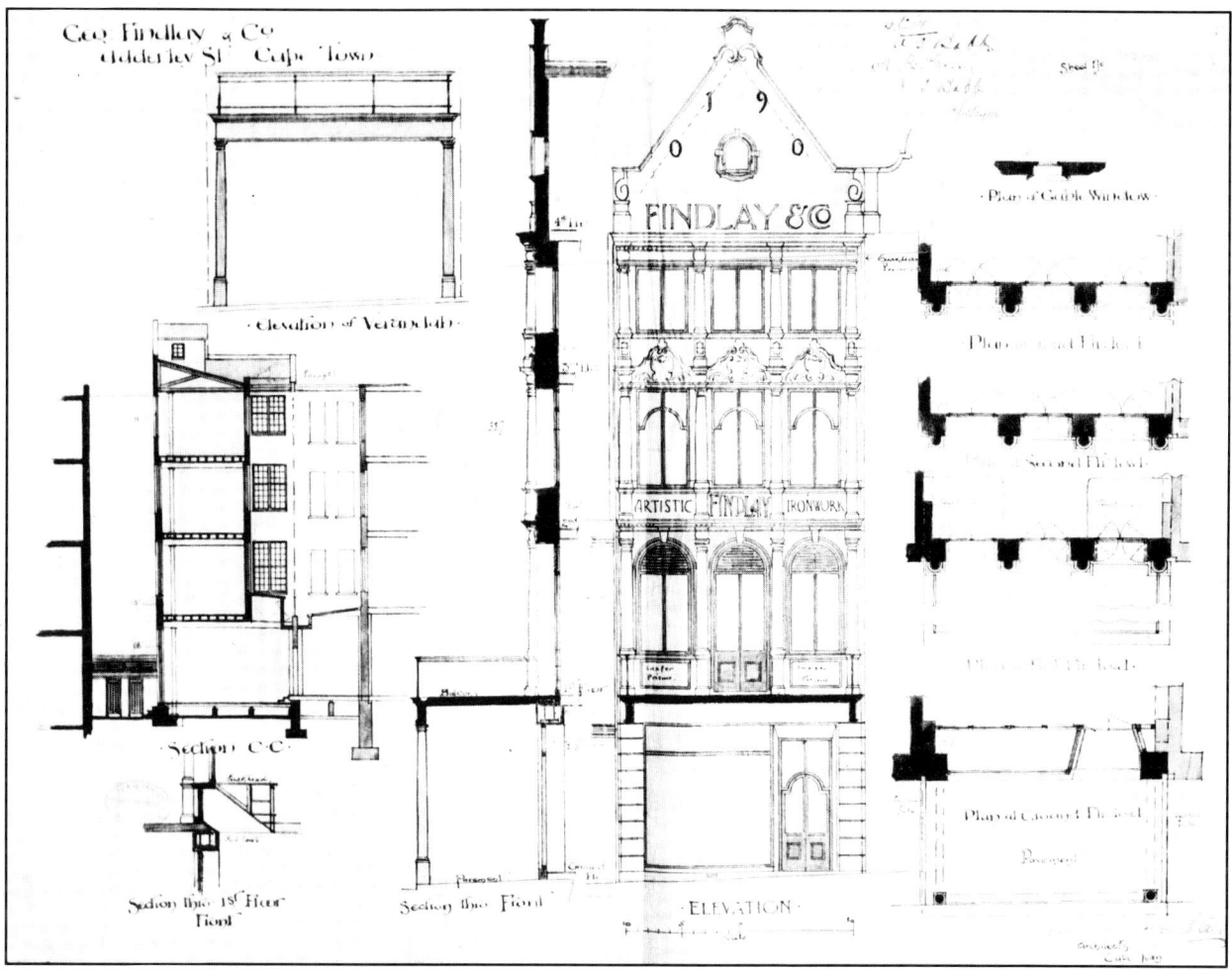

*Findlay Building, 27 Adderley Street, Cape Town, elevation
details.*

redolent of Kelvin Grove and the main façade of
Groote Schuur. Larger than the central one, the
flanking gables have venetian windows upstairs,
vertical sliding sash windows downstairs and semi-
circular air vents to the roof space. In the entrance
hall, too, one is reminded of Kelvin Grove, with its
wooden columns and arches, whilst the reception
room has a bow-topped mantelpiece, as can be seen
at Groote Schuur.[11]

In parallel with the Entrance Block, Baker and
Masey designed a Works Boarding House, in which
Greig sees 'the hand of Masey...in this large,
friendly-looking white building: the small cupola
which marks the centre of the high-pitched roof is
the same as that used by Masey in 1905 for the bell
tower at St James's in Maseru.'[12] Works Offices, too,
were designed by November and a Works Labora-

tory by early the following year. Further work at the
dynamite factory was to follow in 1901.

The new century began well for Baker with his
application for Fellowship approved by the Royal
Institute of British Architects. His election on 8 January 1900 no doubt gave him considerable satisfaction. But with war in the land that pleasure must
have been tempered by apprehension: even though
far removed from the theatre of war, building works
rapidly declined in Cape Town and its surrounding
suburbs. By the end of the war in May 1902, the
number of plans approved by the various munici-
palities had fallen to less than half their pre-war
level, which ironically had reached an unprecedented peak in the year before war began.[13]

As things turned out, Baker's own practice seems
to have been scarcely affected by a war which was

71

DESIGN SUGGESTED BY TOMB OF THERON·
AN OLYMPIAN· VICTOR·AT AGRIGENTUM. SICILY.

F.

DESIGN SUGGESTED BY THE PHILIPPEION
ERECTED AT OLYMPIA BY PHILIP OF MACEDON.

D.

*Top. Design suggested by Tomb of Theron, an Olympian victor
at Agrigentum, Sicily. Bottom. Design suggested by the
Philippeion erected at Olympia by Philip of Macedon. Sketches by
Herbert Baker.*

South African Association Building, Cape Town, elevation.

being fought far away in the interior and domestic commissions continued to come Baker's way despite the political uncertainties of the moment. Very little is known about how Baker viewed the war, apart from the insights to be gained from his *Cecil Rhodes by his Architect*, although this was published in 1934, many years after the event. But even here one can only interpolate his views from those he enthusiastically attributes to Rhodes, whom he idolized the more with the settled hindsight of over thirty years.

Kimberley was not relieved until 15 February, 1900; the Spioen Kop débâcle had taken place less than a month before and an early end to the war was by no means certain although its military outcome was by now predictable. Yet Rhodes was immediately back in Cape Town to commission his biggest building project of all, an office block to house the headquarters of all his companies and financial interests. Baker later recalled how Rhodes, on his first morning after his return from the siege, went with him on the new road he had made on the side of Table Mountain. It was a beautiful morning and Rhodes gazed silently over the sea of mist that covered the Cape Flats, then said, 'This will be all one country now; we must make this its beautiful capital.' Within a month Baker had done his first drawings for the building which still stands at the corner of St George's and Wale Streets.[14]

CLASSICAL INTERLUDE

Baker had hardly begun when his client made one of his most extraordinary gestures, revealing what even today is a little-appreciated side of his character. Early in March, 1900, he wrote in Baker's sketchbook: 'I desire you to see Rome, Paestum, Agrigentum, Thebes and Athens. I am thinking of erecting a mausoleum to those who fell at Kimberley, a bath and a copy of Paestum. Your expenses will be paid and in case I undertake any of these thoughts you will receive the usual architect's fee of five per cent. C J Rhodes.'[15]

On 18 March Baker sailed for England with Rhodes, parting company on their arrival in London.[16] The tour of the classical sites of the Mediterranean lasted some four months. In Egypt he visited Cairo and Thebes; in Greece he saw Athens, Delphi and Olympia; in Sicily he saw Palermo, Agrigentum and Segesta; in southern Italy he saw the Doric temples at Paestum, 'etc', as he put it in a letter to Pearse.[17] Baker described his pilgrimage in his book on Rhodes: 'For the Nymphaeum [Baker's term for the Bath] in the Siege Garden I studied the buildings characterized by Ionic grace; and for the Lion-temple [the copy of Paestum] on Table Mountain the immutable power expressed in the buildings of Thebes and Karnac, and the heavy Doric of the Grecian temples.'[18] In the Paestum-inspired Lion House, or Temple, '...the king of beasts would be admired in his natural strength and dignity...moving through great columns...' But Rhodes's idealized notion appears to have blinded him to the peculiar incongruity of lions living 'naturally' in a Greek Temple on the slopes of Table Mountain!

Rhodes's ideal of a memorial to the Kimberley siege in the form of a Roman 'bath' was translated by Baker into a fountain temple, '...amidst pools of lilies and papyrus...designed as a focus to the brilliancy of the gay garden of cannas and as a framework of white columns to the vista through a long avenue of oranges, backed by red-flowering eucalyptus-trees; and beyond to the illimitable desert.' Plans and estimates were prepared; white marble from Mount Pentelicus was to be used, as it had been on the Acropolis at Athens, for this beautiful oasis in hot, arid Kimberley.

Neither of these building projects, of which Rhodes spoke so idealistically and which 'occupied much of his mind during his early rides' got far under way. They came to naught because the war dragged on and Rhodes's health was declining; perhaps if he had lived longer they would have been realized. But if ever there were a case for building unbuilt dreams, it is surely the so-called Kimberley Bath, which would look so splendid in Kimberley today.

Near Rome, a tomb on the crest of the Alban Hills had struck Baker on his travels; he had thought of it as an idea for the Kimberley War Memorial. 'It consisted, I found, of a high stone podium; on this were ruined masses which I was able to reconstruct on paper as four great cones. These cones represented the metae, the turning-points and goals of the Roman circus, and on a monument became symbols of victory.' Rhodes read into Baker's design 'the goal of the war', the end of which he thought was then in sight, 'and the union of two equal races on the enduring foundation of South African federation within the Empire.'[19] In the monument eventually erected in 1904, known as the Honoured Dead Memorial, '...a four-square columned tetrastyle temple stands on a tall podium somewhat after the manner of a Greek tomb which he had seen and I had sketched at Agrigentum.'[20]

Baker relates how he was 'privileged to meet' Lord Cromer at Cairo. Cromer apparently regarded the Pyramids with some disdain, describing them '...as the most stupendous work of human folly... while [Cromer's] dam at Assouan is one of the greatest works of human wisdom.' Baker added his own comment: 'No human ingenuity could devise a form as ineffective in proportion to its mass as the upward-tapering polished pyramid; the same amount of masonry would have built walls, towers, and domes innumerable, to embody some vast artistic conception.'[21]

The sketches Baker drew on his travels confirm the impressions made on his mind. One in particu-

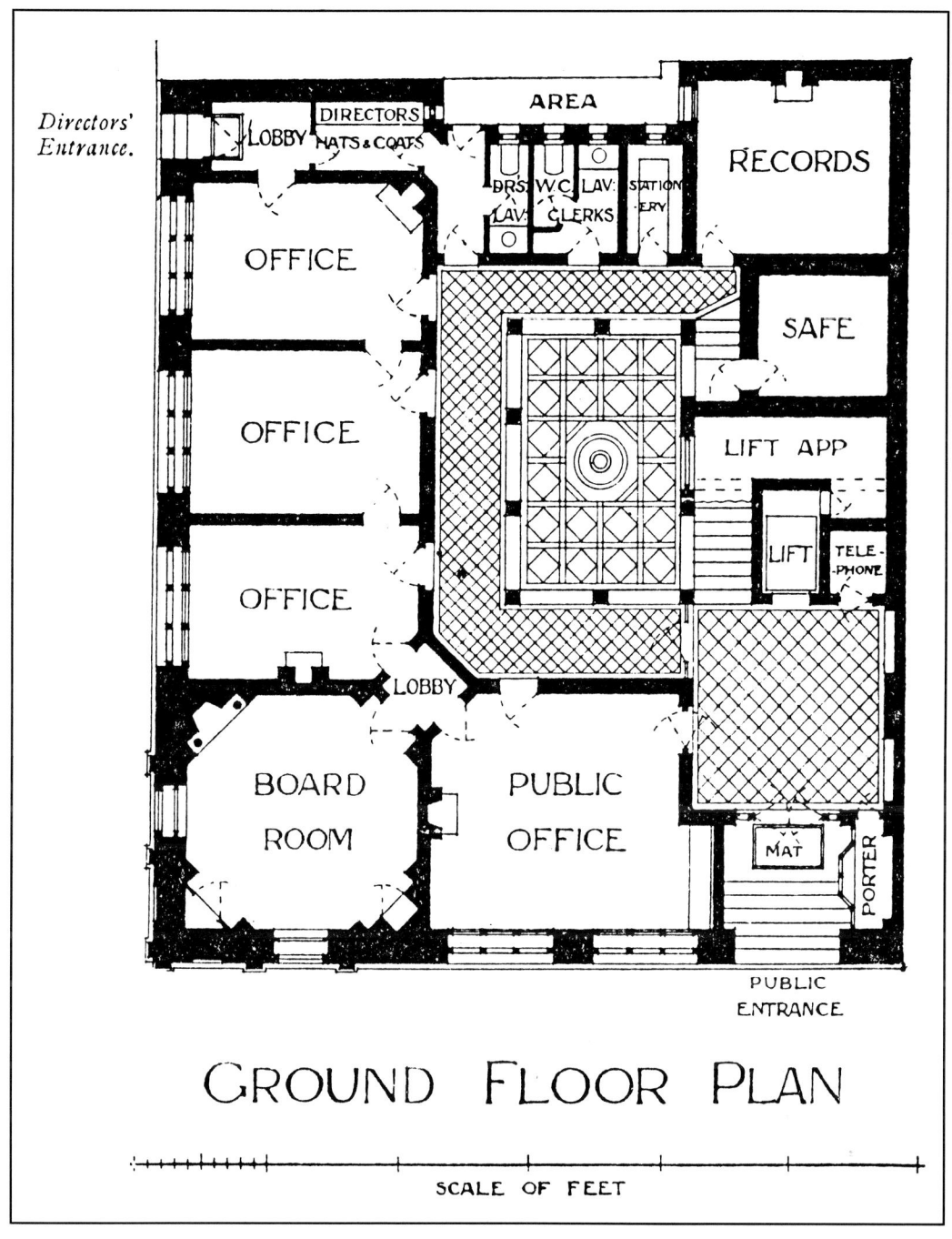

Directors' Entrance.

LOBBY

DIRECTORS HATS & COATS

AREA

RECORDS

DRS. LAV. WC LAV. CLERKS STATION ERY

OFFICE

SAFE

OFFICE

LIFT APP

LIFT TELE-PHONE

OFFICE

LOBBY

BOARD ROOM

PUBLIC OFFICE

MAT PORTER

PUBLIC ENTRANCE

GROUND FLOOR PLAN

SCALE OF FEET

Rhodes Building, 125 St George's Street, Cape Town, ground floor
plan.

lar, that drawing of the tomb at Agrigentum, was to have a profound influence on his architectural persona for the rest of his career. His sketching and sightseeing was interspersed with prodigious background reading. Kendall recalled: 'After his first homeward trip to Europe in about 1900 [Rhodes's tour] I remember he returned to South Africa with a couple of boxes of architectural and historical books, which I helped him to sort and place on his shelves. With some curiosity I asked him when he expected to get time to read all these momentous tomes, to which he replied with a half guilty air "Well you see, I have read them on my tour!"'[22]

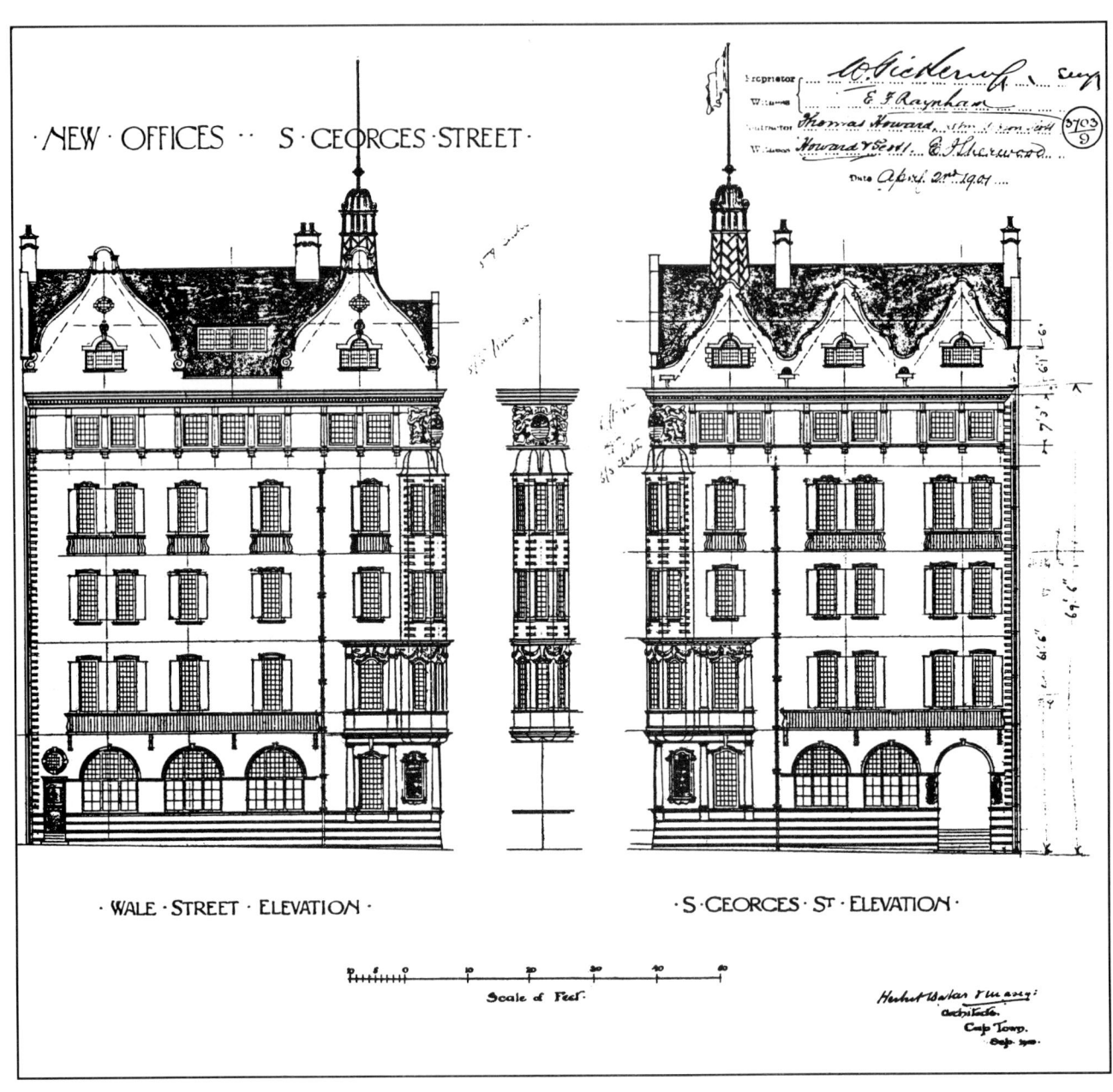

·NEW·OFFICES·· S·CEORGES·STREET·

·WALE·STREET·ELEVATION·   ·S·CEORCES·ST·ELEVATION·

Scale of Feet.

Rhodes Building, elevation.

THE RHODES BUILDING

Returning to Cape Town in July, Baker, with his partner Masey, had the designs for Rhodes's new offices to complete. By September a fine set of drawings showing the building, essentially as we see it today, had been completed. These, coloured up and augmented by later, more detailed, drawings, were signed by the contractors, Howard and Scott, on 2 April 1901. The plans show the accommodation arranged around an inner courtyard, twenty by twelve feet in size, small in relation to the height of the building. Although an obvious asset in a hot climate, it was, at that time, a unique feature for an office building in Cape Town. The building was in many ways a pace setter, both technically and aesthetically.

Each façade resembles the tall shuttered elevation of a house of the Low Countries, pivoting on a three-storey corner oriel. Both street fronts are topped with differing sets of gables, each of which is pierced with identical venetian windows. Less domestic are the broad-arched windows on the ground floor, which both look commercial and give a satisfactory firm base to the Table Mountain sandstone elevations above. In its overall composition, and even in the Dutch-Flemish gables and venetian windows, Rhodes's building could be a regional variant of an 1880s Richard Norman Shaw office block in the Queen Anne manner.[23]

The courtyard was paved in black and white marble in a diagonal checkerboard pattern. In its centre was a splashing fountain of red Verona marble, surmounted by a Zimbabwe Bird, as befitted the founder of Rhodesia. The building provided octagonal boardrooms for each of the two main companies it housed. These were situated on the ground and first floors and were similar in design. Teak panelling and joinery was used throughout and some well-known English firms provided furnishings, such as polished steel fire grates by Messrs Elsley of London; the massive brass door furniture by Gibbons of Wolverhampton and the sanitaryware by Tylor and Co of London.[24]

The *Cape Times* welcomed the 'Rhodes Building', the name it had been given by the time of its completion some six months after Cecil Rhodes's death, calling it 'a magnificent structure.' But reservations were expressed about the building's style: 'Viewed from the outside the Rhodes Building does not strike the casual observer as a particularly handsome one, but its simplicity of design and its huge proportions immediately arrest the attention. It has been specially desired to spend no money in unnecessary ornament, though at the same time preserving the building from anything that might offend the canons of good taste.' Referring to the way the building appeared to reflect its 'utilitarian' commercial purposes, the article declared the style of architecture it employed as being 'distinctive only in this sense, that it seems well adapted to the country.'[25] Though it was not meant to be, that should have been praise indeed.

As it is with so many designs produced by busy architectural practices the question of actual authorship in Baker's office is often confused. The Rhodes Building is just such a case. In a letter to Pearse, Kendall wrote 'As to the Nat. Mutual in Church Square, and Rhodes Building – Masey did

all the original drawings, but Baker "took over" the elevations and improved them immensely.'[26] This would not seem unreasonable on account of Baker's Mediterranean tour taking place so soon after Rhodes's return from the Kimberley siege. Whatever progress Baker had made would have needed furthering during his four-month absence. However, on the list Baker annotated for Pearse's proposed book the two buildings appear consecutively; Baker very clearly attributed the National Mutual building to Masey and placed a 'more especially mine' tick against the Rhodes Building. The English architect and designer, C R Ashbee, a leading member of the Arts and Crafts movement, expressed his uncertainties in his journal whilst visiting South Africa in June 1903: 'Masey's building is fine, but here again presumably there is the imagination of Cecil Rhodes behind it – at least I choose to believe so for I don't think Masey looks like a man of fire – perhaps the work is Baker's! – But the open court of the Barghello and the Palazzo Massimi applied to a place of business in such a dull humdrum, dawdly city as Cape Town is a fine notion. I envy the architect of the Rhodes Building.'[27]

At the time of Ashbee's visit Baker was in Johannesburg and it was Masey who showed him round Groote Schuur and the Rhodes Building. Could it be that Masey, a proud man with his master out of the way and wishing to impress, over-emphasized his own contribution to the design? On balance Kendall's remarks seem closest to the truth, with the proviso that in all probability Baker had laid down the basic concepts of the building before he departed.

THE WOOLSACK AND OTHER HOUSES

Another project Rhodes initiated soon after his return from Kimberley, was The Woolsack, also on the Groote Schuur estate. During the siege Rhodes had the idea of building a cottage in the woods where poets and artists might be encouraged to stay. He explained to Baker: 'If they live in beautiful surroundings they will be better able to interpret through their art the beauty and grandeur of the country.'[28] Rhodes had told Rudyard Kipling that he could 'hang up his hat there' whenever he visited the Cape. Indeed every year from Christmas 1900, when the house was completed, until 1907, Kipling and his family would spend five or six months

Highlands, Tennant Road, Wynberg, early photograph.

away from 'the peace of England, to the deeper peace of the "Woolsack", and live under the oak-trees overhanging the patio, where mother squirrels taught their babies to climb, and in the stillness of hot afternoons the fall of an acorn was almost like a shot.'[29] It has been claimed that it was here that Kipling wrote his famous poem 'If', having in mind Dr Jameson, who had led the infamous raid. The Woolsack is thus inseparable from Kipling memories.[30]

Indeed it was Kipling's wife Carrie, who accompanied Baker to 'select' a site for the proposed cottage on 7 March 1900. If it had not already been earmarked by Rhodes it appears they chose the site of a much older dwelling, possibly in a state of serious disrepair. Like Welgelegen, nothing now remains of the house which had previously stood on the site of The Woolsack.

The house is built with all its rooms leading off a central open court, in winter just as impractical as his own Sandhills was when the wind blew in from the sea. On two sides of the house was a continuous stoep, expanded and roofed over on the north-east, where the shaded, asymmetrical elevation enhances the relaxed atmosphere of the house. Seventeen Tuscan columns surround the atrium and support the outer veranda roof, like seventeen chubby friends standing in waiting. The main elevation faces south-east, onto the open stoep, where the central focus is a fine gable, pierced with a half-round vent and decorated with an inverted flower motif, not unlike Baker's Nooitgedacht of a year before.

Rhodes had instructed Baker 'not to be mean' and no expense was spared by Baker in the detailing of his built-in fittings or the carefully selected antiques which originally furnished The Woolsack. With its roof beams, stable doors, shuttered windows, blue-and-white bedroom fire surrounds; its built-in dressers and half-height cupboards, surviving photographs show it to have been a comfortable and homely summer retreat. Lionel Curtis's diary

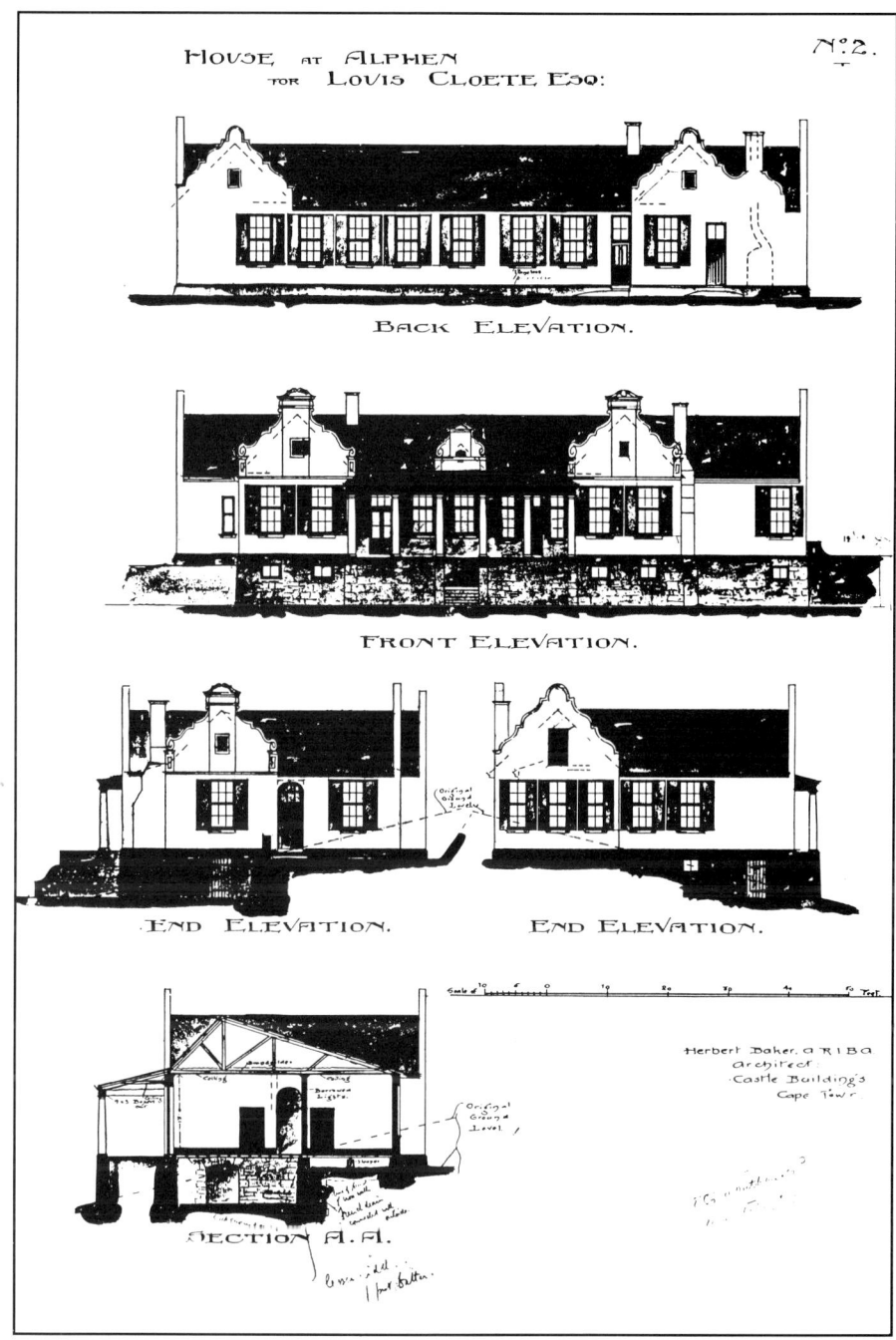

HOUSE AT ALPHEN
FOR LOUIS CLOETE ESQ:

Nº 2.

BACK ELEVATION.

FRONT ELEVATION.

END ELEVATION.

END ELEVATION.

SECTION A.A.

Herbert Baker, a RIBA
Architect
Castle Buildings
Cape Town

Glen Dirk in the Cape, for Louis Cloete, elevations.

for 25 August 1901 records that he 'Lunched with Baker at Rondebosch. He took us to see a house he had designed built by Rhodes for Kipling. It is even better than the Government House's cottage and in the most perfect situation overlooking the isthmus to the Hex Mountains...The bath is lined with Dutch tiles and you descend into it by steps and the furniture is of a piece with the rest.'[31] Today the house is occupied by part of the University's Department of Architecture, who may do more to restore it and keep it that way than many others.

It was during Baker's overseas trip that a plan, dated 19 May 1900, was prepared for the house named Highlands in Tennant Road, Wynberg, for

Rhodes Building, St George's Street, Cape Town, gable detail.

M W Searle. Johnson observes that Highlands has a number of features not previously encountered in Baker's architecture and which may be accounted for by his 'not only returning here to English vernacular but introducing Cape features into his "English" designs.' In view of Baker's absence, it seems perhaps more likely that the work is that of someone else, probably Masey. For example, the gables show the concave line of the sprocketed eaves, a common detail in English roofing for its water-shedding properties, with the upper gable area filled with tile-hanging, used here for the first time by Baker's firm. Another novel feature is the way the windows, larger than usual and set almost flush with the outer wall face, are tied together visually with horizontal mouldings.[32]

Other domestic work on which Baker was engaged in 1900 included eight labourers' cottages for Cecil Rhodes on the farm Vredenburg, which now house a Brandy Museum and a restaurant in the old Strand Road, Stellenbosch; and the Staff Cottage (also known as the Secretary's House) in Government Avenue, Gardens, Cape Town. For the latter, Baker once more produced a design composed of a recessed veranda, from which the cottage was entered, flanked in by two rather Flemish gables. The steeply pitched tiled roof, with its three dormer windows, made space for an upstairs living area.[33]

Concurrent with the building of the cottage were alterations made to the Royal Apartments in Government House itself, completed in August 1901, which the *Cape Times* reported as having 'been effected in a strikingly successful manner...'[34] Lionel Curtis's diary records that on 9 May 1901, 'Robinson, the private secretary, showed us a new cottage put up in the garden, in view of the royal visit... I have never seen a more perfect little house, with its deep cool recesses of white and simple massive furniture, equal to anything I have seen in the Arts and Crafts Exhibition.' Curtis also records that after lunch on the same day, '...we went and saw Baker who took us back to Government House and showed us the royal rooms furnished by him, a masterpiece of dignified simplicity. Then we took train to Muizenberg where Baker has lent Perry another exquisite cottage [Sandhills]. You could throw a stone into the sea from it.'[35]

It seems likely that it was also in that year that he did alterations to Glen Dirk in Klaasens Road, Wynberg, for Louis Cloete. These involved turning the house into something approximating a single-

storey Groote Schuur, by creating a small central gable flanked by two larger ones. Another minor project was to enlarge the chancel and complete the tower of the Church of St Paul in Bree Street. It is possible that Baker and Masey also added the aisle to this unusual South African example of Victorian polychromatic brickwork by E B J Knox of 1878-80.[36]

Baker began 1901 with the design of a Manager's House for the Somerset West Explosive Works, where he still had earlier work in progress. The plan is compact with a recessed veranda contained between two projecting rooms on the south side, leading to the entrance hall and on to the central circulation area containing a simply detailed wooden staircase. To the left as one enters is a wooden screen. The eaves are at constant height, as at Highlands and The Lilacs.[37]

Soon after, in May 1901, a house named Madawaska for W B Hall, in Lovers Walk, Kenilworth, was designed. It has been described as one of Baker's 'most important informal houses. It lacks the heavy and square masses of his other two contemporary houses, Highlands and The Lilacs, as well as the heavy stonework of the Rectory and Trovato.' Entrance to the house is gained from the south, through an arched recess. To the left is a double-storey section, the upper part of which is tile-hung; to the right was a single-storey wing, which has since been added to. The roof is extended over the veranda by means of a catslide, integrating the whole prismatic composition most successfully.[38]

The Lilacs in Camp Ground Road, Rondebosch, was designed in July 1901 for C F Sedgewick. An Italianate tower is the most striking feature of this house, now a Rondebosch Boys Preparatory School hostel. The Romanesque character imparted by this tower is enhanced by the round arches, three on the lower floor level and four on the upper, which remind one of a Roman aqueduct. In plan the projecting rooms contain a veranda to the east and another to the south, from which the house is entered via a small porch. By now this veranda form can be regarded as a typical Baker architectural feature. On entering one is confronted with the staircase across a long, narrow hall.[39]

1901 also saw Baker and Masey design a further commercial building, this time on a narrow site fronting onto Darling and Shortmarket Streets, for D Isaacs and Co, the furnishers he used on many of his commissions and from whom he had bought a table in August 1892, soon after he had opened his first office in Cape Town. The façades were decorated in terracotta modelled in England by Doulton of Lambeth and Burman Tofts of Leeds. Each floor has large windows separated by Corinthian pilasters, and shaped with shoulders in the upper corners of the large panes, giving a faint hint of Baker's favourite detail – the venetian window. The round-headed window in the gable also has a surround which echoes the shouldered forms below. Hopkins and Co were the contractors for this steel-framed building which was fireproofed with concrete. The first sketches were drawn that August and the single gable over the three-bay façade indicates that the building was completed in 1902. The Isaacs building was later occupied by the Wellington Fruit Growers.[40]

A further immediate outcome of the Boer War was a commission to build the Memorial Church of St John the Evangelist in another town made famous for its siege, Mafeking or Mafikeng as it is now called. Baker and Masey's design can only be likened to the Romanesque or early Gothic style, but with flattish, pointed arches in the nave – rather than the round arches characteristic of the Romanesque throughout western Europe.

Like Baker's first church, St Andrew, the curious shape of the chancel arch is not quite semi-circular, and not quite pointed, almost as if a contractor's error had been made. The locally baked red brick suits the style they chose giving it a gaunt nobility. The plan is what Greig has called basilican, that is to say they have a 'narthex at the west end leading into a wide high-aisled nave, a chancel the width of the nave and separated from it by a strong arch; from the chancel lead a large splayed apse, vestries and organ chamber...'[41] The plan of St John was similar to St Michael and All Angels. Again, as in so many of his churches, Baker uses small windows set high in the chancel walls or apse. In the nave the windows are narrow and set well forward to the outside walls, with splayed reveals to reduce the contrast between exterior brightness and the interior shade.

MEANS AND ENDINGS

With his churches, more so than with his houses and offices, Baker's architectural philosophy was crystallizing. St George's Cathedral was still dormant, but he had already committed himself to a Gothic style, with small, high windows – a contradiction to the northern European tradition which sought to let in as much light as possible. St George was the closest he would get to the Gothic Revival as it had been practised in England. But the style had passed its peak of fashion in the 1860s although it still had devoted adherents.[42]

Baker was still far from having arrived at a single unified consistent approach, unless one considered it all Queen Anne, a term which would serve as a catch-all for his work had it been part of the English architectural scene of those years. His houses fall into two fairly distinct types, his 'English' and his 'Dutch', one presumes, according to a client's preference.[43] His churches seek to be 'English' only through their Gothic-cum-Arts and Crafts spirit, but never 'Dutch'. But then he was building mainly for the Anglican Church; one wonders what a Dutch Reformed Church commission would have looked like in Baker's hands!

Baker took on more staff as his practice grew but, according to Vernon Rees-Poole, there always seemed to be too much work to be carried out within the allotted time. Rees-Poole was one of Baker's first articled pupils, joining the firm in 1896, between the arrival of Franklin Kendall and Francis Masey. As an impressionable teenager in the closing years of the nineteenth century Rees-Poole has left us the clearest picture of life in Baker's office in those times. Particularly interesting is his account of Baker's encouragement of students at a time when organized facilities for the training of architects were non-existent in Cape Town.[44]

Consolidating the interest he had aroused towards architecture in general, and early Cape architecture in particular, Baker promoted competitions open to all students in related disciplines. The competitors, who included engineers, surveyors and students in the Municipal Works Department, were required to prepare accurate measured drawings of well-known local historical buildings. Rees-Poole relates that following the initiative of both Baker and Masey, an architectural section was established by the Eisteddfod Association. Other competitions followed and the successful candidates received valuable books on architecture; '...they were called the Baker Prize and the Baker and Masey Prizes.' Various societies began to take an interest in architectural matters, and 'from then onwards, architecture gained a place in the thoughts and doings of a large section of the community.' On many occasions they were invited to

Herbert Baker with Milner's Kindergarten. Baker was a friend and confidant to several of the group who called him 'Grandpa'.
Back row: Lionel Curtis, Nel Hitchens, Peter Perry, Hugh Wyndham, Herbert Baker, Geoffrey Dawson.
Sitting: Lord Selborne, Robert Brand, Patrick Duncan, Lady Selborne, Lord Long, Richard Feetham.
On floor: Philip Kerr, John Dove, Dougal Malcolm.

The Grotto, 'where interesting talks were given on architecture, trees, plants, garden designing, etc.' Visits were also arranged to works in construction.[45]

In all these activities Baker's energy and endurance were remarkable. In his work, 'schemes were thought out and sketches produced in no time; like his walking, no one could keep pace with him. The only recreation he took was walking and horse riding on Muizenberg beach. One day, whilst galloping, his horse came down. Baker was thrown and broke his collarbone; he had to rest for a time, and that was the only short holiday I remember him taking.'[46]

In early July 1901, Rhodes sailed to England. Among other matters of a political and private nature which needed attending to, he was to see a heart specialist. He was told his condition was very serious and the specialist recommended a long rest and constant change of surroundings. In consequence, after a spell in Scotland, a trip to Europe and Egypt was undertaken. On his return journey Rhodes sailed from Southampton with Jameson on 18 January 1902.[47]

He caught a severe cold at sea, and suffered a bad fall one night when he had chosen to sleep on a table in the hope of enjoying a cooler breeze across his cabin. By the time the ship reached the Cape, he was already gravely ill. Rose Innes later described how on the visit he made to him at Muizenberg in early March, Rhodes sat on 'the narrow stoep of that tin-roofed cottage...mortally stricken and in sore need of spacious and airy surroundings, one of the most famous and wealthiest men in the British Empire.'[48] And Baker wrote, 'I said my last farewell to him there in that humble cottage, and I shall all my life be haunted by the remembrance. Rhodes died on 26 March, 1902, whispering "So little done, so much to do."'[49]

The war, now in its guerrilla phase, was not to end finally till the end of May. It had attracted to South Africa many thousands of men from all parts of the world. Along with the soldiers, speculators and adventurers, came servants of the Crown to assist in reconstruction once the fighting was ended. Alfred Milner had arrived at the Cape as High Commissioner for South Africa in May 1897, moving his headquarters north to the Transvaal in March 1901, as the end of hostilities came in sight.

By the end of that year Milner had gathered the nucleus of his Kindergarten.[50] Baker, though not one of the Kindergarten, was to become closely associated with the group. Recalling the events of that time Baker wrote: 'Just before L'd Milner went up to the Transvaal he sent for me and said the new colonies wanted architectural advice. That the political condition being settled people would want to make houses and thus architecture would have its influence on the political stability and prosperity of these countries.'[51] Baker paid several visits to Johannesburg and Bloemfontein during 1901-2 and, 'early in 1902 I went to live in Johannesburg and bought with Lionel Curtis the land of Stonehouse and commenced building; the first to build on that Kopje.'[52]

PART THREE
TRANSVAAL

Pilrig, Parktown, Johannesburg, for Max Balfour.

CHAPTER SIX

1902-1903

NEW BEGINNINGS

STONEHOUSE

'So, with the prospect of abundant work I set forth once again on my adventures', wrote Baker, not without some regrets at having to leave his 'dear little house at Muizenberg and comfortable quarters in the Castle Shipping Company's newly built offices...', the construction of which he had supervised for the London architects, Dunn and Watson.[1]

On 13 December 1901, Lionel Curtis, who had been Acting Town Clerk of Johannesburg since April, wrote in his diary: 'Baker...has been with me and we have just got today a most beautiful site, the last left on the great northern ridge looking forty miles to the Magaliesberg. We are going to build together, with a studio which Max [Balfour] can use, and start at once if possible. All Baker wants is a *pied-à-terre* when he comes to Johannesburg. I must not write more as I have to go up with him and look at the ground. Karri Davis [*sic*] will be our neighbour. He is rather a romantic and interesting person who languished for months in prison sooner than apologise to Kruger.'[2] Curtis bought two acres overlooking a young plantation of firs and gum trees and it was agreed that Baker would take over the land and build a house 'in which he and I and other friends could live together.' And so, during 1902, Stonehouse grew out of the rocky ridge between what is now Rock Ridge Road and The Valley Road.[3]

Baker's designs for Stonehouse were quickly completed and by March 1902 he was seeking a contractor. He also had in hand designs for several other houses in Johannesburg. Contract plans for Inanda House in Forest Road, for W Wybergh, Commissioner of Mines, were complete by 6 March.[4] Also that month, he began to design a house for the Chairman of the Braamfontein Company, R W

Schumacher, later to be known as Pallinghurst.[5] He wrote to Curtis on 12 March about their joint venture: 'This is my first job at Johannesburg and there are naturally so many difficulties that it would be a great comfort for me to have full confidence in the Contractor.'

On the same day Baker wrote to Sir George Farrar, the mine owner and Progressive politician, for whom he was designing a house in what then was still open country. The house was later known as Bedford Court, and today forms part of St Andrew's School for Girls.[6] In his letter Baker referred to one of the most important and immediate tasks he had to undertake before he could open an office in Johannesburg, namely, to 'obtain a good assistant to help...meet the amount of work I anticipate.' To that end, 'I leave for England today...', he informed both Curtis and Farrar.[7]

Baker planned to be away on his search for a suitable English architect for about seven weeks. He had not been home for nearly two years, during which time Britain and the Boer Republics had been at war. And it was an opportunity to enjoy a relaxing voyage and renew contact with his relatives and friends, which no doubt included seeing Edwin Lutyens in London.

On 7 May he wrote to John Dale Lace, another influential and well-to-do client for whom he had begun sketches of a house shortly before he left for England, saying that he had just returned and expected 'to be up in Johannesburg early next week and hope to be able to go ahead at once with all my plans.'[8] The same day Baker wrote to the Transvaal branch of the Permit Office in Cape Town to confirm that 'a permit has been arranged for myself and my assistant to proceed to Johannesburg. My assistant's name is Mr E W Sloper.'[9] It seems strange that this is the only clue in Baker's business correspon-

Stonehouse, Parktown, Johannesburg, early photograph with Florence Baker.

dence of those months that the war was not yet officially over. Neither is there any mention that, during his brief absence abroad, his friend and patron Cecil Rhodes had died at Muizenberg and been buried in the Matopo Hills.

Curtis's house, as strictly speaking it still legally belonged to him, was in Baker's own words, '...planned round a long-windowed hall with two-storeyed wings of small rooms on either side; and to the north, facing the kopje-terrace, the sun, and the distant view, there is an arched stoep, and forming the entrance to the south a white-columned atrium under and through which steps lead up from the front door in the rock wall below.'[10]

Whilst the design of Stonehouse incorporates elements of his Cape domestic work, such as an H-shaped plan, verandas contained by steeply roofed projecting wings, Tuscan columns, bay windows and an Arts and Crafts feel about its detailing,

there were new ideas too. Most striking of all is the entrance approach which winds its way around the atrium. The absurd criticism often heard, that this south-facing atrium is on the wrong side of the house, is given lie to by virtue of a north-facing stoep on the opposite side of the central section, providing choice of use according to season. What could be more ideal! The steeply-pitched, shingled roof has hipped ends, sprocketed eaves at constant height and not a single gable or dormer window to break the surface. Sprouting upwards are Baker's tall chimneys, transforming from stone into brick as they pass the line of the eaves, finishing in round chimneypots.

The house stands rock-solid and fortress-like, literally growing out of the site from which its walls were hewn, and into which holes had to be quarried to plant trees and flowers in the crevices, making a natural rock-garden. When C R Ashbee visited

Stonehouse in July 1903, it was already looking mature. He was moved to write in his journal: 'I wipe out of my mind all the foolish preconceptions as to the ugliness or vulgarity of upstart Johannesburg for I have today seen Baker's buildings, the red sandstone crag sites, the fir and cypress, and the rolling purple hills of the Rand. Baker's own house...springing like a jewel castle from out of the rock, its arcades, and stoeps, its red shingle roof, the open court, the white columns and pergola with the circular garden below...is one of the most exquisite pieces of architecture I have seen.'[11] Baker had built an undoubted masterpiece.

But Baker did not move into Stonehouse until 16 March 1903 when, after much exasperation with the contractor, it was finally completed and the furniture he had had at The Grotto was sent up and installed.[12] This was augmented by pieces he had ordered from Mrs Keightley in London, which he specified to be 'very simple, as cheap as possible, strong for rough wear and carriage and very well seasoned to stand exceptional dry inland climate.'[13]

Stonehouse was the first 'Moot House', the intellectual and social meeting place of Milner's young Kindergarten. The group was the core of an almost exclusively male fraternity which administered the Transvaal and Johannesburg. They were bound together by their common purpose and the fact that all eleven members had been educated at Oxford; and all but two at New College which was, in their day, the most esteemed of the Oxford colleges.[14]

LIFE IN JOHANNESBURG

At first their lives were filled with official duties which left little time for leisure. What recreation time they had, tended towards vigorous outdoor activity such as riding, hunting trips and long treks into the interior. From the ridge they rode their horses early each morning into the valley, cantering among the blue gums, before their long office hours began. In the evenings they often met at leisurely dinners, the erudite conversation spiced with classical quotations. Despite Baker's deficiencies in the classics and his lack of a university education, not to mention his age – he would turn forty in June that year – he was the close friend of several members of the group. When completed, the house which he and Lionel Curtis were building would become for a time a centre for their activities. In the meantime Curtis was staying at the home of J F Perry, who held the post of Imperial Secretary to the High Commissioner and was the first of the Kindergarten to have arrived in South Africa. It was thus through Curtis that Baker usually stayed with Perry and his wife when he visited Johannesburg before moving into Stonehouse.[15]

Apart from Lionel Curtis, who affectionately christened him 'Grandpa', the other members of the group who lived with Baker at Stonehouse were Lionel Hitchens, Richard Feetham and John Dove. 'Living with and being able to share the enthusiasm of these young men', wrote Baker, 'was a great enjoyment to me as well as an education in the broader issues of political and social affairs.'[16] Baker had known many exceptional people in Cape Town but apart from these he had found Cape society 'a little narrow and self-sufficient. Nature's bounty did not inspire all with high thoughts and breadth of view.'[17] Baker had moved into a vibrant new society with a guaranteed clientele; Milner and his young men could open every possible door for him, and they did. The day-by-day growth of his practice was phenomenal, reaching into every sphere of building activity, through every possible route. One of the earliest records of his Transvaal years concerns his virtually immediate election to the Rand Club in March 1902.[18] In July he was invited by E B Sargant, Commissioner of Education for the Transvaal and Orange River Colony, to address the Teachers Congress, held in Johannesburg, on the topic of 'Architecture and Education'. Baker had high ambitions for the publication of the paper he had read, but was greatly dissatisfied with its eventual printing early in the following year.[19] If his friendship with Rhodes had made his success in Cape Town possible, his circle in Johannesburg would make it certain.

But it would be wrong to deduce that, in the first years of his life in Johannesburg, Baker's social circle consisted solely of bright young men. On 24 January 1902, Curtis wrote the following entry in his diary: 'Baker asked me to lunch to meet Miss Flora Shaw. She is prepossessing in person and has a flow of continuous and brilliant conversation...She is withal a very fascinating lady.'[20] Flora Shaw was a little older than Baker and a British journalist on the staff of the *London Times*. Though later that year she was to marry the British explorer and Colonial Governor, Sir Frederick Lugard, she was a friend Baker had known since her early contacts with Rhodes in her role of special correspondent in 1895. Her intellect and maturity made her the kind

Watercolour of Stonehouse, 1902.

Stonehouse today.

of woman who, on the face of it, would have appealed to Baker, himself a serious-minded person.[21] But nothing has come to light to indicate any love interest in Baker's life at this time, nor for that matter at any other time thus far. In the meantime Baker was to remain a bachelor, and Stonehouse and the way of life it contained would suit him and his companions perfectly.

Added to the stimulus provided by his local friends Baker derived much satisfaction from the continuing correspondence with his friend Edwin Lutyens. Some of the best known expressions of Lutyens's architectural philosophy have come to us through his surviving letters to Baker. In one such, dating from February 1903, Lutyens exclaimed: 'In architecture, Palladio is the game!! It is so big – few appreciate it now, and it requires training to value and realize it. The way Wren handled it was marvellous. [Richard Norman] Shaw has the gift. To the average man it is dry bones, but under the hand of a Wren it glows and the still materials become plastic clay.

'I feel sure that if Ruskin had seen that point of view he would have raved as beautifully as he raved for the Gothic, and I think that he did have some insight before he died; his later writings were much more gentle towards the Italian Renaissance.

'It is a game that never deceives, dodges never disguises. It means hard thought all through – if it is laboured it fails. There is no fluke that helps it. So it is a big game, a high game...'[22] Always impressionable in the company of intellects, Baker could not fail to be influenced by such enthusiastic erudition. Lutyens continued to expound on his discovery of classicism in another letter to Baker in December 1904: 'It means hard labour, hard thinking, over every line in all three dimensions and in every joint; and no stone can be allowed to slide. If you tackle it in this way, the Order belongs to you, and every stroke, being mentally handled must become endowed with such poetry and activity as God has given you. You alter one feature (which you have to always) and then every other feature has to sympathize and undergo some care and invention...it is no mean [game] nor is it a game you can play lightheartedly...'[23]

No doubt the lessons sunk in deep, adding to the experiences he had absorbed in the Mediterranean in 1900. But it would be a while yet before he could try his hand at the sort of substantial building where the 'high game' could be played to effect.

Returning to July 1902, we find Baker working on a house for his Stonehouse neighbour, the popular, swashbuckling Major Karri Davies, who was the first to ride into Mafeking. The house, alas, has since given way to the Kenridge Hospital in Rock Ridge Road. By 7 July he had completed the drawings and quantities for W Wybergh's Athol House, which stood in Pretoria Avenue and Linden Street, Athol, also demolished in recent times. Wybergh's house was another of the H-plan type and, in Doreen Greig's belief, '...the only house in the Transvaal...unaffectedly Cape Dutch in conception.' Its centre gable had a 'strong kinship to the one over the front of Die Oude Pastorie in Paarl.' White walls and a corrugated-iron roof, through which massive plastered chimneys sprouted, contrasted with the dark beamed interior, much in the Baker and Masey Cape manner.[24]

Of the original Inanda House – built for a Mr Myberg – little of the original design remains, because of the many alterations. It was square-planned, with an internal courtyard and a long stoep across its north side, and also white-walled under iron, with tapered plastered chimneys and elongated gables.[25]

As the year wore on, the work multiplied as more and more new projects were begun, adding to the complexities of finishing earlier, uncompleted, contracts and keeping in touch with what Masey and Kendall were doing at the Cape Town office. Bearing in mind that Baker still had only one qualified assistant, Ernest Sloper, and an office boy, but no typist, which meant that all correspondence was written – often as many as half a dozen letters a day – and tissue copies pressed by hand, the performance was awesome. Yet, somehow or other, design schemes, documentation, and the buildings were produced.[26]

On 10 July Baker put forward development proposals and costs for a site on the corner of Pritchard and Eloff Streets for Major Livingstone, whilst, on the same day managing to find time to write to the Royal Institute of British Architects on the subject of commissioning work in the colonies.[27] Then, towards the end of August, Baker and Sloper travelled together by train to Lydenburg, to visit the Reverend Vyvyan in connection with additions to his church, for which they posted drawings a week or so later.[28]

On 29 August Baker wrote to Rudyard Kipling: 'I am so glad you will undertake the tablet [on the Kimberley Memorial]. I think the cost you mention £90 will do. We must be careful as we have a niggardly committee to deal with.'[29] There were further schemes for houses for W Pennant, for which tenders were invited early in August and in September, and for Sir Percy Fitzpatrick at Irene, a scheme which was soon to be abandoned when Sir Percy transferred his home building interests to a farm near Harrismith. Then, in the same month, construction began on Dale Lace's house, eventually to become The Lodge to the larger mansion Northwards.[30] Only slightly behind was the house at Bellevue for Lieutenant-Colonel C M O'Brien, President of the Military Tribunal, for which a contract was signed on 1 November.[31]

It is surprising to learn that in September that year an invitation to compete in a limited competition for a new church of St Augustine, in Doornfontein, was declined, even if only for reasons of a professional technicality![32] In mid-November, however, he was pleased to accept a similar invitation, but with different conditions, from the directors of The Standard Bank of South Africa.[33]

Baker's fee income was now steadily growing, yet his expenses were such that he found it difficult to raise relatively small sums of cash. He had undertaken to lend to his relative, Herbert Nicholson, two hundred pounds for a farming venture in the Orange River Colony, just as his father had done to help his brother Lionel establish a farm at the Cape in 1892. But, wrote Baker, 'I will give you the money during the next twelve months mortgage upon my Cape Town property.'[34]

One feels for the Oxfordshire-born Raymond Schumacher when, wanting to change his mind yet again and omit the tower and battlements from Baker's design for his Parktown house, he was strongly rebuked by the architect. In one of two letters Baker wrote to Schumacher on 29 October (the other was in regard to the fees for it all) he declares, 'I should never have dreamed of building such an expensive house, had I not been keen, in conjunction with Karri Davies and others, on improving this prominent part of the estate, in fact preserving the beauty of these ridges has been the talk of everyone who takes an interest in [the] future of Johannesburg.' Baker's persuasive tone now borders on the bullying: 'If this bit of vandalism is perpetuated we had better all chuck beauty and architecture to the winds and go in for tin villas at once.'[35] There is nothing quite like it in all of Baker's voluminous correspondence over several decades.

In the matter of obtaining work, it seems there were few disappointments to be borne in his early Transvaal days. There is one worth mentioning, however, for the light it sheds on Baker's attitude towards his art, and dare one say, business. It came from a Mr Littlewood and, three days before his first Christmas at Johannesburg, elicited the response: '...I can only reply as frankly, that nothing hurts the feelings of an honest architect more than to be told that he cannot be trusted with small jobs because he is expensive. In the first place alterations to the back of a building require as a rule more skill in economic planning than do complete new designs, and secondly there is only one market price for building; there are broad cloth and shoddy and all an architect of principle will refuse to give his clients is shoddy hidden by tinsel. I write this privately but I hope you will read it to your Board.'[36]

Despite the Christmas season – which incidentally gains no mention in any of Baker's correspondence – Littlewood must have replied quickly. For Baker, distinctly hurt, wrote on 2 January that he thought the alterations were to be made without an architect, '...but now understand another has been employed and myself thrown over.' Baker continues: 'I may employ artistic and expensive details for private clients, who I may think have the taste to appreciate them, but I have always considered it dishonest to do so to any intent in [sic] purely utilitarian structures where economic planning and good construction are the first essentials. I must however thank you personally for your long and candid letter.'[37]

Inevitably there were criticisms too, of inadequate supervision for example, as in the case of Lt-Col O'Brien's house. Here, Baker's defence seems sound when he wrote to the Director of Public Works about the contract, which was 'signed on 1 November, a week later we inspected the trenches and shortly after approved a sample of masonry in the foundations. We find that we have since visited the work upon the following days: November 16, 24, 27, December 2, 6 and again today – in less than six weeks no less than eight times.'[38]

One senses, behind Baker's ostensible altruism, the hint of a tout in the letter he wrote to John Begg on 8 December: 'I am practising up here now. I am distressed about the carrying out of a church – St Mary's which you designed. The plans have been put in the hands of a firm of architects...completely without knowledge of church architecture – or possessed of any training of architecture at all on the artistic side', ending, 'I hope you are more than satisfied with your Indian venture.'[39] Years later Begg would appear on the sidelines of the Lutyens and Baker New Delhi saga.[40] So incensed was Baker that he wrote to the editor of *The Star* and very possibly made covert approaches to the church authorities. The work eventually went to the English architect G H Fellowes-Prynne, but a seed had been sown for Baker's eventual, if not inevitable involvement in the building of the Anglican Cathedral of St Mary in Johannesburg.[41]

But behind all this varied and intense activity in the second half of 1902 two of the biggest plums of all continued to ripen, the Governor's Residency in the Transvaal and the Cathedral of St George in the Cape.

PRETORIA STRIVINGS

Long before Stonehouse or any of his Transvaal projects was complete, Baker had received a letter of appointment to design a new Government House in Pretoria. He could hardly have been surprised. This, after all, was the sort of work Milner had invited him to the Transvaal to do. To arrive in a new country and know that the most prestigious building of the moment is to be yours, as if by right, is a strange position for any architect to find himself in, and almost bound to dramatically affect his self-confidence.

The letter from the Lieutenant-Governor, Sir Arthur Lawley, was dated 29 July 1902, but referred to earlier informal discussions. The brief was for an eight-bedroomed mansion with appropriate drawing and dining-rooms. Included was a large hall, eighty-five to ninety feet long and thirty-five to forty feet wide. There was also to be substantial servants' accommodation, an office for the Private Secretary, an ADC, and their supporting clerical staff. For all this a working budget of £25 000 was stipulated, rising to £35 000 if unavoidably necessary.[42]

From the beginning Baker had to work against an inadequate budget and a conflict between client and architect. His clients thought they knew what they wanted, and Baker, arguably with greater experience, knew what was needed. Besides, was he not Lord Milner's Architect? For his strivings he has often been accused of extravagance, and for this reason it is important to examine quite closely the sequence of events by which a building adequate for its practical and symbolic purpose was achieved.

Baker replied the next day accepting the commis-

sion. In his letter he immediately launched into a discussion of the house's requirements and size, saying: '...I ask that the size of the Hall suggested will necessitate a larger proportional scale to the whole house', pointing out by way of comparison that 'the Ballroom at Cape Town is only fifty by forty feet.'[43] Within a few days Baker was in a position to discuss his plans with Lord Milner, which he did on Sunday, 3 August. During the following week Baker was injured when his horse shied and fell, with him partly under.[44]

Notwithstanding this setback Baker pressed on with a sense of urgency and, on 12 August, informed W E Davidson, the Colonial Secretary, that he would 'work out plans to a larger scale on the basis of a seventy by thirty hall and send or bring them to Pretoria for your approval before the Lieutenant Governor arrives.'[45]

Typical again were the remarks he made in a letter dated 27 August 1902, to Major G H Fowke, RE, who had charge of the new Public Works Department: 'I am glad you think the bedrooms too few. My instructions were eight. I can easily I think get more. The hall I know wants lot more thinking about...' Baker had already questioned the adequacy of septic tanks and queried the irrigation of the site; he now concluded to Fowke: 'I hope you will arrange for a drainage system. There must be water closets in this house.'[46]

Sir Arthur Lawley took up his appointment on 1 September and, once he and Lady Lawley arrived on the scene, there were many more requests for further embellishments to the brief, and not a few suggestions from Baker. Indeed, on Christmas Eve, Lawley and Baker inspected the site and decided on nothing less than a new position for the building. Within a month Baker submitted 'another set of plans and sketches...upon the new site...', with a long letter listing all the improvements that had been made, but pointing out that the levels he had requested had still not been received. In May 1903, a start was made on the foundation works for Government House, only to be halted in August.[47] But in the meantime Baker continued to consolidate his position in the Transvaal.

THE GENERAL'S HOUSE

Also in Pretoria, and before the actual appointment for Government House had been received, another prestigious imperial commission came his

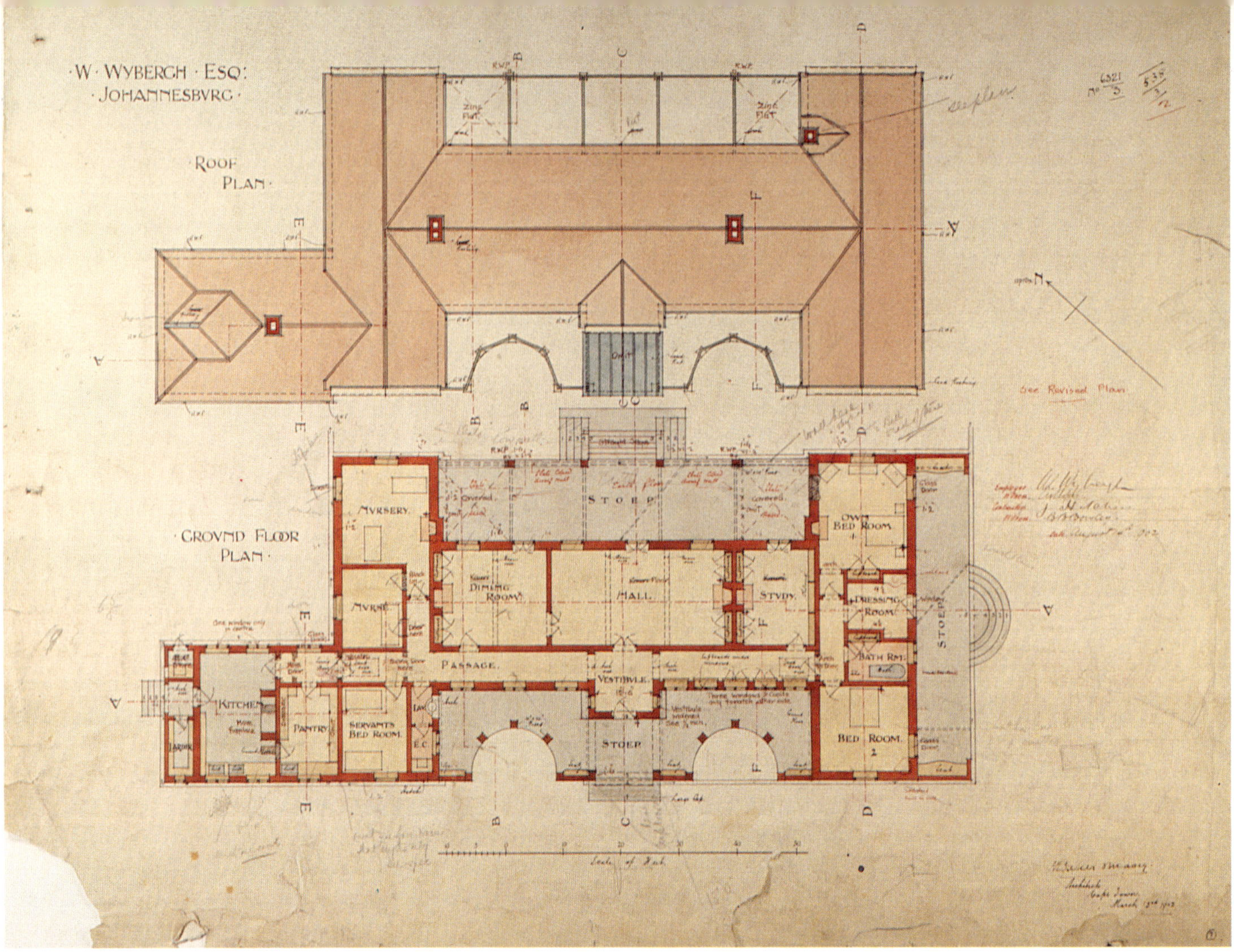

Top. *House for W Wybergh, esq. Roof and ground floor plan, March 1902. Bottom. Stonehouse, for Lionel Curtis. Plans, March 1902.*

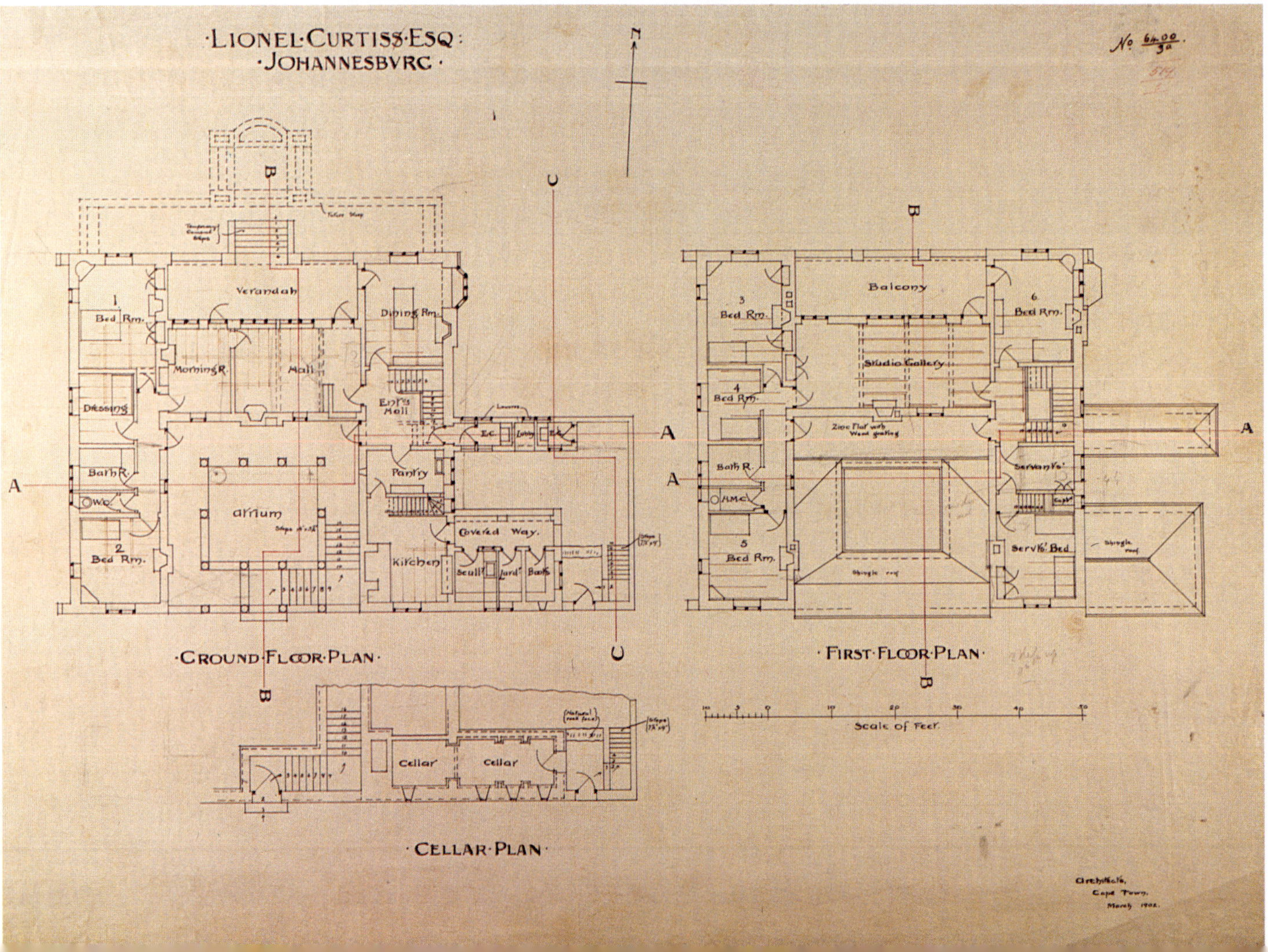

Stonehouse, Parktown, Johannesburg, entrance courtyard looking
west.

way: The General's House. On 20 June 1902 General Sir Neville Lyttelton took command of the British forces in South Africa, succeeding Lord Kitchener. Barely a fortnight later Baker was writing to Masey: 'I have not yet heard anything from the General.'[48] Not long afterwards Baker was asked to design a new house for the Lytteltons at Roberts Heights, the military station near Pretoria, now known as Voortrekkerhoogte. Then, by 19 July, Baker was discussing how savings could be made to the house he had designed by using 'government and military labour.'[49] Construction began in November and immediately Lady Lyttelton required revisions amounting to an extra £800.[50] The plan was again H-shaped with stoeps, on both the north and front sides, arched on the ground floor and columned upstairs. Otherwise, the finishes were according to formula: white plastered walls under iron. In the original colour scheme all the external woodwork was stained green and all the internal walls painted white.

Baker also knew that the General and his wife were very good friends. 'Lady Lyttelton took a helpful interest in planning the house.'[51] Indeed she did! As the bulging files attest she made numerous, and to be fair, intelligent requests. For example, she wished 'an alteration to be made in the position of the windows on the first floor which come over the dairy and service room. It is thought that the reflection of heat from the iron [roof] will be less if the windows are grouped in the centre with a 14 inch pier between.'[52] She and 'some of her three charming daughters' stayed with Baker in his 'little house at Muizenberg' and Baker 'spent many happy hours with them in Pretoria...' General Lyttelton's command expired in 1904 when Lord Methuen, whom Baker equally admired, succeeded as the 'kindly host' at Roberts Heights.[53]

FIRST MINERS' HOUSES

In stark contrast to Baker's work for the Johannesburg wealthy, were the groups of 'mine houses' he was commissioned to do in his first year and subsequently. The earliest and best known of these, commissioned in groups from October 1902 onwards, was the collection of thirty-eight cottages for mine workers, popularly known as 'Eckstein's Compound'.[54] These low-cost family homes, built for the Corner House Mining Group, of which Schumacher was a director, and situated between what are now

Barkly, Doveton and Frere Roads, were built amid much local opposition. But through them Baker demonstrated that brick and plaster construction, embellished with columned stoeps, was a viable alternative to the wood and iron houses which were being built by the company's mechanical engineers department.

The plans of Baker's houses were variations of three types, whilst the constant pitch of the corrugated iron roofs, the stable doors and the white Tuscan columns gave the housing scheme a uniform identity which persists to this day, despite the many alterations since made to individual houses. The success of Eckstein's Compound was followed by a number of further commissions for similar schemes spread over several years, and for other companies.[55] Such low-cost work would eventually save Baker's practice from disaster.

MUIZENBERG TO MARIENHOF

Before leaving Cape Town to live and work in Johannesburg Baker, with Masey, who was to remain in Cape Town, had had further work to do on a number of projects, including the development of the design for the Kimberley Memorial to the Honoured Dead, which he had started for Rhodes a year before. There had also been plans to prepare for two important houses at Muizenberg. One of these was for the wealthy businessman Sammy Marks, the other a summer residence which Cecil Rhodes had commissioned before his death and which was now to be completed for the mining magnate Abe Bailey.

Although the Marks house was never built, existing drawings dated 17 February 1902 show it was intended to be one of Baker's favourite types, with projecting bays flanking a veranda. It was to have had double-storey bay windows and, upstairs, the four bedrooms were to have shared a single bathroom.[56] As Baker later wrote regarding the 'witty, large-minded and generous' future Senator, Marks: '...of the building schemes we discussed, his offices at Cape Town [which Baker and Masey began to design in October that year] alone were realized.'[57]

Marks's house project, and that for Rhodes, were two of the last to be done by Baker working with Masey from the same office, although there is some doubt as to the part Masey played in Baker's Johannesburg work before he opened his office there in May 1902. But thereafter the polarization of archi-

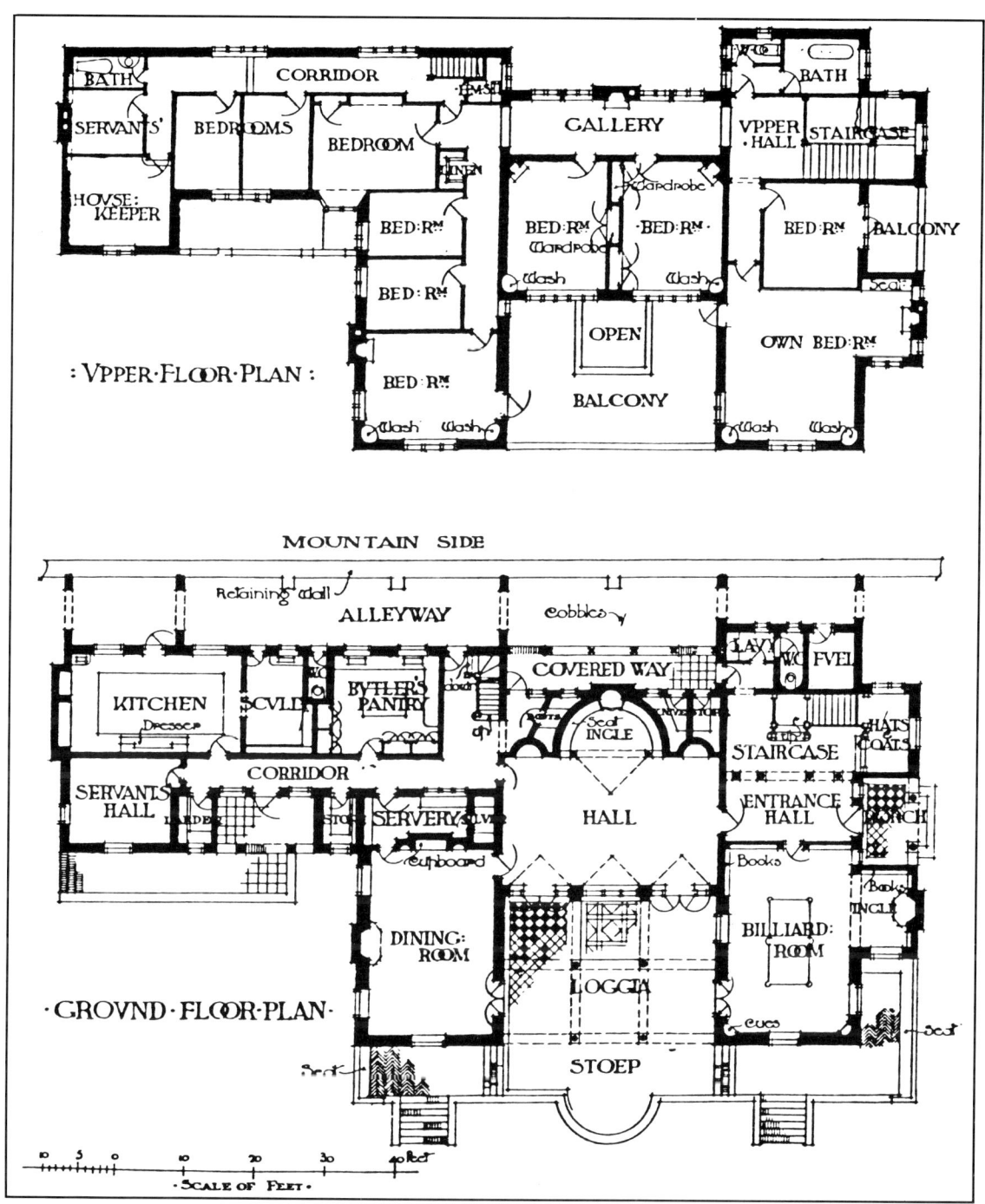

Rust en Vrede, Muizenberg, plan.

tectural ideas began in earnest and, for us, the problems of design attribution become more complex. As will be seen, Baker continued to exert a critical influence on the Cape Town office; but once his physical presence was removed the effect of it must have lessened considerably. Masey would have to initiate the design work commissioned in his sector and, in the main, Baker's considerable correspondence on it could only be superficial and concentrated on the most important commissions. However, in Baker's Transvaal work, now free of Masey's more subtle influence, some new directions could be seen.

97

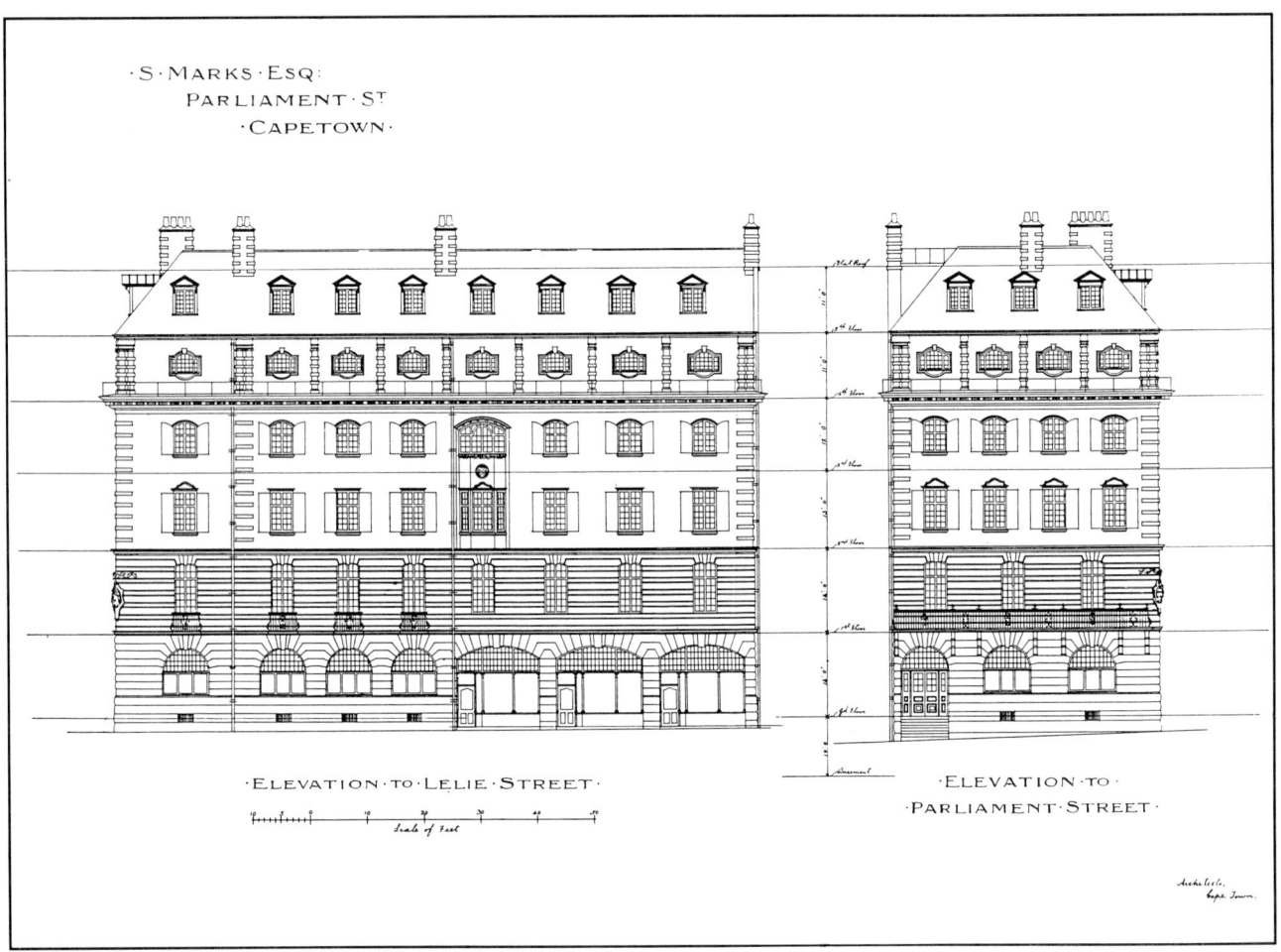

·S·MARKS·ESQ·
PARLIAMENT·ST
·CAPETOWN·

·ELEVATION·TO·LELIE·STREET·

·ELEVATION·TO·
·PARLIAMENT·STREET·

Marks Building, Parliament Street, Cape Town, elevation.

The other Muizenberg house was Rust en Vrede.[58] Before Cecil Rhodes's death on 26 March 1902 Baker had done sketches for a summer house for him above Main Road. He had planned to build Rust en Vrede, 'near his little cottage, but higher up the hill in better air, and I raised for him a terrace with a high retaining wall overlooking the surf...' But, Baker continued, Rhodes 'never built the house on it which I designed for him, owing to the continuance of the war, and his desire to save his money for the endowment of his Oxford scholarships.'[59] Baker remarks elsewhere that during all the years he had previously worked for him, Rhodes had called him 'mean', because he would not spend enough. Now, '...in this last phase I became "damned expensive," if I designed in the same liberal scale he had before desired.'[60]

Rhodes's site and the scheme, completed in its details by Masey, were subsequently taken over by Abe Bailey. On that terrace, wrote Baker, '...we built a deep arched and white columned stoep so that the road below was hidden and nothing marred the view of the waves breaking on the rocks and the blue sea beyond.' From this fabulous site 'the view stretches over the wide expanse of False Bay to the high-cliffed promontories of Cape Point and Danger Point, the far-distant outposts of the bay.'[61] A sketch of Rust en Vrede, drawn in November 1902, shows that Baker's design closely resembled the pristine white house we see today, but which Rhodes never saw.[62]

The plan is a basic H-shape to which are added various projections, each terminating in a narrow Flemish-looking gable. The groin-vaulted loggia gives the house Italian overtones, reinforced by the venetian windows – a favourite Palladian device –

Marks Building, Parliament Street, Cape Town.

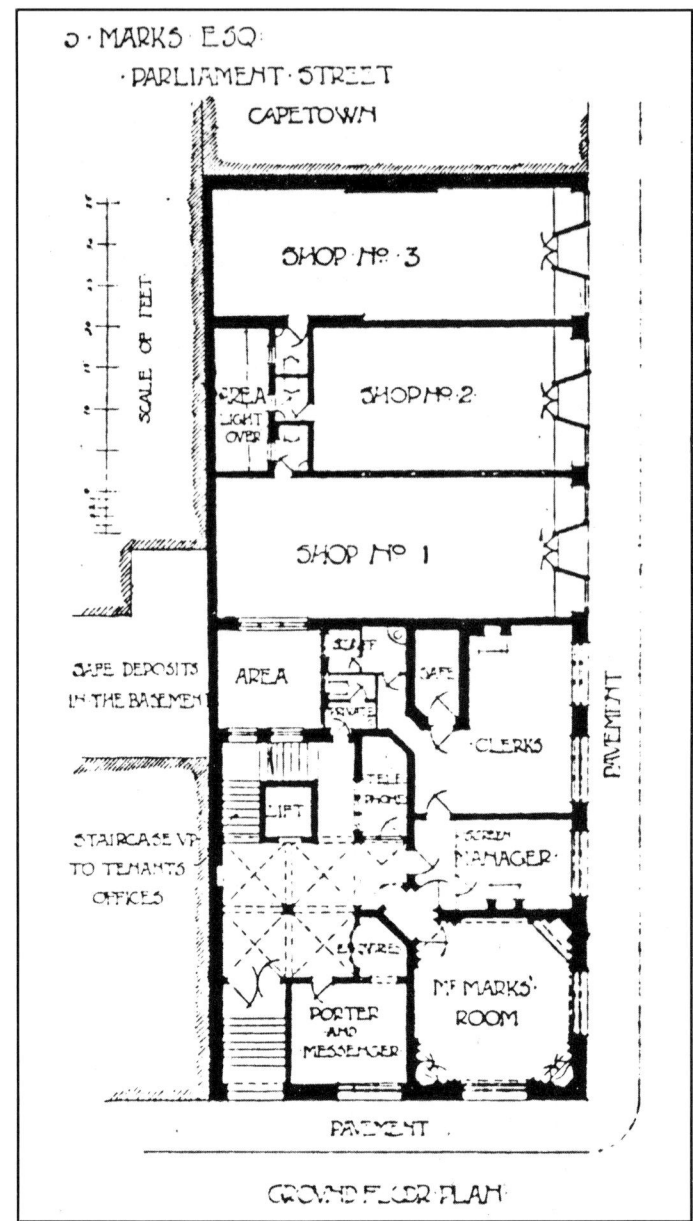

Marks Building, Parliament Street, Cape Town, ground plan.

in the front gables. On the first floor a 'long gallery' connects the projecting wings. The contrasting Englishness of this feature is enhanced by the exposed timber tie-beams and 'antler' posts, reminiscent of Lutyens's Munstead Wood. The house was furnished largely to Baker's designs, which included several bedroom suites, a dining table, billiard table and many cabinets. Most was made locally but some items were made in England by the Guild of Handicrafts at Chipping Camden, again to Baker and Masey's design, a direct result of Ashbee's visit to South Africa in June and July 1903.[63] A contemporary account remarked that: 'Messrs Heal and Son of London have supplied some excellent bedsteads in copper and bronze which at first sight have the appearance of unpolished oak or walnut.'[64]

Rust en Vrede was to a large extent a prototype for Marienhof, the Johannesburg house now known as Brenthurst. However, before Marienhof was begun, another project which had similar characteristics, despite its greater size and imperial purpose, would impose itself: the new Government House at

Pretoria, the designs for which were still to be finalized.

But the most important new Cape Town commission of 1902 was the office block for Sammy Marks. Situated on what was once the corner of Parliament and Lelie Streets, it stood directly opposite the Houses of Parliament.[65] The building, which the Baker and Masey firm began to design in October 1902, and which Marks eventually donated to the State, was later much extended and more recently has been sensitively absorbed into a greater parliamentary precinct. Fortunately the original building is still discernible from its extensions and new context. Franklin Kendall recalled in 1946 that Masey 'did the original design...and Baker hardly touched it.'[66] That being so, it provides a useful measure to gauge the inherent differences in style between Baker and his partner.

Completely faced in stone, the building stood on a heavily rusticated ground-floor base, on which was a layer of less rough, striated, rustication. The upper floors had smooth stone walls and Ionic pilasters, and projecting quoins; the roof was pierced with dormer windows, reflecting the window spacings below, and emphatic slabs of chimneys. Between the third and fourth floors projected a massive dentilled cornice. All in all, it is a fairly typical Edwardian Renaissance building, if anything, decoratively restrained compared with the standards of the London of its time. The Marks Building, the name by which it is still known, was completed in 1905.

BLOEMFONTEIN BEGINNINGS

With the foundations of the Johannesburg practice firmly in place, came work from yet another sector which was undergoing post-war administrative reconstruction, the Orange River Colony. During October 1902, Baker was commissioned to design extensive additions to the Government Buildings in President Brand Street, Bloemfontein, where Sir H F Wilson was Colonial Secretary to the Orange River Colony.[67] In parallel came a request to design alterations to Wilson's house and its garden. There was promise, too, of some substantial work at Grey College, comprising laboratory additions to an educational institution which dated back to the 1850s and ran courses through to university level, and possibly a complete relocation of the outgrown college on another site. By the end of the month the Government Offices scheme had already been revised to omit the law courts which were originally included, '...leaving a suggested colonnade on this side'.[68]

After Baker's initial conception the scheme was passed to Masey to develop its details. There would inevitably be some problems in sorting out the distribution of fees in proportion to what each office had done, not only on this project but on many others. With regard to the transfer of funds from Johannesburg to Cape Town, Baker wrote: '...I suggest subject to your approval that to simplify accounts these be set off against the work done here on Marks – but as you decide. I have divided all my rail expenses between two offices, which seems fair particularly as Bloemfontein goes to Cape Town. With any luck we will pay off £500 soon.'[69]

The firm also had the task of dealing with the heraldic symbolism of the Fourth Raadsaal, inaugurated in June 1893. This building was designed by F Lennox Canning and considered to be the pride of Free State architecture. That Baker had no qualms about overriding his partner on matters of artistic principle, which to him went hand in hand with sentiment, when he saw fit, is illustrated by his letter to Wilson of 13 June 1903.

'Masey has suggested to me', wrote Baker, 'that there should be no carving on the pediment of the Raadsaal, and that the space instead should be left perfectly plain. Although I agree with him that a great deal is to be said in favour of this, my own preference is for a concentration of ornament in the form of a Scroll Shield and Coat of Arms, in accordance with our original design. This is in my opinion an essentially English way of treating the pediment of a classical Renaissance building. Our design I suppose would have been executed some time ago, had it not been for the idea we started in conjunction with the Kiplings to design a fresh Coat of Arms for the ORC. Kipling told me that the model for this had been sent to you, but I have not yet heard your criticisms upon it. I most strongly hope that you will consider the proposal, as it seems to me very tame to have nothing but the Royal Arms for the different Colonies. In the meantime the sooner the old carving is cut away the better, and the surface left plain until the new stones can be let in for the new design.'[70]

The letter illustrates, too, Baker's complete acceptance of the imperialist implications of the proposals; uppermost in all his thinking is his architectural pragmatism, with which he disguises notions of both art and politics.

Top. *Church-cum-school at Westminster, Orange Free State.*
Bottom. *Cottage at Westminster.*

Left. *Westminster, Orange Free State, gable window detail.*
Bottom. *Westminster today, gable and veranda.*

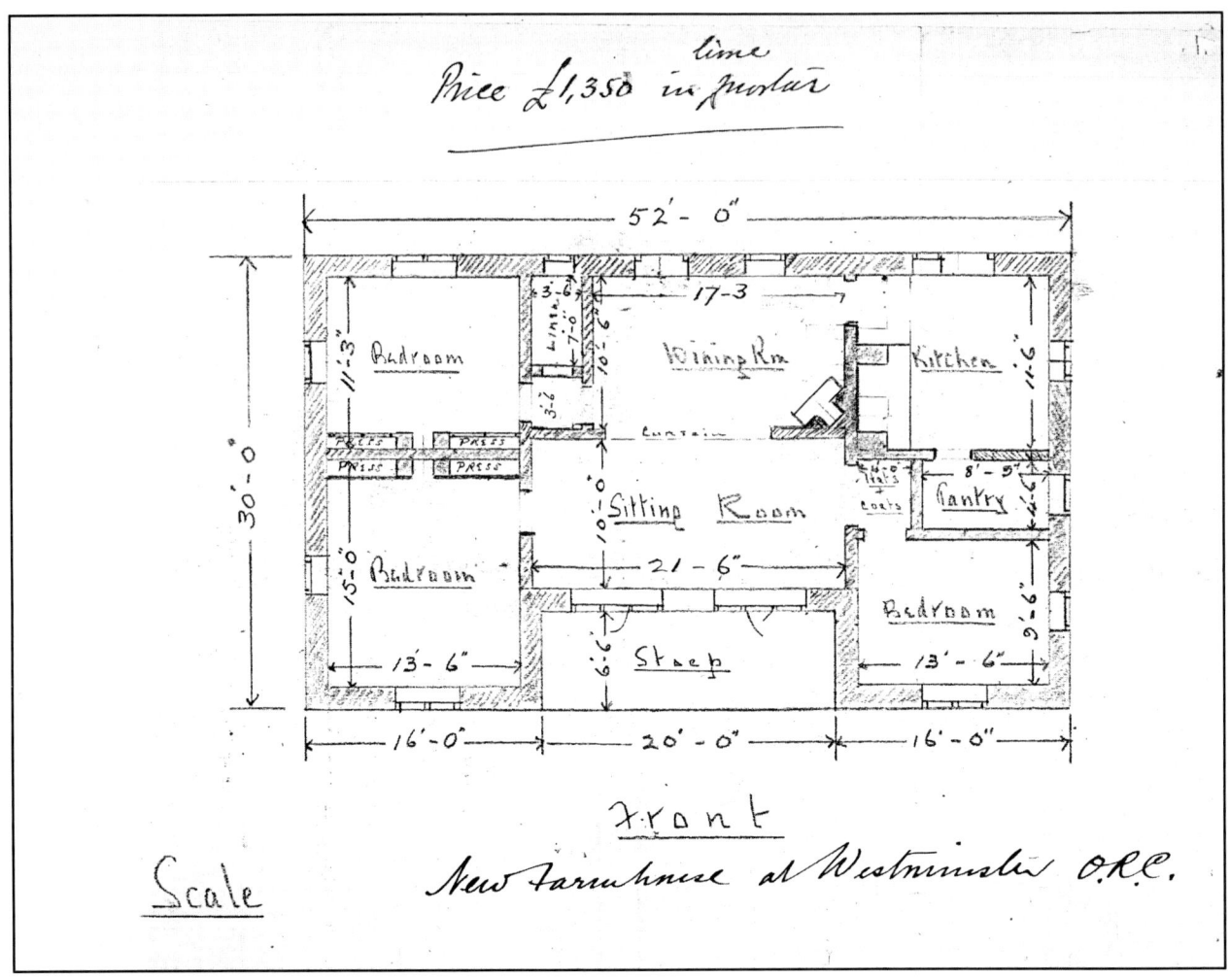

Westminster, Orange Free State, cottage plan.

Baker's revised design for the Government Buildings was to complete a large quadrangle to the rear of the existing two-storey building of 1893. The space formed was surrounded by a colonnade which, with the simplicity of the detailing, gave the building the look of a schoolhouse. Inserted into the accommodation immediately behind the old building were two atria to light toilet facilities which 'with their four white columns seen through the gloom of the [existing] passages with the large court beyond, will be attractive', wrote Baker to the Colonial Secretary.[71] On 20 August 1903 Lord Basil Blackwood, then Acting Colonial Secretary, wrote confirming that Baker's fees were to be 'fixed at the rate of four and a half per cent on the total cost of the proposed extensions.' By October 1903 working drawings were completed, a year after design had first started.

During that year Baker had had another request from Wilson, to which he replied on 28 April: '...we shall have much pleasure in making suggestions for Settlers' houses and will prepare some plans as soon as possible. Our Mr Masey expects to be in Bloemfontein next week and will see the types of wooden houses which have been ordered from Australia.'[72] In view of Baker's previous reactions to the suggested use of what he considered to be inferior and impermanent materials, this must have sounded ominous. Nothing seems to have come of the suggestion and by September Wilson had approved Baker's plans for the cottages in Margraf Street, Bloemfontein.[73]

Another opportunity to do work in the Colony came soon after from G A Wright regarding a church at Harrismith, where Baker was assisting Sir Percy Fitzpatrick in building a house on the farm he had acquired in November and had named Buckland Downs, but without full professional services. Although the church proposal of May 1903 came to nothing, Baker's reply is significant for its common sense and candidness, given when he sent a 'sketch plan of the proposed new Chancel, with the object of showing in what manner the temporary structure you now propose to erect should be built', even though he was unable to do a perspective as yet. 'The Chancel will be considerably higher, but the space between the roof of the temporary building and the ceiling of the Chancel, could be filled in with match boarding and zinc, so as to leave an ever present inducement to those interested, to try and complete their Church.'[74] Here was a clear, and probably the first, statement of the church-building formula which Baker was to calculate on over and over again.

The contrast between the Bloemfontein Government offices and the Cape Town office block for Sammy Marks, designed just a month or two before, indicates clearly the widening divergence of taste between Baker and his partner Masey, and it would be fascinating to know the processes by which they arrived at design solutions at this particular time. As the contract reached completion in September 1905 Fred Masey, Francis's brother, who by then was responsible for its supervision, wrote: 'The Government never expresses satisfaction at the progress of the work although possession will be six months before time. His Excellency is, I think, responsible for this attitude which I am glad to say is now less marked than in the past. Individually the Government is pleased and as friendly as possible, it is collectively that they are hard.'[75] If the administration was happy with the building so was its architect, who later wrote: 'I may be forgiven for saying I was pleased with this building, a quiet contrast to the remainder of the old offices.'[76]

On 28 October 1908 the building was destroyed by fire and then subsequently rebuilt, to a similar arrangement and in the 'style of Baker', but by the Public Works Department. Alas, the 'Bakerish' building to be seen today, even though successful in its own right, gives us only a hint of what the original synthesis was like. An invitation to design a house for Blackwood himself soon followed, and prospects for further work in the Colony looked good.

Also from Bloemfontein had come the promise in November 1902 of additions to Grey College from W A Russell, Assistant Director of Education in the Colony. But there were delays and confusion in sending Baker the plans and photographs of the existing college buildings, which he needed before he could make a start on the laboratory extensions Russell required.[77]

WESTMINSTER IN THE VELD

The General's House, like the war memorial schemes, was a direct consequence of the South African War. Indeed Baker's move to the Transvaal was itself made as a result of that war: at Alfred Milner's invitation to Baker lay one of the less tangible aspects of his intrinsically idealistic imperialism. A further component of Milner's post-war Reconstruction was his policy of Anglicizing the rural areas by means of the settlement of British farmers, both immigrants and colonists, in the Orange River and Transvaal Colonies. The policy was a costly one and Milner realized the importance of enlisting private enterprise to this cause.[78]

One individual wealthy enough to give substance to this expensive form of idealism was the Duke of Westminster, who had served in South Africa as ADC to Lord Roberts and in which capacity had actually raised the Union Jack in Pretoria on 7 June 1900. Whilst holidaying in 1902 and reliving his memories of a beautiful country, the Duke bought a tract of grassland large enough to divide into eighteen farms of 1 000 morgen each. The farms on this estate were to be offered at a generous rent to suitable settlers, who would find water and all the essential facilities needed, including a farmhouse, established on their arrival.[79]

The Duke had admired Baker's architecture in the Cape and indeed, as ADC to Milner, after Roberts, must have stayed at the staff cottage which Baker had built in the grounds of Government House in Cape Town. That, and Milner's backing, made Baker's appointment to build the Duke's estate inevitable, and by December 1903 he had produced his first sketches for the Duke's agent, Colonel Byron, to peruse.[80]

At the centre of this transplanted squiredom was to be The Big House, the Duke's own country home in South Africa. Replete with home-farm buildings, stables and dairy, and with a schoolhouse-cum-church soon to follow, it was all to be set in a home-from-home 'English' landscape.[81]

The Big House is one of Baker's finest stylistic inventions, combining Jacobean English with

Courtyard view of stable block at Westminster, Orange Free State.

Dutch Colonial in a peculiarly South African blend of Queen Anne. On the entrance court side the house is symmetrical. The U-shaped plan has projecting wings terminating in chimneys modelled like huge pilasters, tapered in steps as they reach upwards. Over the central entrance arch is the Duke's coat of arms, carved in stone, and a leaded window set in a simple shouldered gable which tapers to a rounded top, on which is carved the date, 1904.

In complete contrast is the garden front, informally composed with a long, columned veranda, terminating at one end in a twin-gabled projection; each gable shaped similarly to that over the main entrance. The materials are brickwork, faced in coursed random-rubble and plastered or panelled internally. The long veranda wall and the chimneys are faced in smooth stonework. In the dining-room the fireplace and the surrounding built-in cupboards are remarkably similar to those at The Woolsack. Sharing the same character and materials, Baker's home-farm buildings are as successful as the main house, forming an oasis of charm which speaks well of the Duke's courage and imagination.

Construction on the estate began in December 1903, with The Big House completed by March 1905.[82] The following month Baker was requested to design a schoolhouse which 'would probably be used for Divine Service on Sundays, by ministers of the various denominations.' The brief received from Colonel Byron also requested accommodation for the schoolmaster, sanitary arrangements for a mixed school and stipulated that the total cost, inclusive of fees, should not exceed £1 250.

In terms of appearance the schoolhouse fits its brief to perfection. To the uninitiated it is indeed difficult to tell whether it is a school or a church. Its arched entrance is set in a flush west-wall, which tapers to a small open-sided bell-gable, similar to the one he found at St Saviour, Claremont, and which he was to use again at St Andrew's College chapel, Grahamstown.

By comparison the farm cottages were a dismal failure. Early in November 1904, E W Sloper reported to Baker from Bloemfontein: 'You approach them in general from such odd angles that the long symmetrical front loses half its value and it seems to me cannot have the adjuncts it cries out for.' Sloper suggests there should be no difficulty in getting Byron 'to adopt still another design' with a 'considerably larger pantry than I did and also...the

type of settler will in many cases demand a bath room.' Sloper suggests too that a small extra room would be valuable: 'I am sure the Duke will wish to provide every inducement to the proper peopling of the land!'[83] It appears that Baker did not design all eighteen farmhouses. When, as early as January 1905, structural faults were observed, Byron wrote to Baker that 'several of the farmhouses on this Estate have been badly built, that is to say the foundations have not been properly looked to and the masonry is not up to the mark...' Byron went on to request an 'opinion as to the masonry of the various farmhouses, here, not only those of your own design but also of the first lot generally, most of which have come under the notice of Mr Baker or Mr Sloper at various times.'[84]

Byron was indeed willing to make architectural changes to the plans, born of his own 'experience of the settlers' views of the cottages...' He proposed in a letter dated 17 July 1905, with an attached plan, what he saw as '...but a slight departure from the last square cottages you designed – which takes the form of a double gable in front instead of a single...' But still the house had no bathroom![85]

UBIQUE

Work was now coming in from every quarter; only Natal Colony had eluded Baker. By the end of 1903 Baker and Masey had opened an office in Bloemfontein under the supervision of Franklin Kendall, now a junior partner. Kendall had moved up from Baker's Cape Town office in order to control the proposed extensions to the Orange River Colony's government buildings in Bloemfontein.

Then, in November 1903, Baker received a letter from Natal. It came from E Hugh-Jones, Rector of Michaelhouse, and concerned a new chapel for the school which, in the previous year, had moved from Pietermaritzburg to Balgowan in the rolling hills of the Natal midlands. Hugh-Jones had sent Baker a photograph of the recently completed buildings, which formed an open-elbowed L-shape, the first half of the future Founders Quadrangle.[86]

The reply, in Baker's absence, was dealt with by Ernest Sloper, who appears to have drawn the original 'slight pencil sketch showing what might be done for your Chapel...' The letter continues: '...we imagine there must be some internal quadrangle to the school building, and have thought therefore that a corridor which would give access to the chapel and also to that quadrangle, might be a convenience, and it would certainly link the new building to the school building conveniently, whilst allowing freedom in the treatment of the chapel.'[87]

Clearly the new school had never been seen, which should put paid to the misconception shared by architectural historians, and others, that it was Baker who designed the original buildings of Michaelhouse. The fallacy probably stems from Baker's remark that he had 'enjoyed little beginnings, which Fleming has carried to great ends at the Boys' School, Michaelhouse...'[88] Indeed it was Frank Fleming, who joined the firm in the following year and later became a partner, and the firm's successors, who designed some of the best work at Michaelhouse, as he did at many other great private schools. But that was some years after Baker himself had left South Africa for good.

The original buildings, which established the pattern this beautiful school continued to follow until the late 1940s, were in fact designed by M B Price and F Kent, two young English architects practising in Pietermaritzburg.[89] Nevertheless, Baker's chapel, when it was built in 1909, blended well with the work of Price and Kent, making a distinctive addition at a crucial stage in the school's architectural development.

Back in the Cape, the firm in 1903 did some minor restoration and alterations at the historic Groot Constantia, including the selection and acquisition of some old Dutch furniture.[90] At Muizenberg, next door to Baker's seaside cottage Sandhills, they built Swanbourne for H E S Free-mantle, now number 20 Beach Road. Swanbourne once had a plan and appearance similar to that of Sandhills, except that the gable tops were verged whereas its predecessor's had parapets. The cottage has now been altered out of all recognition.[91]

Also at Rosebank, Koreelah was built for J A Baraclough at 21 Pillans Road. Koreelah is noteworthy for its entrance, an arched opening into a recessed porch with a seat, and its upper windows which rise to the eaves of a high roof. The attic floor has windows on either side of the tall chimneys which rise from fireplaces situated on internal partition walls.[92]

1902 and 1903 had been momentous years for Baker. One feels almost breathless contemplating the enormous range, quantity and, indeed, quality of his achievements in those early years in the Transvaal. But the strain of it all was beginning to tell on him. Besides, he was now financially secure and had made only two visits to England since his arrival in 1892; and even those were made in passing; on his way to the Mediterranean at Cecil Rhodes's expense, and recruiting Ernest Sloper.

Baker was now over forty and ready to settle down and enjoy the fruits of his labours and success. On 4 December 1903 Baker wrote to his partner Masey: 'I selfishly want, after eleven years of incessant work here, to take things a little more easily.'[93] The tone may be slightly querulous, but perhaps it simply reflected tiredness; or perhaps he was forcing on himself a realization that he was no longer a young man and that aspects of life were passing him by.

CHAPTER SEVEN

1904

CONSOLIDATIONS

A LONG VACATION

Baker had already booked his passage to England and expected to be away for about five or six months. He was to leave Johannesburg on 13 January and stop off at Cape Town for a week or so to catch up with developments since his last visit two months before.[1] Whilst there he would give some further thought to the new house John Dale Lace had commissioned nearby his Stonehouse, and which would become known as Northwards. 'I have been working down here', he wrote to Mrs Lace regarding her dining-room, 'and have sent a complete drawing up to Mr Sloper. In carrying out your ideas I have made this a Dutch room with beams, cupboards, curved recesses for china and whitewashed walls.' Seeking her permission to buy in London some pieces 'to suit the design', he gave his forwarding address as the Arts Club, Dover Street, London.[2]

Before leaving he and Masey had agreed partnership terms with Ernest Sloper and, from mid-January, the firm was to be known as 'H Baker, Masey and Sloper'. Baker had found Sloper to be not only a reliable assistant but 'an excellent fellow with great character and distinction in his work.'[3] Moreover, he had shown 'great gifts in educating builders and craftsmen to better methods of building and the use of local materials. The excellence of the walling built of koppie stone was largely due to his perseverance and encouragement to the masons.'[4]

Now that Sloper was in charge, one of his first tasks was to get the new buildings for Roedean School – tenders for which had been submitted before Christmas – started on site by the end of January.[5] J Barrow was to be the contractor for the school, as he would also be for J W Kirkland's house a month later. Sloper also had to send the

Sister Superior at the Diocesan School for Girls, Pretoria, an estimate of costs and get her authority to commence working drawings for a new school block, chapel and cloister.[6]

Then, in the Orange River Colony early in February, the foundations for the Duke of Westminster's house were put in hand; whilst Kendall had come up to Bloemfontein to discuss the proposed extensions to the Government Offices there.[7]

Later in the month Sloper wrote to the Reverend A F Newton in Krugersdorp: 'I am sending you a further sketch for your church. It is an attempt to obtain some dignity of effect, as is suitable for a town church, without incurring too great cost.' The church was eventually to be called St Peter. Sloper then explained a feature which was to recur in Baker's church design and which probably originated during his absence: 'The curved buttresses – of which the lower portion is pierced so as to form small side aisles, giving access to the seats – would, I think, give character to the building, and by taking the thrust of the roof...prevent the necessity of tie beams, and allow the maximum height to be obtained in the interior.'[8] The church was also graced with a tower of a type and character which, as will be shown, recurred in the work of Baker and his partners.

At the time of the St Peter commission a design for Archdeacon Michael Furse's house, to be known as Bishopskop, had just been approved and was about to be built in Gale Road, Parktown. Although designed in Baker's absence, Bishopskop portrayed several Baker characteristics of plan and appearance. The house was basically on an H-shaped plan under a square roof, hipped with dormer windows and logical deep eaves on its northern side, and gabled on the south. The walls were of stone quarried on the site and the symmet-

*Northwards, Parktown, Johannesburg with venetian window in the
north gable.*

Northwards, Parktown. Above. Fanlight, veranda door, north side. Left. North veranda door looking east.

rical twin chimneys were built in brick. Timber-stud partitions, covered with hair plaster on a lath of wire mesh, were used for the internal walls upstairs. This form of construction was unusual for the firm, although its use was universal domestic practice in England, and it was therefore likely to have been Sloper's idea. The study near the entrance had timber panelling and cupboards with brass fittings by George Ness.[9]

Furse was later to become Bishop of Pretoria, and commissioned the firm to design a number of churches, including the Anglican Cathedral there and the Church of Christ, in the suburb of Arcadia, where side aisles similar to those at St Peter were to be used.

Thompson's house was completed in March and let immediately to Lord Harris, who took occupation on Friday, 4 April, the day on which documents for a 'small house at Bryntirion [Pretoria] for Mr F C Dent', were sent to Kirkness for pricing.[10] Construction of the two judges' homes at Bryntirion was about to start, but not without some intervention from officialdom.

On 5 April Sloper wrote to the Director of the Public Works Department in answer to objections which had been raised in regard to the size of roof timbers and floor joists employed in the Bryntirion houses, for which building contracts had by now been signed. Objections which 'we know fully well that from an English standard of building...would be thoroughly justified.' But, 'we have to point out that unless we depart from such English provisions it is impossible for us to meet the crying need of local conditions.' Sloper admits, with somewhat less conviction, that 'the scantlings and dimensions which we have adopted are such as could hardly be employed in a building intended to stand for centuries', as if that had ever been the case! At any rate, he argued, the dimensions are 'the universal practice in Johannesburg...'[11]

Almost immediately came similar intervention from another quarter. The Town Engineer of Pretoria was insisting on ceiling heights of ten and a half feet. Sloper was dismayed at this apparent backwardness and there followed a battle of words. But the authorities stood by their specious arguments on grounds of health, whilst Sloper insisted that with good ventilation from correctly positioned openings, nine feet was perfectly adequate. This he backed up with reference to the firm's recent experience in Johannesburg, examples of which he invited officials to see for themselves.[12]

Ironically, the house the firm was building at Muckleneuk for Lionel Curtis, the then Assistant Secretary for Urban Affairs – now called The White House, or the Pretoria Moot House as it was known then – on which construction had started in mid-November, was also affected by this revelation. Though it was suggested by Sloper, Curtis felt it was inappropriate to use his high office to influence matters, an example of the high integrity of Milner's men.[13] It was then discovered that in fact Bryntirion lay beyond the Pretoria Town Engineer's area of control, so the judges' houses were unaffected by the regulation.

Work was now falling off a little, an eventuality Baker had predicted before his departure for England. Sloper was trying hard to persuade Reverend Newton that 'we have an especially good opportunity of developing the design', for the church at Krugersdorp. Pressing home his plea, Sloper writes: 'We frankly say that we are anxious to have the opportunity of doing church work in this country because we think we may lay claim to a training which qualifies us to do such work appropriately, and we must say that we do not ourselves know of any really successful example of an English church in the Transvaal. We enclose a photograph showing some additions which we have just completed, of a church near Cape Town, originally built by Sir Arthur Blomfield [sic]. The chancel and the transept are new.'[14] Sloper was referring to St Saviour, Claremont, but in fact it was Sir William Butterfield who earlier had designed extensions to the original church by Sophy Gray. In May J W Kirkland's house 'on the Berea' was under construction, as were those in Pretoria for Curtis at Muckleneuk, and the three Bryntirion houses for Rose Innes, Mason and Dent. Then, in June, the house of yet another official, Mr Justice Solomon, was designed for this enclave of high officialdom.[15]

Sloper had written to Masey in Cape Town on 25 May agreeing to 'go and see the Church authorities at Maseru the next time I go down to the Westminster Estate, which will not be for six weeks or two months' time.' But it appears that Sloper was too busy or forgot, since he advised Kendall at Bloemfontein on 6 September that he knew 'nothing whatever about the Maseru Church, except that such a Church was in contemplation. Masey never sent any sketches here.'[16]

At the same time Sloper was attending, on behalf of his absent senior partner, to some problems which had occurred at Stonehouse. On 1 July

Sloper wrote urging these to be 'completed before he brings Mrs Baker to her new home.' This matter-of-fact statement is the first intimation of Baker's intended marriage, to be found in the firm's letter books.[17]

MARRIAGE

Whether or not marriage had been on Baker's mind before going home to England is difficult to tell, though knowing his frame of mind in the latter part of 1903, it seems a strong possibility. Baker had known his cousin, Florence Edmeades, of nearby Nurstead Court in Kent, since his boyhood, but nothing has come to light about a continued relationship of any kind. It is likely therefore that his marriage to her came as a complete surprise to his partners and associates in South Africa.

In the month of his marriage to Florence, Herbert Baker turned forty-two. His father, Thomas Henry Baker, now in his eightieth year, had seen little of Herbert in recent years but had lived to see his son married. A few weeks later, on 25 July, whilst his son and daughter-in-law were at sea returning to South Africa, Thomas died at Owletts. As soon as he heard the news, Sloper put a notice of the death in *The Star*.[18]

On 6 August Sloper wrote to Baker, who had stopped off at Bloemfontein on his return journey, with news of Government House: '...what Sir Arthur has decided is to build the whole of the private portion of the house, the omissions will be the big hall and the suite to the east, together with the rooms over', which, he thought, would bring the cost down to about £37 000. Sloper continued: 'Kendall writes to say that he is arriving here on Sunday [7 August], and I know he will be anxious to run down in time to meet you at Bloemfontein, but I shall try to keep him here, if possible.'[19]

Sloper had one more thing to do before his chief returned: he had decided to make the bay window being inserted at Stonehouse 'my wedding present to Mr Baker.' He had to write to the builder, requesting that the cost be kept separate from other work.[20] Meanwhile Masey in Cape Town, and Kendall in Bloemfontein were deciding on their wedding present – a warming pan.[21] On Saturday, 13 August, Herbert and Florence Baker arrived back in Johannesburg. Baker had been away for exactly seven months.[22]

TRANSVAAL HOMECOMING

One of the first matters to be attended to on Baker's return was to write to Frank Fleming, a young English architect who, having begun to practise in Kent in 1901, had been encouraged by his sister to come out to South Africa to help her organize an orphanage for Boer children at Irene. 'I presume your brother [Owen Fleming, an architect also practising in Kent] wrote to you to say that when I was in London, I was making enquiries about an assistant and gathered that you were in this country looking out for some such position...' Baker, not wishing to commit himself so soon, went on to state: 'Since my arrival here, I do not see any immediate prospects of requiring an assistant with your qualifications but, at the same time, I should be very glad if you would, when you are next in Johannesburg, kindly call and see me or Mr Sloper.'[23]

Apart from keeping up with what Masey was doing in Cape Town there were two new projects to attend to in the first month after his return. First, Sir George Farrar, who had taken occupation of Bedford Court only five months before, was thinking about a new house in Pretoria, and then there were the plans to look over for Howard Pim, a new client who had come to Sloper in Baker's absence. Pim's house in Gordon Hill Road, known as Timewell, was clearly designed by Sloper, who had signed the drawings. Northwards was nearing completion for Dale Lace and there was also the new house and stables to design for Drummond Chaplin – Marienhof, as it was to be named. By early September Chaplin had provisionally approved the design and Baker was anxious to proceed with working drawings.[24]

There seemed, after all, to be enough work to justify taking on another assistant and Frank Fleming, whom they had since interviewed, had impressed them. On 12 September Baker wrote to him: 'Sloper and I...have decided that we shall be very glad if you could see your way to come and help us in the office', at a salary of £30 per month. There was only one snag; they would now need larger premises from which to operate.[25]

Just as tenders were about to be invited for the Krugersdorp church, Baker sent out sketches for yet another church proposal; these were for a church hall at Randfontein, the future Church of St John the Divine. Baker's letter to Reverend Henry Johnson presented another aspect of the 'longer view' argument which had first been put to G A Wright in

St Peter, Krugersdorp, nave. Opposite. St Peter, Krugersdorp, tower.

May 1903 regarding the Harrismith proposal, and which had come to nothing. 'You know what we have done at Parktown', wrote Baker on 11 October, 'There the proposal was at first, to build a purely temporary building because no one could see how the money was to be raised. But the money was raised and there is no one in the parish...who does not feel that in what we have done, we pursued a wise course. Therefore I strongly recommend you to take a similar line at Randfontein.'[26]

In the closing months of 1904 a house at Bellevue was designed for J de Villiers, for which construction began in December. In November, Drummond Chaplin's Marienhof was begun, and in the same month the contractor J Barrow began to build both St Peter at Krugersdorp and a sanitorium for Roedean School.[27] The larger premises the firm needed were found and, from 1 December, the office address was 161 Exploration Buildings, in Commissioner Street.[28] From there the firm applied to enter the competition for a new synagogue for Johannesburg, which had been advertised in the *Rand Daily Mail* on 28 December. But by far the most important work of those months was finalizing the design of Government House.

GOVERNMENT HOUSE TAKES SHAPE

Having seen the foundations pegged out the previous June (1903) Baker and Lawley decided to reposition the house on the edge of the kopje. Today the dramatic consequences of that move are magnificent, but, unlike the ridge on which Baker had built Stonehouse and its neighbours, the Pretoria kopje is precipitous, presenting a virtually unperceivable elevation to the north. Moreover, the new position provided space for only a narrow stone-paved terrace for social functions to spill out onto.[29] Then, in August 1903, without apparent reason, work had stopped altogether. The likelihood is that Lawley, no doubt encouraged by Baker, was having second thoughts about the scope and scale of the project and was scheming for something more grandiose and more appropriate to the national and imperial role the building would have to play.

If the reason had simply been that funds were running short in the days of Milner's post-war reconstruction programme, then the changes and delays could only have made matters worse. Besides, there was Baker's fee account to be paid.

On 22 September 1903, Baker had written to Colonel Fowke: 'His Excellency has informed us of the abandonment for the present of the building of Government House, and has asked us to suggest a fair settlement for payment of our work up to the present time. The position is that we first made sketch plans for a different site; then entirely fresh set of plans for the new site upon the kopje; these plans were approved, and contract drawings have been drawn in pencil...'[30]

Though it has been suggested otherwise, Baker was quite right to charge his fees on the basis of the building costs to date, even though much of the design work done had been abortive. It was correct too, for Baker to explain: '...we make no mention now of fees for laying out the grounds which must be a matter of separate arrangement.'[31] This was customary; as it was the responsibility of the client to enter into a direct contract with an electrical contractor to install the electric lighting, the layout of which – in most cases – was designed by the architect.

A month after his return from England Baker was able to confirm the instructions from Sir Arthur to proceed with the revised proposals and invite tenders. Baker then wisely prepared drawings which would enable his clients to see where their money would be spent and where the protracted discussions were leading, giving them some choice in the matter which was in danger of getting out of hand.

Accompanying the drawings was a letter dated 5 December 1904, in which he explained the fundamental aesthetic problem posed by partial completion of the scheme. 'The main points', wrote Baker, 'are that the portion of the building at present proposed to be built is bound to look very ugly as the kitchen quarters are meant to be a simple block in subordination to the main fronts of the building, which will not now be built.' The drawings he had prepared were coloured up to show 'the part already sanctioned red, the suggested completion without the Hall and Stoep blue, and the Hall and Stoep yellow. Our estimate for the red part is £27 000, for the blue £13 000 and the yellow £10 000, the total cost being about £50 000.'[32] These were building costs and did not include furnishings and the land costs, nor the landscaping of the site which had by now been extended by a further one hundred and thirty-eight acres at a cost of £18 000.

Then, on 10 December Baker requested that the main angles of the building should be set out in

Government House, Pretoria (now called the Presidency). View of entrance front from the south-east. An early photograph.

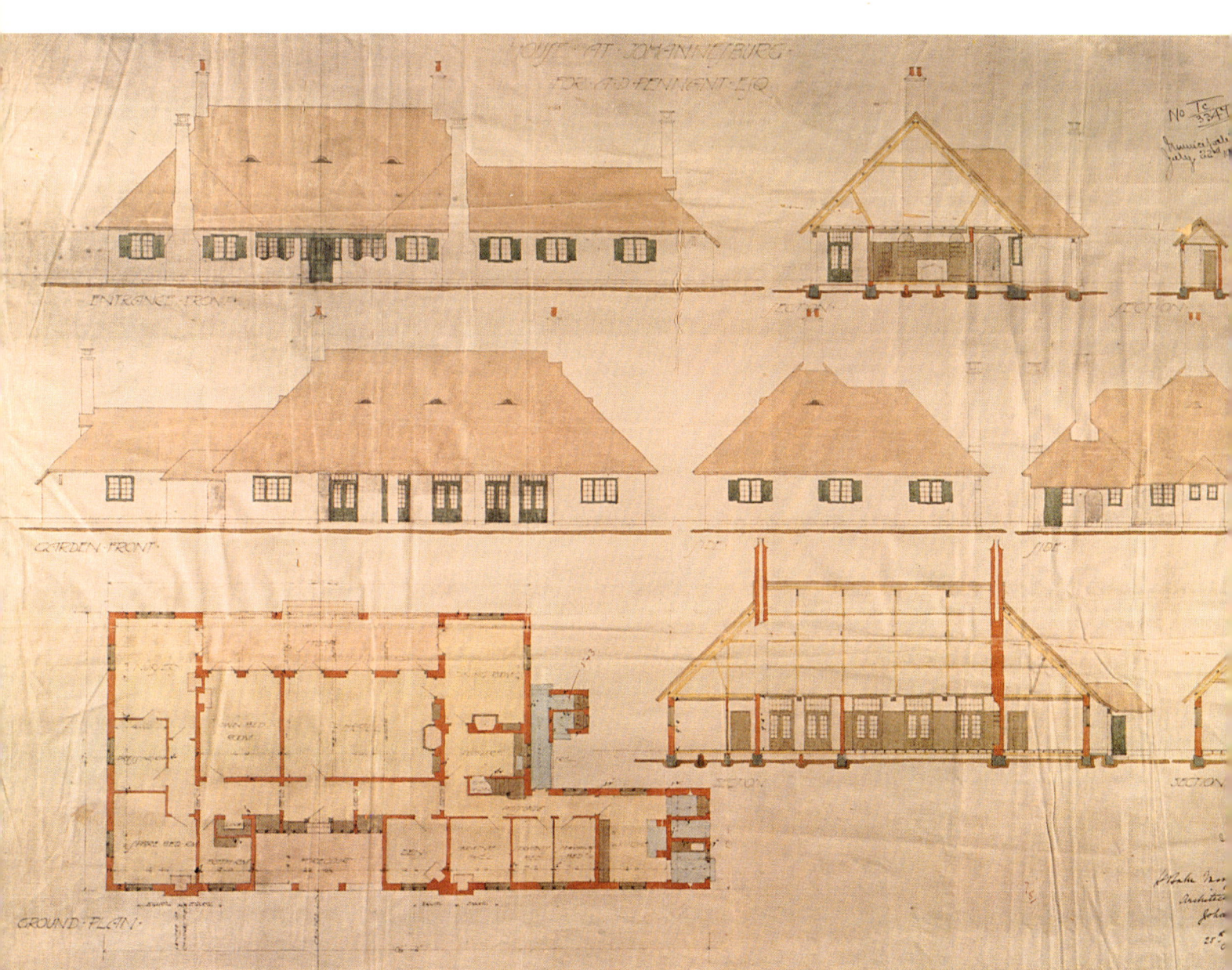

The Thatched House, Riviera, Johannesburg, 1904,
drawn for A D Pennant.

relation to the adjoining gardens so that the whole design could be assessed on the site itself. On 19 December Sloper was able to report to Baker, who was in Bloemfontein after a fortnight away in Cape Town, that the setting out had been completed as asked.[33]

Baker argued sensibly that exclusion of the hall would be a false economy when taking into account the cost and inconvenience entailed in the regular erection of a temporary ballroom. Time has proved him right as the building is now considered to be too small for state occasions, and an additional block of banqueting and conference accommodation may soon be added to the building now known as The Presidency. On 14 March 1905 a contract was signed for the full scheme with builders Edmanson and Thomas and the house was completed the following year.

During the course of construction Baker constantly had to assimilate into his plans many additional client requirements such as a block of stables, a refrigeration plant and cold room, a servants' hall, a plate safe and numerous minor items and changes. There were unforeseen additional costs for drainage and water supply to the vast site to contend with, and the cost of carpeting, furnishing and light fittings increased proportionally too, until the final total cost approached £94 000.[34]

It is doubtful whether much of this additional expenditure can be blamed on any misplaced wilfulness on Baker's part, still less on his negligence or incompetence, or even whimsicality.[35] Even an over-reaction to Rhodes's stricture of 'meanness' is unlikely, for the building remains a house and not an extravagant palace. And it would seem unfair to compare the final total cost with the inadequate original budget, which had allowed for so much less; one would simply not be comparing like with like.

It was Baker's duty to follow his client's instructions, and approvals were granted accordingly, even if progress on site demanded that some had to be given retrospectively. No doubt Baker himself provided some ideas for improvements, particularly with regard to the quality of materials and finishes and the suitability of furnishings, but that was to be expected from the architect imported to do the job to the highest standards possible. Still, some official eyebrows were raised on completion and a call for an inquiry was made by the Treasury in 1906.

In response the Colonial Treasurer, Lionel Hit-chens, could only conclude that too many people seem to have been involved and that 'no one person and no one department was responsible for deciding what was to be done and what was to be omitted.'[36] However, if Baker was fortunate to find such rare equanimity in the higher reaches of officialdom it must be remembered that Hitchens had been one of the Kindergarten who had lived with Baker at Stonehouse, and remained a lifelong friend.

Certainly nothing was wasted in producing this magnificent colonial dreamhouse, and it is ironic that Sir Arthur and Lady Lawley, who 'helped with the plans', but whose taste Baker distrusted, never lived there and that its first occupants were Lord and Lady Selborne.[37] Indeed, to Baker's relief, it was Lady Selborne who furnished the house. As was the case with Abe Bailey's Rust en Vrede, Baker had many items of furniture made to his own designs in Cape Town and London. Baker relates that Lady Selborne aimed at 'simplicity' in furniture and furnishings; and '...when I revisited the house during the Athlones' term of office [1927] it was pleasant to be told by Princess Alice that she had left everything as Lady Selborne and I had originally designed it.'[38]

In the design of Government House Baker illustrated once more his superlative gift of being able to extract from a sensitive political context all that was symbolically significant and to synthesize it into appealing architecture.[39] Baker believed that Government House should be a permanent architectural monument thus necessitating special workmanship of a kind which had not usually been employed in the Transvaal. In the words of Graham Viney: 'Baker was adept at producing that delicate combination of the domestic yet grand. Nothing could have been more apposite for the new colony, especially where at least half the white population was likely to view askance Government House and all it stood for and disposed to take quick affront at the smallest hint of ostentation from the new governing cadre. To this end too, Baker's skilled synthesis of English and Dutch vernacular architectural style was nothing if not felicitous.'[40]

Disregarding the sheer size of Government House, there are some interesting comparisons to be made between it and Rust en Vrede, not only in the basic H-shaped plan arrangements, but in the wavy-topped parapet walls over the respective loggias, linking the pierced narrow gables. In both cases they span across arcades of Tuscan columns

Marienhof (now named Brenthurst), Parktown, perspective sketch.

and are set flush with the flanking projections, making the whole front a continuous white surface resembling an applied cardboard cut-out.

The compositions of these elevations are fresh and rich with invention, as are the gables themselves. In both designs, and indeed elsewhere, Baker was using historical motifs in much the same ways as his European contemporaries were. Therefore it would seem misguidedly purist to condemn him for the lack of 'authenticity' in his gables, a criticism so often levelled at him. Logically, there is no more reason for his drawing inspiration from local historical prototypes than from others in Holland, or for that matter, from the Queen Anne style of England. These forms break free from the constraints of Cape Dutch, for which there was no real multi-storey precedent anyway, and in them one may see something of the sinuous lines of Art Nou-

veau, the style which prevailed in all the visual arts at the turn of the century.

MARIENHOF

Rust en Vrede was nearing completion around the time the Bakers passed through Cape Town on their homeward journey to Johannesburg from England. A short while later the first discussions with Drummond Chaplin (later Sir Drummond) took place regarding the building of his new house and stables on some forty-five acres of land not far from Stonehouse in what is now known as Gordon Hill Road. Drummond Chaplin, a young rising star who became President of the Chamber of Mines in the following year, named his house Marienhof, the name it enjoyed until it was renamed Brenthurst by

Sir Ernest Oppenheimer when he acquired the property in 1922.[41] The house was the third to share important characteristics with Rust en Vrede and Government House.

Although Marienhof's main façade is strikingly similar to that of Rust en Vrede and Government House, there is a remarkable and quite unprecedented 'Gothic' bay window to the hall at Marienhof. This high-roofed hall, or drawing-room, forms a projecting wing similar in principle to, but much smaller than the Big Hall of Government House, which was still in gestation when Marienhof was designed in September 1904. The house was estimated to cost £16 000, befitting the Manager of Consolidated Goldfields and was paid for by that company.

Chaplin appears, however, to have kept a close hold on his company's expenses. Some penny-pinching was done in the construction, which began early in December – particularly in the outbuildings – and parts of the main house were omitted to effect further savings. Elsewhere less expensive materials were used to keep costs within the estimate, which was very nearly achieved, despite the numerous changes made by Chaplin's wife Marguerite. Baker remarked, in view of these changes: '...those [extras] which have been from time to time and after much discussion, definitely settled by Mrs Chaplin but which have involved so many changes in the plans and complicated measurements before it was possible to arrive at a definite price...[involving] enormous amounts of labour to us.'[42]

The need to get authority for each stage of the work and to confirm everything in writing was characteristic of Baker's highly professional approach, which, with his firmness and masterly tact, serves as a model to this day. Certainly it paid off when disputes relating to fees occurred. On the whole Baker's clients paid up promptly and without much argument. Even though many were his friends or became so, there was no question of special favours. He was careful to keep business strictly separate from his personal life, and there can be no doubt that he was respected for it in the long run.

Indeed, that week Baker took time to consider, as he did periodically, the question of unpaid fees. This affords three instances to illustrate Baker's attitude toward the claiming of fees for abortive or abandoned work. In the case of the house for Douglas Pennant, for whom two quite separate designs had been prepared, he was forthright in saying he did not think it right to make any deduction 'on account of the fact that you have already paid us for a former design.' C L (later Sir Llewellyn) Andersson, who had commissioned a house in April 1903 but who subsequently abandoned Baker's scheme in favour of an extraordinary design by J A Cope-Christie – the house named Dolobran, which stands today at the corner of Victoria Avenue and Oxford Road – likewise received a demand for the payment of fees in full. Nor was any reduction offered to W Dettlebach who, after a year, had still not paid Baker's fees 'for design, working drawings, specification, bills of quantities and tenders' in connection with his abandoned project.[43]

In early December Baker and his wife travelled to Cape Town for a fortnight at Muizenberg. Kendall seemed slightly put out by the news, as he wrote to Masey from Bloemfontein, on 5 December: '...I do not know if the Bakers little jaunt down to Cape Town will make it impossible for me to get down for Xmas. I hope not.'[44] But Kendall was more sympathetic when a few days later he wrote: 'I was very sorry to hear of Mrs Baker's seediness – but I hope her trip to the Cape will do her a lot of good. I shall be sorry not to see her here with H B. Where are they staying now?'[45] Florence was experiencing her first African summer and probably finding the December heat and dust somewhat overpowering.

Top. *St George, Groot Drakenstein, apse end.* Bottom.
St George, nave.

CHAPTER EIGHT

1905-1906

YEARS OF DEPRESSION

BLOEMFONTEIN 1905

Early in the new year Kendall had been talking to Masey about the future of the Bloemfontein office, and Masey in turn discussed it with Baker. Referring to these discussions in a letter to Baker dated 9 January 1905, Kendall wrote somewhat diffidently: 'I hope you will not mind my saying a few words about it? I have always been rather chary about Bloemfontein's future – i.e. as a quickly growing or highly prosperous town, and therefore have felt some doubts as to our advisability in staying here. We came considering the Grey College work a certainty, as well as the Government offices – with some sort of prospect of the Law Courts in the future – all of which would of course have been an admirable nucleus on which to build a practice, supposing of course, we came into demand. In the event of our doing Grey College I suppose all might be well, but without it, I do not think the Government will have been treating us quite rightly.'

Then, as an aside, Kendall adds a serious criticism: 'We should never have thought of opening up an office here on the strength of the Government offices alone...if we do not get Grey College they will have scored pretty heavily over us. I wonder if they quite appreciate this?' Then comes a hint that the relationship between Masey and himself may perhaps have been a little strained. Kendall adds: 'In the event of my going back to Cape Town I really think that Masey and I should do much better if our respective work was more clearly defined – to avoid that very unsatisfactory "overlapping" of duties which I am afraid has often been evident in the past.'

Kendall remarks that Masey had suggested to him an office in Wynberg or Claremont, from which certain suburban jobs should be directed, but adds:

'This might be a way of meeting the difficulty – but I am not very certain about it. It might be a mistake to be away from the town itself.'[1] The letter reached Baker just as he was recovering from a bad attack of influenza, and was unlikely to have been at his optimistic best. Would his own condition somehow have assisted in opening his eyes to Masey's physical and emotional need for a holiday, just as he himself had needed a year before?[2]

Because Sammy Marks's new office building which Masey had supervised in Cape Town was now complete, it was an opportune time for Masey to be away. Marks himself was in Pretoria at Zwartkoppies when Baker advised him, on 2 March, that 'Mr Masey is staying here for a few days on his way to Delagoa Bay from whence he goes Home by the east coast for a four-month holiday. You may perhaps like to see Mr Masey about the Cape Town offices [Marks Building], and he would very much like to see you...'[3] But on 24 March Baker revealed in a letter to Sammy Marks that it was rather more than just a holiday that Masey had embarked on: 'Mr Kendall who is taking charge of the Cape Town office in the absence of Mr Masey who has gone Home ill, sends us a report...'[4] Just as Baker had made Sloper a partner before leaving the Johannesburg practice in his care for seven months during the previous year, so Kendall was made a partner on Masey's departure from Cape Town.[5]

Arrangements for Masey's holiday must already have been made when Baker was commissioned to design one of the most important buildings of his career, the Rhodes Memorial. It had taken until January 1905, almost three years since the death of Cecil Rhodes, for those who were organizing his principal memorial to form a sub-committee, a group which would investigate the various propo-

Grey College, Bloemfontein, entrance front.

sals that had accumulated regarding its form and location.

'It is not clear when the idea of having a memorial building on Devil's Peak and asking Herbert Baker to design it first arose', write Langham-Carter and Rennie in their recent study of the Memorial's history.[6] After final agreement on the siting of the memorial had been reached, the sub-committee met on 20 February to consider Baker's first rough drawings, probably prepared during the preceding week, of a suitable building, and found the ideas they embodied most acceptable.

Baker, who was in Cape Town to design the memorial and present his sketches to the sub-committee, was instructed to draw up detailed plans for a building that 'would last forever', but not spend more than £20 000.[7] He and Masey immediately returned to the Transvaal, with the customary stopover at Bloemfontein; Baker on his way to the impending start on Government House at Pretoria and Masey en route to Delagoa Bay. With Masey away from the country on extended leave the Memorial design was to be developed at Exploration Buildings, Baker paying a further visit to the Cape in April.

In March 1905, whilst Masey was abroad, drawings for 'alterations' to the Bloemfontein Cathedral of St Andrew and St Michael, comprising a parish room, Lady Chapel, and a tower were begun in the Cape Town office. Most notable of these works was the tower, a red brick campanile built in a Romanesque style and which housed the organ chamber. As Dr Greig remarked: 'The tower had the special merit of uniting the two different parts of the cathedral which were built at different times.'[8] Lord Selborne, Baker later recalled, said that it gave Bloemfontein 'a soul.'[9] It was demolished in 1965 after developing cracks similar to those which the Campanile in the Piazza San Marco, Venice, had acquired before its collapse in July 1902, after standing for almost a thousand years.[10]

Baker's thoughts must have been very much engaged with the memorial to Rhodes when his second great patronage, and a phase of Empire history, came quietly to an end when Lord Milner left Johannesburg for England, via Lourenço Marques, on 2 April 1905.[11] Milner's tenure as High Commissioner for South Africa and Governor-General of the Transvaal and the Orange River Colony had ended with 'reasons of health' given as the main cause of his retirement.

The goals of Reconstruction, and the unification of South Africa under British authority, had not yet been fully achieved. But changing political conditions in Great Britain had convinced both the Colonial Office and himself that these objectives, for which he had striven so energetically, were less likely to be attained with his retention.[12]

HARD TIMES

With most of Milner's help already given, and Baker's practice having established a momentum of its own, the event was unlikely to have much effect on Baker's career. If work was short it was so for everyone and the head start he had been given was still keeping him going. From 'Randlords' to Archdeacons and Bishops, Baker without doubt had the best contacts it was possible for an architect to have in South Africa.

Not that it was plain sailing. Work had to be fought for, even bargained for. On 24 July Baker advised Kendall, still in Cape Town, that Grey College had offered £100 in settlement of the firm's claim for fees, which did not even cover out-of-pocket expenses let alone the work done. Baker instructed Kendall to suggest the compromise that 'we agree to a payment of say £200 plus bare out of pocket expenses in settlement of all claims of work previously done in connection with Dale College on condition that we are appointed architects not only for the present...but for any work which may be done in future...either to Dale College or to other schools, within say ten years.'[13]

Meanwhile, in Cape Town, the Cape Times had published a piece entitled 'The New Grey College: Architects Crumble'.[14] The article concerned the removal of Baker and Masey as architects for the project in favour of the Public Works Department. 'For some reason or other the plans and drawings submitted by this firm failed (as is frequently the case with even the very best firms) to meet with the approval of the Government, who have now given the work of preparing plans to their own...Department...[an action] which architects complain of.' The article continues to argue for public competitions to be held for large undertakings, adding that the Public Works Department is not 'of a size capable of dealing with such a contract.'

At the foot of the cutting from Baker's files has been written 'No one knows who the grumbler is!' Equally of interest the piece concludes by drawing attention to the Government of the Cape Colony's

Rhodes Memorial, Groote Schuur Estate, Rondebosch, Cape Town.

Rhodes Memorial, Rondebosch, portico.

call for submissions from South African architects for the new University buildings, '...and are bringing out from England an expert nominated by the RIBA to assess the different plans. Advantage might have been taken of this gentleman's visit to the country to secure his services in the assessment of open drawings for the new College buildings.'

FRED MASEY

Late in August 1905 Kendall, after three years – barring his return to Cape Town during Masey's four months of absence – of running the firm's office at Bloemfontein fell ill and returned to Cape Town. His place was taken by Masey's younger half-brother, Frederick William Masey, who came up from the Cape Town office. Fred Masey had been an assistant there since his arrival in South Africa from London in 1903.

The younger Masey had never, on his own, wound up a building contract – as he admitted in his report to the Cape Town office from Bloemfontein , dated 25 August 1905. Remarking that he had submitted the firm's account for the Jagersfontein Bank of Africa, he asks for advice in connection with quantity surveyors' fees, '...as this is the first time I have wound up the affairs of a building...'[15]

In the same letter Fred Masey remarks on the cut-throat methods architects were using in order to obtain work in those difficult times. From Reid, who was representing the contractors for the Bloemfontein Cathedral work, Jacobs and Beebe, Fred Masey had learned that 'Sterkstroom and Steynsburg are contemplating church work. As their places are near Queenstown can you approach Mr Price asking him to recommend us to their Committees?'

Masey continues: 'I may say that outside Cape Town and Joburg striving for work is most barefaced, it is a case of fighting, the retiring Practitioner being misunderstood and despised. In Mr Kendall's time we lost the maternity home because we were too dignified and allowed others to step in, although this work was in Mr Wilson's gift and appeared in our list of Office work. During the last month another nice piece of work that mentally I had earmarked for ourselves was nearly robbed. A local man sending in Drawings, Specs and estimates to a provisional committee who were only meeting to consider the raising of the money for the scheme. Fortunately I had knowledge of this and so

exposed the man (who as a further bait had promised to do the work free) that the meeting decided to regard his propositions as "not received". I state the above, as I believe the Molteno district, if tapped, may prove a rich one and if you do not care to work it from Cape Town I should like to try from here.'[16]

In a report to the Cape Town office from Bloemfontein, dated 1 September 1905, Fred Masey writes: 'The Colony having to face a deficit all new work here is closed down...the Johannesburg branch knows that this is not for want of trying, as they also tried to get embellishments passed...' Masey's use of the impersonal 'they' and 'the Johannesburg branch' for Baker, indicates a style markedly different from his elder brother. He adds proudly: 'We have been successful in doing some hundreds of pounds worth of fittings under special votes. The Museum looks well...fittings £480 instead of £200 in provision...'[17]

In the same report Fred Masey describes a novel way of touting for work he had shamelessly devised: 'I have recently instituted (and it is doing us good) Wednesday afternoon teas to the Chief Families of the Town. Mid-week is the half holiday here and I receive at 4 p.m. During tea in the office I lecture on the large number of C.T. and Joburg photos of the firm's work, Kipling's House, Carl Jeppe's, Dale Lace's, Rhodes's Buildings etc., etc., and afterwards a descriptive tour of the buildings.'

But the report contains other brief comments on the progress of work in Bloemfontein, including the Cathedral, and is worded almost as though neither Baker nor Masey had any knowledge of the commission, yet it is known that drawings were completed in March. Masey blandly writes: 'Here a Lady Chapel, Chapter House and Organ Chamber all of the most modest order are just being finished. A tower of 75 feet high is going on next week. I am very friendly with the Bishop and resident Canon and am quite at ease over the new Dean. The Bishop is most anxious to meet Mr Francis Masey.' Also mentioned is the Kroonstad Bank, which 'I hear is starting, I understood this was to be mine.' Finally, he adds the quaint remark that 'The Joburg office has made me a member of the Bloemfontein Club, this I am sure will be a wise move.'[18]

Still with very much on his mind the battle to get work, Fred Masey writes again from Bloemfontein: 'I hear today [7 September 1905] that a large building scheme is afoot here in Market Square. In the hopes of receiving the work Stucke and Harrison are making sketches. This is one of the firms who undercut us by offering to do work free when they hear our name mentioned as probable Architects. The financial backer of the scheme is named Wickert...can you find him in the Directory and do anything with him? The work is not yet given out. S and H are working in presumption. H.E.[His Excellency] is unwell and unable to see anyone. Shall I bespeak a bedroom in the Club for you?'[19]

PLANS AND PROSPECTS

During August Francis Masey returned from England to find that the commission they had received from the National Mutual Life Association of Australasia, on which they had begun to work in January 1899, had been resurrected and was going ahead. Masey was working on the design of the building when, on 21 August, Baker wrote to him saying: 'I am very much grieved that my suggestions with regard to this building have caused you so much extra trouble but I am glad that you think on the whole they effect an improvement. It seems to me that by increasing the pitch of the roof you would get almost as much room in the top offices as with the Mansard roof.'[20]

Baker had planned to visit Cape Town later in August 1905 but found himself under too much pressure and, to make matters worse, he was 'bothered very much' with an impending law suit which he felt would come to a head at any moment. The action concerned Dale Lace's refusal to agree to the issuing of the final certificate for payment, on the grounds of Thompson's alleged non-completion of Northwards, which had been occupied for over a year. In due course the arbitration went against Lace and Baker was able to press for his fees.[21] There was also an apparently important project to attend to before he could leave for Cape Town – a new school.

In his letter of 11 September 1905 to the Reverend Howell Griffiths, Rector of Parktown, confirming his brief, Baker outlined the school's initial requirements, 'for 10 boarders and 50 day boys', with eventual classroom accommodation for 150 boys.[22] The project had originated in the mind of T H (later Sir Thomas) Cullinan, churchman and friend of Howell Griffiths. In his history of St John's College, K C Lawson writes: 'Mr Cullinan, realising the pressing need for educational facilities in the growing northern suburbs of Johannesburg, had offered to subsidise a Church School either in Park-

town or farther out towards Rosebank...'[23] However a decision was made in favour of 'the even bolder proposal that, instead...the whole of Mr Cullinan's gift should be devoted to refounding St John's on ...Houghton Estate.'[24] And so, for the moment, the scheme came to nothing. It would take almost another year before Baker would be asked again to design the first buildings for the Diocesan Boys' College of Johannesburg.

No opportunity to win work through competition could now be dismissed and, on 26 September, Baker wrote requesting the conditions of a competition for a new church in Arcadia, Pretoria. Baker had just enough time to study the competition requirements and to outline his scheme with Sloper before leaving to join Florence, who was already at the Cape.

In Cape Town there was not much work and Baker, apart from considering the Rhodes Memorial project, had ample time to get involved with the design of the small church of St George at Groot Drakenstein, where his brother Lionel 'first enlisted the help of his neighbouring farmers to build a church.'[25] The result was the charming Cape-cum-Arts and Crafts country church, unique in Baker's repertoire for being the only 'whitewashed' church he built. It is a delightful experience to chance on this simple, but elegant building and to enjoy its cool, restful interior. It is utterly at home among the white-painted houses of Rhodes's wine-growing valley.

Plans for St George were presented to the Parish Building Committee during Baker's stay at Sandhills. Things must have moved very quickly at Groot Drakenstein for a foundation stone was laid on 19 November. Two days later, on 21 November, Baker returned to Johannesburg where, in the meantime, Sloper had submitted their design for the Pretoria church competition on 30 October, accompanied by a long explanatory letter describing the materials which had been chosen, and the fees which would be due to the architects.[26] These two churches, so unlike in character, and yet so much bearing the Herbert Baker imprint, were in fact to start a flood of new church work for Baker's firm.

RHODES MEMORIAL

In the sense that the Memorial building did not house any functional activity, other than generating heroic thought and patriotic emotion, it was not a building at all; it was a stage-set erected against a backdrop of some of the most magnificent scenery in the world. And, since the visitor to this theatre of Empire was intended to feel something approaching a religious experience, the temple-like form it was given was entirely appropriate. It would never have occurred to Baker to question the motivations that lay behind the concept of a shrine in memory of the Empire Builder. Nor – at that time – did such questions occur to Kipling, who wrote this understandably little-known, but affecting poem in a letter to the architect, whilst the form of the Memorial was still under discussion[27]:

As tho' again – yea, even once again,
We should rewelcome to our stewardship
The rider with the loose-flung bridle-rein
And chance-plucked twig for whip,

The down-turned hat-brim, and the eyes beneath
Alert, devouring – and the imperious hand
Ordaining matters swiftly to bequeath
Perfect the work he planned.

From the first it was Baker's avowed wish that the Memorial should reflect the beliefs and aspirations of the man to whom it was dedicated, Cecil Rhodes.

Baker and Rhodes had discussed the building of a lion house on a site some fifty feet above his favourite viewpoint below Devil's Peak. That his project should be for the King of Beasts was itself symbolic for Rhodes, but he had hoped that visitors, being attracted to the site and absorbed in its beauty, would be inspired by the breathtaking view to think noble thoughts there, just as he himself had done so often. There was no time for Rhodes to start the scheme in his crowded final months, but Baker regarded it as a sacred duty to come as close as possible to fulfilling his master's wish in the design and spirit of his memorial.

The events of February 1905, and the first sketches shown to an approving committee before Masey left for his English holiday, were mentioned earlier. Meanwhile from Cape Town, on 28 August 1905, Francis Masey had written to Baker regarding the Rhodes Memorial design which Baker had developed during his partner's absence in England, and on which he had been invited to comment.

Apart from indicating the stage the design had reached, the letter is highly significant for the points of detail Francis Masey articulates, and which were incorporated in the design. The tactful, if not deferential expression of his ideas is worth studying for the insights it provides into his own architectural philosophy and his relationship with Baker. One can imagine too, that having recently visited Egypt, Masey's vision may have been coloured by the breath of that other extremity of the African continent:

'Dear Baker, Thank you for yours of the 23rd. instant [August], and for the consideration which you are prepared to give to my criticism from within on the design for the Memorial. In regard to the style, I did not intend to convey the idea that we should imitate Egyptian architecture in detail, but only that as the circumstances governing the treatment of our Memorial were so very similar in many respects, we should lean to a perfectly simple treatment of the Egyptian work rather than try to get our effect from features such as one finds in Greek and Roman architecture, especially as we have neither the material nor the money to do justice to such treatment. With the beautiful climate and sunshine and surroundings, it seems to me that the chief problem is one of grouping and proportion, doing without moulded work as far as possible, and the more we bend ourselves to effect this the more we should be working in accordance with Rhodes's own ideas. The Egyptian treatment has an additional appropriateness in view of the fact that although far distant, Egypt itself is part of Africa.

'In regard to the blocking course, I think it ought to be omitted, because it gives a touch of commonplace to my thinking, to the design, and detracts from its dignity.

'I cannot see what necessity there is for allowing people to walk on the top. Would it not vulgarise, and also desecrate it? Supposing the monument were on a flat plain then there would of course be a reason for getting on a height. As however, the same view which the top of the temple would command, could be obtained in the near vicinity, the excuse for admitting people up there does not exist. I do trust that you will eliminate this feature. It quite destroys the sentiment which we both like to see connected with such a solemn erection.

'In regard to the approach, my fear is that the platform in the original sketch instead of leading up to the temple tends to hide it from view, whereas one of the most sure sources of effect should really be the arrangement of the steps forming the approach. I enclose a sketch of the Propylaea which will illustrate what I have in mind.

*Rhodes Memorial, Rondebosch, detail of columns and
niche.*

'In regard to the position of the Temple, the original reason for placing it far back was our idea of getting it with its back at the mountainside. As the slope is not sufficient for this to be done, I quite agree that the further the monument is brought forward the better it will look. For this reason I should have brought it even more forward than shown on the tracing which you sent. I should then be inclined to arrange the platform in a series of terraces. The monument should stand on one of the lower slopes of the terraces, so as not to compete with the Temple too much, in fact like the pedestal in front of the Propylaea.

'Another point I notice is that the steps are of a very easy slope, which I think is a mistake. In a case like this, one should not I think adopt a rule which would apply to an ordinary staircase, but make the steps steep. This much enhances its dignity, and I have often noticed has been adopted in antique buildings in cases where people were quite well acquainted with the advantages of easy steps. The very act of climbing steep steps in a case like this gives a certain sense of achievement, which all helps to impress the visitor. I think the steps ought to be about 12 x 9, and of course we can have a landing on each terrace to allow people to rest.

'I feel I really have no business to raise this criticism on it at this stage when you have given so much patient study to the problem. I will not of course think of raising these questions to those in authority. If we talk the matter over we may agree to make such modifications that really [sic] be desirable and practically feasible.

'In regard to Watt's [sic] Statue, it is not the Bronze itself but only the cast which is in Burlington house. I should not have thought that a copy of it would have been very expensive. It is even possible that the model may still be in existence, however I leave the matter to you. Yours sincerely, F Masey.'[28]

Owing to the Dale Lace arbitration, Baker was unable to get down to the Cape until mid-October where he joined Florence, who had been relaxing at Sandhills since the beginning of the month. Whilst there Baker and Francis Masey concentrated their efforts on the Rhodes Memorial, no doubt taking into account the observations Masey had made in his letter.

On the Bakers' return to Johannesburg early in November, Masey wrote a series of letters on the design and construction of the Memorial which illustrate how well aware he was that whatever heed Baker might take of his partner's advice, and heed it he did, the master was still in charge. Masey's letters are full of phrases like: 'I shall be glad if you will look it over and send it back...' Or, 'The following are the points on which I would like your advice...'[29] Masey even went to the extreme of saying: '...I do not like to take the responsibility of doing anything without first consulting you.'[30] Yet, when he felt it necessary, he would tactfully emphasize his own point of view, as he did in a letter dated 23 November: 'On giving more study to the order [of classical architecture] I am convinced that your decision to have an architrave is a correct one...', but, he adds later in the letter: 'There is one feature which I venture to think would best be modified, and by doing so we might pay for the extra cost of the architrave. I propose instead of making columns to the openings at the back [of the Memorial] to have them square on plan, with the edge slightly taken off, similar to the Sun Temple of the Pyramids.'[31]

And so on, but in the end the column and entablature system, or order, he employed at Devil's Peak was identical to that which he had previously devised for the Kimberley Memorial: a Tuscan or Roman Doric which, in its finest detail was of Baker's own invention.[32] No less remarkable was the detail design of the steps, where the practical human need is set into the monumental scale of the giant steps.

Kipling's initial reaction to the sketch which Baker had sent him was that it was an 'atrocious imposing monument', and, 'being florid in my tastes I should like, against the dark green [of the mountainside] a vermilion entablature and columns sheathed in bronze after the insolent Egyptian fashion. Something that to the vulgar suggested Cape to Cairo and to others – other things. No need to make it Dutch. Make it Continental.'[33] Perhaps we are fortunate that Baker had his own firm views on the matter!

By December 1905 design work had progressed, and funds were secured, to call for tenders for building the first stage; the colonnade, and a terrace on which to stand Watts's statue 'Physical Energy', which had been presented for the purpose of incorporating in the monument. For this an eighteen-month contract was signed on 27 March 1906. The contractor was J R McKillop, who also secured the contract to build the steps, terraces and bastion, taking in all some twenty-eight months, from April 1906 to July 1908.[34]

SCHOOLS AND CHURCHES

Returning to Johannesburg Baker wrote to Colonel Bell expressing 'pleasure that the Committee have passed a resolution in favour of our plans' of the Arcadia church and agreed to meet the Committee at 4 p.m. the following day provided he was able to catch the 5.5 train back for an engagement in Johannesburg![35] To Baker all seemed well, but behind the scenes the Committee were not yet convinced. On 12 December Baker wrote to Bell in astonishment, saying: 'We fully understood from your previous letters and our meeting...we had been selected as the successful architects.' Baker added firmly that it would be 'unprofessional on our part to do any further work under the competition without being definitely appointed your architects.'[36]

Clearly this firmness worked and a week later Baker was writing again to Bell, and to Archdeacon Hamilton, regarding the 'very satisfactory letter' he had received and, as was by now his usual practice, confirming that he would 'proceed at once with working drawings, details and specifications...' Though some sample stonework construction, using 'refuse slate', was put in hand later that month, full-scale work did not begin until the following October. The sample work was to 'consist of a portion of an arch, a pier and a buttress...', as shown in a sketch. 'The arch might be elliptical so as to experiment for different radii which would suit the nave arches and the smaller windows.'[37]

At Randfontein, in October 1905, the construction of St John the Divine had begun, but there were still doubts about ventilation and comfort in the church. Baker was suggesting additional windows and ridge ventilation to the roof, writing: 'It is true that we have taken felt as a precaution against heat, but with an iron roof this additional precaution we think would more than fully justify the additional costs involved.'[38]

Whilst a new St John's College was maturing in the minds of its founders, another school of quite a different kind had been commissioned, The South African College of Music, in End Street, Doornfontein. By 9 December Baker was able to instruct the contractor who had submitted the lowest tender (£3 450) to start building immediately.[39] Work on this remarkable little building, which in this writer's view has been treated hideously in recent years, was completed in April. Inspired by the need to cater for the social arts among the youth of the mining city, the school was built under the patron-age of Mrs John Dale Lace, and situated in what was once a fashionable area. The accommodation was built around a hall designed to seat 195 people with a further 45 in the gallery.[40]

Its special architectural interest lay in the soft red brick with plaster trimmings; Baker rarely used brick at all in the Transvaal. The brickwork was particularly suited to the fashionable Queen Anne style which Baker had attempted here with more deliberation than anywhere else. Round-topped gables, each surmounting symmetrical venetian windows, flank a larger central venetian motif, all in the same plane. The impression is given of an upper-floor recessed terrace behind this central feature, which straddles the recessed arched entrance below. The effect is enhanced by the large ornate central gable of the hall within, which looms over the flat-roofed central section.[41] The great irony is that a building conceived to serve artistic accomplishments should have been treated so barbarously. It is to be hoped that some more enlightened age will rescue this charming and unique gem from its present tartish mockery, and restore it to its rightful position as one of Johannesburg's most attractive buildings.

The year 1906 found Baker still concerned about the flow of work. Writing to an applicant for employment, he advised: 'I much regret that we have ourselves had to curtail the assistants in our office and that we see no prospect at present of making fresh additions to our staff...'[42] He was concerned, too, about Bishop Robson's difficulty in paying the fees for the Kimberley church.[43] To Masey in Cape Town he wrote: 'I am very glad to hear that the King Williamstown School [Dale College] is going on after so many years of fruitless endeavours on our part.'[44] There was an invitation from the chairman of the committee of the church of St Andrew, Pretoria, to act as assessor in the competition for a new church, for which he would charge fifty pounds, plus expenses. In April the Wesleyan Trustees made him a similar offer to act in the same capacity and for the same fee.[45]

Baker even wrote to E Bradshaw in February noting that the land opposite the stock exchange, on which he had earlier designed Farrar Bros' abortive office scheme, had been bought, offering his original plans for its development and drawing attention to the savings that might be made in such a deal.[46] Then, after a fortnight in Cape Town and following the award of the arbitrator in his favour, he made an offer 'open for a day only' to Dale Lace

Rhodes Memorial, Rondebosch, detail of steps.

Rhodes Memorial, Rondebosch, a copy of 'Physical Energy'
by George Frederick Watts.

to reduce his fee to £400, in view of their old friendship. Lace accepted, probably with gratitude.[47]

Baker was away when the Lady Warden of St Anne's College at Hilton Road, Natal, called at Exploration House in connection with a new chapel for the school and a proposed church for the village at Hilton Road. In his letter to her dated 24 March, Baker observed that building in Natal 'should be considerably cheaper than up here', adding the coercive proviso: 'I presume that it will not be always so low as it should be during the present depression.' Remarking on how busy he was he wrote: 'Mr Sloper however could manage quite easily to run down during the next fortnight before he goes Home to England.'[48]

It is not clear whether Sloper was merely taking a holiday at a convenient low ebb in the firm's fortunes or had planned to leave the country for good. It is even possible that Baker himself had suggested the departure, though in view of Baker's high opinion of his partner this seems unlikely. Whatever the true reasons were, Sloper never returned to South Africa. Later in the year Baker described him as 'my late Partner...who has changed his name to Willmott, and is acting as my agent in London at present...'[49] Ernest Willmott set up a practice in England, represented the Transvaal Institute of Architects at the Seventh International Congress of Architects, held in London later that year and, in 1911, wrote an indifferent book entitled *English House Design*. He died at Great Missenden in Buckinghamshire, in 1916.[50]

Ernest Willmott Sloper had left by the time Baker, with Frank Fleming as his senior assistant, prepared plans of a house for Capt H R N Bourne of the Colonial Secretary's Office at Pretoria: 'I have worked out two plans, one of your idea and one of my own.'[51] Conditions had also been requested for a competition for new buildings for the Transvaal Technical Institute, and plans had been sent to the Reverend A H Gallagher for a church hall at Florida in April.[52]

It was not until May that Baker was able to fit in a visit to Hilton Road. 'I am going to combine my Natal visit with one to Cape Town so as to save railway journeys and go by sea', wrote Baker on 17 May to the Lady Warden of St Anne's, regarding the 'two little churches at Hilton Road...' He was to 'meet the Bishop on Tuesday afternoon' and was 'much pressed owing to my partner being in England...Tenders have just come out for the Cape

Town Cathedral and I have to fit in my journey with a meeting of the Committee there.'[53] Hilton Road must have been impressed, as no doubt they were meant to be, by the connection of their own modest churches to the most important Anglican building project in the land!

On 19 June Baker wrote to the Reverend Douglas Ellison of St Peter's Home, Grahamstown, reassuring him that 'with Masey looking after the designing of the work and giving an occasional visit, and with a thoroughly practical energetic fellow like Marshall in the neighbourhood to supervise the work you need have no fear that whatever is done by the firm will be satisfactorily designed and built.' But it appears that there was another architect to dispose of. Baker continues: 'I should only like to repeat now that both Masey and I are anxious to act as considerately as possible in every way to White-Cooper, both in connection with his present interests and with any building in connection with [which] we may have to build. He is a man we both very much respect both in his work and personality and there is nothing we should regret more than to interfere with him in any inconsiderate way.'[54]

There were to be one or two setbacks before the Hilton Road schemes could get under way. To St Anne's, where building plans had been deferred, he wrote: 'It is a great disappointment as it is seldom one has the opportunity of building in such sympathetic surroundings and conditions.' With regard to fees, '...the account will be merged into any future commission if the chapel is built at all in accordance with our original design.'[55] But there was worse to come. On 30 July Baker wrote to thank the Reverend H Hammersley for 'informing me in advance of the decision of the Hilton Road Church Committee not to pay us for any designs for the completion of the church. As a matter of fact, I have practically completed these designs...' The Committee, Baker added, were 'acting rather on the side of meanness.'[56] By September, however, the church project was proceeding and Baker was explaining that the roof pitch was the same as 'a rather similar Tower which we have recently added to the Cathedral at Bloemfontein, and we have received more praise of this Tower from people whose opinion is worth having than perhaps for any other work we have done.'[57] Alas, as has been seen, in time the Bloemfontein tower became unsafe and was demolished in 1965.

REPORT OF WORKS

IN PROGRESS AT

The Rhodes Memorial. Rondebosch. C.C.

For Week ending *March 2nd.* 190*7*.

HERBERT BAKER & MASEY, F.F R.I.B.A.,
ARCHITECTS,
CAPE TOWN.

WORKMEN EMPLOYED.

Foremen at Quarry & Memorial Site

	No.	Days.		No.	Days.
	3	6.	FORWARD ...	39	6
Excavators ...			Smiths and Lab's ...	2	6
Bricklayers ...			Plumbers and Lab's		
Masons ...	26	6	Plasterers ...		
B'klayers' & Masons' Lab's ...	10	6	,, Lab's ...		
Carpenters ...			Tilers ...		
,, Lab's ...			Painters ...		
			Electricians ...		
FORWARD ...	39	6	TOTAL ...	41	6

WEATHER REPORT.

Monday . . *Fine*
Tuesday . . ..
Wednesday ...,,....
Thursday . . *Windy*
Friday . . . .*Fine*
Saturday . . .*Fine*

REMARKS.

Mr Masey visited the Memorial on 27th ult.

DRAWINGS RECEIVED.

(No. need only be stated.)

—

DRAWINGS REQUIRED.

SKETCH PLAN.

PROGRESS OF THE WORKS.

Since my last report considerable progress may be recorded. The accompanying plan will shew to what extent the work has already been carried. All except four Columns on South Side where Crane is placed, have been fixed with Caps Complete & with their exterior & interior lintols. Portion of the granite Ceiling has also been done. The Columns in Centre with their lintol have also been fixed & on the North Wing the erection of the four front Columns is in progress. The Stair to Roof has been Completed & the Mountain Stone paving at rear of Memorial begun. Portion of the Cornice with a model of the parapet is being prepared and erected for the approval of Mr Baker.

J M Solomon
CLERK OF WORKS.

Rhodes Memorial, report by J M Solomon.

Baker had already been responsible for the beginnings of the Parktown Girls' School, Roedean, and had been in contact with the two Diocesan schools in Natal, St Anne's and Michaelhouse. He had also been involved with the earlier ideas which had led to siting a new St John's College in Houghton. Moreover he had had more than a fair share of just about every Diocesan pie; his choice as architect was inevitable. On 18 August 1906 he was invited to view the Houghton site with Archdeacon Furse

Top. *St John's College, Houghton, 1907.* Bottom. Church
at Turffontein, Johannesburg.

School of Music, Doornfontein, Johannesburg, as it is today.

Left. *Christ Church, Arcadia, Pretoria, nave.* Right.
Christ Church, clerestory windows.

and immediately prepare plans for new accommodation for the school which had begun life in St
Mary's Church, Eloff Street, in August 1898.[58]

On 19 November Baker's plans were approved by
the Diocesan Board and, in the following year, on
10 August 1907, the new buildings, which today
form part of the Preparatory School, were opened
by Lord Selborne.[59] A contemporary description
held that they were 'of a beautiful coloured hard
stone quarried from the spot. The ground is on a
slight slope, so that one wing, consisting of classrooms, is only one storey high, while the other, containing the schoolhouse, has two storeys. Between
the two wings, and connecting them, stands a massive square tower with a large central doorway, and
above, the Chapel.'[60]

Whilst the Hilton Road Church Committee was

deliberating, and in little more than a week or two,
three more church projects materialized. For Turffontein the Reverend A T Hare of All Saints, Booy-
sens, requested a parsonage and church hall that
August. This was followed by George H Hull's
request for Baker to design a new church at Christiana, in the south-western Transvaal. Then the
Reverend J A Cutter of Premier Mine, near Pretoria,
asked the firm 'to act as architectural advisors in
connection with a new Hall and Rectory.'[61] On top
of all this came a request from the Reverend A Hankey for a wooden candlestick 'with possibly a silver
emblem' on it for the Community of the Resurrec-
tion, of Sherwell Street, Johannesburg; yet another
request, for a font and lectern, came from the Reverend W P G McCormick.[62]

In a slightly different vein came a request from Archdeacon Furse to comment on a design for St Mary's offices, of which Baker declared he would prefer to see a 'wholly brick building which I know could be built for the same price as a wholly plaster one, if the useless Turrets and ornaments were missed out, but these seemed so dear to the heart of the Architect!'[63]

Meanwhile in the eastern Cape at King William's Town, A J Marshall was persevering with the elevation of Dale College, which 'you seem to have improved...very much on the lines of my suggestion, with the exception of the height which I think is rather a serious matter. I should certainly recommend you to reduce the height by scale or otherwise. I am sorry you are worried with inconvenient office accommodation, but hope that the College contract is now settled and that you are more comfortable.'[64] Baker wrote again to Marshall on 4 October about re-tendering for the Dale College contract and, asking, '...is it too early to do anything about Bedford?...I am sorry about Grahamstown...is it that we specified too high a standard of work? We must be very careful in entering a new country to keep near to the limits of the usual building custom there.'[65]

Two days later, on Saturday, 6 October Baker left again for the Cape with the intention of being away for two or three weeks but in fact not returning until 22 November. Fleming was in charge and during Baker's seven weeks of absence produced drawings of two alternative designs for a parsonage at the tiny south-eastern Transvaal town of Wakkerstroom; the church hall and another parsonage for the township of Cullinan, where the Premier Mine was situated; and drawings of the St John's College scheme for the Bishop's consideration.[66] Fleming was also able to report that the Secretary of the Witwatersrand Agricultural Society had called, saying, '...it is proposed to ask you to act professionally for them...'[67] On his return Baker sent another sketch and estimate to Wakkerstroom. Meanwhile, in the south of Johannesburg, the Florida church hall was complete but for some minor defects, whilst in another remote country town the Christiana church was finished bar its painting.[68]

But above all, and at long last, his most important Transvaal building to date was nearing completion in all its details of furnishing, decoration and landscaping: Government House was to be occupied on 1 February 1907. There were a number of minor details to attend to, like the removal of all temporary buildings, a cottage for the under-gardener, and an article to prepare for the British magazine *The Builder*.[69] In total contrast, were two items for this grand house which, in their own way act as poignant symbols of the era. One was his design for a zodiacal sundial, incorporating what resembled an Empire clock which told the time in South Africa, London, India, Australia, Canada and New Zealand.[70] The other was described in his letter written just before Christmas to the contractors Edmanson and Thomas: 'We authorise you...to build a small cook shed for the Kaffirs [*sic*], near the Rondavels, consisting merely of a rough wall and a piece of iron for a roof. This must not exceed a cost of £10.'[71]

CHAPTER NINE

1907-1908

LIGHT AND SHADOW

TO ENGLAND AGAIN

It is pleasing to reflect on the fact that even in the rush of meetings, tasks and duties, which demanded his attention daily, Baker could find time to think of wild flowers. Recalling the 'Hilton Road daisies' he had seen in Natal, he wrote to R H Cooper of the Hilton Road Church Committee on 7 January 1907, requesting some 'large scarlet, with dark centre...Gerbera?', to be sent up for his garden, and for others, including Government House.[1]

Early in the new year Baker sought to make a simple improvement to the Hilton church, which was then well under way. 'We feel very strongly', wrote Baker to Cooper, 'that you ought to have the stone window even at the extra cost of £4.10.0. We think, however, that this extra is very unreasonable and that you ought to put pressure on the contractor to reduce it, or else we should try to devise some other means of forcing his hand...Do you think you could threaten him with having it made here unless he is reasonable about the price? This might appeal to his *amour propre*.'[2]

That week Masey had been in Johannesburg to discuss the future of the firm now that it was clear that Sloper – or Ernest Willmott, as he now was – had no plans to return to South Africa. On 5 January Baker had advised his bank manager that in future the name of the firm would be 'Messrs Herbert Baker and Masey', and as Baker would be the sole partner at the Johannesburg branch, 'he only will sign on behalf of the Transvaal Firm...'[3] In the event he now decided to dispose of 'one office in excess of our needs' at Exploration House; it seemed pointless to hold on to it when prospects looked so bleak. He had just written to yet another prospective employee: '...we very much regret to say that we have no work in the Transvaal, nor do we know of the immediate prospect of any upon which we could engage your services...'[4]

Masey's memory of that visit seems to have been coloured by a relatively minor irritation, but nonetheless he had felt sufficiently slighted to remark peevishly: 'When I was in the Johannesburg Office I was a little sorry to see the photograph I sent you of the Cathedral consigned to a dusty shelf, and to think that my poor drawing was such an unworthy one!'[5]

Also early in the new year the municipality were asking questions in regard to the design of the classroom windows for St John's College. Baker responded by pointing out that he had 'carefully worked out the figures in connection with the main rooms' and had based his designs on 'the standard proportions...given from Clay's Model School Buildings.' But, he added – giving us some insight into how architects established such matters in times when no standard briefs and norms existed – he had also taken account of the requirements set out 'in the recent competitions for two Secondary Schools in Johannesburg.' The issue was 'whether or not it would be better to have three instead of two windows in the classrooms, not for the sake of more light, but...more distribution. I put 2 large instead of 3 smaller windows for architectural effect, but do not in the least mind altering it if you should think it desirable.'[6]

At the end of January Baker was again in Cape Town to attend to events there. First, there was much detail still to be agreed on the Cape Town Cathedral superstructure, the construction of which had begun the previous June, two months after the Rhodes Memorial had begun (1906). He had also to attend a meeting of the Rhodes Memorial Committee on 2 February. With the extra funding made available that month by the Beit Bequest, and making possible the second phase of construction, it was decided to place Watts's statue on the bastion, where it was erected in August that year.[7] There was still the question of the bronze lions which the English sculptor J M Swan had been invited to make. At the meeting Baker was asked to travel to London to finalize the commission with Swan and also to discuss the possibility of his sculpting the large bust of Rhodes which was to be the focal culmination of the long climbing progression to the heart of the temple. Baker was to be paid £150 for his expenses in England and for his return steamer passage.[8]

Before his departure from Johannesburg on 25 March, political currents were flowing fast in South Africa and some notable events had occurred. In the Transvaal self-government had already been granted in December 1906 and the Orange River Colony would receive the same status in June. On 20 February the long-awaited Transvaal election was held, with General Louis Botha emerging as Prime Minister, and General Smuts as his chief lieutenant in the Cabinet. In the air were important Memoranda, and much talk of a future federation of the British and former Boer Colonies. These were events which the ruling British Liberal Party welcomed. But for many British and Colonial conservatives they were to mean that the Boer War had been fought in vain, shattering the dream of a South Africa with a British future.

Rudyard Kipling, who had travelled to the Cape during December to winter at The Woolsack, was among the disillusioned; and it was with the returning Kipling, and their respective families, that Baker sailed to England from Cape Town in the *Kenilworth Castle* on 3 April 1907.[9] That same month Botha was in London to attend the Imperial Conference, receiving a rapturous welcome from British Liberals. The conversation on board the *Kenilworth*, coupled with the continuing economic depression in South Africa which had stilled the growth of his practice, must have caused much soul-searching for Baker on his journey to the country he and Florence still regarded as 'home'.

Towards the end of February, after instructing his lawyers Webber and Wentzel to take action against Dr Posnet for long outstanding fees,[10] Baker spent a week at Lionel Phillips's farm at Woodbush, near Pietersburg, where he was advising on the building of a cottage 'in the middle of the forest.'[11] In the week before leaving for England instructions were received to proceed with working drawings for the

church at Cullinan, and yet another new church commission was in the offing, this time from the Reverend Fitzwilliam Carter who had contacted Baker regarding the proposed church of St Luke, Orchards. Just before Baker left he advised Carter, who had been headmaster of St John's College from 1904-5, that if he could not get to the meeting proposed, 'Mr Fleming, my Manager will be there...'[12]

It was to Owletts, Baker's family home in Kent, that Fleming addressed his report dated 8 July 1907.[13] St John's College was 'very nearly finished' and St Mary, Rosettenville was 'going steady and well.' Most interesting is the confirmation of the authorship of St Luke, which was progressing slowly, 'but he has brought through all the essential points in the building as you designed it for him.'[14] The Cullinan church, however, had 'come to a sudden stop', indeed work had not yet begun owing to a lack of money.[15]

MICHAELHOUSE CHAPEL

Baker was on his return voyage to South Africa when Hugh-Jones, the Rector of Michaelhouse wrote again after a silence of almost four years. Arriving back in Johannesburg on 11 September 1907, Baker immediately advised the school that he was sending Fleming down to Balgowan.[16] By 27 September plans of the proposed chapel 'in brick, similar to the present buildings, inside and out' were prepared, along with modifications to Hugh-Jones's house 'in cheap local bricks, plastered and whitened', and a new sanitary block.[17] In the following weeks some discussion took place on the orientation of the choir seating and of the chapel itself, in relation to the original buildings, designed by the Pietermaritzburg architects Price and Kent.[18] Also discussed were ways of dealing with its future expansion, for which Baker advised that 'a north aisle would certainly be the most convenient enlargement...without much extra expense now...[we] could arrange the necessary arches in the wall so that enlargement could be very conveniently managed at any time.'[19]

It was not until December that year that Baker himself was able to see the site, combining his visit with one to St Anne and the church at Hilton Road, and meeting with the Governors of Michaelhouse in Pietermaritzburg. Considering that he was travelling by train, it was a programme that would seem unthinkably tight today. 'I suppose if I got out at

Michaelhouse Chapel, Balgowan, Natal.

Balgowan', he wrote to Hugh-Jones on 17 December, 'I could get on this [?] evening – but I should not like to arrive very late, having my wife with me. I do hope the trains are punctual – I arrive at 2.8 and there is a train that leaves at 2.59. This will enable me to see the site, which is all I want...perhaps you might meet the train...on Fri. 20th. Thanks for interesting book. I will write separately about the Chapel.'[20] On the day following his brief meeting with Hugh-Jones he explained his proposals to the Governors in Pietermaritzburg. The final design of the chapel and associated works was an ingenious piece of infilling, providing a chapel of great simplicity and character.

Its walls were pinkish-apricot brick, inside and out, with a high beamed roof and segmented apse containing small high windows. In his report dated 15 January 1908 Baker writes, perhaps a little defensively, but nonetheless with interesting perception: 'In anticipation of any criticism as to the absence of elaboration in the design, we would answer that beautiful architecture depends more on solid construction and good materials and workmanship, than on multiplication of detail. And in our opinion, this principle should be of the greatest educational value to South African boys, who too often have examples only of an opposite nature before their eyes.'[21] But Baker's architecture went well beyond those minimum requirements, giving dignity cheaply where decoration might have been applied expensively. Sadly, one of Baker's most successful smaller churches was destroyed – arguably needlessly – in 1952 to make way for the new and much larger Memorial Chapel. One wonders if the loss of such simple and appropriate beauty has made any less likely the repetition of similar acts of enthusiastic thoughtlessness, at that school or any other.

The month before making his trip to Natal, Baker had dined with a new client Mrs Haarhoff, following which he wrote: 'I have lost no time in working out another plan for you much cheaper than the

Michaelhouse Chapel, Balgowan, Natal, interior.

last.' Baker's design for her proposed house was in the 'scale and style' of a gabled and tiled 'Dutch design inside and out.'[22] He had also heard some extraordinary news from Cullinan, a matter which needed to be nipped in the bud immediately. Writing to the Reverend J A Gutten, Baker expressed sympathy '...in your disappointment about the loan...we think it may be wise...to reduce the size of your church. We must however point out to you that you are taking...a very unusual course...in appropriating and using our plans for another church, without reference to us. We cannot possibly agree to such an unprofessional proceeding.' The right course, he explained, was to make reductions to the present scheme, rather than to become responsible for 'fresh commission on the Copyright and necessary alterations of Turffontein Church.'

As is expected, his stern but utterly correct letter was accompanied by his detailed fee account for a church, hall and rectory.[23]

RISING TENSIONS: 1908

As the year 1908 began Francis Masey was again upset by what he felt was a lack of recognition on the part of his partner. The incident concerned a public address given at the Mansion House whilst Baker was in London, and which had been reported in the *London Times*. Baker replied on 3 January 1908 that he regretted the 'omission of the Speaker's [sic] of your name', maintaining that 'such things happen in architectural partnerships.' Baker illustrated his point with the example of Ernest

Church of St George, Parktown, Johannesburg. View of apse and tower.

Cathedral of St George, Cape Town, roof.

George, in whose office he had once been a senior assistant, and of G F Bodley, where 'it was the rule.' In both these firms, he contended, neither of the respective partners, Harold Peto or Thomas Garner, '...though their share of the work was large – predominated in some cases – ever cared I fancy. Nor should I if it were the other way.' As a sop, Baker added: 'A correction ought certainly to be put in the Cape Town papers, although there everyone knows. They wouldn't put it in the *L Times* – because the speeches were personal, not official.' Understandably Masey was still not satisfied with this explanation and wrote again.[24]

Baker then moved to the subject of the Cathedral roof: 'I am sure the 55 degree pitch should look very bad in the gables and from many points. But you are right about the apse...I confess myself wrong in not seeing that there the roof was steeper, as is usual in hips.' These, Baker asserted, 'should always be 5 or

7.5 degrees steeper than the main roof. I always make them so here when I can overcome the tile difficulty of the hips and the true lining.' Baker asked if it was too late to make it so. 'The hips and tiles can be humoured to the change of pitch. You know the difficulty in fitting the hips and changing the gauge to keep the line. It seems to me this being over the groining that there is no difficulty – either as to time or construction – in doing this. So I would suggest it.' The steeper pitch round the apse meant the tiles were a little closer, 'and that of course adds to the appearance of it, gaining variety and better texture. So it is worth doing in every way.'

If Baker had begun his letter with a qualified apology to his injured partner, these latter remarks, which were tantamount to instructions, would do little to restore Masey's pride. But now he was to close it with a rebuke, reminding Masey that he had asked him to 'kindly send me particulars of the work done before I signed the certificate, as I ought not to sign anything in the dark. Reid will not mind waiting a little.'[25]

Three days later his tone was sterner, and his handwriting even more difficult to read than usual. On 16 January 1908 Baker wrote: 'You did not understand I think, the point of my telegram. "Humour" implied that I knew the roof was cut out but my letter will explain my point that in the common roof over the groining you could at little expense ease or even fir up the rafters to get increased pitch...as is often done in old roofs...if you can manage the tile, as I think you can as I have often done it here. It is worth thinking out, at any rate and I have no doubt you have done so.' Finally, again the reminder: 'I am waiting for details of certificate.'[26]

Then, just four days after, on 10 January 1908, Baker virtually repeats himself: 'I shall be pleased at any letter that may be in the local paper and will write one if you like – but everyone at Cape Town knows. But as I said, it is difficult to correct personal speeches...I enclose a letter – put it in if you wish – but it would come better from the Committee.' Baker reiterated the cases he had quoted, which he considered to be 'parallel...as both Junior Partners were mainly or wholly responsible for much work the public gave the senior partner all the credit for...' Returning once more to the roof, Baker declares: 'I don't understand – you say you made the Eastern hip 55 degrees corresponding to that of the main roof – does that mean you leave it alone and don't want to alter it?'[27]

Several letters later the tone is similar. In that of 10 February he writes mystifyingly: 'Thank you for yours of 5, 6 and 7th. Re J.B.R. I...hope you will make peace and get the job. Try [?] as mediator – a true one. He has just left here – the papers say, for Cape Town. Or I would try, though it is difficult for he locks himself up like a despot and is very rude by letter. No, his ruling passion is revenge – but only averice [sic] against us.'[28] Although it is not certain who or what this was all about, in all probability it was J B Robinson, the mining magnate, for whose Wynberg home Masey had prepared designs and tenders in the previous May. But Baker once more reproves the errant Masey: 'Again you have failed to send statement with certificate. So I must ask for it again please. It can only take ten minutes.'[29] Baker then thanked Masey for the photograph of the sketch he had sent, adding: 'Though I take exception to many details of the architecture,

I think the drawing is admirable, especially the Tower, and I congratulate you on it. But don't make any geometrical drawings until I have seen and approved.' Baker closes with a report that '...we have just signed a contract for £10 000 for 26 miners' cottages and £950 for a stone church for Premier Mine [Cullinan] and £1 100 for the Guild of Loyal Women also at Pretoria. That's all that's new and signed for. The cottages are I hope a promising and permanent connection in a new and profitable field.'[30]

The frequency of their correspondence is astonishing. The following day Baker, referring to Masey's letter of the 8th, writes in regard to the seemingly forever unfinished Cathedral: '...we must not raise alarms to the Committee now – we have all along taken the view that the work can be stopped at the stages proposed at different times. We have always treated the temporary work as light...see that they have a complete usable stable building for the limit they fix.' Baker ends his letter on a high note, despite the implicit challenge: 'My hopes as to the miners' cottages proving a good connection have come quickly true – as I am asked to design more cottages and a boarding house on one of the Eckstein mines, provided I can do them as cheaply as their engineers – a hard task and their prices are bedrock.'[31]

Throughout this correspondence, of which we have only glimpsed fragments, one is aware of an underlying tension between these men, an unspoken war of wills, no less ruthless for being fought with the weapons of icy politeness and professionalism. There are clues, too, in Baker's highly erratic handwriting, which varies from the almost indecipherable to the clear and strong. Masey's letters, however, are generally typed or written in a cool, elegant hand, concealing his own deeply emotional nature.

THOUGHTS OF CHANGE

Behind the tensions created by the artistic rivalry and personal ambition of these two highly motivated architects must have lain Baker's concern about the lack of new work and his doubts about his future in South Africa. Whilst in England six months earlier, Baker almost certainly would have broached the subject of entering into partnership with his old friend Edwin Lutyens, now almost thirty-nine years old and with a successful London

Top. *St Boniface, Meyer Street, Germiston, tower.*
Bottom. *St Boniface, interior.*

practice heading for great achievements. On his return Baker wrote to Lutyens mentioning the possibility of partnership, but Lutyens's reply of 10 May 1908 made his lack of commitment to the idea apparent:

'It is absurd for a man of your calibre to stay out [in South Africa] and put up tin buildings or at the best stone apses to tin naves', alluding to Cape Town Cathedral. 'Human nature prompts me to hope you won't come! and this remark is probably the instinct of self preservation which prompts me to pray you will stay out in Africa and at the same time prompts you to come home!! Things are quiet here – yet London is being rebuilt! You'd have a splendid chance; you have reputation and would start, with all your experience, on a clean slate. Your danger might be to be too conscious of texture', warned Lutyens in thinly veiled criticism of his friend's architecture. 'For yourself I should dearly love to have you home in England. My position is not so good as to enable me to say I would be jealous – but you would like that? and I shouldn't like you less!!...I should gladly lift you to my "well fortified heights" in a partnership. But I don't think, when behind my works, they look either high or well fortified – I should never say this to another man...But I cannot justly judge what is the true state of affairs in Africa and what you stand to lose...If I had work enough for two I should make you an offer at once, on an equal basis. But I haven't, and I don't know, even if you are willing, how a partnership could be effected. I should dearly love working with you and having the endless fun and discussion – a process I have long felt the want of.'[32]

In the same letter Lutyens made some suggestions for a Pretoria church, presumably the new Anglican Cathedral of St Alban which Baker had been commissioned to do early in April. Lutyens comments too on the Rhodes Memorial: 'Your Rhodes should be like a Christ in a Byzantine apse – colossal and impassive', an opinion he enlarged on in a later letter, of 15 July, when he remarked that: 'A seated figure of Rhodes in your structure sounds impossible.'[33]

Three months later such a partnership was still a remote possibility. On 24 August 1908 Lutyens wrote to his wife Emily: 'I have written to Baker. I have never shown you his letter. The proposal is that on a joint income of £3 000 he takes £1 000 and I take £2 000 and then as the income increases he takes 1 500 – 2 250; 2 000 – 2 500; 2 500 – 2 700;

3 000 – 3 000, and then equal. He puts in a plea for £300 a year to start with as a living wage which is fair I think. He is coming home and then we can talk it over. Then for us there will be the question of Bloomsbury Square, whether we move or the office moves as B.Sq. won't be big enough for both...'[34] Lutyens suggested they each put £6 000 or £8 000 into a joint capital fund. Baker replied that '...if you really want help, – if beautiful Amelia really wants to marry Captain Dobbin', he might be able to contribute half that amount, assuming that Fleming continued as his resident partner in South Africa.[35] Though a decade later Baker and Lutyens would begin working in collaboration on the world's largest and most prestigious building project of its time, New Delhi, nothing was to come of the ideas now being considered. It will be seen that, to use Baker's phrase, 'the fates intervened.'[36]

THE GLOOM BEGINS TO LIFT

Throughout the early months of 1908 the work situation remained gloomy. There were continuing problems with numerous septic tanks of the Johannesburg houses and Sammy Marks was complaining about the 'continual expense of repairs' to the Marks Building in Cape Town, leading to Baker's demand for an 'exhaustive report' on the matter from Masey.[37] But although he informed Masey in January that 'the diamond depression has hit us now and Mrs Haarhoff writes that she has put off building the house...', February saw some exciting glimmers of hope in Pretoria and Germiston; and there was some more building for the mines to be done, including a new boarding house for Crown Deep Mines and some mineworkers' cottages for Simmer and Jack in March.[38]

ST ALBAN

From Pretoria the Bishop's Chaplain had sent Baker plans of the Schoeman Street site, where a temporary brick and iron Cathedral had been started with the help of the Royal Engineers in 1878.[39] The commission, confirmed early in April, was to build a new chancel eastward from the old building which would serve until funds were available to build a complete new church.[40] Baker's designs were prepared in parallel with those of St Boniface at Germiston, for which he had completed plans and per-

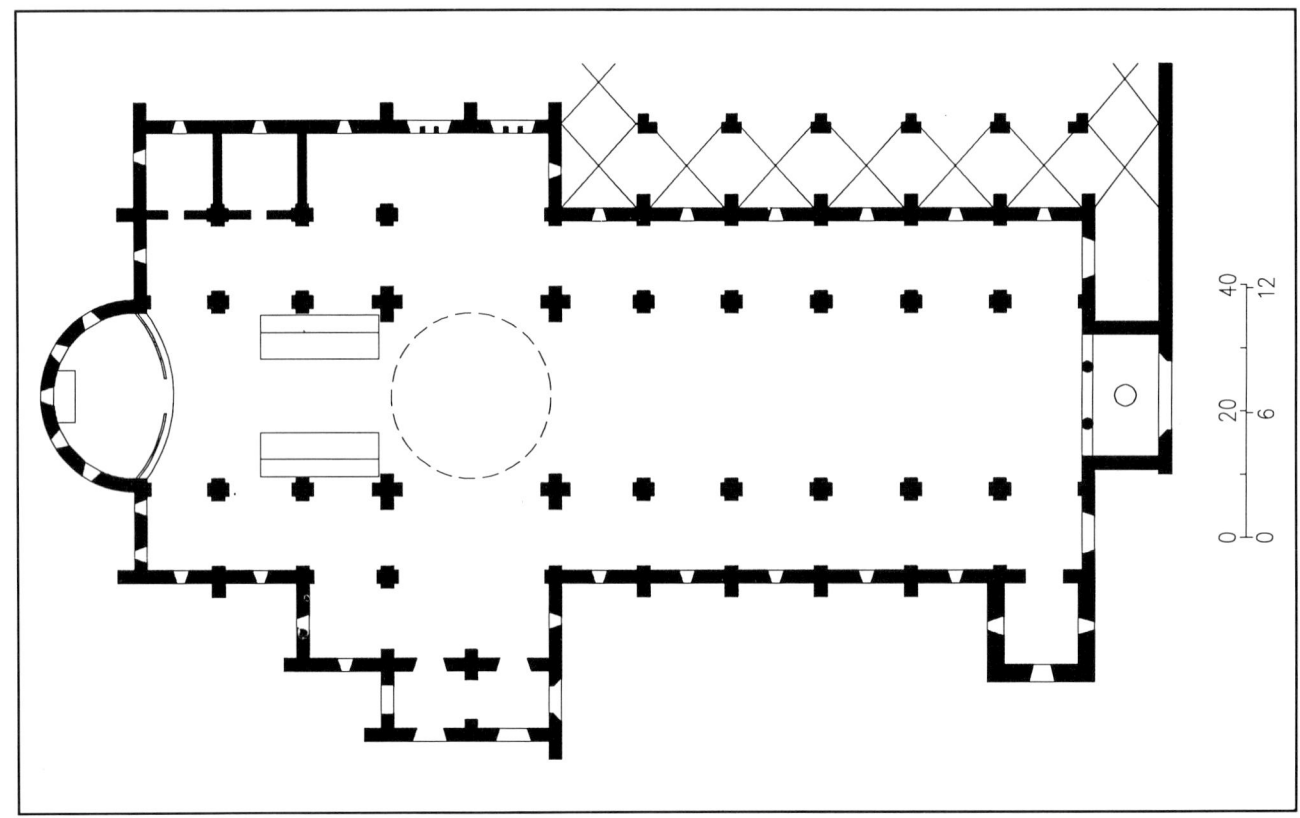

Cathedral of St Alban, Pretoria, plan of the original design.

spectives of the new church, with sketches of the vicarage and additions to the hall, for submission to Canon Farmer by 7 March 1908.[41]

For the Pretoria Cathedral, Baker's plan was to add an apsidal chancel, a sanctuary and choir to an eventual seven-bay, barrel-vaulted nave, with transepts crossing beneath a shallow dome. Of his designs only the sanctuary, chancel and a side chapel were built, further work being postponed by the 1914-18 war. The remainder was completed in a contrasting modern style by E N Wilfred Mallows in 1957, with an aisleless sloping nave, separated from the stone-walled chancel by Baker's strong wide arch.[42]

Baker's walls were built of local kopje stone, rough – even rougher than those in Cape Town – and full of subtle blues, greens and greys and burnt sienna. The windows have simple stone tracery, set in surrounds of smooth reddish freestone. The apse has a semi-circle of small, deeply splayed, windows set in the curved concrete vault. In the bright light of Pretoria the stained glass by Christopher Whall glows with·'saphire tints and amethyst and

ruby', redolent of a Romanesque or Byzantine church. Baker had written to Whall in England, on 5 October 1908, inviting him to do the windows and pointing out that: 'The climate is very much hotter and brighter than Cape Town, and might be compared with that of South Italy. For this reason the windows are deeply recessed both inside and outside.'[43] This was the first of Baker's churches to have concrete vaulting, a device which reinforces the Byzantine feeling of the church. The vaults were covered with low-pitched roofing in red tiles. In July a foundation stone was laid by Lord Selborne, and Bishop Carter consecrated the new chancel on Easter Monday, 1909.

For both the Pretoria Cathedral and that of St Andrew and St Michael at Bloemfontein, Baker designed a common design for a memorial to the South African Constabulary. Baker was anxious that 'Gill, who is a careful and expert craftsman at such work should do the tablet if possible.'[44]

In June, in his capacity as Diocesan Architect, Baker was asked by Archdeacon Furse to comment on a 'Proposed Parish Hall at Rose Bank' and another at Boksburg North. Baker's comments are interesting examples of his method of innocuously damning with faint praise; offering suggestions as to how the unfortunate designs might be improved. He also made it clear that his advice was indispensable, with the probable intent of wresting the jobs from their original designers! Of the Rosebank scheme he wrote: 'We have looked at the sketch plan for the above. The design seems suitable, though...a few massive buttresses would both be useful and interesting.' For Boksburg his observation was similar: 'The plan is simple enough and would seem to give a serviceable hall. All the three little projecting features are rather puny...', and inevitably he suggested improvements.[45]

SUNNYSIDE

In August that year Baker advised the Reverend W R Gibbons, Vicar of the Church of St Michael at Sunnyside, Pretoria, that he was 'always prepared to make liberal terms' for the Anglican Church. He was therefore willing 'to make sketch designs free of charge so long as we are your architects and no other is employed.' Baker then shrewdly used an alternative phrase to describe his services, and leave his client little room to manoeuvre without accepting their financial responsibilities, which would otherwise be Baker's loss to carry: 'Should you change your professional advisors we should charge for whatever work we have done...'[46]

Although not necessarily arising from any action of the St Michael Church Committee in particular, Baker's warning was born of his experience with a number of impoverished but nonetheless grasping committees. Some of these had tended to regard architects' services as coming from a charitable institution with no expenses to cover, in producing designs to suit their every whim. Indeed it was intended as a safeguard against the very situation which now arose at Germiston. On 28 September Baker wrote to Canon Farmer regarding the Germiston Church of St Botolph which he had designed in March. 'In my capacity of Diocesan Architect, plans and additions for your Church have been put before me. I must say I consider it very extraordinary indeed after the large amount of work which I did for your Parish in designing the Church, Vicarage, and alterations to your Church Hall, that you should employ another Architect without any word of explanation or apology to me.' Baker's indigna-

tion was perhaps justified but ironically the boot was, for once, on the other foot.[47]

The Church of St Michael and All Angels was built in stone quarried from Meintjeskop, the rocky outcrop not far from Baker's Government House. This stone, uneven in texture and variable in colour, contrasts with the smooth fine-grained red sandstone used in the chancel vault and the nave arches. His original plan was cruciform with a nave of six bays, aisles, transepts, choir and sanctuary. Like so many of his churches, only a portion of the Sunnyside church was built initially, leaving completion to future generations. In this case the last three bays of the nave were completed in 1961. 'Internally the roof is open to the apex and all the timbers are left in view', wrote Baker, who described the nave arcade as 'regular from west to east up to the Sanctuary arch, and is carried out in red Warmbaths stone, with plain caps of the same, borne on rectangular pillars of the local stone.'

The arcade is surmounted by a clerestory of 'simple pointed windows', similar to those of the aisles and transepts. A wide flat arch, nearly semi-circular at the head, separates the nave from the five-sided apsidal sanctuary, which is vaulted in the red Warmbaths stone. The same stone is also used for the two cusped sanctuary windows. As for a tower, which Gibbons desired, Baker thought it 'impossible to get a tower at all in proportion to the size of the Church built over the nave at the west end...'[48]

On 31 October news came of the fire which had destroyed the Government Buildings at Bloemfontein. Baker immediately wrote to '...express our regret and sympathy at the destruction...We had rather an affection for the building, and particularly for the Quad, which we felt was to be one of our best pieces of public building in South Africa...If it were built again, we think the whole design might be immensely improved, and kept simpler, and rather more distinctly South African in Character like the work in the Quad.'[49] Baker still had the plans, but these came to nothing when the Public Works Department rebuilt the offices themselves, based largely on Baker's previous work. There appears to have been some evidence that the fire was caused by an electrical fault, a factor which probably prejudiced Baker's position in the eyes of the Department.[50]

During October, Masey was working in Cape Town on the Richmond church in Natal. Baker's tone is again reprimanding when he writes: '...I presume therefore, you did not then take the steps on

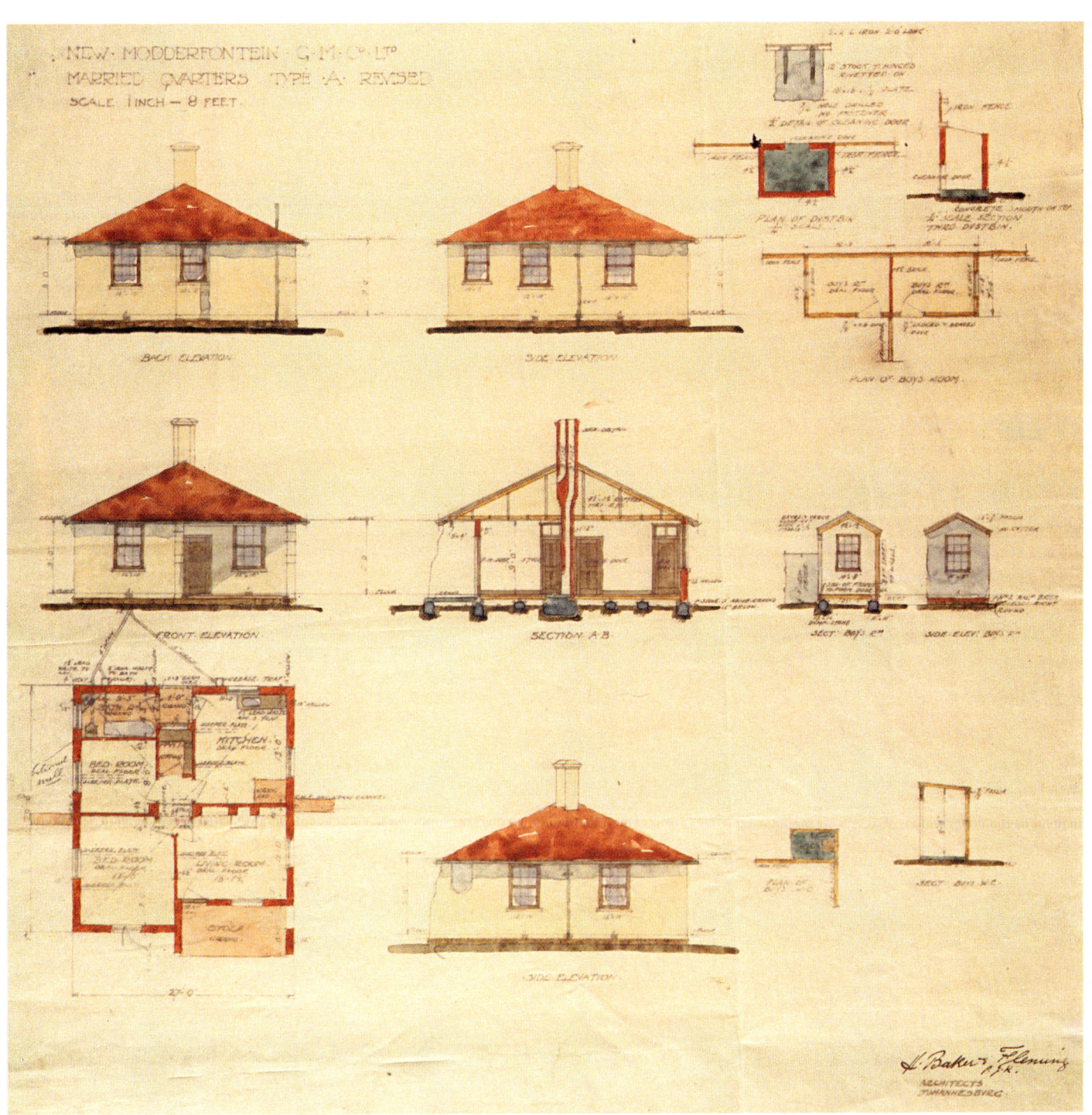

*New Modderfontein G.M. Co. Ltd. married quarters, Type 'A' plan,
revised. Sections and elevations, February 1912. Previous
page. St Michael and All Angels, Sunnyside, Pretoria, apse end.*

the lines I suggested. I am quite in the dark about the matter because you did not let me know anything about what you had done, or proposed to do...Barrow [who was building the Michaelhouse Chapel] should be asked to give a tender for the little piece of the church which they think they can build...therefore I propose to make a sketch and give it to him for a tender.'[51]

That month, with mine work still bringing in much of the firm's income, Baker sought to make some basic improvements to the standards provided. Regarding some cottages proposed for Village Deep, he wrote: 'On some of the mines we are now making the Boy's room not only a brick building, but also a little larger in size than the minimum, with a view of it being useful if required either for a white servant, or other white person. This can be done at a very small increased cost per cottage.' Whatever the stated motives for this move, it did provide a highly desirable improvement over the unlined 'tin box' commonly provided at that time.[52]

Baker left Cape Town on the night of Saturday, 24 November, and passing through Bloemfontein on Sunday morning, met Fred Masey on the station platform, where they briefly discussed the fire and resultant damage to the Government buildings. Baker learnt that an enquiry was to be held.[53]

Baker was in Cape Town when Fleming advised him that the assessors for the Pretoria Station competition had been unable to reach agreement, and that 'Reid is anxious that you alone should be asked by the Assessors to help them on a definite reference to come to a unanimous decision...' Baker immediately advised the General Manager of the Central South African Railways that he was returning from the Cape via Durban, sailing on Wednesday, 2 December 1908, and that he would arrive in Johannesburg on the following Tuesday.[54]

Announcing his return on his first day back, Baker in the meantime turned to other accumulated correspondence. He was delighted to read a letter expressing the Synod's thanks for his services as Diocesan Architect and to find that his old client at Turffontein, the Reverend A T Hare, required his services for a new church and rectory at Benoni. This was to be followed in December by a rectory for St George in Parktown, for which, owing to its proximity to Stonehouse, he was prepared to 'make a present to the Parish of that proportion of the fees which were for supervision...'[55] He was glad too, to learn that Abe Bailey's Friedenheim was to be occupied before Christmas.[56] The Christmas of 1908 was to leave an interesting relic of Baker's moral rectitude in a letter he wrote to the contractor, E N Ostend: 'I am much obliged to you for your kind thought in sending me a Christmas present, but I think it is a good rule that presents should not be received from people with whom one has business relations. I am quite certain you acted on the best intentions but I should be glad if you would receive the parcel back.'[57]

CHAPTER TEN

1909

VISIONS OF GREATNESS

COMPETITION DERAILED

In January 1909 Dr Engelenburg, the Editor of *Volkstem*, translated into English an article he had written on railway stations for Baker to read. In his publication Engelenburg, whom Baker admired as a man of high taste and culture, wrote disparagingly of early Victorian architecture. The article elicited from Baker a revealing defensive response: 'But seventy years have passed since then, and I think that most critics, even many good Continental ones, would acknowledge that this activity, misplaced at first in many ways, has given birth to a really good school of Architecture in England. The work of Norman Shaw and his school, it will I believe some day be realized, has added to the Architectural wealth of the world. It can hardly be called a "style", but rather an ideal or attempt to get at the basic truths of the Art and Craft of architecture, and for this reason, if intelligently understood, it should be peculiarly suitable for adaptation to the different conditions of this country.'[1]

Baker was given a further opportunity for reflection when, during the following month, Engelenburg invited him to write an article about the architecture of Pretoria's Government Square. As Baker saw it, his task was to write on the general principles of the 'Grand Manner' of Architecture. 'By this I mean...large principles of unity and symmetry, which has always prevailed in the great periods of the Art, but which was killed by the Romantic and Gothic revival at the beginning of the last century. The reaction has now set in, and these noble principles of Architecture are beginning to be revived all over the world, and now is a very good opportunity to teach the lesson in South Africa.'[2]

These remarks reveal Baker's thinking at the precise time of receiving his first large commission for a secular public building in the Transvaal. Baker gives 11 February 1909 as the date on which 'first negotiations' over the Pretoria Station took place, and 19 February as the day the abortive competition plans were inspected.[3] Between these dates Baker had written to Charles Murray, the Acting Secretary of the Public Works Department, stressing that Piercy Eagle, the Department Architect, 'must study the plans and reports, more especially my report.' Baker added: 'The Railway Department have apparently no architect, and it is no use reporting that things are to be done to the plans if there is no one of Knowledge and Taste to see that they are carried out.' The calculated wording made the job as good as his. Once more Baker had managed to get a direct commission out of a competition which had been bungled.[4]

There followed a brief correspondence with the Institute of Architects regarding the ethical question of his taking over from where the abortive competition had left off, and he began his sketch plans for the railway station on 17 March 1909.[5] They were virtually complete by the time he left for Cape Town three weeks later on 7 April, returning to Johannesburg on 12 May. Baker delivered the contract drawings to Pretoria on 11 August and construction began soon after.[6]

Though it is almost certain that, during the five weeks Baker was at the Cape, Masey was consulted on the station design's finer details, any suggestions he may have made could only have been of a minor nature. Now with the station secured and Lionel Phillips at last ready to build a new house, it seemed that the tide was turning and any thoughts of returning to England could at least for the moment be dismissed. That month (February) Baker was able to write to his friend: 'Dear dear Lutyens, the facts are intervening...'[7] Baker would now stay

Villa Arcadia, Parktown, Johannesburg, courtyard.

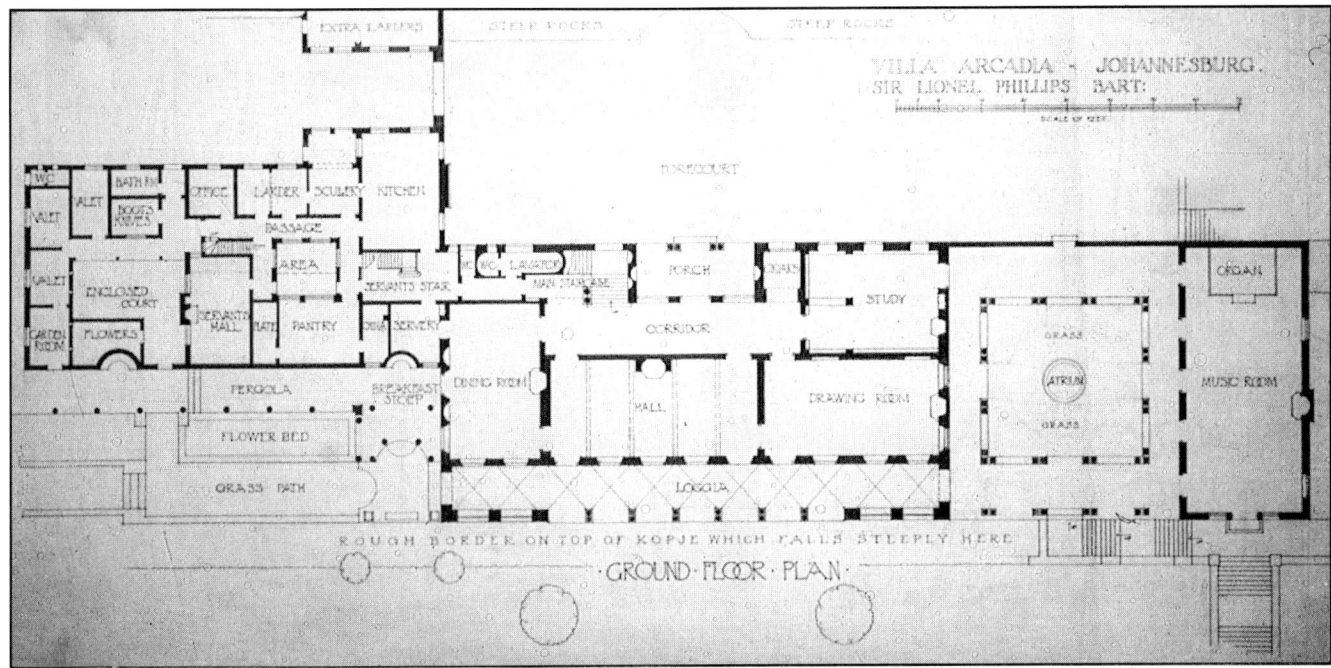

Villa Arcadia, Parktown, for Lionel Phillips, ground floor plan,
April 1910.

on in South Africa, writing to Lutyens: '...though working with you where are summer and winter, flowers, spring, birds, and the prospect of being buried under a yew tree, all pull'.[8]

But Christopher Hussey, in his *Life of Edwin Lutyens* puts it among his reasons that 'the Convention had raised the ideals of the Government and they were more inclined to trust Englishmen...'[9] Hussey then puts it even more colourfully: '...the fear of a bump between two stools, and the folly of throwing up good connections, and the feeling that he filled a gap in the imperial wall, joined in inducing him to remain at his post. He didn't want to desert, couldn't face Kipling if he did, and realized Rhodes's scorn of colonists "who desert to useless swamped lives at home".'[10]

VILLA ARCADIA

Most encouraging was the news that Lionel Phillips's house, Villa Arcadia, was to go ahead. On 23 February 1909 he wrote to Marshall requesting him to come up from the Eastern Cape to act as clerk-of-works for the house 'quite close to where I live.'[11]

The Villa Arcadia is today a children's home. Although the first Arcadia was a large house in the Swiss chalet manner, it was too small for the lavish life style of Lionel Phillips and his wife Florence. In 1909 it was demolished to make way for Baker's Mediterranean mansion. The house took some eighteen months to build and several more years before it was finally completed. Its magnificent garden setting, on its vast twenty-six acre site, was the creation of Baker and Mrs Phillips. Dorothea Fairbridge described the view from the stoep, '...seen through its columns the blue line of the Magaliesberg Mountains shut out the distant veld...and below me, falling sharply away from the stoep and melting into the blue green eucalyptus of the Sachsenwald stretched a garden of exquisite charm ...Terrace after terrace lay below us, with flights of steps paved with the accommodating Transvaal sandstone...Tall cypresses marked the line of the terrace, but in the Italian fashion and flanked by Italian oil jars in which fuschias rioted and gleamed in rich purples and reds and pinks. On another terrace was a Rose Garden...At the end of the long grass walk was an alcove formed by clipped cypresses, in which a group of leaden figures took one back to the gardens of England...'[12]

159

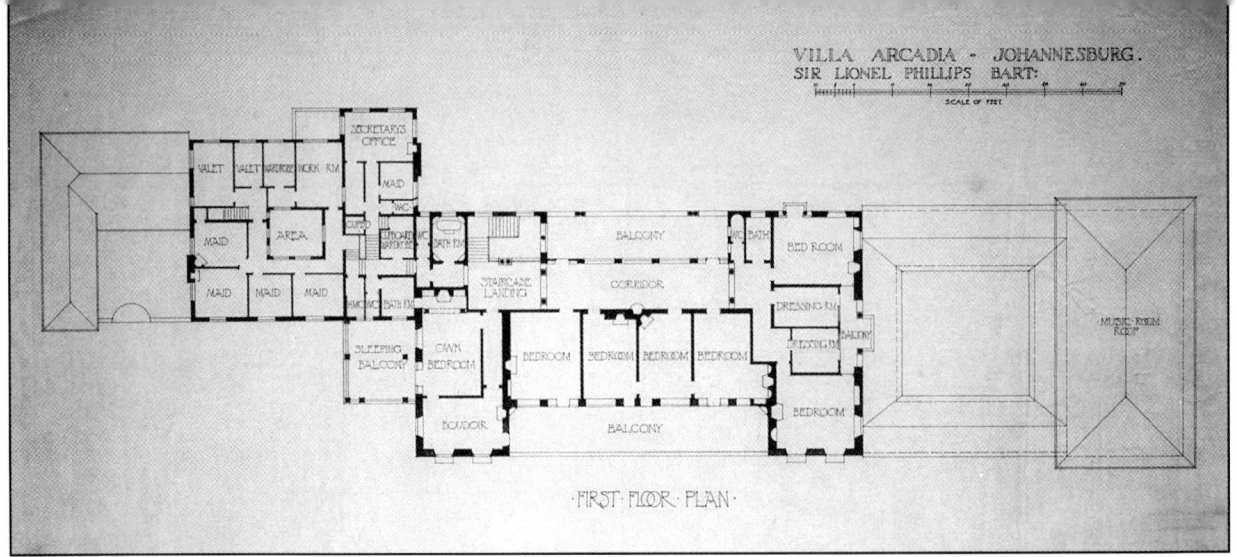

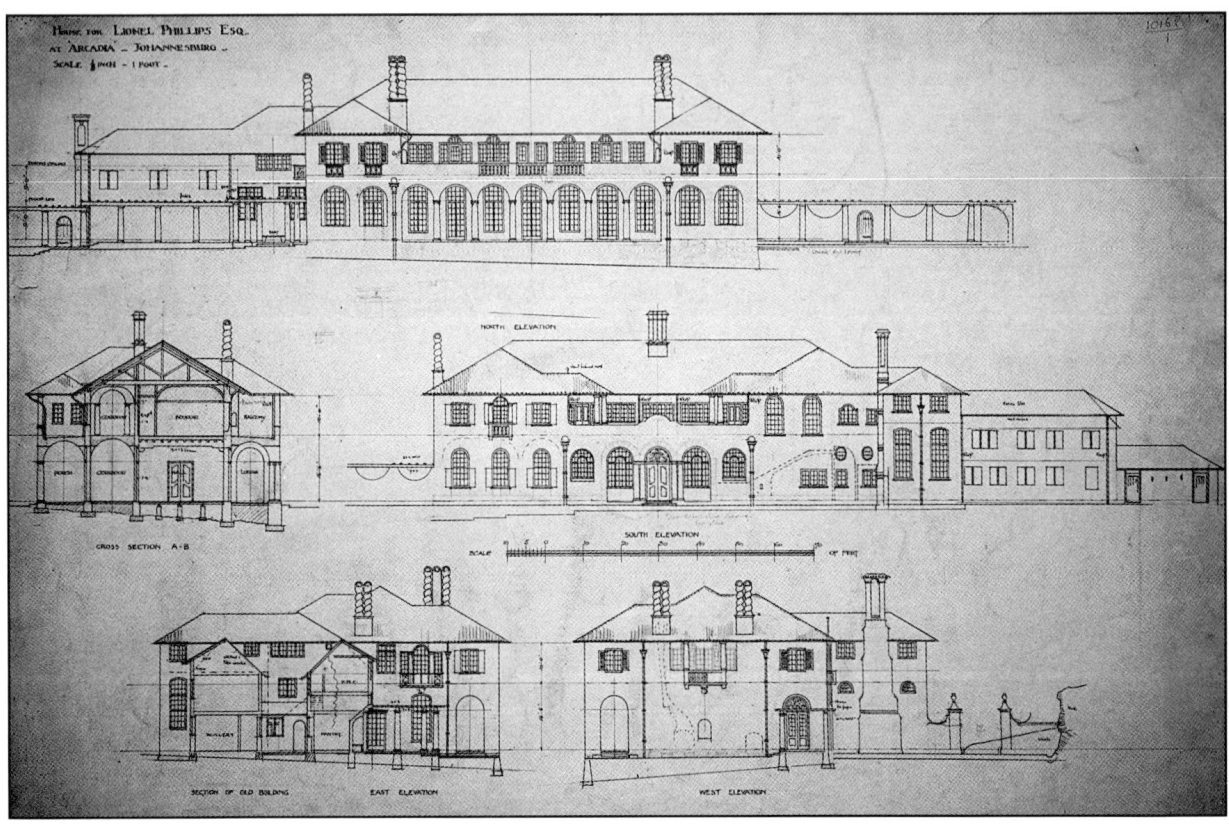

Top. Villa Arcadia, Parktown, Johannesburg, first floor plan, April 1910. Above. Villa Arcadia, elevations and sections. Bottom. Villa Arcadia, the Music Room. Elevations, plans and sections, April 1910.

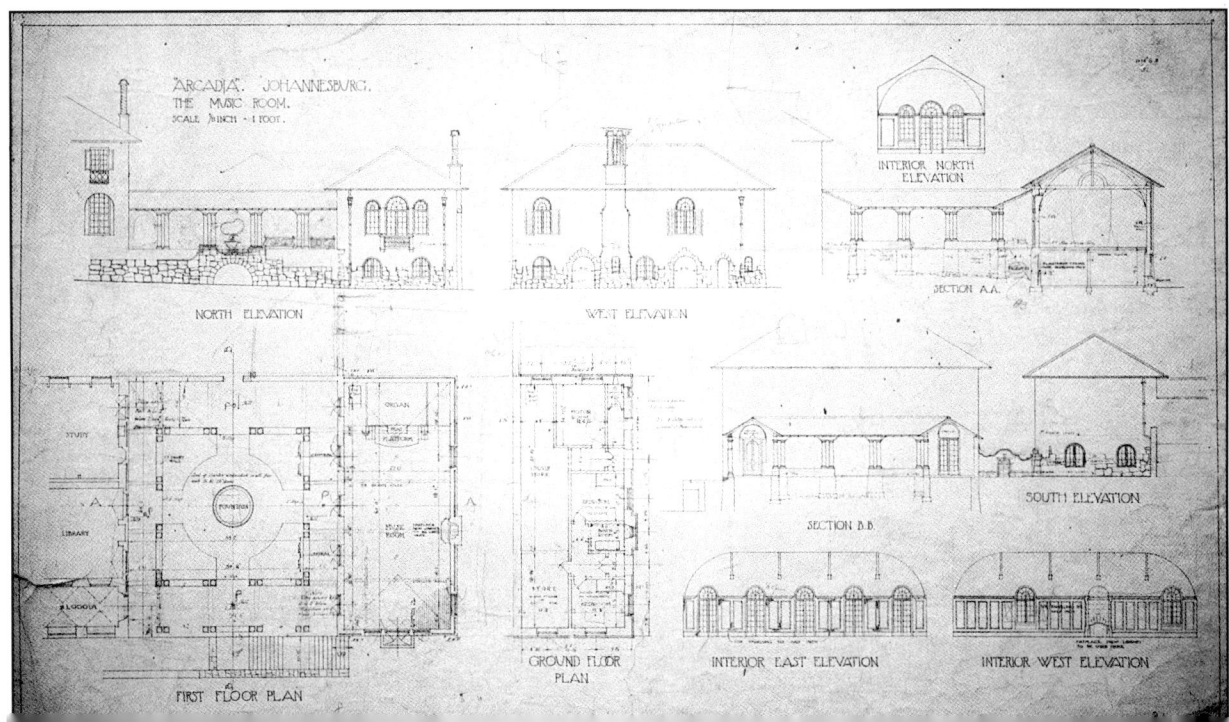

Villa Arcadia, Parktown, vaulted roof over loggia.

Top. Villa Arcadia, Parktown, balcony detail. Bottom left. Villa Arcadia, chimney detail. Bottom right. Villa Arcadia, twin columns.

This description does indeed give the keynote of the house and the setting in which it was built: Italianate Arts and Crafts. It is a long, north-facing villa with a formal rhythmical façade in gleaming white. In its centre section is an arcaded galleria-like loggia of Ionic columns, paired at right angles to the façade, from which spring concrete vaults. The red-tiled roof is low-pitched in the Mediterranean manner, topped with barley-sugar chimneys. At the western end is a 'columned cloister', which 'led to an organ-room where its owner sought recreation from his business cares', writes Baker.[13] Here Baker's favourite Doric columns are again grouped in pairs, but in line with the wide eaves, around the single storey Roman atrium. It was thus at Villa Arcadia that Baker first experimented comprehensively with the Italianate style, with the use of materials and constructional techniques that go with it. But that said, the hints of Arts and Crafts, even of Cape Dutch, are still felt in the details and in the dark beamed interiors. The Villa Arcadia was Baker's high peak of eclecticism.[14]

MUTUAL RELATIONS

With work picking up again, and the tensions and minor irritations becoming ever more frequent, it is not surprising that mutual relations between the partners were being reviewed as the year 1909 began. 'I have been so very overworked the last few weeks', wrote Baker on 18 March, 'that I have found it impossible to draw up the promised final statement of the changes we propose...which began with my letter of December 14th 1908, and yours of January 25th 1909.'[15] Baker made it plain that he now had no intention of returning to England, with the consequence that '...we have only to meet the circumstances at present existing which are that I have my office and chief sphere of interest in the Transvaal, and you your offices and sphere of interest in [the] Cape Colony.'[16]

The main points of the agreement, which was to date from 1 January 1909, were that the name of the firm was to remain unchanged 'for the present' and Frank Fleming was to come into junior partnership in the Johannesburg office. Baker would now receive one-third profit from the Cape Town office, instead of one-half as hitherto, and Masey would in future 'resign all profits upon ordinary work' carried out in the Johannesburg office, with the exception of a one-third share on all church and Cathe-

dral work, but excluding work done on rectories and detached church schools in that office. Masey was to have a 'generally free hand' in the Eastern Province, though he was required to submit all important matters and designs for Baker's approval.

As the year progressed Masey became more and more aggrieved at what he believed to be his unfair treatment by Baker. Following a minor blunder over some china which had 'vexed' Lord Selborne, Masey wrote: 'I am sorry that I should have misunderstood you. It is very disheartening to get scolding letters of this nature when I am trying my best to help.'[17] Masey clearly did upset Baker with his careless or wilful omissions and constantly contradicted his master, in the politest of terms; yet Baker's frequently sarcastic manner was hardly conducive to goodwill and communication.

On 23 July 1909 Baker writes in connection with the Rhodes Memorial: 'Thanks very much for your sketches...In both cases they are ideas which I discarded at the outset...'[18] That same day, in another letter to Masey, Baker writes: 'I certainly do not think you ought to have promised to be a guarantor having devoted 10 years of your life to such exceptionally strenuous work on its [the Cathedral's] behalf, but if you think it is right to do so, I must of course do the same.'[19]

Then, regarding a proposed book, he adds: 'I do not quite understand all the points in your letter, as I do not know what Millar, Batsford and Mrs Trotter intend doing, but I am quite prepared to leave it to you and Millar to do whatever you think best. I think there are some points in my introduction which should not be buried, though I should of course like time to add to both the illustrations and notes. Before anything is done I shall read it over. I hope you will get on quickly with your book and not leave it too long.'[20] Writing again to Masey on the subject of 'mutual relations', Baker's tone is brusque: 'I do not know what there was in my letter which caused you to gather from the remarks that it was the second alternative I had adopted in the accounts of the last year.' Baker was referring to the 'one-third share of church work' agreed in January that year.

Baker then makes a 'final proposal – That in return for renouncing all share here I give you three-quarter share of the work at Cape Town. In addition to this I will renounce all my share for 1909, or, if you think this is not liberal enough, I will renounce a part of the amount due to me in the past in your books, so that you can start afresh in 1910 on a new

Villa Arcadia, Parktown, music room beams.

basis with a very small or no debt.'[21] On the face of it Baker's terms sound fair, even generous. But bearing in mind that Baker had turned the corner and was now in a very sound position, with endless bread and butter work coming in from the mining houses, and the Pretoria Station and Union Buildings now secured, Masey could be forgiven for feeling he was getting the worst of the bargain. Yet these new circumstances meant Baker needed Masey, possibly more than ever before.

Masey was now determined to seek his fortune elsewhere, some territory where Baker had not yet gained supremacy as he had virtually done throughout South Africa; and Rhodesia seemed to offer that promise.

CLASSICAL JUNCTION

If the Shangani, Kimberley and Rhodes Memorials, and on a more domestic scale the Villa Arcadia, had been progressive five-finger exercises in the language of classicism, Pretoria Station was Baker's first symphony. Sited on the axis of Market Street (now Paul Kruger Street) the north front terminates a vista from Church Square of nearly a mile. Without a glazed shed to cover the platforms in the dramatic manner of King's Cross or other well-known stations, the architectural interest of the station is centred on the main building itself. From the facing square the building is entered from beneath a flat-roofed *porte-cochère*, which juts out from a heavily rusticated ground floor, arcaded almost to its ends, and built in a dull granite, quarried south of Pretoria. At this level are all the usual public spaces for tickets, waiting, baggage and refreshment — some faced in a variety of marbles. There are a number of beautifully conceived rooflights and a surprising, tiny, columned court beneath a ventilating eye in the roof of the gentlemen's toilets, only to be enjoyed by the appropriate gender.

Pretoria Station, concourse.

Above are two floors of official accommodation, faced in a smooth Flatpan stone, and separated on the north elevation by a deeply recessed central loggia, across the front of which are placed four pairs of Ionic columns. The wide eaves of the Italianate roof and the loggia and arcaded plinth combine to cast splendid shadows on the north face of the building, giving a feeling of cool in the oppressive summer heat. The ends of this façade are given emphasis at first-floor level by means of balconied venetian windows and pairs of oval apertures beneath the eaves. A Wren-inspired flèche, a little on the small side, caps the Mediterranean-looking roof.

Apart from giving its architect a chance to try his hand at classical design on a non-domestic scale, it provided useful experience for Prentice and Mackie, one of the two firms of contractors employed on the Union Buildings. Doreen Greig is right in her suggestion that, despite some failings,

'Perhaps that is what makes it interesting: it breaks new ground. Baker was experimenting with forms and building methods which he was preparing to use on the Union Buildings; the station occupied a transitional position in his development and equipped him with the experience which was necessary for an even more exacting task.'[22]

UNION BUILDINGS

It was while waiting for approval to begin the production of detailed contract drawings for the station that Baker received possibly the most important commission of his life, the new Government Buildings in Pretoria, universally known as the Union Buildings. He gives 2 June as the day when negotiations began, which is borne out by the letter he wrote on the following day to E P Solomon, Minister of Public Works. Baker's letter confirmed that

Pretoria Station, porte cochère and clock tower.

Top. *Pretoria Station, rooflight. Bottom. Pretoria
Station, rooflight in Gentlemen's toilet.*

Pretoria Station, bend in east elevation.

he 'should act in some way in collaboration' with the Department's Architect, but firmly dismissed the idea that he should be appointed as the Consultant Architect only: 'Personally I would recommend the course now being adopted with the...Station, with the difference that the PWD should take the place of the Railway Department in settling the several plans showing...arrangement and accommodation of the building.'[23]

Baker relates that he was given a free hand in suggesting sites in and around the city. He was shown 'the block of land...where the Museum and Town Hall now stand. But with the high ideals we all had at that time I thought the site unworthy of a united South Africa.' Baker explored the surrounding kopjes and selected 'two ideal sites' overlooking the city. Despite the advantages of the southern site 'for extensions' and 'sunlit front façades' he set his heart on Meintjes Kop, which was near his Government House and his Bryntirion houses, and which dominated the city 'as did the Acropolis the city of Athens...' He recalls his attraction to the concave

depression in the rock platform 'such as the Greeks might have chosen for an open-air theatre.'[24]

His vision brought to his mind Segesta with its temple and theatre, and Agrigentum 'with its rows of temples on the hillside, both overlooking the Sicilian seas.' These sights had fascinated him on his study tour of the Mediterranean. And so the vision came to him 'of two great blocks...connected round the top of the depression by a semi-circular colonnade overlooking an open theatre...' Baker showed his rough sketches to General Smuts and then went with him to the site. His notion found sympathy with Smuts, who 'with his quick insight and imagination, at once visualized the idea and its power to give dignity and beauty to the instrument of Government and the symbol of the Union.'[25]

Meanwhile, on 9 June, Baker wrote to the Chief Engineer of the Central South African Railways with regard to pressing on with drawings: 'As I understand that both the Administration and the Department have approved the 1/8" scale sketch plans...As soon as I receive the formal instructions

Top. Union Buildings, Pretoria. Perspective drawing by Baker's assistant, Gordon Leith. Bottom. Aerial view of the group and its dramatic setting. An early photograph.

of the Administration, I will proceed with the contract drawings.'[26] Small wonder, then, that with the station still very much on his mind, his initial scheme for the Union Buildings should bear some resemblance to their predecessor in the composition of the twin blocks, about to be presented to the Government for the first time.

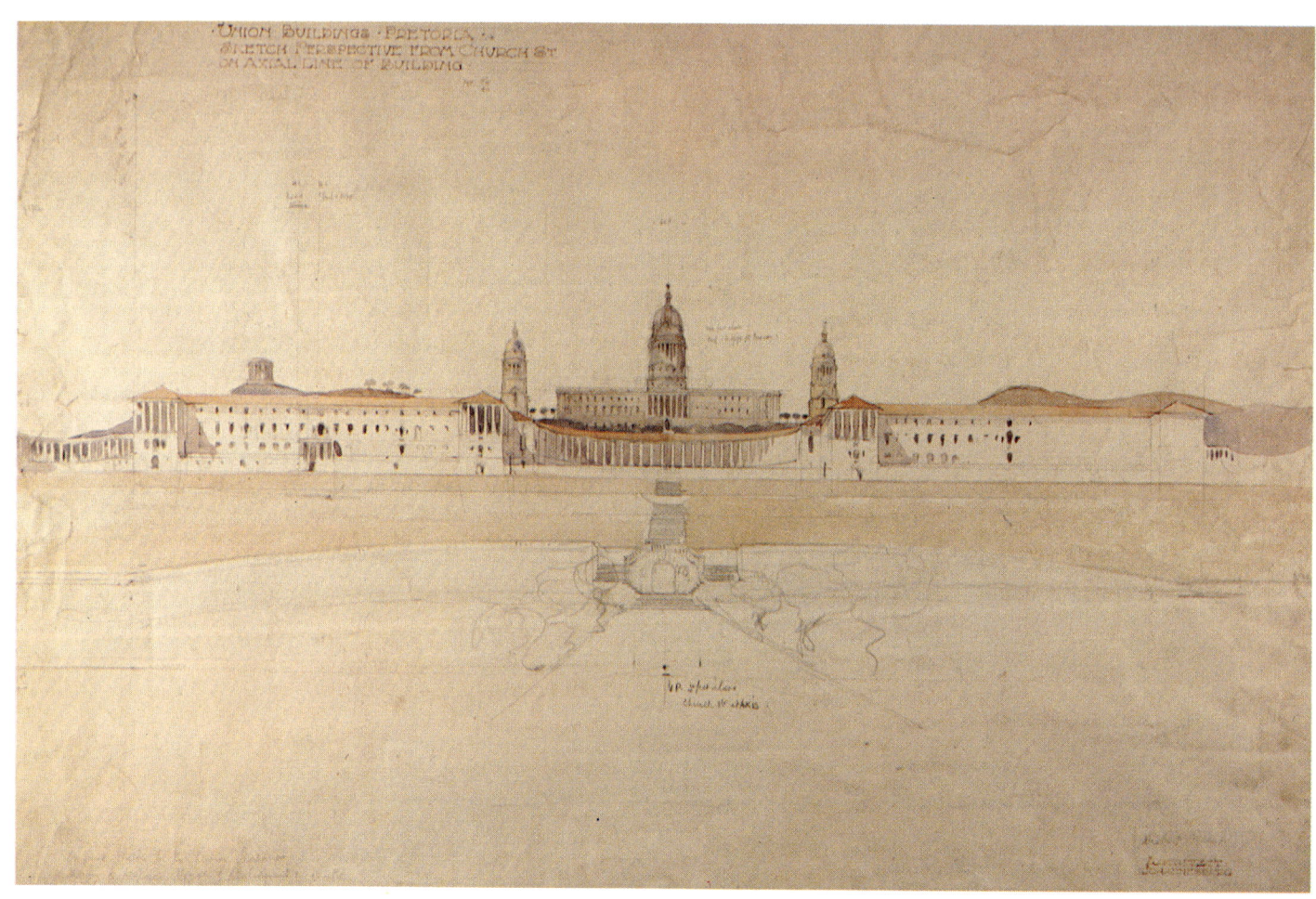

Union Buildings, Pretoria, sketch perspective from Church Street on axial line of the building. Design of 25 September 1909, showing Baker's full scheme which included the never-to-be built Temple of Peace.

Union Buildings, Pretoria, termination of the axis at rear.

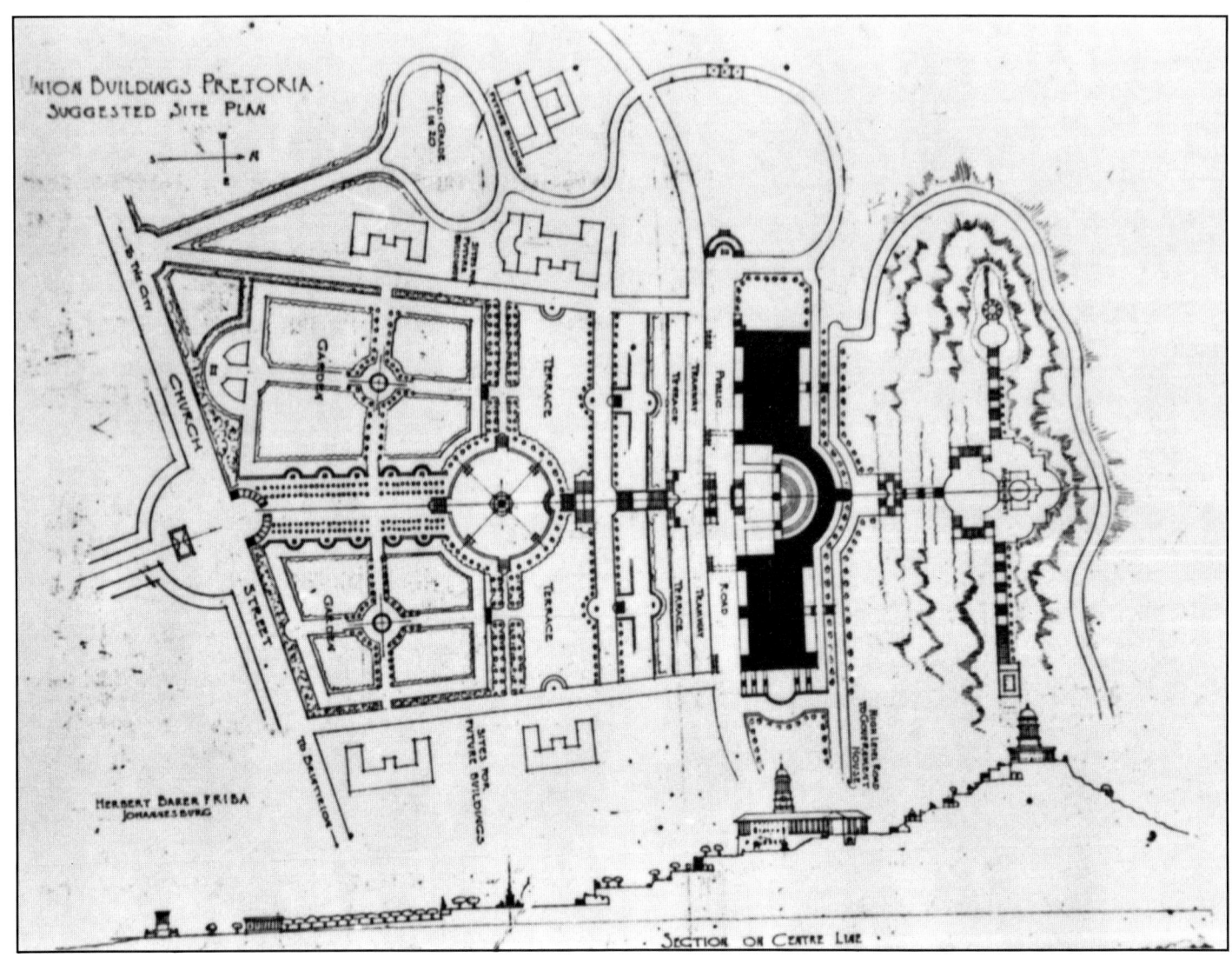

Union Buildings, Pretoria, layout plan with Temple of Peace.

On 26 June Baker wrote to the Prime Minister, General Louis Botha, from the Pretoria Club suggesting a site 'on a plateau, which is broken by a small kloof which is a natural amphitheatre.' Baker's plan suggested placing 'one block of buildings, to hold the new offices immediately required ...on one side of the kloof', adding that 'at some future date a second corresponding block can be added on the other side.'[27] Baker's remark that in the future these 'could be linked together by a semi-circular colonnade' seems to suggest that he regarded this element as of secondary importance.[28] Indeed in Baker's accompanying perspective, dated 25 June, the colonnade appears as little more than a

minor visual link in a scheme dominated by a substantial domed building on the top of the kopje, crowning the whole composition. As he had written to Edwin Lutyens, and also sent a sketch, the previous day, he hoped to place the group 'on a kopje acropolis overhanging Pretoria.'[29]

Three months later, on 25 September, Baker's revised scheme showed the twin clock towers, with their 'two domes, designed to lead up to a greater dome.'[30] It is possible that these were introduced at the suggestion of his friend Edwin Lutyens, to whom he had sent drawings for comment, and who had incorporated similar domed towers in his unsuccessful competition design for County Hall,

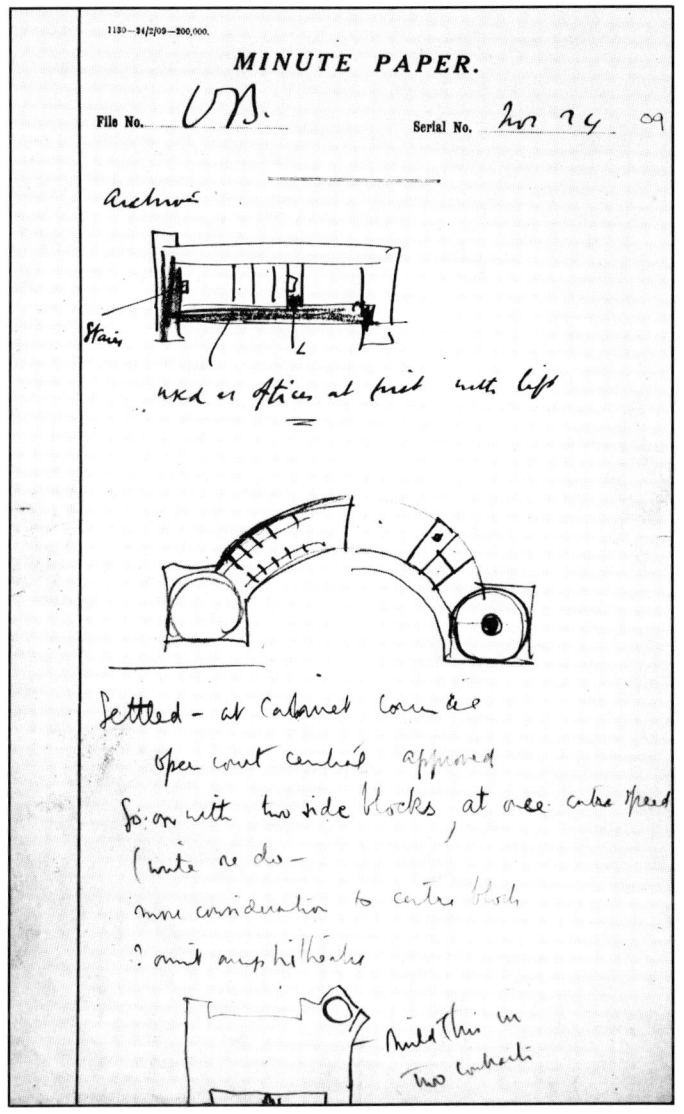
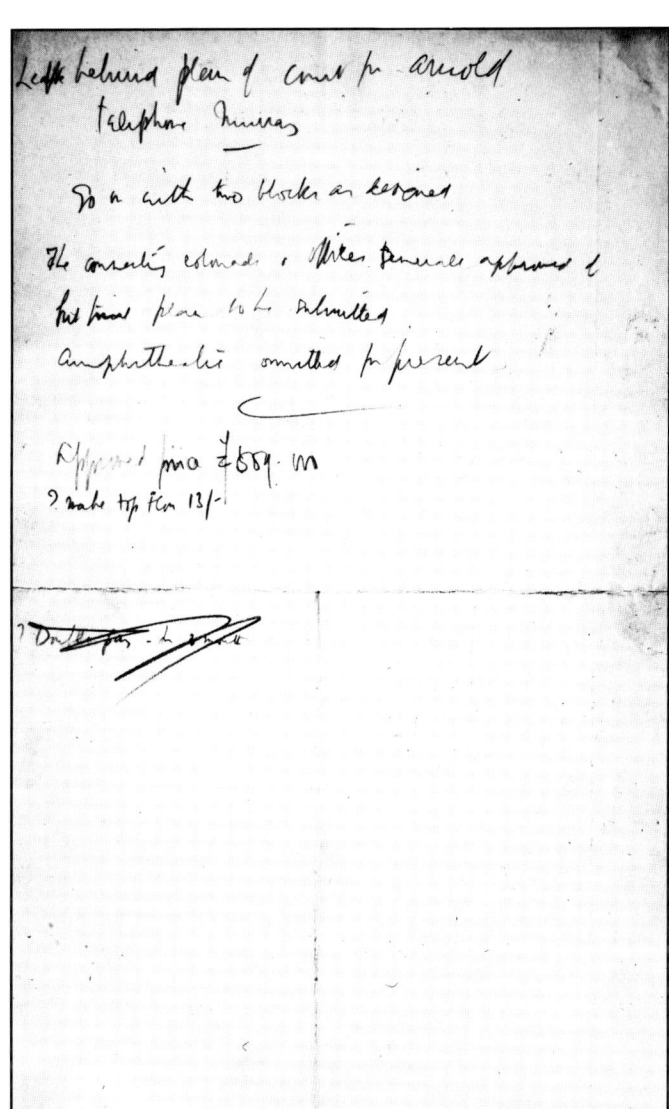

Union Buildings, Pretoria, Minute Paper dated 24 November 1909.

London, in 1908. But it is equally probable that his inspiration came from the Royal Naval Hospital at Greenwich, attributed to Wren but more likely to have been the work of Hawksmoor, an etching of which hung in Baker's office.[31]

HIGH IDEALS

In his autobiography, written in later life, Baker describes his conception thus: 'There on the central axis, where it would be seen from below between the two high dome-capped towers, symbolizing the two races [sic] of South Africa, I imagined a large low dome, a greater symbol of final union, a Hall of Fame or Heroon, a shrine of the Great of all races in South Africa.'[32] But Baker is misleading on this point; by no stretch of the imagination can what he drew be called a 'low dome.' It is interesting too that nowhere in the early documentation can the notion of the towers symbolizing the unity of the two white language groups be found, although he does write later of the idea. The likelihood is therefore that it was a romantic afterthought.[33]

Besides the imagined domed Heroon, another unrealized vision was 'a *Via Sacra* along the ridge

173

Union Buildings, Pretoria, projecting portico with window.

Union Buildings, Pretoria, window detail.

Union Buildings, Pretoria, basement columns.

of the Kopje to its apex overlooking the city...a broad stepped pathway with bastions and pedestals on either side for sculpture as it neared a little circular columned Temple of Peace, as we called it, crowning the summit'. The fading of that dream, with its echoes of the Rhodes Memorial, was perhaps fortuitous for it would have blurred the outline of the present, charming composition, despite providing the climax it now lacks.

But there were still doubts in the minds of some high officials, and the understandable jealousies of the local architectural profession to contend with.[34] There was widespread feeling that a competition ought be held for this, the most important building in the history of the about-to-be unified colonies; many thought too, that Baker had already had more than his fair share of the pickings. In response, the Government appointed in October an advisory board to consider the matter. The board consisted of two members, the Department Architect Piercy Eagle and Willem de Zwaan, a prominent Pretoria architect.[35] A month later, in a strictly confidential report, they strongly urged that alternatives should be considered before Baker's plans were accepted, expressing the view that his design was 'out of harmony with the topographical nature of the site and the skyline in the background.' Being south-facing and in the shade for the greater part of the day, they claimed that the building would present a 'dark, uninteresting square mass'.

Going on to criticize the 'extravagant and expensive scale' of the colonnade, they condemned the amphitheatre as having 'no practical value' and doubted whether such an auditorium would ever be used. 'The tiers of stone seats, unprotected from the weather offer very poor comfort to the visitor as they will either be too warm or too cold for sitting upon.' They concluded with the suggestion that a layout modelled on Washington should be considered.[36] Ironically, they were probably influenced by an American Government report Baker had acquired and shown to the Secretary, Charles Murray, and to Piercy Eagle.[37]

The board's report came into Baker's hands and, on 1 December, he rebuffed the charges in a letter to the Minister of Public Works, saying that he had already considered and rejected many alternative schemes. Defending the colonnade as 'the covered passage connecting the two blocks of offices', Baker suggested that if the Government wanted 'a monumental or ideal treatment, a plan on the following outlines might be more impressive on the site.'[38]

But Baker drew attention to the effect such a plan might have on the compactness and convenience of the office accommodation, remarking that 'if its beauty were its sole object, is the Government wholly to banish architectural embellishment from the Buildings of the Administrative capital?' Baker had in the meantime written again to Lutyens, on 21 October, describing the site and enclosing a sketch contour map and details of the plans and elevations.[39]

Matters were virtually clinched when, on a Government Minute Paper, dated 24 November 1909, Baker recorded that the design was 'settled – at Cabinet Committee', a meeting which he attended. He had approval to go ahead 'with two side blocks at once', and for speed of erection these should be built as two separate contracts.[40] However, there was still some more consideration that Baker wished to be given to the central colonnade block. In the meantime Baker was trying to assemble a team to produce the numerous drawings which were soon to be required. Masey had wanted some help with Parliament House but Baker found it impossible to oblige.[41]

Baker had just 'got two new men' and was 'just on the point of starting the big work, which will occupy all of us fully for the next six months, at the very least. There is Poole, and a clever young fellow named Leith, in the Public Works Department at Pretoria; Poole is still on the temporary staff and although he likes Pretoria, I doubt if the climate agrees with him, and he might possibly come. Leith

is a very nice, ambitious, capable young fellow, and he wanted to come into my office some time ago, but as I was collaborating with the PWD I made a half promise that I would not attempt to draw away their assistants. Either of these might possibly like to come down and help you.'

But, wrote Baker, 'Unless they contemplate an entirely new scheme I should have thought that you and Kendall could have drawn it out, and saved the cost of assistants: it was all carefully measured up before if I remember right.' Baker felt that the best solution was to try and get Morris. 'If you can take him back it is quite possible that he might help you to solve the difficulty of doing work in places as far apart as the Eastern Province, Cape Town and Rhodesia.'[42]

A few days later, on 8 November 1909, it all seemed settled and Morris had been recruited to help Masey. There followed some comments about the Parliament Building, particularly about what Masey proposed to do with the 'sham marbles in the Central Hall: I hope nothing will be left to disgrace the Union Parliament.' And with regard to Rhodesia: 'I do not see how you can do this work and go up there at the same time. Therefore, I think you might reconsider your decision about Kendall. You must do something or you will never get the work unless someone is there on the spot, particularly at the beginning, and that I fear you cannot be with this new big job.'[43]

In a letter to Lutyens dated 23 December, Baker expressed his feeling that there should not be two buildings for the new Union Government, one at Cape Town and one at Pretoria, but only one in Pretoria. In his view Parliament should sit in the central domed building he had shown surmounting Meintjes Kop.[44] Again his memoirs are at odds with the documents of the time: 'Rumours that I designed a Parliament House there are unfounded. For my part I favoured the dual capital, that Cape Town should be the seat of Parliament; this I thought would help to remove the mutual prejudices of the folk who lived at the coast and on the high veld.'[45] But the evidence of his drawings makes it clear that Baker felt this culmination to be an essential aesthetic element of his composition, whatever the political considerations such a scheme might entail.

Little did Baker know that within four years he and Lutyens would be in India, collaborating on the building of the new capitol there. At New Delhi, their planning scheme and their working and per-

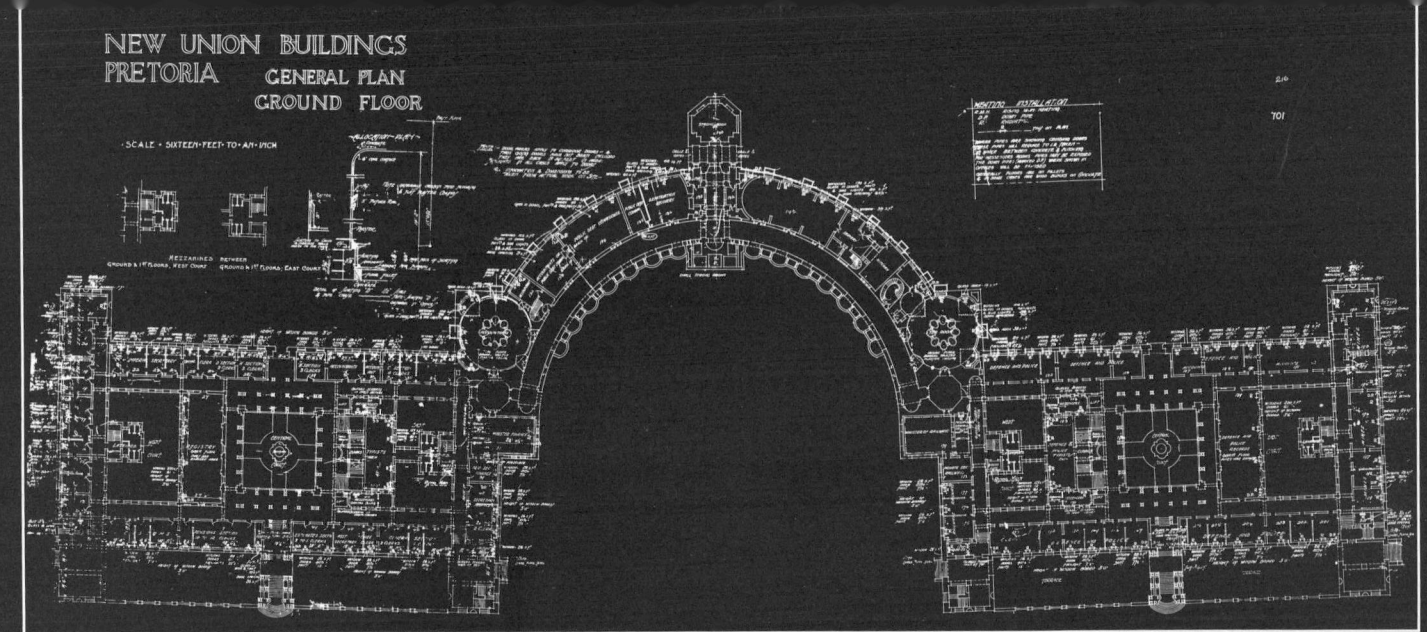

NEW UNION BUILDINGS
PRETORIA   GENERAL PLAN
GROUND FLOOR

· SCALE · SIXTEEN·FEET·TO·AN·INCH ·

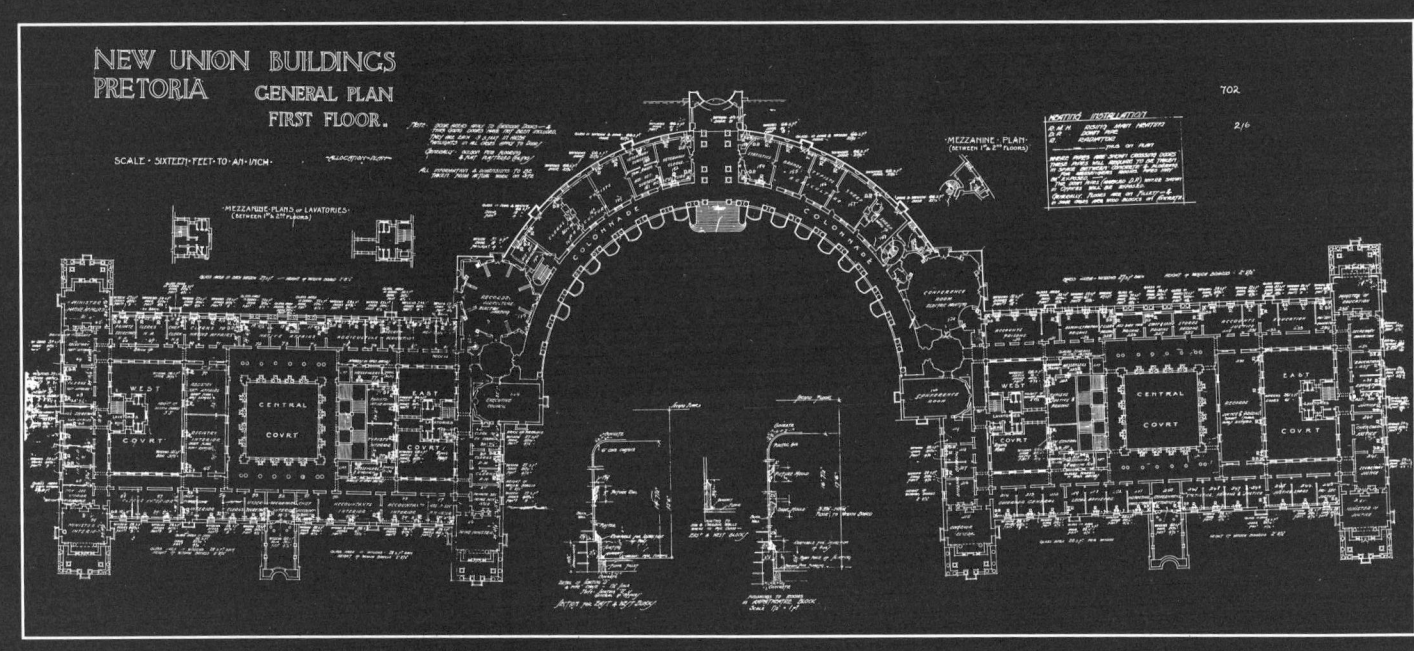

NEW UNION BUILDINGS
PRETORIA   GENERAL PLAN
FIRST FLOOR.

· SCALE · SIXTEEN·FEET·TO·AN·INCH ·

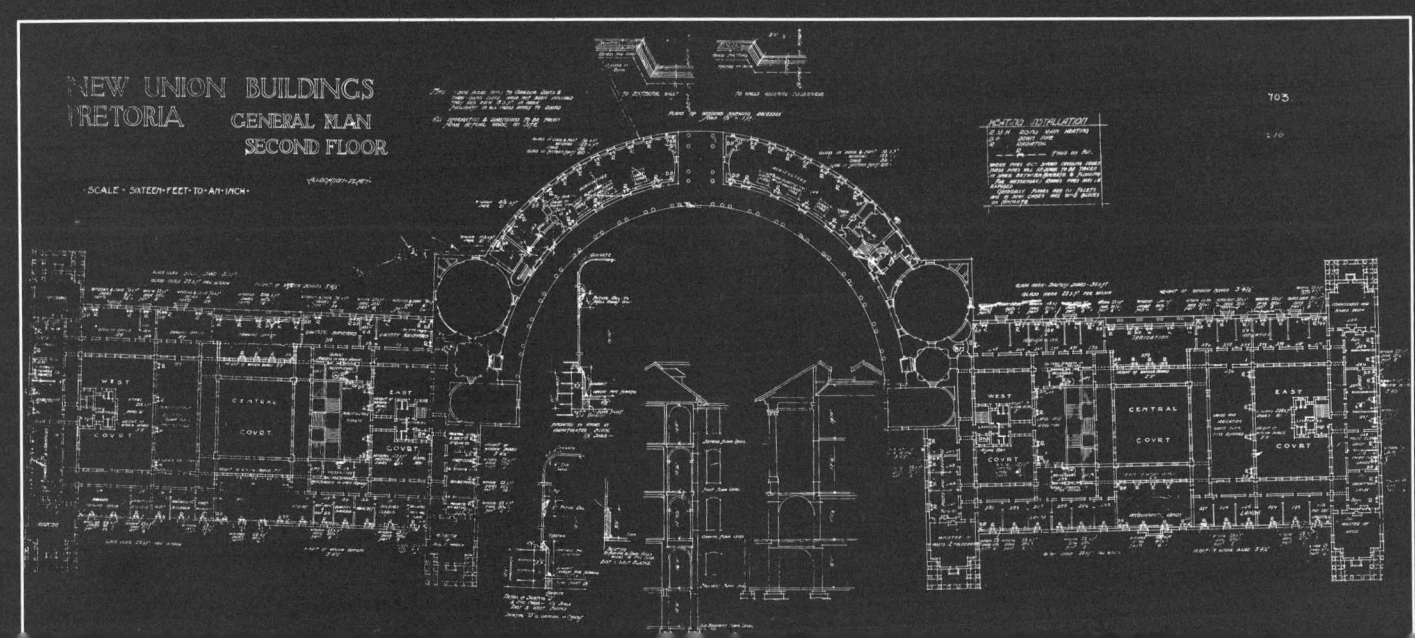

NEW UNION BUILDINGS
PRETORIA   GENERAL PLAN
SECOND FLOOR

· SCALE · SIXTEEN·FEET·TO·AN·INCH ·

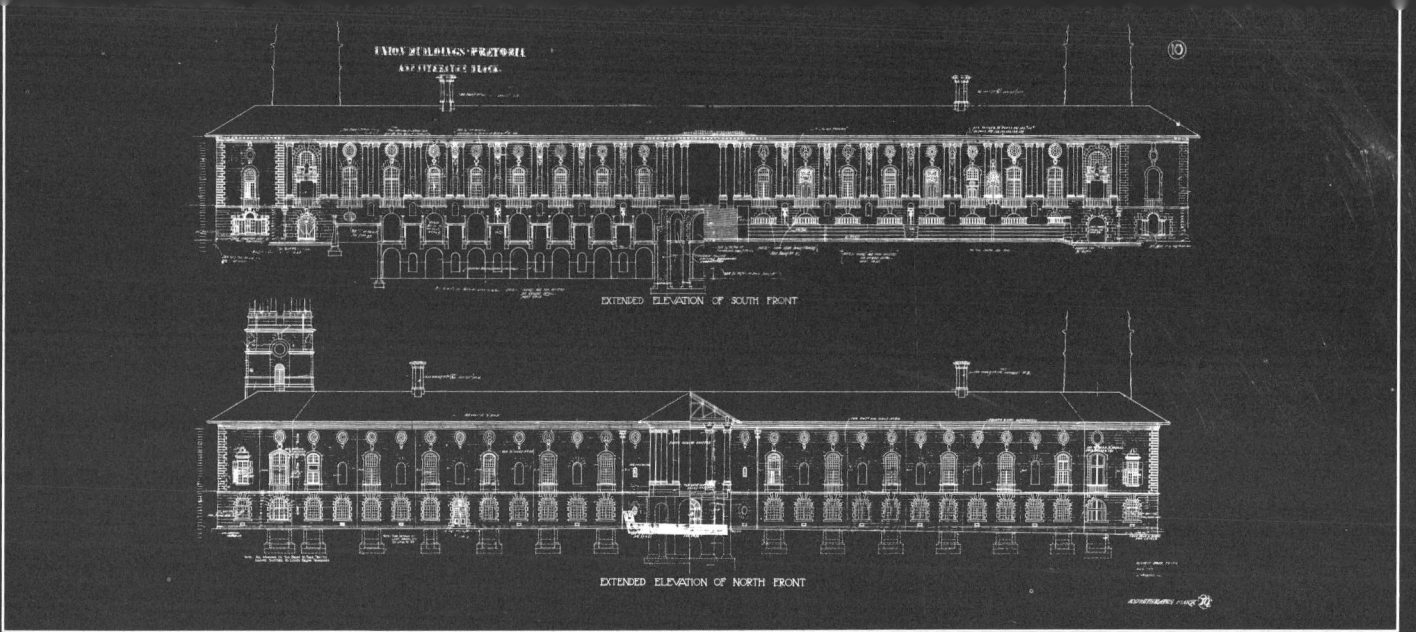

UNION BUILDINGS · PRETORIA
EAST CENTRAL BLOCK

EXTENDED ELEVATION OF SOUTH FRONT

EXTENDED ELEVATION OF NORTH FRONT

10

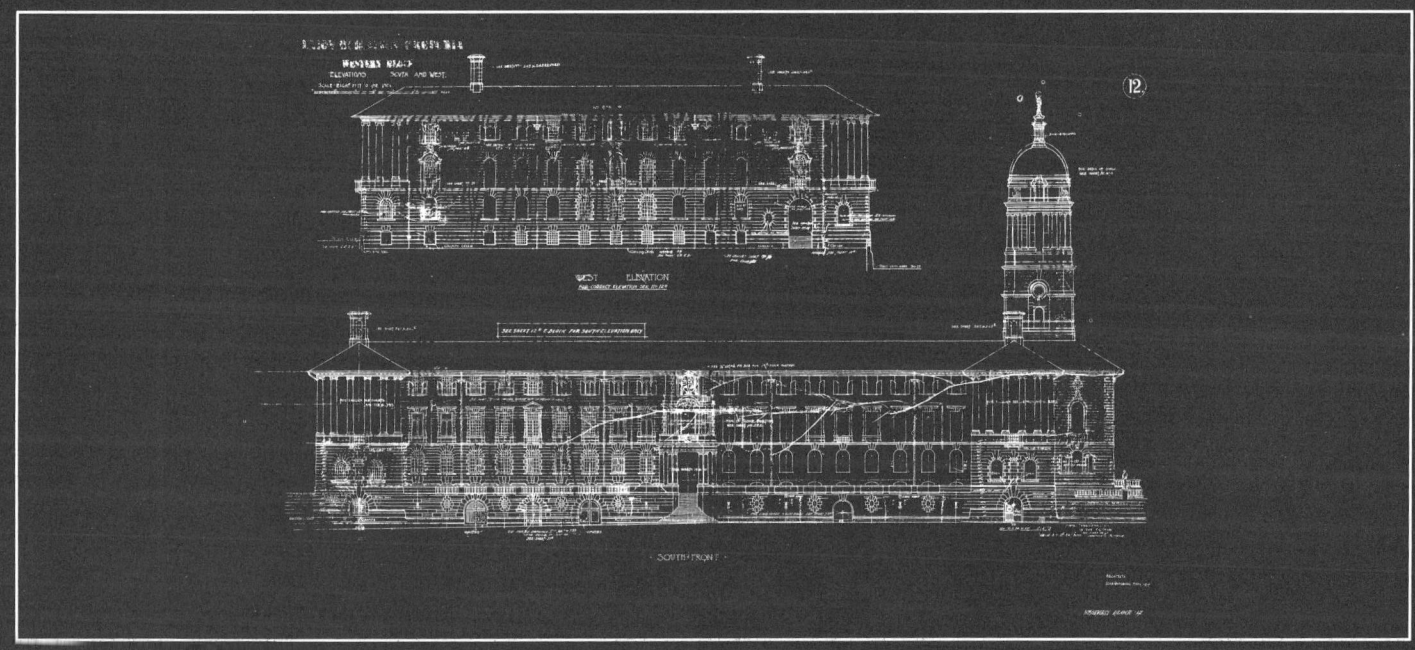

UNION BUILDINGS · PRETORIA
WESTERN BLOCK
ELEVATIONS · SOUTH AND WEST.

12.

WEST ELEVATION

SOUTH FRONT

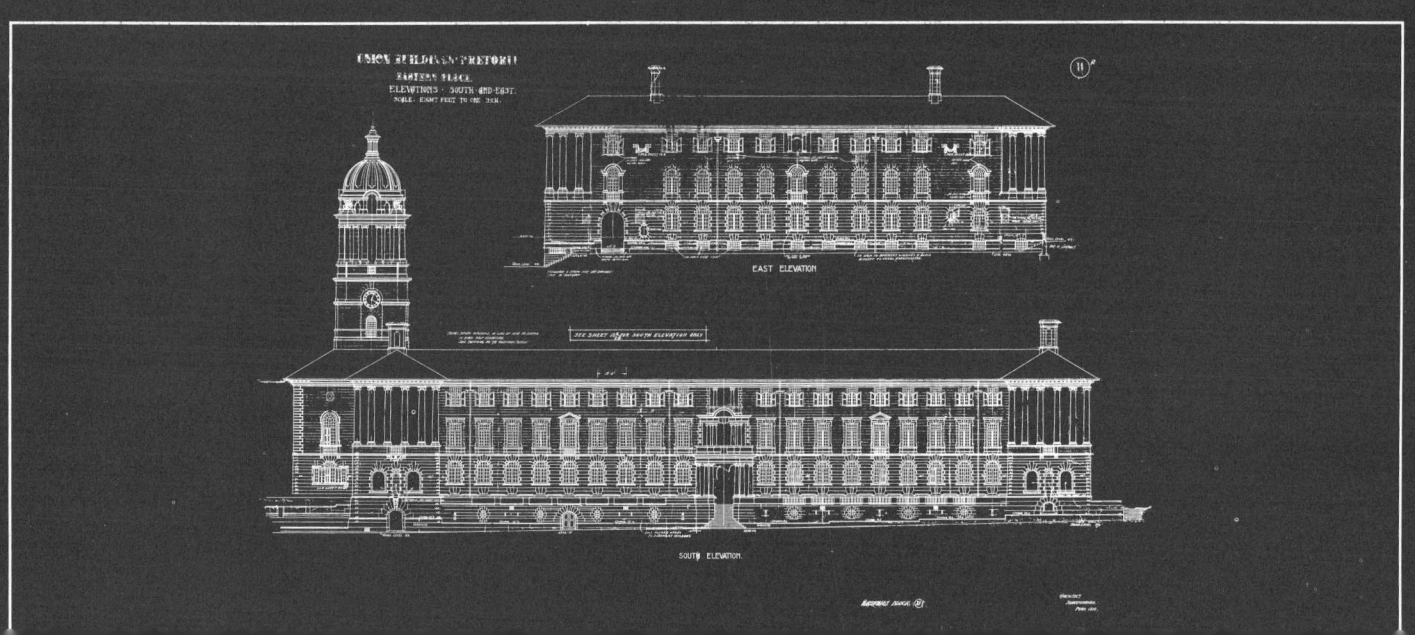

UNION BUILDINGS · PRETORIA
EASTERN BLOCK
ELEVATIONS · SOUTH AND EAST.
SCALE · EIGHT FEET TO ONE INCH.

11

EAST ELEVATION

SOUTH ELEVATION.

sonal relationship, were to hinge on the very point Baker now made to his friend and confidant: 'The dome would be seen from the town and valley but not from the terraces – but must there be no surprises in architecture? no hiding and then revealing? It all grew from that colonnade!'[46] Lutyens would have done well to have those words imprinted on his mind, for they were, in not unsimilar circumstances, to lead to one of the most celebrated disputes in architectural history: the design of the ramped approach to the Viceroy's House at New Delhi.[47] But, always at pains to throw in his own ideas, Lutyens writes, on 1 February 1910, 'I am rather fond of an entablature with the frieze omitted and the top member of the architrave becoming the lower member of the cornice', which he illustrated with a sketch.[48]

In a sense then, the form of Baker's Union Buildings group, as we know it, was evolved in series of happy accidents. Certainly the elevations of the large twin blocks, as originally conceived, bear a strong resemblance to Pretoria Station, with central, six-columned, recessed loggias beneath low-pitched tiled roofs, on which slender cupolas were positioned, each block terminated with projecting loggias.[49] On the central axis of the curved linking element was another small cupola, set above the small entrance indicated by the wider spacing of columns and tiny pediment at that point. The real climax of the composition was intended to be the 'Parliament' House, itself almost as large as the foreground blocks, and surmounted by a tall – rather than flat – dome on a relatively slender drum. This was intended as 'the emblem of the Capital and of Unity' with a Union Monument or 'Temple of Peace' on a point to the left.[50]

With such a climax above and beyond, the timidity of the focus in the linking element is understandable, although the group has an ungainly uneasiness about it. Then with the Parliament Building removed, the twin clock towers appear in order to give more weight to the centre of the group, but not on the axis itself, which lost its focus – of entrance and cupola – altogether. With the clock towers, the need for the smaller cupolas on the main flanking blocks fell away. Thus the end result is a design with a recessive and totally unimposing centre, and an axis which leads the eye to nowhere in particular.

But having gone through that process of change,

what is left is indeed a characteristically Baker composition. As at the Rhodes Memorial, even as at Sandhills and Stonehouse, and on many of his subsequent axial or symmetrical compositions, the centre is 'soft' and undemonstrative, giving more visual weight to the flanking elements than to the centre. At the Union Buildings the curved loggia which embraces the heart of the group, the so-called amphitheatre – a misnomer which seems to have become a part of South African English, and since which all outdoor theatres have become known – is its most memorable and endearing feature.[51]

The second major characteristic of Baker's Union Buildings is his use of projecting porticoes. No longer with the regularly spaced sturdy Tuscan columns of the earlier monuments: here they are Ionic, graceful and spaced with unexpected subtlety. Even on the south front of the building they reflect the northern sun and magically illuminate the porticoes, as if by curling rays of sunlight round their shafts. Baker revealingly described them as 'columned temples – they are hardly porticoes; loggias perhaps better describes them – leading out of the Ministers' rooms.'[52] His inspiration, he writes, was Rhodes's habit of telling men of narrow vision to look at The Mountain. 'So here, high above the city with its narrower interests, Ministers can lift their eyes up to the surrounding hills and the vanishing distances and splendours of the high veld, from which they may gather inspiration and visions of greatness.'[53]

Baker's concluding sentiment regarding the future role of the Union Buildings might best be seen in an address he gave at the Royal Institute of British Architects on 21 November 1927: 'The South African Dominion is yet young, and who knows what yet may come there? A capital expressing some great national, Greater-African, or Imperial ideal, or a Parliament House, when the centre of gravity moves northwards with the union or federation with the younger British Colonies which are growing up – realizing the dream of Cecil Rhodes – on the highlands of Central Africa from Rhodesia to Kenya and the source of the Nile.'[54] The language sounds strange to post-imperial ears, and the eventuality impossible in the terms expressed. Early in 1910, the year of the foundation of the Union of South Africa, construction began – an episode remarkable in itself.

CHAPTER ELEVEN

1910-1911

MASTERED DREAMS

STONEWALLING

In the final weeks of 1909, whilst events were fast gathering momentum for the Union Buildings, and construction had started on Pretoria Station, Baker saw the completion of two more churches. He had been in Cape Town, staying at Rust en Vrede, where no doubt the deteriorating relationship with Francis Masey was causing him concern, returning in time for the opening of the Pretoria Church of St Michael on 9 December.[1] Also, at Benoni, St Dunstan was nearing a final inspection. Walter Reid had asked him to comment on the 'architectural educational syllabus', to which he replied dwelling on its historical aspects. Baker's opinion was that the sections dealing with Asiatic architecture, and the difference between Scots and Irish architecture were likely to confuse students, who should concentrate on the mainstream of European history.[2]

Perhaps the Christmas season had given a moment's leisure to reflect and to indulge his love of literature. Somewhat surprisingly, for someone who declared his lack of enthusiasm for the theatre and his deficiency in the classics, he wrote requesting Gilbert Murray's translations of Greek plays from the Cape Town bookseller, Maskew Miller. But in translation they were a vital part of his cultural background; an extension of English literature and poetry itself, and something which perennially delighted him.[3]

Early in January 1910, the unhappy Francis Masey travelled to Rhodesia 'for some weeks.'[4] Ostensibly he was to report on the preservation of the Zimbabwe Ruins, which were being 'destroyed by tourists.' Baker had been asked by the Rhodesian Government to undertake the study the previous year but was far too busy to go himself and Masey

had gone in his stead. Baker also wished him to see about 'some other' work, but what that was is unclear.[5] No doubt Masey would have spied out the land with a view to starting a practice there, before returning to Cape Town at the end of the month. On his return Baker wrote to him in connection with the alterations to the Houses of Parliament, strongly expressing the view that he 'should certainly, without hesitation, build groins in concrete...', in a building of such importance.[6] News that the church at Creighton, in Natal, was to go ahead was welcomed, and Drummond Chaplin was making extensions to his Marienhof. On 15 February, the contract for the house designed in The Valley Road, for H G L Panchaud, to be named Blackroofs, was ready for signature.[7] And there was much else of a minor nature, matters which a year or two previously would have seemed of vital importance to the survival of the firm, but which were chicken-feed by comparison with the Union Buildings.

In February 1910, Sir Ernest George, now President of the Royal Institute of British Architects, and in whose London office Baker had once been a senior assistant, was prompted to write to General Botha. George's primary purpose was to say how thoroughly the action of the Transvaal Government was appreciated in the appointment of an 'exceptionally gifted' architect for the Union Buildings. '...I formed a high opinion of Herbert Baker as a young man. He has knowledge and experience with the fine sense of the artist', adding, 'Your Government's action is more likely to result in the production of a dignified and appropriate building than if a competition had been resorted to.'[8]

The remark seems slightly odd since George would have had no knowledge of such a possibility, unless he had been primed by Baker. And it does seem likely that Baker would have enlisted any

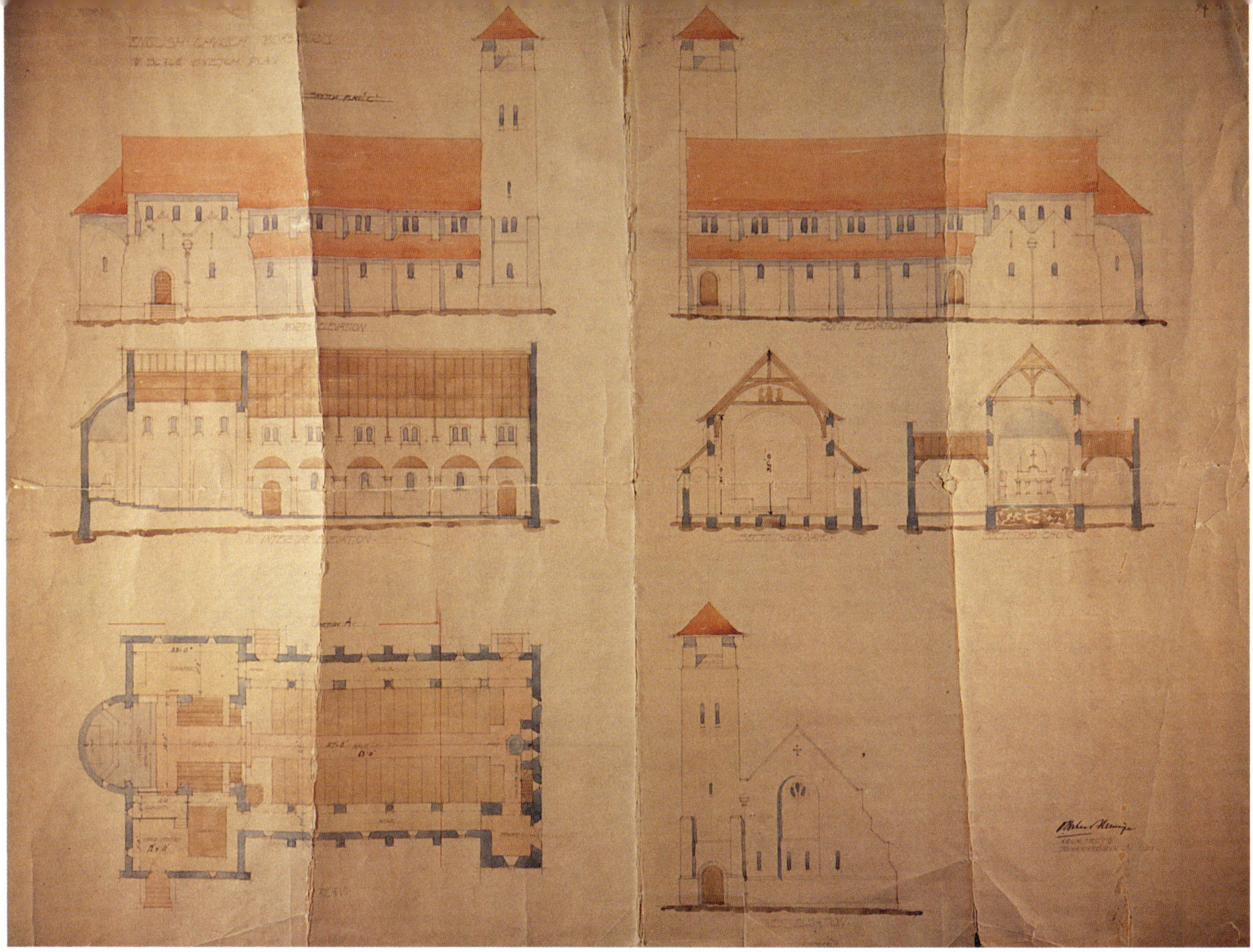

Top. *St Michael and All Angels, Boksburg. Elevations,
sections and plan. Bottom. St Michael and All Angels,
west front and tower.*

St Michael and All Angels, Boksburg, nave and font.

support he could, to avoid being involved in any way in a competition. Too much was at stake this time; an opportunity on this scale might never come his way again. It was virtually his and he did not want any intrusions. A repeat of the Station experience was the last thing he wanted. Besides, he might even have lost such a contest, and he knew all too well that the opposition were more keen to prevent him from gaining the appointment than to ensure that the right man got the job. Although Baker knew the stated intention of the Eagle and de Zwaan Report was to open up the whole question of siting and design, he must also have realized that a competition could be the only real alternative.

But George's letter of support was in any case too late to have any influence; it arrived after the east and west blocks had been put out to tender on 15 February. On 4 April Meischke's tender of £622 500 was accepted, and on 17 May that of Prentice and Mackie for the central colonnade was accepted at the sum of £256 224.[9] The contract was thus effectively in three sections. Charles Murray later explained that 'it was considered probable that no single Contractor could finance the whole...In some ways we would have had less trouble if Meischke had got the whole, but there was an advantage in having two Contractors, especially as they were not on good terms with each other and we were able to play off one against the other in questions of price, etc.'[10]

The agreement between Baker and the Public Works Department limited his responsibility to 'the designing and supervision of the architecture, as apart from all purely practical and business matters, such as the strength and quality of the

Church at Sabie, Eastern Transvaal.

materials. Notwithstanding...I was the first to warn the Government of the uncertainty in the quality of the stone', wrote Baker to the Minister in September 1911.[11]

The selection by the Government of the stone to be used was a thorn in Baker's side from the beginning. Since August 1909 Baker had repeatedly warned of the care needed in selecting a stone of exceptional quality. 'In the conversation I had with you on the 22nd instant', wrote Baker in the same letter, 'you implied that I was responsible for the quality of the stone...', and, 'After all that has passed between myself and the Government on this subject, I cannot understand how such a suggestion could have been made by you, and I must, therefore, put it on record again that I have no responsibility in the matter whatsoever...My letters to the Secretary ...will show what my position in the matter is, and I can only repeat that I do not accept any

responsibility for what has been done, and cannot allow any statement to pass which would seek to fix any responsibility on me.'[12]

Speaking at the RIBA on 21 November 1927, Baker describes the stone: 'The basement and ground floor of the buildings above the granite plinth are faced with a local light-coloured sandstone, which, when the work was some way advanced, was found to contain nodules of iron pyrites. Fearing discoloration and possible decay from this cause, the stone was changed above the ground floor. But after the test of 18 years our fears have fortunately not been justified, as the iron has caused no decay and has dyed the stones with an infinite variety of light tints of yellow and red amid the natural cream white of the stone, with only an occasional strong patch of brown green iron stain.'[13]

Baker's remarks cannot, however, be applied to many of the other stones which were thrust on him by the Department. In fact, an astonishingly wide variety of stones was used in the buildings and their adjuncts, making the complexities of their origins and subsequent failures and successes a subject in itself.[14] Baker's misgivings were justified for there have been notable and highly disappointing failures, and replacement continues to this day. In particular the 'Balmoral' from east of Pretoria, used for retaining walls in the amphitheatre, and lower down the site, has weathered badly. Neither the Orange Free State 'Steenpan', used for internal retaining walls, nor the 'Flatpan' of the amphitheatre parapet walls, have fared well.

Many of Baker's problems arose from the fact that he was not allowed to have any direct dealings with the contractors; all communication was to be through the Department. Inevitably this caused delays. 'If I were in sole charge of the building, I could often make a detail drawing in a day or two, and settle it direct with the Contractor; whereas, under the present system, weeks are taken preparing laborious inked-in drawings on linen...you will appreciate the time spent in their preparation.'[15] And to turn out the drawings required for this enormous undertaking, Baker had to mobilize all the architectural talent he could find, and his team included men borrowed from the Public Works Department.

For this work Baker's fees were basically three and a half per cent on the buildings and one three-quarters per cent on external works; but there were also various additional sums, amounting to something over £3 000, for alterations and revisions, for his town planning schemes, for furniture and fittings etc., and of course all his out-of-pocket expenses.[16]

After completion Charles Murray, the 'hard headed Aberdonian' Secretary of the Public Works Department, summarized the success of the building operation thus: 'I imagine it is pretty well a record for a building costing £958 000 to be finished within the Estimate and without a Lawsuit...it is also to the Contractors' credit that during the operations (at one time there were over 90 cranes at work on the building) there was only one fatal accident and a few of a minor character.'[17]

A tribute entitled 'The Union Buildings and their Architect' was written by J M Solomon in *The State*, July 1910. The article included the remark that Baker's work 'is now at its most equable level of good architecture, matured by considerable experience and study. This is evident both in the studied simplicity and quiet dignity of the Villa Arcadia now nearing completion in Parktown.'[18] The article evidently pleased Baker who sent copies to Willmott, who was still doing the odd favour, as a sort of 'London agent.'[19] Willmott replied with news of his own achievement; he had written a book on *The English Country House* which Baker wanted a copy of, insisting that he pay for it from his London account, and adding his hope that Willmott 'will have luck in selling Enstead', the Johannesburg home he had designed for himself in 1903.[20]

LUTYENS'S VISIT

Lutyens's visit 'originated with a telegram from Lady, then Mrs, Lionel Phillips that he had got in Rome in 1910, inviting him to design the Johannesburg Art Gallery', wrote Christopher Hussey in his *Life of Sir Edwin Lutyens*.[21] Hussey adds that 'a competition was held for its design among local architects. By the autumn of 1910 matters had progressed so far that [Sir Hugh] Lane went out to help judge the competition. When none of the designs proved satisfactory, it seems that Lane, with Baker's agreement, suggested calling in Lutyens, in view of his work with the Royal Commission on International Exhibitions and as the coming man in the eyes of many *cognoscenti*.'[22]

Edwin Lutyens arrived in Cape Town on 7 December 1910, to be welcomed by Baker with great warmth. After two days' sightseeing in Cape Town, discussing the University of Cape Town prospects and lunching with General Smuts, Lionel Phillips and Dr Malan at Parliament House, and calling on the Prime Minister and Mrs Botha at Groote Schuur, they took the train to Johannesburg.[23] There he was immediately introduced to Mrs Phillips at whose Villa Arcadia he was to stay. Lutyens was entranced by the land in all its variety, by its wonderful beauty and strangeness; by the black people, the Karoo he had travelled through, by the moon which he described as 'a revelation.' He found it hard to believe that only twenty-three years earlier, Johannesburg had been limitless veld. 'No wonder the Boers fought for their country', he wrote to his wife, Emily.[24] Although apprehensive about the official meetings he had to attend, he found that despite warnings – from Baker, one wonders – his 'silly innocent jokes' had been a great success.

But 'the town council etc. are all dead against Baker and they want to rope me in without Baker. This makes my position difficult – Baker is as good and generous as gold and I must be careful not to hurt him however advantageous to myself.'[25] Lutyens was horrified that a local newspaper should head a column on him 'A great architect.'[26] On 15 December he wrote that he had 'got sailing orders to go on with the design...I must get the designs inside before I go for the Gallery, its extensions, the laying out of Joubert Park and a bridge across the railway and connect the Union ground with it...' Lutyens remarked on how busy he was, on how he had 'offered to go over the whole town plan of Johannesburg!'[27]

He confidently listed the work he anticipated thus: '1. University, Cape Town; 2. Pretoria – layout; 3. Rand Regiments Memorial of the Park; 4. Art Gallery. Joubert's Park and Parade ground; 5. The great Church; 6. Mr Phillips's garden'.[28] Of these, only the Memorial, built in 1911, and the Gallery came to fruition, both supervised on his behalf by Baker. The Johannesburg Art Gallery was begun in 1912 and extended by Lutyens in 1929. It has recently been greatly enlarged by Willie Meyer in a bold but sympathetic post-modernist style. But Lutyens's idea of bridging the chasm of railway tracks to give some civic space in front of the gallery is, at least for the present, still a lost dream. On 26 December, after a hectic fortnight, Lutyens left Johannesburg for Cape Town on his homeward journey. In 1919 Lutyens went again to South Africa to report on designs for the University of Cape Town, a commission he had hoped for, but which had been given to J M Solomon, Baker's former assistant. Whilst in Cape town he stayed with Solomon at The Woolsack, which he found 'A nice little house', but, he added in what was by then his totally scornful and patronizing manner towards Baker, 'full of schoolboy errors, a sort of early me.'[29]

LAST SOUTH AFRICAN CHURCHES

In the East Rand mining town of Boksburg, Baker built St Michael and All Angels, one of the largest of his numerous churches.[30] The church has a Romanesque character, with small high, round-headed windows and a tall campanile, its tall-arched belfry topped with a pyramidal tiled roof. Both externally and within, the walls rise from a cruciform plan in a yellowish local freestone. Its

twenty-six foot wide nave leads to a narrower chancel, and terminates in a semi-circular vaulted apse. Seven king-post trusses spring from stone corbels to support the red tiled roof, which is ceiled below in dark boarding. Beneath the corbels are the supporting columns, alternately square and round, which articulate the bays and the side-aisles, and which, compared with Christ Church, Arcadia, are generously wide. A small double-gabled chapel projects southwards from the chancel crossing, as does the vestry to the north, giving the plan its overall cruciform shape.

Each bay of the arcaded nave is lit with high clerestory windows, which appear as pairs of narrow windows on the outside, but are set in single, wider-arched, openings internally. This apparent contradiction between inside and outside treatments, a typically Bakerish device, in fact serves to correct the scale appropriate to each respective face. The chancel is framed with strong semi-circular arches where, in the words of Dr Greig: 'The interior displays a high degree of beauty and drama in the inspired handling of the heavy chancel timbers, the crucifix under a triumphal arch, and behind a raised altar, in the reredos composed of glowing mosaic figures which are framed in the three centre arches of the apsidal arcade.'[31]

The west wall of the nave is pierced with a small, clear glazed, rose window set between internal buttresses which are joined by a low arch to form a font recess. On the outside this stone-traceried window appears too small for the vast west gable wall, made larger still by being placed flush with the tower, at the foot of which is the entrance to the church. The expanse of vigorous, dark-jointed, stone walling is relieved by a shallow – again arched – recess which rises to full height, to curve around the rose window, thus giving modelling to an otherwise bleak but powerful front and reflecting the buttressing within.

In this Transvaal Arts and Crafts-cum-Romanesque style Baker concocted for St Michael, there are, enlarged and elaborated, the same basic elements he first deployed in the design of St Andrew in the Oaks at Newlands. The church recalls, too, the Germiston church, which, though brick-faced internally, has several common characteristics, such as the brick chancel and relationship of the tall stone campanile to the gabled west end and in its overall planning and massing.

The first Anglican church at Fort Salisbury was little more than a hut, built in 1891 by Canon Bal-

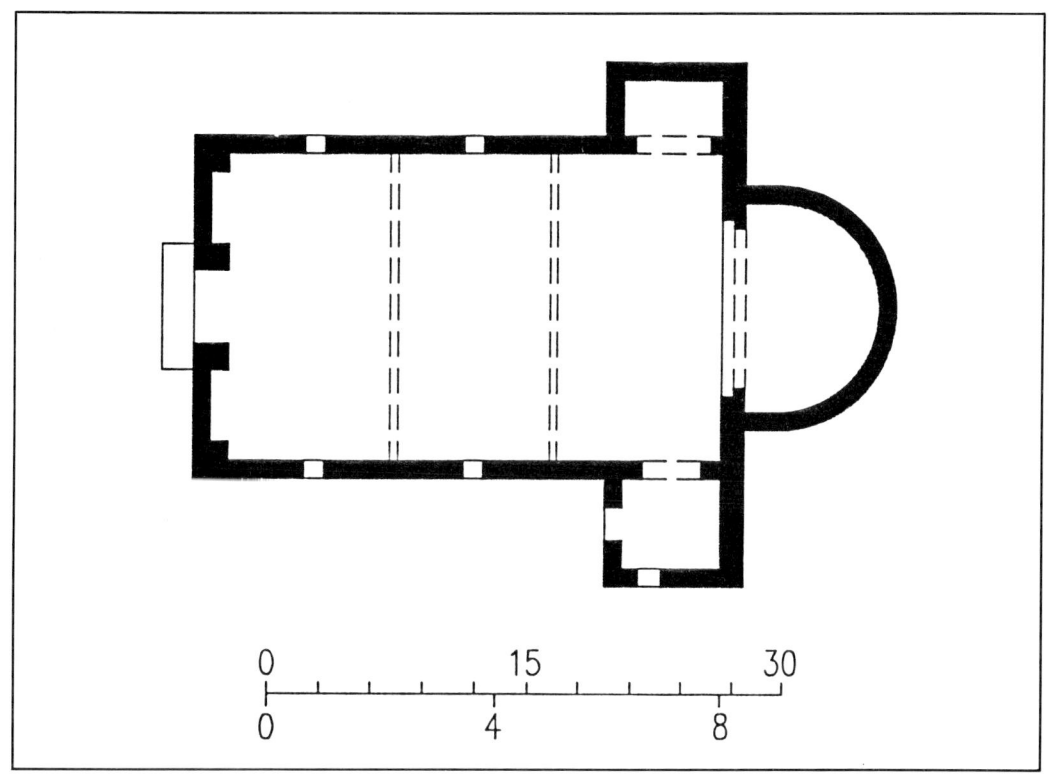

Top. *Church at Sabie, Eastern Transvaal, redrawn plan.*
Bottom. *Church at Sabie, tower.*

four. In the following year a Pro-Cathedral was begun, receiving an iron nave in 1898 and extended in 1911. Francis Masey, who since his break with Baker in 1910 had been practising on his own in Salisbury (now Harare), was approached to design a new permanent cathedral church.[32]

At the time of their dissolution agreement, Baker recorded on 20 March 1911, 'concessions' had been made in Masey's favour in respect of Rhodesia, '...in order that you should have a free hand in devoting yourself to that country, in return for which...it was certainly understood that Kendall, with my help, should work in the Cape Colony. At all events, it could never have entered our heads to have made an agreement in the other direction... favouring your interest in the Cape Colony. However, I think this unprofitable discussion had better close.'[33]

The circumstances in which Baker, who had refused ever again to work with his former partner, ousted Masey are somewhat vague. However, there is a letter which Baker wrote to E A von Hirschberg, dated 10 May 1911, thanking his 'Committee for their kindness in requesting me to undertake this work. I should like to think over the matter a little before writing to you officially, and I ought also to explain the circumstances to Mr Masey before accepting the work. In the meantime', Baker adds, 'would you kindly send me pictures, or photos, of the Cathedral at Nagpur?...'[34] This was the last straw for Masey, who appears to have initiated a lawsuit against the Cathedral Committee in 1911 on account of their rejection of him in favour of Baker.[35] Once more Baker prevailed and the defeated Masey died of pneumonia two months later at the age of fifty-one.

Baker's design for the Salisbury Cathedral was in his characteristic Romanesque style with round-headed windows and arches, half-round apse and a detached campanile, a tall tapering cylinder topped with a conical roof, on the apex of which was a cross. The tower, with its obvious reference to the Zimbabwe Ruins, was felt to resemble a lighthouse, and the idea was abandoned. Baker built a first phase consisting, as usual, of the building's east end; a choir, sanctuary and side chapels, with a temporary nave taken from the Pro-Cathedral. These were built in a rather drab grey granite and roofed with red tiles. Round-arched barrel vaulting covers the nave, with a shallow concrete dome on pendentives over the crossing; the strong semi-circular stone arches springing from cruciform columns are redolent of his St Albans in Pretoria. The foundation stone was laid on 23 April 1913 and Baker's contribution was completed in 1914 after he had left South Africa for India. Further phases were built in 1934, 1947 and 1950.

One of the last parish churches Baker designed in South Africa was that of St Peter at Sabie, in the old prospecting region of the Eastern Transvaal. St Peter is a small church, cruciform in plan, with an aisleless nave, twenty-foot wide, divided by two timber trusses into three bays. Each truss consists of two rafters which rest upon stone corbels and the shingled roof is ceiled with dark boarding. The walls of the church are of a local mountain stone, plastered internally and pierced by round-headed openings. More Arts and Crafts than Romanesque, is the square tower over the vestry, with its horizontal, slot-like openings beneath the wide eaves of its low-pitched pyramidal roof, reminding one more of a watch-tower or blockhouse than a campanile. The round apse containing the altar is framed by a stone chancel arch which rests on white walls up to its springing level. As in so many of Baker's early churches it is, awkwardly, not quite pointed, and not quite semi-circular.[36]

RHODES UNIVERSITY COLLEGE

Apart from parts of the South African College in Cape Town, Baker's only university work in South Africa was in Grahamstown. Rhodes University College was endowed by Cecil Rhodes and received its charter in 1904, becoming a fully independent university in 1951. In another book concerning Grahamstown history, R F Currey relates that Baker first approached the College Council seeking 'authority to draw plans for a university...'[37] The Council's reply was to hold an architectural competition 'with prizes of £200, £150 and £100, for plans of the Rhodes of the future.'[38]

Currey writes: 'When the sealed envelopes containing the names of the competitors were opened it was found that the plan which had been awarded the first prize was that submitted by Baker and Kendall.'[39] Although in Kendall's 'territory', and although Kendall appears to have been chiefly responsible for the design and wanted to do the work, Baker retained the production of the firm's entry in the competition in Johannesburg, where it was drawn up in October 1910, by 'Gibson and two others [who] are now hard at work on the plan. It is coming out very well, and I really think it would be the best thing for you, and the best chance of getting the job, if you let them complete it.'[40] On that point Baker was triumphantly right and there were bonuses for all concerned when the result of the competition was announced. Baker wrote to congratulate Kendall on winning on 6 February 1911.[41]

But the competition had an unpleasant sequel for one of the team, Gordon Leith, who appears to have made an unfortunate remark, eliciting the immediate response: 'Until you apologise for the disgraceful insinuation you made today against Mr Baker's honour, we must ask you not to come to the office again. We enclose a cheque for your salary this month, and a further cheque of £10.0.0, being your share of the bonus distributed on account of the firm's success in winning the Grahamstown Competition.' A fortnight later, on 13 March 1911, a blunt letter and 'a book from Lutyens' was sent to Leith at an address in Doornfontein.[42] No doubt the young Gordon Leith relented, for he was to become one of Baker's most valuable and respected assistants and the first recipient of the Herbert Baker Scholarship, founded by Baker in 1912.

Rhodes University, Grahamstown, perspective drawing.

Union Club, Plein Street, Johannesburg, perspective drawing.

Top left. *Glenshiel, for Col W Dalrymple in Westcliff, Johannesburg. North-east wing of the 'butterfly'. Top right. Glenshiel, twin Doric columns supporting the double-height loggia. Bottom. Glenshiel, triple-arched loggia and attic dormer windows.*

Glenshiel, Westcliff, Johannesburg, entrance hall.

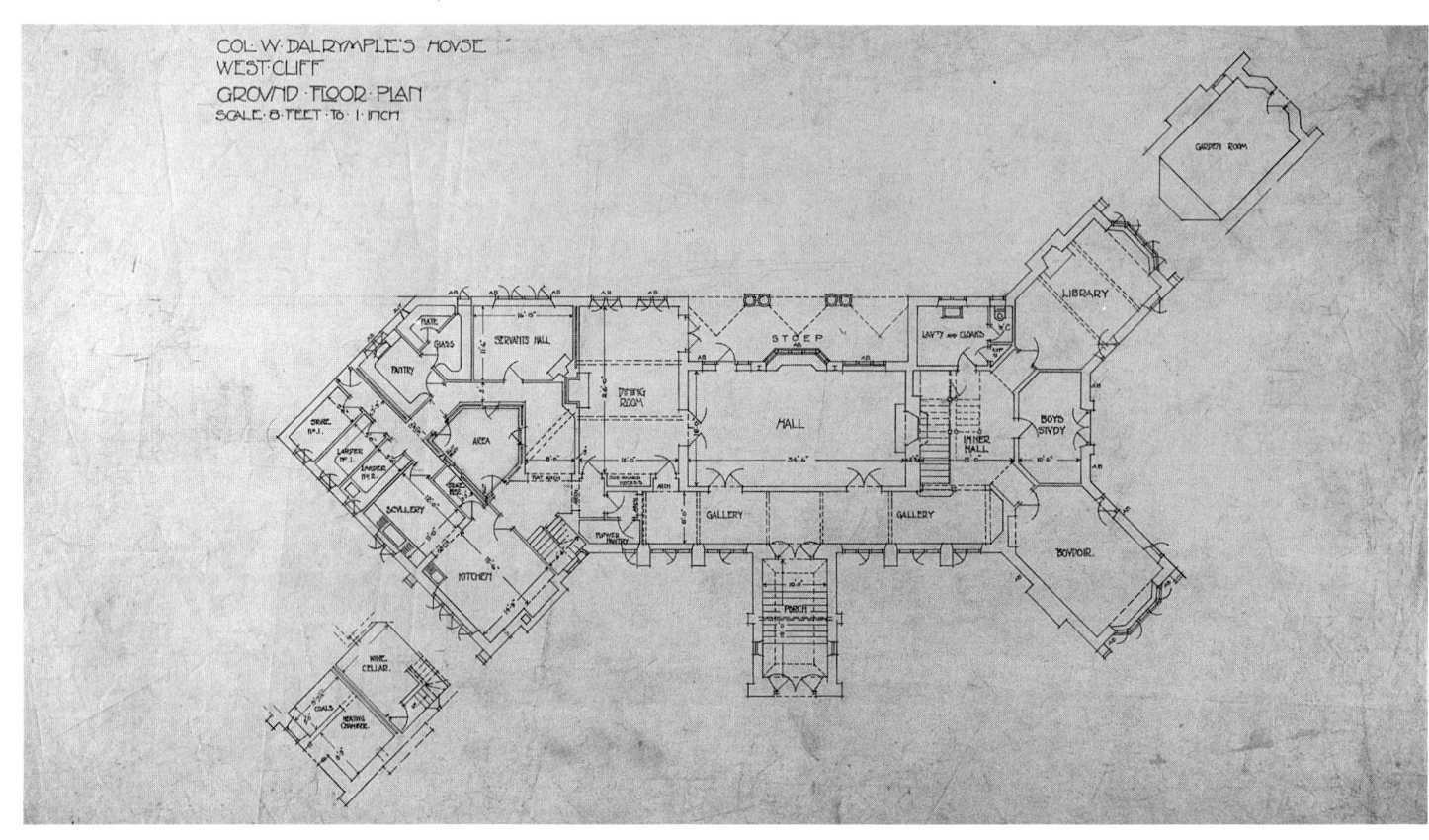

Top. *Glenshiel, Westcliff, Johannesburg, ground floor plan,*
1910. Bottom. Glenshiel, elevations, 1910.

The Rhodes University scheme was first published in *The African Architect* in September 1911.[43] It was a splendid design of great individuality, characterized by its use of the hard local sandstone, a blue-grey quartzite such as had been used for the Grahamstown Cathedral by Sir Gilbert and his son John Oldrid Scott; a contrasting lighter stone from Bathurst was to have been used for columns, balconies and dressings. Alas, in order to effect savings in cost the building, much depleted in character, was constructed in plastered brick on a more refined ground floor base of stone. Nevertheless, the design as built makes a fine contribution to the townscape of this small university town. The central tower over the entrance to what is now called the Old Arts Block, on the axis of the Cathedral at the opposite end of the High Street, creates a satisfying vista.

LAST HOUSES

Baker's domestic architecture of his last years in South Africa occurred mainly in the Parktown and Westcliff areas of Johannesburg. The houses are generally on a modified H-plan. A modification of a different kind was made for Glenshiel, one of Baker's larger houses, designed for Colonel (later Sir) William Dalrymple in June 1910 and completed in May the following year. Here the plan has splayed the legs of the H and formed a butterfly-wing pattern on three corners. Twin Doric columns support the arcade of the double-height loggia, over which three dormers form an attic (third) storey. The rusticated ground floor is faced in stone, as is the unusual two-storey, projecting, entrance wing which thrusts toward the visitor, barring his way with large forbidding doors in an arched opening. The shingled roof is hipped at every end, with a massive volume, containing the dormers, in the connecting 'body' of the butterfly. The eaves are tilted upwards, shading the plastered walls of the first-floor level.[44]

Later in the year Baker and Fleming's assistant, J M Solomon, did a particularly fine set of drawings for Kleine Schuur, in Rhodes Avenue, a much smaller house designed for Dennis Santry. The stone-walled house was roofed in a single square, with hipped ends, from which emerged symmetrical brick chimneys and hipped dormers. Beneath this simple roof-form was an H-shaped, south-facing plan, with recessed stoeps in the characteristic Baker manner. Baker's partner Frank Fleming altered the house in 1935.[45]

H G L Panchaud's house, Blackroofs, in The Valley Road, was designed on a basic north-facing H-plan. Faced externally in stone with a steeply-pitched hipped roof, covered in wood shingles, with dormer windows and symmetrical brick chimneys, it bears a likeness to Kleine Schuur and the more rambling St Margarets, near Stonehouse, in Rockridge Road. Earnholme, also in The Valley Road, was similar in character and materials.[46]

CHAPTER TWELVE

1912-1913

FROM PRETORIA TO NEW DELHI

OVERTURE

It was in February 1912 that Edwin Lutyens first told Baker: 'I believe I am fixed up for Delhi...As regards the building, who does it, they won't commit themselves. There will be more than one man can do...Oh what fun if we could come together on it.'[1] Lutyens first sailed for India on 1 April as one of a 'Commission of Experts...to advise the Government of India as to the site of the new capital and the laying out of the same.'[2] In the fortnight before travelling Lutyens hurriedly cleared up his commitments. Writing to Baker, he remarked: 'Sending perspectives of Johannesburg. Hope we shall meet in Delhi some day.'[3]

But Baker's assumption was still that it was Lutyens who would design the buildings, and he wrote speedily to: 'My dear Conqueror of 3/4 of the Universe...full of the hugeness of my congratulations.' And: 'It is really a great event in the history of the world and of architecture, – that rulers should have the strength and sense to do the right thing. It would only be possible now under a despotism – some day perhaps democracies will follow...I wonder what you will do – whether you will drop the language and classical tradition and just go for surfaces – sun and shadow. It must not be Indian, nor English, nor Roman, but it must be Imperial. In 2 000 years there must be an Imperial Lutyens tradition in Indian architecture, as there now clings a memory of Alexander...Hurrah for despotism! On the day you sail you should feel like Alexander when he crossed the Hellespont to conquer Asia.'[4] Baker would now take the opportunity to outline his own ideas about a style for New Delhi, and now had to wait and see what would turn up. In the meantime, and until he heard more than just a faint wish from Lutyens, Baker had his own imperialism to pursue.

ST ANDREW'S COLLEGE CHAPEL

The new chapel for St Andrew's College, Grahamstown, had been designed by the local architect W White-Cooper in a red brick neo-Gothic style, and a foundation stone had been laid in 1905. Lack of funds had prevented further progress on this relatively expensive design.

The story goes that Baker, who happened to be passing through Grahamstown early in 1912, was lunching with the Headmaster, Canon P W H Kettlewell, when he was invited to look over White-Cooper's plans. R F Currey, in his history of the College, writes that Baker gladly consented to do so, and that: 'One glance at them was sufficient to show Baker that every line of the projected building was a denial of his whole architectural credo', which not surprisingly was duly expounded for Kettlewell's benefit. 'There and then Baker sketched out in pencil the Chapel he wanted St Andrew's to build', converting Kettlewell instantly to a stone design in his Romanesque style, inspired more by the south of Europe than the north.[5] The Cape Town office under Kendall was duly commissioned to carry out the work, along with a block of two classrooms, a large dormitory, the Principal's study, Bursar's office, book-room, a changing room, and art room. There were also studies for twenty-four boys, living quarters for two masters and the cricket professional. The block was later to be named Merriman House.[6]

The chapel was built in a local fine-grained quartzite on a cruciform plan[7], with a high aisled nave of six bays under an open timber roof covered in tiles. At the west end the buttressed wall is topped by a narrow bell-gable such as had been built for the Westminster Estate schoolhouse and at Randfontein. The heavy buttresses enclose a projecting baptistry, over which is a large window. At the opposite end is a splayed apse, arcaded and vaulted in concrete, with buttressed walls and small traceried windows. When tenders were called for, it was found that reductions needed to be made and 'in a bad moment' it was decided that 'the height of the proposed Chapel be reduced, the interior be lined with brick, and the vestries, porches, and side-aisles curtailed.' These were lamentable decisions, writes Currey, 'and it is not possible to look at the truncated arches in the nave today without a pang of regret.'[8] Fortunately it was later decided to build the chapel in stone throughout. The War Memorial tower, which now stands sympathetically detached and in matching stone in front of Baker's apse, was built by Kendall and Morris in 1926.

In the Transvaal the flow of commissions for new houses was incessant. In July 1912 the design of Byeways, in Torwood Road, Forest Town, was completed for R A Lehfeldt. Byeways was shingle-roofed, with dormers and splayed chimneys finished in plaster. The house was built on a less typical T-shaped plan, its double-storeyed walls of mountain stone and rough-cast plaster, and fronted with a stoep and pergola carried on Tuscan columns: the Baker formula in one of its countless variations.[9] Eclecticism, if you like, but beautiful and enduring. Dr Greig comments that the eclecticism of the Transvaal houses is 'neither Cape Dutch, English nor Italian; it is Baker's own...They were the first original contributions to domestic architecture in South Africa since the days of the Cape Dutch builders.'[10]

Standing outside the mainstream of his Transvaal work, and harking back to his first years at the Cape, Baker, with Fleming, built his last important house before leaving South Africa. Many years later he was to design Noordhoek for Sir Drummond Chaplin, but that was by mail order, as it were. At Rietbult, near Balfour in the south-eastern Transvaal, he designed a white gabled farmhouse, complete with harmonizing whitewashed outbuildings, for the Mostert family. The house was designed on high ground with terraced gardens and fine views over surrounding farming country. In a most curious way Baker had finally come full circle, as he wrote: 'I built a country house in which I was able to embody many of the characteristic features

of his [Mostert's] ancestral homestead on the Groote Schuur estate.'[11]

Years earlier Baker had rebuilt the former Mostert home, Welgelegen, for Cecil Rhodes. Notwithstanding the understandable preference of his client for a whitewashed farmhouse in the Cape Dutch style, which Baker appears to have relished providing with some degree of purity in the main house, he still managed to compromise in details of the accompanying cottage on the Rietbult farm. His English Arts and Crafts vocabulary speaks out in the hipped dormers in the red-tiled roofs, covering doors onto balconies linked to the shuttered sash windows of the floor below, and in the great chimney piece.

TIME FOR CHANGE

On Sunday, 9 June 1912, Herbert Baker celebrated his fiftieth birthday. Nearly a month later, on Friday, 5 July, the Rhodes Memorial was finally inaugurated, although it had, to all intents and purposes, been structurally completed in 1908.[12] 'Although the Union cabinet was conspicuous by its absence', write Rennie and Langham-Carter, 'the Afrikaans population was well represented by the mayors of Laingsburg, Paarl, Tulbach, Worcester and several other towns.' After a long and impressive speech Lord Grey unveiled the bust of Rhodes and many hundreds of Cape doves were released from cages on the roof to circle in the sky while, led by an African choir, the gathering sang 'God Save the King'.[13]

Baker had laboured for twenty years in South Africa and was tired and in need of a long rest. With his work on the Union Buildings virtually over, although construction was not finally completed until November 1913, he felt able to take one. In a letter to Edwin Lutyens he expressed a feeling of anticlimax: 'All seems dead now...I have lived through three great periods here – the Rhodes, the War and Milner. Botha has no courage left.'[14]

However, the thought of collaborating with Lutyens at New Delhi was kept alive by what Baker called 'hints', apparently from sources other than Lutyens's enthusiastic letters, and unknown to Lutyens himself. 'I knew that on the strength of my Pretoria buildings my appointment had been recommended by Lord Hardinge, but on great pressure from home, he, rightly, appointed Lutyens. When he was out there, however, the

Viceroy decided that Lutyens must have a collaborator, and then I also was appointed.'[15]

On 3 October 1912, *The Times* published a lengthy and eloquent article written by Baker regarding the building of the New Delhi. Entitled 'The problem of style', the piece was reprinted in his autobiography, noting that it was 'written before the architects were appointed.' If the letter was motivated by a desire to support what he believed to be Lutyens's point of view, it was surely also calculated to enhance his own prospects of being appointed. This reality came about some four months later. In the article Baker argued for a new style of architecture, '...a blend of the best elements of East and West.' Baker relates that he advocated that there should be no direct imitation of Indian styles of building, nor the following of any orthodox classical period. The aim should rather be, he contended, 'to build according to the great elemental qualities and traditions, which have become classical, of the architecture of Greece and Rome, which grew out of the needs of a southern climate; and to graft thereon structural features of the architecture of India as well as decoration expressing the myths, symbols, and history of its people.'[16]

But *The Times* letter, ostensibly intended to support Lutyens's own contentions, nevertheless took him by surprise; nervous as he was of the repercussions it might have on sensitive ears in India and Whitehall. Lutyens, wrote Hussey, was 'assiduously avoiding any public expression of opinion and did not entirely welcome this sudden antiphon from South Africa. It was one thing to further Baker's claims as an accompanist; another when the accompanist treated himself to a prolonged prelude on the soloist's instrument.'[17] Lutyens now had to act to regain the initiative, especially as there was still a possibility of a competition. Lutyens cabled Baker, who, on 29 October wired back that he would 'willingly co-operate subject difficulties explained my previous letter.' These were that he still did not want to be parted from his family, nor would he consent to being a sort of junior partner to do the 'hot work.'[18]

Baker revealingly added: 'I shall find it difficult to collaborate with you. You the quicker and I the older. You rather heartless in ignoring the human side of clients, I too tender-hearted perhaps. But we agree so in principle, and if our spheres could be separate, with general co-operation, I think our work together would be for the good of the job.' Baker suggested they meet in India to agree on their spheres of influence, then, 'You go North, I South, to work out the building of our spheres.'[19]

With that possibility in mind, writes Baker: 'I went home in the autumn, and on to Italy to refresh my memory at the home of the Mother of the Arts.'[20] In the last week of November 1912 Baker left for England and Italy, expecting to be away for about three months, but as ever, his absence was extended and he was not back in Johannesburg until about 7 May 1913.[21] But in that six-month absence events that would change his life, and the lives of all with whom he was associated, were to take place in London. It was whilst he was in Rome that he received a telegram from the India Office, asking whether he would collaborate with Lutyens. It is probably no coincidence that in December, during his absence, his Johannesburg office prepared for their own refresher course in classicism, ordering from Batsfords in London, W J Anderson's *Architecture of the Renaissance in Italy*, and both Banister Fletcher's history and Simpson's three-volume history of architecture.[22]

Baker was summoned for interview by the Under-Secretary of State at the India Office in Whitehall on 17 January 1913. Baker recollected that he had 'some hesitation and qualms of conscience in the foreknowledge that my acceptance would mean forsaking a trust and allegiance to South Africa, then the happy home of my wife and three sons. South Africa had welcomed and given me of its riches in full measure; and the interests of her art I felt to be a trust imposed on me by the spirit of Rhodes.' Baker went therefore 'with conscience a little pulling against the glamour of the great Imperial Quest. But conscience weakened as I waited in that great room hung with portraits, and stood gazing upon the face of Warren Hastings, vigilant, enduring, and not unacquainted with grief. Who could think of difficulties in his presence! And any lingering irresolution was at once dispelled by the charm of Sir Thomas Holderness, and by the kindness of Lord Crewe.'[23] Baker was officially appointed by Lord Crewe on 22 January 1913. From England he sailed for India, on his 'second Great Quest', aboard the steamship *Egypt* three days later, arriving at Bombay on 7 February. At Bombay Baker was met by Lutyens, as he had met Lutyens at Cape Town two years earlier.[24]

On 21 March the two architects left Delhi to return to London, where their contract was drafted and considered at the India Office, and by 7 May Baker had returned to Johannesburg. Three weeks

South African Institute for Medical Research, Hospital Street,
Johannesburg, front.

Left. South African Institute for Medical Research,
Johannesburg, south side. Right. South African Institute for
Medical Research, tower.

later, his partner Frank Fleming, on whom he was going to rely heavily in the months to come, sailed for England from Cape Town for a well-deserved holiday.[25]

CLASSICAL INSTITUTIONS

After Pretoria Station and the Union Buildings, Baker's third most important public building was the South African Institute for Medical Research, established primarily for the investigation of miners' diseases. The design, with which he was greatly assisted by Fleming, was completed early in 1913, whilst Baker was overseas. Like its predecessors it is in the classical style which marked his final years in South Africa.

The Medical Institute is planned around a series of three quadrangles, the first of which is open to the garden approach from the east and is enticingly seen through a screen of paired Doric columns over which is a graceful dome in which the water tanks are ingeniously housed. The approach has a 'soft' Baker centre, flanked by columned porticoes, relating it formally to the Union Buildings and the Rhodes Memorial. Greig remarks that 'However strange it may seem, the "English Renaissance" plan functions adequately here in a building devoted to scientific research and administration. In this elegant, gleaming white Renaissance building which for Baker, was of an unusually homogeneous nature unlike any of his earlier public or private buildings, we see a further extension of the change in his architecture which began at the Villa Arcadia with the use of Italian forms. Now the vernacular element has disappeared altogether...a revelation of a latent talent in the handling of a classical theme.'[26]

Greig sees, too, the 'undoubted' influence of Lutyens's Nashdom, built in Buckinghamshire in 1909, in the long side elevation facing De Korte Street. Like Nashdom, the Institute was constructed in white plastered brickwork, possibly in reaction to the problems Baker was experiencing with building-stones at the Union Buildings, at the time it was designed. Also in the grounds of the Institute is the Director's House, designed in an appropriately subdued Italianate style sympathetic to the main building. The double-storey, iron-roofed house, built on an H-shaped plan and finished in white plaster, is entered from the south through the gardens and onto a columned portico.

The Union Club was one of Baker and Fleming's last important works in South Africa and following the Rand Club, designed by Emley in 1898, the second important club to be built in Johannesburg and one of the city's most successful central buildings. Standing on the corner of Bree and Joubert Streets, the building today strikes a forlorn note. Now in a part of the city long past its heyday, the building has been spoiled by the insensitive stack of additional floors and a flat roof.

But the strength of the ground floor rustication, and the massive quoins, like plumped cushions, still prevails over the bric-à-brac of modern advertising. Where once Baker's strongly modillioned cornice and a steeply pitched tiled roof, with dormer windows and tall chimneys tied the composition together, the eye now slides off the bland walling to the sky without hiatus. The plastered brick exterior is still set off by the fine-grained Elands River stone of the Italianate quoins. By arranging the openings in sets of three and accenting the central group with semi-venetian windows and balconies, or the tall columned portico facing Bree Street, Baker established strong rhythmical effects. It is Baker in his best Cape-Palladian style, which in the England of that time would have been described as Queen Anne.

Perhaps the most beautiful feature of the building was the marble-lined internal court, forty-six foot square around a central pool, and surrounded by three floors of access arcades, supported by Doric and Ionic columns, redolent of the Rhodes Building in Cape Town or the Union Buildings. Within the building was a wide groined staircase, a panelled dining-room with a wide barrel-vaulted ceiling, intersected by smaller vaults which ran into the arched openings, and President's Rooms opening on to a loggia. Greig observes that: 'Its grace derived from good proportions, elegant vaulting, such details as fanlights carved by Benjamin Smith, wrought iron balustrades by Ness and the use of forms suitable for the climate...It is in scale, a most happy compromise between such intimate clubs as the old Arts Club in Dover Street, Picadilly, and those of Pall Mall.'[27]

FINAL DEPARTURE

During the months of correspondence with Lutyens over the designs for Delhi, Baker's youngest son Alfred was born on 14 August 1913 and baptized two days later by Bishop Michael Furse, in St

George's Church, Parktown.[28] Lutyens had expressed the wish to be godfather to the child in a letter, dated 22 August, largely devoted to arguing detail points of design in terms of politics and sentiment, so dear to Baker but which 'frightened' Lutyens.[29] Baker's letter to Lutyens of 26 September was seminal to their differences of which Baker was so aware and so often expressed through the years:

'My dear colleague who can write so nicely. I like your being outspoken – when it helps the cause. But don't when fighting an enemy, and when annoyed, turn and rend your friend. I by taking a rather less obdurate attitude, and recognizing the standpoint of sentiment and politics, can help fight the arch – the devilish ones – best. You must recognize the political standpoint in a political capital, or, if you don't, the reasonableness of politicians, our masters, in doing so. And you get your way best by doing so, and showing that there are more vital things than the mere accidental shape of an arch. Ungeometrical arches and vaults in conjunction do not express a scientific logical government which the Government of India is or should be. That is the line of attack I think. Give them Indian sentiment where it does not conflict with grand principles, as the Government should do.'[30]

Baker's letter, and the fact that he wrote to *The Times* in October 1912, reveal an imperial attitude quite different from his outlook at Pretoria. It has taken years to come to terms with the politics it implied, and is enshrined in the stones of both buildings. Both buildings have benefited from time and changing fashions in taste and idealism.

Interest in the colonial architecture of India has greatly increased in recent years. No longer is this aspect of the subcontinent's heritage considered to be a mere jumble of eclecticism, unworthy of serious study. Its history is rooted in politics, classicism having been deliberately used to impose imperial order on perceived Indian chaos since British dominion became a reality in the eighteenth century. But policy received a change of direction after the uprising of 1857. Reconciliation, expressed through the semi-indigenous Indo-Saracenic style, a bizarre hybrid interpretation of the exotic East, became the ideal. Though Baker, from the beginning, was fully able to accept the inevitability of a British departure from India, his thoughts represented the apotheosis of colonial architectural idealism. His own imperialism in South Africa was tempered by the British presence and the influence which a semi-English society brought to bear on his architecture. His understanding was deepened by his role in a society of which he felt a part. Unlike at Pretoria, in India he was a complete outsider when New Delhi was conceived. There is thus a fundamental distinction in his attitude towards his two great quests portrayed in his two greatest buildings.

Baker's sailing was delayed by an attack of eczema and a sudden flood of new work, for which arrangements had to be made for its execution. Fleming and another assistant were to accompany him on the voyage to India, via London, which they reached on 4 November. Baker and Lutyens, and their assistants, set off from Victoria Station for Marseilles on 13 November and arrived again in India on 28 November 1913.[31]

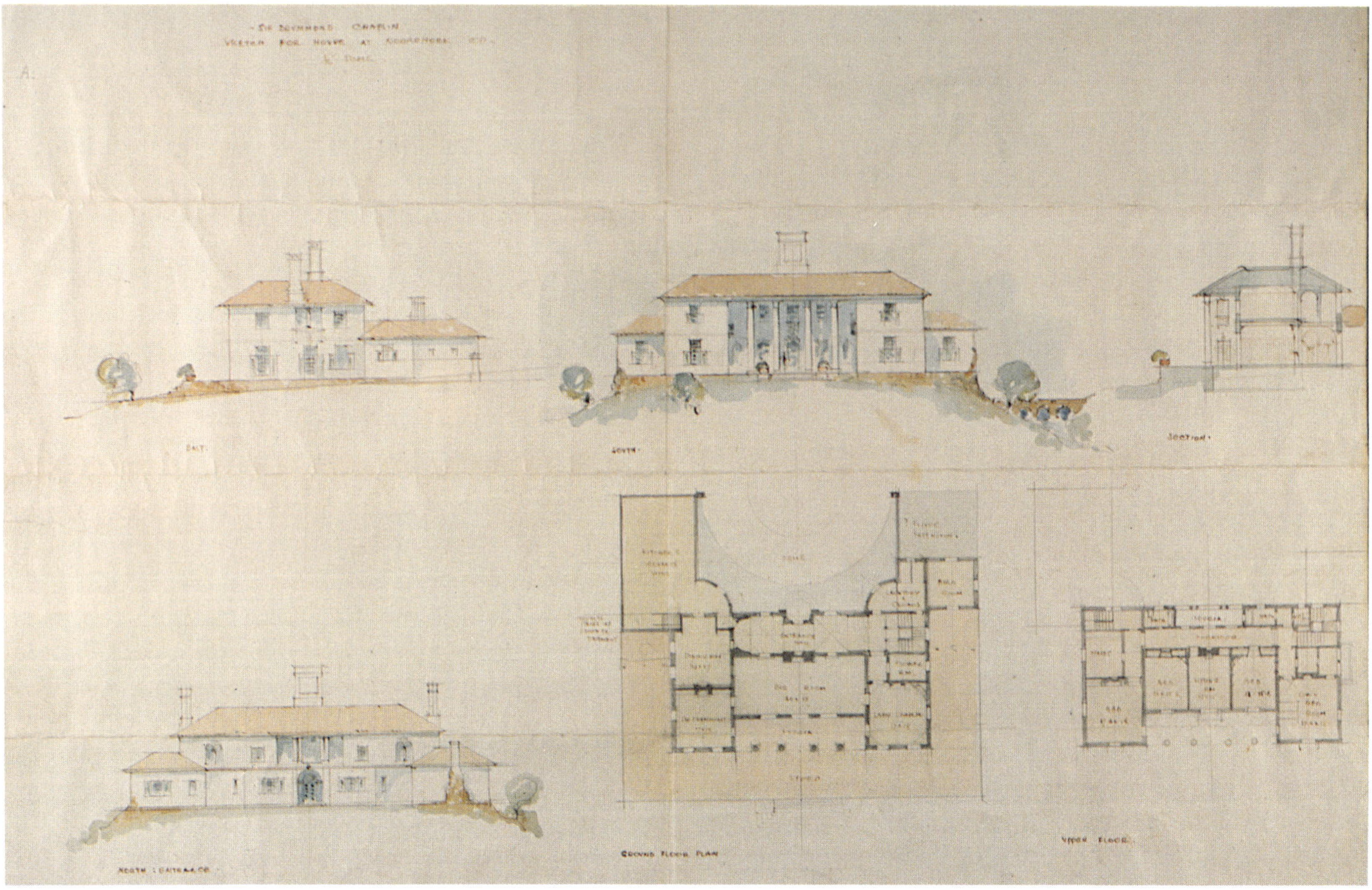

Top. Noordhoek, for Sir Drummond Chaplin, Noordhoek, preliminary plans
and elevations. Bottom. Noordhoek, entrance front.

EPILOGUE

STICKS, STONES AND LAURELS

After 1913, except for a few short visits, Baker never returned to South Africa. His Cape Town partnership with Kendall was ended in 1913 and that with Fleming in Johannesburg, which continued to include his name in the firm's title, was not dissolved until 1921. In those intervening years scores of fine buildings were designed by the firm in its own right, but with Baker's name on every drawing title and letterhead. Inevitably this has led to much confusion in the public's mind as to who designed what, explaining how many 'Baker' buildings could never even have been seen by him.

The buildings in South Africa designed by Baker from his London base are few and include the Adderley Street Barclays Bank, completed in 1933 and now the flagship of First National Bank; the old Reserve Bank in Church Square, Pretoria, begun in 1927; and a large, white-walled, classical house on the mountainside at, and named, Noordhoek, designed in 1921 for Sir Drummond Chaplin, for whom he had earlier built Marienhof (now called Drenthurst) in Johannesburg.

The full story of Baker's subsequent career must be told elsewhere. It spanned another thirty years or more, producing buildings in many countries and equalling his already prodigious output in South Africa. Baker was knighted in 1926 and received the coveted Gold Medal of the Royal Institute of British Architects in the following year. On his death in 1946 his ashes were interred beneath the nave of Westminster Abbey, perhaps the ultimate accolade.

Sir Herbert Baker's experience in South Africa was indelible and can be detected in all his subsequent work. His churches of St Paul at Woldingham, Surrey, and St Andrew at Ilford could be mistaken for those he designed in the Cape and Transvaal. His memorials designed following the Great War when he was a principal architect to the Imperial War Graves Commission, particularly that at Delville Wood, could have been sited on Meintjeskop or Table Mountain. His cricket pavilion at Lords might have been at Newlands, and his 'Cape-Queen Anne' house at Port Lympne – all in warm red facing brick – which he designed for Sir Philip Sassoon, could equally have been at Rondebosch. Even to the point of being incongruous, the Cape Dutch mansion for W Mein at Woodside, California is a superb transplant from the Groot Drakenstein Valley.

In this epilogue I will dwell briefly only on his most important work: New Delhi, which was his reason for leaving South Africa; the Bank of England, a seminal but highly controversial work, and those empire houses which relate so closely to his South African connection. Above all I will attempt to show why it was that his later work was regarded as no more than indifferent by some critics and lauded by others.

C R Ashbee had found Stonehouse to be 'one of the most exquisite pieces of architecture' he had seen. Yet about seventy years later one of the most perceptive art historians and critics of this century, Kenneth Clark, described Baker as 'a polite and thoughtful man with a positive genius for errors of design; in his public buildings every proportion, every cornice, every piece of fenestration was (and unfortunately still is) an object lesson in how not to do it.'[1]

It gives one a jolt to think that those words, and what can be seen of Baker's work in South Africa, could describe the work of the same architect. In fact, one can find many such dramatically contrasting comments on Baker's work. He produced, or was associated with, so much that perhaps it should not be so surprising that some of it fell short

Barclays, now First National, Bank in Adderley Street, Cape Town.

of the mark and, even today, remains controversial. Moreover, despite the claims of estate agents, and home-owners to live in Bakerish houses, it is now evident that he had somewhat less to do with the detail design of many buildings than is popularly supposed.

It is in South Africa, more than anywhere, that Baker's work has been best appreciated and assessed, and by no one more than the late Dr Doreen Greig whose pioneering studies have been widely acclaimed.[2] Internationally, Baker has for too long stood in the shadow of his friend, colleague and rival, Sir Edwin Lutyens. Much of the problem is due to the fact that his work has never seriously been considered as a whole. But Baker, assisted by changing fashion and taste, is beginning to emerge from that particular shadow. As Sir John Summerson has said, '...history is likely to judge Lutyens to be the "fluke genius" whereas Baker may be the more representative figure of his time.'[3]

Lutyens – the ambitious, egocentric, sensitive artist-architect, and Baker – the pragmatic, political, literary poet-architect, were astonishingly different in temperament. It should not surprise us that these fundamentally opposed differences should eventually destroy their relationship, and as some would argue, the success of the most important building project of its time.

NEW DELHI

The joint commission of Edwin Lutyens and Herbert Baker to plan the New Delhi and to share the design and execution of its principal buildings, continues to this day to provide rich material for the study of almost every aspect of architectural affairs – artistic, political and practical. Since their deaths, two major works of architectural scholarship have given full treatment to the New Delhi

Dominion Students' Hostel, Mecklenburg Square, London.

project and to the celebrated dispute concerning the ramped axial approach to the capitoline group; that unhappy episode which soured relations between two architects who had been friends for nearly thirty years. The first of these studies was Christopher Hussey's *Life of Sir Edwin Lutyens*, published in 1950 and described by David Watkin as the 'finest architectural biography in the English language.'[4] The second was Robert Grant Irving's *Indian Summer: Lutyens, Baker and Imperial Delhi*, published in time for the magnificent Lutyens exhibition of 1981-82 at the London Hayward Gallery.[5] Sir John Summerson described Irving's book as 'scrupulous...massively documented...the famous quarrel about the inclined way gets a chapter to itself...'

Both these studies appear to share the central assumption that Lutyens suffered the spoilation of his concept through Baker's wilfulness, if not, as others have hinted, through his aesthetic ineptitude. But if the facts are examined in a different light, and in particular with the evidence on which

the misunderstandings and accusations appear to hinge, the perspectives of William Walcot, it is possible to reach other conclusions.[6]

By the time Baker arrived in India, Lutyens, who was appointed first, had already formed a fairly clear concept for the group of administrative buildings on a hill, surmounted by a Viceroy's palace. Both Hussey and Irving relate how, on Baker's arrival, his fresh ideas and strong opinions were stimulating to Lutyens, if not a little startling. Alas, they were soon to have misgivings over the contract for the sharing of fees and expenses which their lawyers had drawn up.[7] Their mutual annoyance over relatively minor technicalities, at a time when total collaboration and communication was essential, may have been significant in the dispute which was to follow.

The root of the problem lay in their final agreement to place both the twin Secretariats and the Viceroy's House on a common, level platform at the crest of Raisina Hill – an eminence which rose gently to the west of the new capital. In Lutyens's

New Delhi, India, steps and portico.

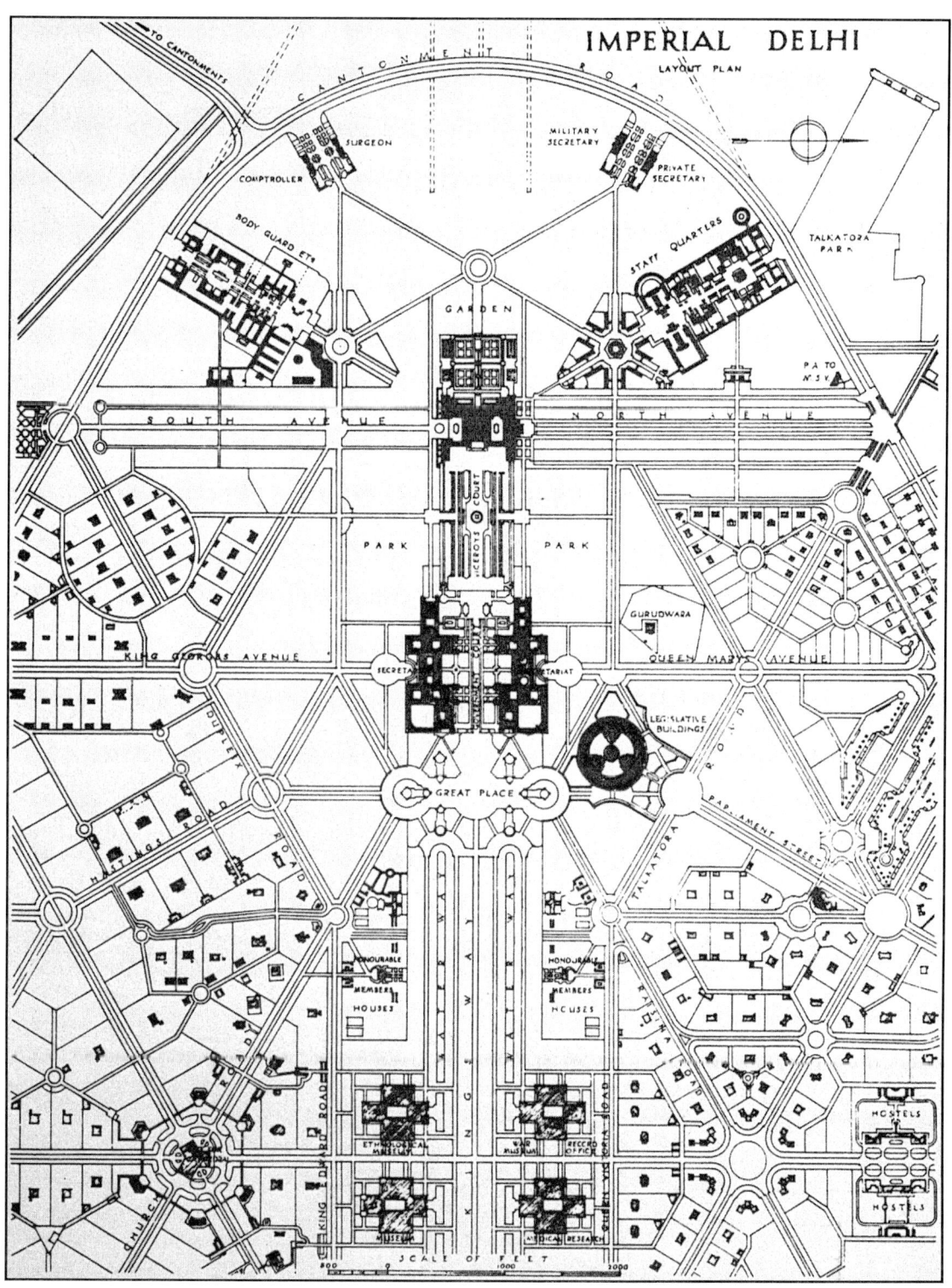

New Delhi, India, plan. Baker was responsible for the twin secretariats on either side of the central axis and for the circular legislative building on the right of the group.

previous conception the Viceroy's House, the design of which he had reserved for himself, occupied a higher, more dominant position in relation to the administrative buildings which Baker was allotted. However, with the experience of the Union Buildings behind him, Baker reasoned persuasively that both democratic symbolism, and the ancient classical precedent of the raised acropolis, on which the main buildings shared the sanctity of the temenos, would be more appropriate.

Although Lutyens willingly accepted the political wisdom of Baker's alternative concept, it seems he never fully appreciated the spatial implications of such an arrangement. The architects then engaged one of the most brilliant perspective artists of the day, William Walcot[8], to prepare presentation views to illustrate their scheme for final approval of the Imperial Delhi Committee. These perspectives, which aroused considerable interest when they were exhibited at the Royal Academy in 1914, were based on sketches roughed out by Baker and two assistants on his voyage to England from South Africa.

It can be surmised that, at least as far as Baker was concerned, they represented faithfully the conception which had been agreed to, and had by now been translated into designs. But according to Christopher Hussey's reading of Lutyens's mind: 'Since the inception of the existing scheme in 1913 when, with Baker, he had prepared a sketch of the three buildings on Raisina Hill as they would be seen from the Great Palace, he had visualized the portico of Government House...being continually visible from the avenue over the crest of the slope between the Secretariats.'[9] Hussey then adds a damning conjecture: 'There was no doubt in his mind that Baker, in whose "area" the actual slope occurred, was equally clear on this crucial point, since the façade was so shown in the perspectives...they had supervised together at Apple Tree Yard.'[10]

Whatever assumptions may have dwelt in their minds at that early stage, Baker, in March 1914, actually wrote to Lutyens seeking firm agreement on the precise gradient of the ramp. After sampling the suitability of various gradients on actual roads around Delhi, a slope of 1 in 22,5 was selected and the work of blasting out the rock went ahead. Amazingly, it was not until January 1916, nearly two years later, that the reality of that agreement dawned on Lutyens and the famous dispute began.[11]

Later, writes Robert Grant Irving: '...when storms of controversy raged over Raisina, one panoramic perspective showing Government House seen between the Secretariats played a conspicuous role in the vehement discussions.' Prepared from Baker's sketches, Walcot's rendering 'showed an impressive view of the palace's eastern façade...'[12] But is it really an 'impressive' view? It seems to be strangely obscure considering the importance claimed for it. Be that as it may, Irving, as does Hussey in similar vein in his parallel account, goes on to say: '...the inclined way actually masked all but the dome' and that 'Lutyens remarked bitterly that the drawing exceeded even the bounds of artistic licence. He felt certain that had Baker submitted a true perspective...showing only the palace dome above the inclined way, the Royal Academy or public opinion would have rejected the drawing.'[13] But, as has been demonstrated elsewhere, the drawing portrays not only what was agreed, but what was built. An important point that vanished in the haze of invective.[14]

Unfortunately for Herbert Baker the misconception has been long-standing and Lutyens's lengthy struggle to persuade the Viceroy, the King and Queen and every power he could find, to authorize expensive 'correction' of the half-built scheme, by flattening and extending the ramp into Baker's level court beyond, gained Lutyens many sympathizers. Most notable among these was the critic Robert Byron, who, in January 1931, described the so-called error as 'little short of a crime...doubtless dictated by base and selfish motives...'[15] A further article by Byron, in the magazine *Country Life* in June 1931, sent Baker hot-foot to his lawyer, but no action was taken.[16] Christopher Hussey quotes a letter which Baker had written in defence and which, claimed Hussey, '...enables us to see how, meanwhile and perhaps throughout, he [Baker] had come to the conclusion that the practical and social value of a level expanse Government Court outweighed with him the scenic value of a continuous sight of Government House.'[17]

Lutyens was deeply soured by the protracted dispute and grew increasingly virulent in his personal criticism of Baker, both for his sentimental idealism and his architecture. Mary Lutyens, in the memoir she wrote of her father in 1980 summed up the sad episode thus: 'Father was to hear in June [1922] that the decision over the gradient had gone against him. He had met his "Bakerloo" as he called it. He did not resign but he never forgave Baker. If this book were a biography instead of a memoir I should feel obliged to try to be just to Baker and put his point of view. I am sure he had a very good one. As it is, I feel no compulsion to do so. We were brought up to look on Baker as a villain who had ruined Father's life's work. It is only now, in going into the subject, that I realize what a small matter the gradient really was and how little the loss of the level way detracts from the glory of Father's achievement.'[18]

BANK OF ENGLAND

It was in the early twenties that Baker became involved in a further controversy, and one which perhaps invited even more criticism than New Delhi. Remodelling the Bank of England, with vastly more accommodation than was provided by the existing buildings, on a congested site in the City of London, would be an exacting task for any architect. But when much of the site was covered with the finest surviving work of Sir John Soane, the problem was virtually incapable of a totally satisfactory solution. The art historian, Sir Nikolaus Pevsner described the virtual rebuilding as, despite the Second World War, '...the worst individual loss suffered by London architecture in the first half of the C20.' After completion of Baker's scheme only Soane's screen wall remained, 'screening now nothing but the huge contraption erected inside by Sir Herbert Baker. Soane's banking halls, the most original secular spaces of their date in Europe, were demolished, and all we have is Baker's paraphrases of their ingenious vaulting conceits.' Pevsner remarks that 'to preserve the screen-wall only and scoop out all the rest strikes one as peculiarly distasteful. The use of Soane's masterwork as the footstool of a Herbert Baker seems unforgivable...yet what could be done?' Pevsner unhelpfully concludes that only by building elsewhere could Soane's work have been saved.[19]

Baker himself reported in phraseology we have become familiar with in South Africa, that 'Long and sympathetic study has been given to the determination of the extent to which the more valuable portions of the old building...could be retained consistently with the creation of a new structure worthy of the bank and sufficient for its needs.'[20] Baker's account of the building in his 1944 autobiography was in turn derided by Pevsner as 'a masterpiece of egregious diddling. Any reader,

from the use of such phrases as "retention", "preservation in the plan", "incorporation of the best features", etc., would think that Baker did indeed preserve Soane's rooms.'[21] One may conclude that if it is true that Baker desired to build a new bank, all of a piece – albeit drawing inspiration from Soane – it was a sad misjudgement.

Alas the beauty and magnificence and the undoubted skilful planning of the new building have been obscured by what is generally considered to have been a disastrous strategy. The Bank was richly decorated with bronze doors, symbolic plaques and numerous sculptures by his protegé, Sir Charles Wheeler, to whom Baker gave 'a young artist's dream' and set him on his illustrious career, employing him on numerous subsequent projects.[22] Baker was rewarded with a knighthood but the furore over the destruction of Soane's work probably shook his confidence; much of the earlier vigour seems to be absent from his subsequent work.

INDIA HOUSE

Like the Bank of England, India House is an important key to Baker's subsequent development, relating as it does to Baker's other Empire Houses, which as a group are of particular interest to his South African architecture in its broadest sense, and deserves a moment's examination. 'India House will not appeal to the ultra-moderns', wrote *The Architect and Building News*, soon after it opened in April 1930. 'It pays no deference to their own particular gods, functional expression, structural truth and impersonality of ornament. On the contrary, it is scenic, heraldic, even romantic in intention; it is meant both to express and impress the Indian mind.'[23]

Two years earlier the same journal had exclaimed that Baker had given some of the chief rooms 'a particularity of form which has never yet been given to a chamber having no contact whatsoever either with the external walls of the building or yet with its roof...surely never before has there been a two-storeyed central hall with a gallery on the first floor surrounding a well, through which we see a vaulted ceiling surmounted by a large lantern of traditional shape. This, however, instead of being open to the sky is five storeys below the flat roof of the building...what has really happened here is that one building has swallowed another whole, and yet apparently shows no signs of indigestion.'[24] In this

Winchester College, England. War Cloister.

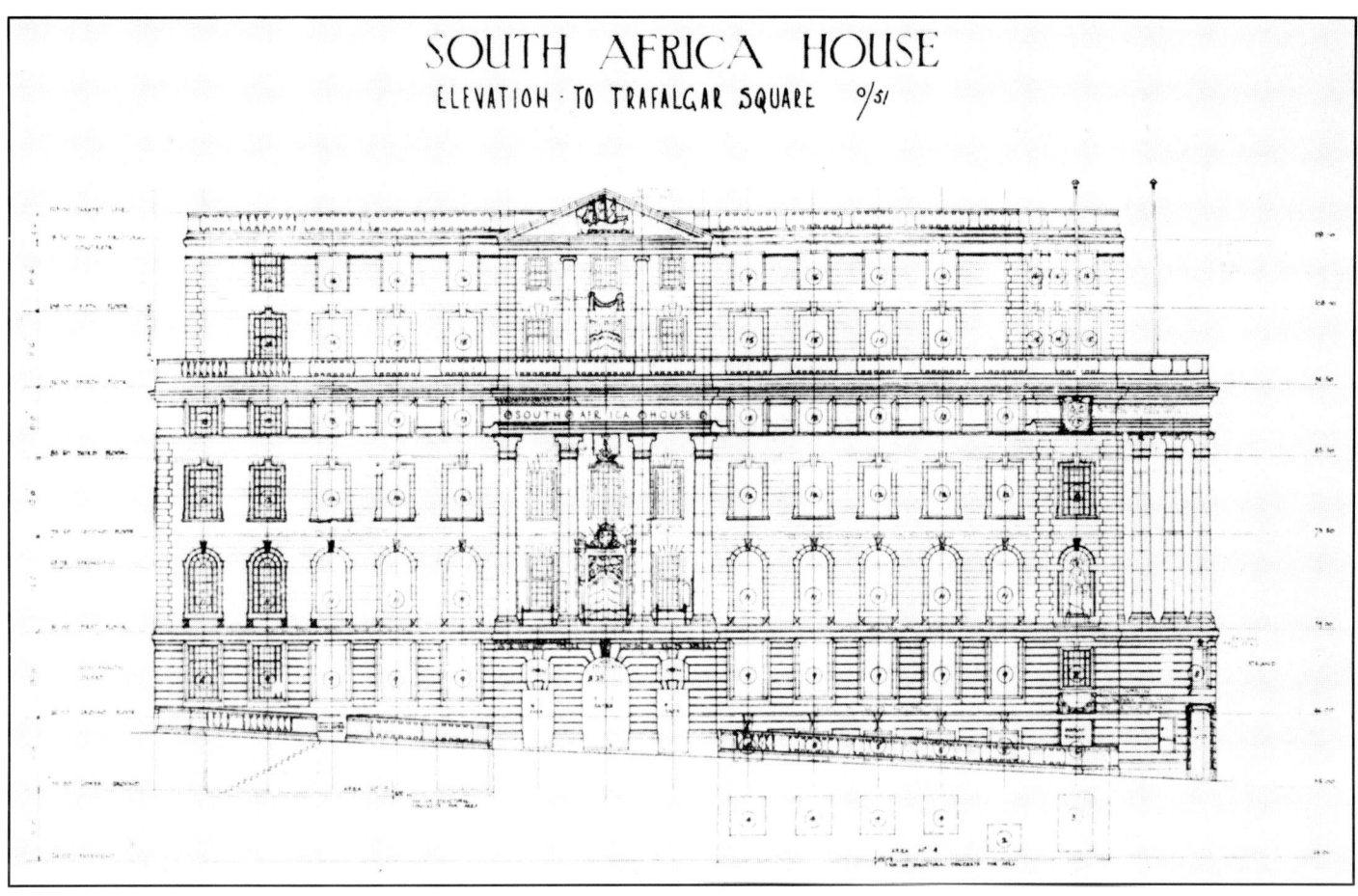

SOUTH AFRICA HOUSE
ELEVATION · TO TRAFALGAR SQUARE

South Africa House, London, elevation facing Trafalgar Square.

extraordinary way Baker had contrived to pack an enormous amount and variety of accommodation into a small congested site, next to Bush House, in London's Alwych.

The complexity of the building is best seen in its cross-section. And yet nowhere on the outside is this achievement apparent; the façade is a mask designed to look pretty and not express anything in particular, other than what many regard as a spurious Indian character. Above the black marble entrance door are two heraldic tigers and Asoka columns by Wheeler and, wrote Baker, '...between the arches of the lower floor of the façades are the arms, cut in stone and coloured, of the twelve provinces of India. Inside are carved, in both stone and wood, animal and floral symbols, and emblems of significance in the myths and lore of India.'[25] Passing through the admittedly striking doors of Indian rosewood, past black columns, one enters the domed hall. Looking upwards through a circular aperture guarded by white jali work, can be seen the distant dome, mysteriously but naturally lit by borrowed daylight. All around are walls of red sandstone, arches and pendentives covered with delicate paintings by Indian artists.

RHODES HOUSE, OXFORD

In terms of its somewhat naive symbolism and, for some, its rather overwhelming sentiment, one might have thought India House a hard act to follow. But the second of Baker's Empire Houses, Rhodes House in Oxford, was to give him just as much scope to exploit these qualities which were now becoming characteristic of his later work, particularly that which had Empire connections.

Arthur Mee's 1942 volume on Oxfordshire, in the popular *The King's England* series, says romantically of Rhodes House, opened in 1929, it: '...stands finely in South Parks Road, surrounded by trees and gardens...on the west front is the craftsman's stone with the names of the architect, Sir Herbert Baker, and those who worked with him to make this place so beautiful. They built it with fine English stone...roof slates from the Cotswolds, and oak from our midland forests; and a wealth of decoration throughout the building symbolizes the British Empire, the United States, and the ideals of Cecil Rhodes. Over the bronze door in the colonnaded porch is carved a Ship of State with the British lion and the American eagle on its sails, and built into the south wall are stones carved with symbols and heraldry of the English-speaking peoples. In the central dome are emblems of the British Commonwealth of Nations, such as the rose and the maple leaf, and in the centre of the floor is a round stone from the Matopo Hills where Cecil Rhodes lies.' The piece concludes that 'nobly planned and nobly built, Rhodes House is a great addition to the architectural glory of Oxford...'[26] But Rhodes House has not always inspired such outright affection.

Writing in the Oxfordshire volume of the *Buildings of England* series Sir Nikolaus Pevsner describes Rhodes House as a 'curious wedding' of high-roofed Cotswold mansion and classical copper-domed rotunda; the building which started the 'regrettable fashion' of squared rubble walling in Oxford. He goes on to say: 'Baker argued speciously that the rotunda should not be out of place in the seat of classical scholarship and that the Cotswold features represent the traditional craftsmanship of the stone-building shires of Oxford and Gloucester.' Pevsner comments: '...architects are so good at finding rational justification after the event.' He concludes his description of the building with a wry note of sarcasm: 'The building is an oddity, but has personality enough to rouse affection in some.'

The one whose affections were strongest was Sir Herbert Baker, who in his memoirs quotes Sir Michael Sadler's calling it 'the most inspiring place in Oxford.'[27] Pevsner wrote that in 1974. More recently, *The Oxford Guide to Oxford* called it 'a boring because unpeopled place, a mausoleum to the imperial ideals of Cecil Rhodes, but insulated by false principles of decorum from the raw energy of those who have come for eighty years to enrich Oxford in his name. Sir Herbert Baker, the architect, must bear much of the blame; he aimed at a harmony between Oxford's classical traditions and native Cotswold craftsmanship and achieved instead a genteel parochialism.'[28]

Looking at the plan of Rhodes House, both its virtues and faults become graphically clear. The rotunda, a memorial to Lord Milner, looks like a stuck-on afterthought. Milner, who had been instrumental in bringing Baker to the Transvaal after the Boer War, had been chairman of the trustees appointed to administer the Rhodes scholarships, a body which included Rudyard Kipling and some former members of Milner's Kindergarten.

If Rhodes and Baker were passionate believers in Sir Christopher Wren's dictum that 'architecture has its political uses', Milner, to his credit, was suspicious of Baker's enthusiasm for grandiose expressions of imperialism, an attitude born of Milner's own experience of the complexities of colonial government. Milner had wanted a flint-walled building after Baker's sublime War Memorial Cloister at Winchester College, or his other splendid Memorial Building at Harrow School. He had striven to prevent Baker from creating a memorial that he considered would be ridiculed by the decadent young men of the generation which followed the Great War.[29]

With Milner's death in 1925 such restraint was removed. Baker now added to his original H-shaped manor house plan the grandiose temple, and decorated the building with meaningful sculptural motifs, the symbols of Empire he so much loved. One can only guess what Milner, himself a distinguished classical scholar, would have thought of the 'no smoking' sign in the vestibule, which solemnly translates from the Greek, 'Let No Smoke-Bearing Person Enter'!

It is, perhaps, just as well that the scale of the portico and the domed hall immediately behind it, through which all must pass, is not carried through the rest of the building. Here is a most happy wedding of Arts and Crafts and English Jacobean, with a hint of Baker's best South African work, in the well-proportioned interiors. 'But no work that fortune brought me', wrote Baker, 'gave me greater satisfaction than that of building the Oxford Home of the Spirit of my first patron and friend, Cecil Rhodes.'[30]

SOUTH AFRICA HOUSE

On 22 June 1933, King George V and Queen Mary

South Africa House, London, panelled vestibule.

opened a new building in Trafalgar Square, London. The King concluded his speech by referring to South Africa House as 'a monument to concord and unity.'[31] In those balmy pre-apartheid days, the building was received as a symbol of Empire and was, to the man in the street, a thing of glory and pride. Perhaps appropriately, the building was sited close to where the coach that had brought Mr Pip to London, had set him down to benefit from his 'Great Expectations' – of a fortune made in the colonies.[32]

The crowds applauded as the royal carriage crossed the square on the return to Buckingham Palace; it was a roar quite different in spirit from the noisy demonstrations which have become associated with the square and the building in recent years. Later that day Baker's client for Rust en Vrede thirty years earlier, Sir Abe Bailey, who was

there as an official guest, wrote to the architect: 'My Dear Herbert Baker, I must write to congratulate you on the excellent work you put into SA House. Really great – I enjoyed it all, & will again be there – Kind regards to Lady Baker, your good self. Yrs, Abe Bailey.'[33]

Baker had already built two of his 'Empire Houses': India House and Rhodes House, Oxford, when the commission to design South Africa House came. In South Africa he had been regarded as the country's 'Architect Laureate' in all but official title. Arguably, with all that, and especially the Union Buildings, he should have been granted a knighthood before he ever went to India, to work with Lutyens on the most important group of buildings in the world in that era. For these achievements, not to mention his work for the Imperial War Graves Commission, and the two more Empire

Left. *Harrow School Memorial Building.* Right. *Village Memorial Cross, Hertfordshire, England.*

Houses still to come, history must acknowledge him to be, more than any other, the Architect to the British Empire. Certainly, for South Africa House, there could be no other architect but Sir Herbert Baker. In due course work on the site began in January 1931.

Assisted by his partner A T Scott, Baker tackled the design with unbridled sentimental gusto. Although its primary purpose was to provide offices for the High Commissioner and his staff, he saw it as an opportunity to symbolize the flora and fauna and the whole history of South Africa, right from its 'discovery' by Bartolomeu Dias in the fifteenth century on his voyage in search of a new route to India. Baker's problem was to design a building which would fit into the existing architectural context of Trafalgar Square, and at the same time reflect its essentially South African nature.

To the north of the square was the National Gallery with its portico of Corinthian columns and, in the north-east corner, the Church of St Martin in the Fields, also with a tall columned portico and pediment.

Facing the square, the main entrance to Baker's building is through three arched openings in the granite-faced base of the building, leading on through a vestibule to a grand staircase. Over the teak doorways are fanlights containing carved tracery similar to those found in many famous early Cape houses. Above the entrance is a two-storey portico which rises past the High Commissioner's Room, the heart and centre of the building, once more an echo of the Union Buildings.

The portico is roofed by a projecting balcony supported by four Corinthian columns, the entablature inscribed with the words 'South Africa'. From the balcony the balustrade is continued around the building, emphasizing the cornice marking the line at which the two attic floors are set back from the floors below. Behind the balcony a smaller portico, or stoep, topped at roof level with a pediment containing a bas-relief of Jan van Riebeeck's ship *Goede Hoop*, leads into a shallow two-storey recess in the attic floors. At the lower, Strand, end of the site is the familiar visitor's entrance, a floor below the main entrance in view of the natural fall of the site. Above the entrance hall, on the first and second floors respectively, were designed a visitor's room and the library, from which access is gained to the loggia, a two-storey semi-circular colonnade, or curved portico. This feature, perhaps the most striking and successful aspect of the whole building

is the pivot on which the eye falls, like the clock-towers of the Union Buildings.

Within the building, white South African marble lines the walls, with columns of green and grey Transvaal marble; the floors too are inlaid with coloured marbles and granites. The main spaces are roofed with domes, in which Latin inscriptions, coats of arms, and other symbols of South Africa abound.

A contemporary description of the building, at the time of its opening, remarked that 'a multitude of interesting materials, many imported from South Africa, have had a wealth of craftsmanship expended on them. The building reveals a kind of Gothic exuberance of detail allied to modern taste in figured woods and marbles. The last thing of which Sir Herbert Baker's buildings can be accused is dullness, though occasionally the visitor may become somewhat satiated with too much colour (in the sculptural sense)...',[34] which, with great politeness, seems to say it all. More recently, Pevsner declared that, despite his efforts to relate his building to the St Martin portico, 'in the end Baker could not suppress his delight in small motifs, odd balconied windows in aedicles, odd bits of meaningful sculpture, etc., and so no harmony with St Martin's is achieved.'[35] Another writer has said that 'although Sir Herbert Baker may still be an unfashionable name amongst the trend-setters...his talents were perfectly suited to the projection of a national image in the grandest and most traditional commercial terms.'[36]

THE EMPIRE AT HOME

In concept nothing could be more of an Empire House than the headquarters of the Royal Empire Society, founded in 1868 as the Royal Colonial Institute by a group of leading Imperialists to counteract the threatening Separatist influences of the time, and to 'promote a better understanding among peoples of the Empire.'[37] As the *Architect and Building News* commented at its completion in October 1933: '...it is not inappropriate that the architect of so many other "Empire" buildings...should have been given the task.'[38] The commission was the fourth of the five touched on here.

Situated in Northumberland Avenue, this is frankly a dull building, '...a straightforward and natural expression of the plan in the classical tradition',[39] meaning that the fenestration indicates the type of room behind, and exercising polite good-neighbourliness with its surrounding buildings. Because the site is triangular and confined, the plan follows a triangular outline, with a cross connection, making it resemble an 'A' on its side. The main space is the assembly hall in the basement, rising through the ground floor to create a double volume with a surrounding gallery on three sides. It is lit from above by laylights. Around the gallery front are the inevitable armorial plaques of the Empire. Apart from the gallery, the ground floor contains only the entrance hall and adjacent lounges reserved for use by the Society, the remaining space being let as banking halls, one on each side of the main entrance. On the first floor was planned a large sage-green and golden-brown library, housing over 250 000 volumes. The upper floors contained a variety of accommodation, including fifty-five bedrooms, bathrooms, etc.

The last Empire House that will be examined here, the first phase of which was completed in December 1937, is London House: 'A hall of residence for British men students from the Dominions and Colonies of the British Empire, together with a limited number of students from the United Kingdom.'[40] Here, on an island site, Baker and Scott were able to adopt a collegiate type of plan around a large quadrangle.

Christopher Hussey, writing soon after Baker's death, when the building was nearing final completion, reflects that the style is 'Baker's modern version of English tradition, which brings together elements and memories of many phases of our architectural history, combining them by an overall feeling for texture and making the whole an honest expression of the purpose and plan of the building.' Hussey observes that a 'quality of modesty is achieved by suppressing any suggestion of the monumental, and by breaking the street façades into distinct but related sections. The flint facing to the basement storey carries the mind back beyond Georgian Bloomsbury to England's mediaeval foundations, while the fine brickwork and generous windows are typical of the Renaissance union of the arts and sciences.'[41]

As he had demonstrated in South Africa, Baker's 'eclecticism produces a retrospective effect, in which allusive charm and homely dignity are the dominating impressions rather than that conviction of inevitability that is found in great architecture of any style.'[42] As one might expect, contemporary descriptions of London House include references to 'an Empire clock telling the time for all parts of the British world', and predictably, 'in the cove of the ceiling are the symbols of the nations of the British Commonwealth...'[43] Externally the building exemplifies Baker's later architecture in its facing brick combined with flints and stone quoins, pitched tiled roofs and dormer windows. It is an architecture wrought from Arts and Crafts and Queen Anne beginnings, matured under the fierce sun of Africa and India and returning to its paler origins in restful quietude. London House was to be one of his last important commissions. With the strange appropriateness we have almost come to expect from Baker, only Church House, the headquarters of the Church of England in Dean's Yard, Westminster, was to follow. Pevsner, comparing London House with India House, South Africa House and the Bank of England, found in the symmetrical south front 'Baker's motifs and foibles ...only too noticeable.'[44]

BAKER AND MODERNISM

Pevsner was Baker's unkindest critic. He condemned the continuation of the classical tradition in the twentieth century as 'the embodiment of the most reactionary of political programmes, spawning a bastard progeny [which] looms large in the perspective of history.'[45] Edwin Lutyens was one of the most brilliant and successful architects in history, yet he is totally ignored in Pevsner's *Outline of European Architecture*. Lutyens was omitted, as was Baker, because he failed to fit Pevsner's *Zeitgeist* ideal, his Hegelian view of historical progress.

Baker, like Lutyens, of course, was never a modernist; he was, therefore simply in the same unfathomably 'reactionary' camp. But in fairness, although still professionally very active, he was already in his seventies when, in the 1930s, modernism began to gain ground internationally. When Le Corbusier wrote his influential, but nonetheless arrogant jumble of poetic insight – and outright nonsense – *Towards a New Architecture* in 1923, Baker was sixty-one.

Baker's attitude to the movement is summed up in the remarks he made during a debate on modernism in architecture in 1928: 'I do not think we need be afraid of Modernism...I think English people are much too sensible. Sir Reginald Blomfield thought it would end in smoke, and Mr Goodhart-Rendel thought it would end in a cul-de-sac. I would...say it will end in an explosion, which will leave some dust behind, and whatever may be good in the movement will be the dust added to the mountain of Tradition, which, in itself, can never be moved, though often a little shaking may do it considerable good.'[46] How prophetic Baker's words sound in the post-modern world of today!

What do Baker's example and experience have to offer the present and the future? Pevsner's day, with the doctrinal form of modernism he espoused, has gone. Architects have only recently relearned the place and value of tradition, and the right of one generation to draw inspiration from another, even if that be the most recent to have passed. It seems the threat to artistic tradition and to individual genius posed by the forces of novelty and conformity has faded. In the fresh air we can rejoice in the values of traditional architecture once more, as indeed the unindoctrinated man in the street always has done. In such a climate, Baker's example may be taken up without fear of derision. For he showed us how to design in tune with nature, how to take account of idealistic aspirations, and, for architects, how to manage a great practice efficiently. His office correspondence is a lasting model for the study of professional practice, and deserves selective publication for that reason alone.

It was Baker's misfortune to be compared with Edwin Lutyens, an architect of undoubted genius. In his own right Baker had an outstanding talent which he was able to harness to an astute political sense to motivate others and get things done. His energy was nothing less than prodigious. Baker has been accused, in his lifetime and since, of being 'expensive', but what is true is that, almost without exception, his efforts were directed at giving his clients the very best long-term solution that they could afford, even though they sometimes thought they could not. Moreover, his clients were invariably delighted with his work, frequently coming to him again many years later.

If anything detracts from Baker's superb achievements, it is surely the effect of his unbridled sentimentality. The derogating label of 'eclectic' cannot dislodge his laurels, for he lived in an age of eclecticism. It was the natural way of doing things then, as it is becoming so again today.

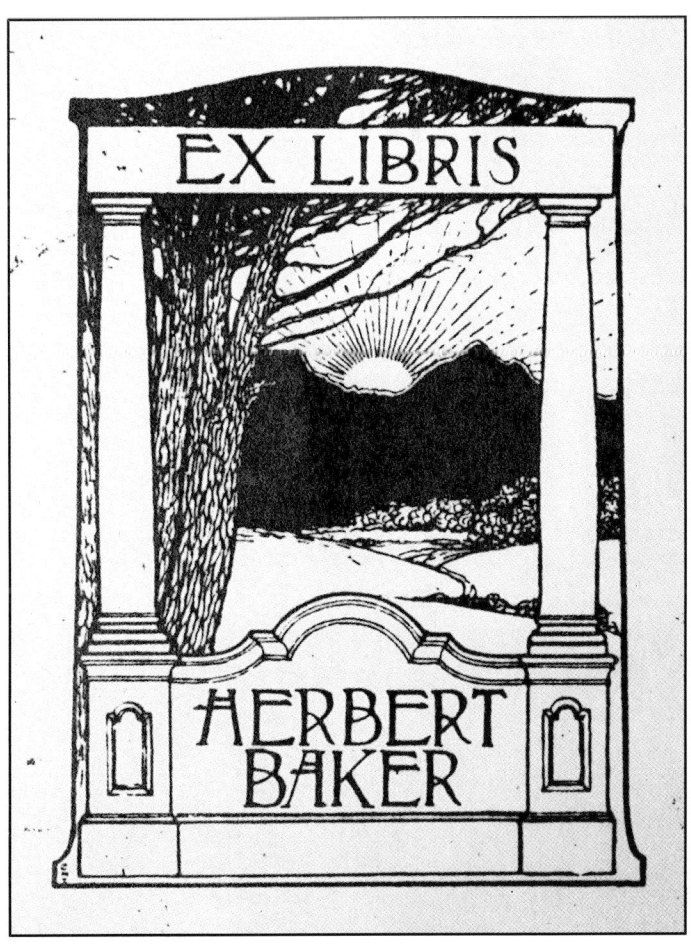

Baker's bookplate.

NOTES AND REFERENCES

PERSONS

CR	Cecil John Rhodes (1853-1902)
EL	Sir Edwin Landseer Lutyens (1869-1944)
EWS	Ernest Willmott Sloper (1871-1916)
FF	Frank Leonard Hodgson Fleming (1875-1950)
FM	Francis Edward Masey (1861-1912)
FK	Franklin Kaye Kendall (1870-1948)
HB	Sir Herbert Baker (1862-1946)

OTHER ABBREVIATIONS

A+P	Herbert Baker, *Architecture and Personalities*.
AR	*Architectural Review*, London.
ASA	*Architecture South Africa* (successor to SAAR *et al*).
CL	*Country Life*, London.
CRA	Herbert Baker, *Cecil Rhodes by his Architect*.
DAC	B A Johnson, 'Domestic Architecture at the Cape 1892-1912'.
DNB	*Dictionary of National Biography*, Oxford.
DPW	Director of Public Works, Pretoria.
HBDW	Doreen Greig, 'The Domestic Work of Sir Herbert Baker'.
HBSA	Doreen Greig, *Herbert Baker in South Africa*.
HSRC	Human Sciences Research Council, Pretoria.
JLMA	Jagger Library Manuscripts Archive, University of Cape Town Libraries.
LB	Letter books of Baker and Fleming, Strange Collection, Africana Museum.
LBID	Robert Grant Irving, *Indian Summer: Lutyens, Baker and Imperial Delhi*.
PWD	Public Works Department, Pretoria.
RIBA	Royal Institute of British Architects.
RIBAJ	*Journal of the Royal Institute of British Architects*.
SA	South Africa, South African.
SAAB	*South African Architect and Builder*.
SAAR	*South African Architectural Record*.
SAJCAH	*South African Journal of Cultural and Art History*.
SCA	Strange Collection of Africana, Johannesburg Public Library.

PREFACE

1 Mark Girouard, *Sweetness and Light: The Queen Anne Movement 1860-1900*, 1977, p 1. Girouard provides a most illuminating background to HB's early training and approach to style in architecture.

2 HB to Prof Pearse, 10 March 1925. Copy in HSRC collection.

3 Dougal O Malcolm, in DNB, 1941-1950, p 42.

4 *Appreciation – HB*, p 4, typescript draft for criticism appended to letter: FK to Pearse, 9 September 1925, JLMA, BC 206.

5 Ibid.

6 Sir Charles Wheeler, *High Relief*, 1968, p 58. HB wrote: '...I was not "literary", and was a poor talker and a bad diner out; but I thought I had one qualification, that of being a good listener', A+P, p 204.

7 Kendall, *Appreciation*, p 4.

8 Vernon Rees-Poole, in a symposium 'Sir Herbert Baker: In Memoriam 1862-1945 [*sic*]' SAAR, vol 31 (July 1946), p 169.

9 Christopher Hussey, *The Life of Sir Edwin Lutyens* (London: 1950), p 181.

10 Ibid, p 182.

11 Gordon Leith, in symposium, *In Memoriam*, p 177.

12 Kendall, *Appreciation*, p 4.

13 Wheeler, *High Relief*, p 53. See A+P, pp 97-8.

14 Kendall, *Appreciation*, p 3.

15 HB was a member of the Kent County Cricket Club, and *Wisden Cricketer's Almanack* published his obituary in the 1947 edition (p 687). In A+P (p 18), he writes: 'I kept up my cricket for a year or two at Cape Town and played in some of the best matches.' *See* also Kendall's *Appreciation*, p 3.

16 Kendall, *Appreciation*, p 3.

CHAPTER ONE

1 A+P, pp 5-7; also, Henry Edmeades Baker, *Owletts* (National Trust guide), 1975.

2 Henry Edmeades Baker, *Owletts*.

3 A+P, pp 9-13.

4 A+P, p 6.

5 A+P, p 14.

6 A+P, p 13.

7 Ibid.

8 Ibid; also, H D Furley, ed, *Tonbridge School Register 1861-1945*, 1951, pp 109, 823-4, 830.

9 HB (A+P, p 13) describes his headmaster as 'Dr Rowe'; *see* Furley, p 3; also A+P, p 14, and Furley, p 9, for Mr Whitmell.

10 A+P, pp 14-15.

11 A+P, p 15.

12 HBSA, p 11. Greig states that Baker's pupilage began in 1879. This error appears to have been repeated by numerous writers in biographical notes in encyclopaedia etc., leading to much confused chronology of HB's early life. *See* also RIBAJ, vol 4, series 3, 1897, p 360; and David Cole, *The Work of Sir Gilbert Scott*, 1980, pp 182, 201, 232.

13 F H Crossley, *English Church Design*, 1945, p 7.

14 *See* Arthur Baker's obituary in RIBAJ, vol 4, series 3, 1879, p 360, for mention of churches. HB gives '1½ years' spent

as clerk-of-works in his nomination papers for election to Associate Membership of the Royal Institute of British Architects, dated 6 December 1889. However, the statement he made nearly ten years later (for his Fellowship class election) dated 26 September 1899, gives '9 months'. The former seems more likely and better fits the known dates.

15 *See* obituary, *loc cit*; also RIBA Associate Membership nomination papers, RIBA, Portland Place, London.

16 These are illustrated in HBSA, pp 21-3. Several of Baker's earlier English drawings are preserved in the University of Cape Town (JLMA).

17 A+P, pp 14-15.

18 *See* Gavin Stamp and Colin Amery, *Victorian Buildings of London 1837-1887*, 1980, pp 121-4.

19 A+P, pp 16-17. The crosses at Winchester College, Canterbury Cathedral Close, Hertingfordbury, and The King's School in Canterbury are all redolent of the Derwen cross. *See* Epilogue.

20 A+P, p 15.

21 Ibid.

22 A+P, p 17. *Plas Mawr* was published by Farmer and Sons in a limited edition of 200 and paid for by subscription – mainly by friends and relatives.

23 HB's RIBA nomination papers, *loc cit*, show a further inconsistency. His Associate statement gives '6 weeks in Italy, 3 in France.' Yet his Fellowship statement gives: '2 months' sketching in Italy, 2 fortnights' visits to France and 1 week in Holland...'

24 A+P, p 17. *See* Robert de Zouche Hall, *A Bibliography on Vernacular Architecture*, 1972, p 128. *Archaeologia Cantiana*, vol xiv, 1886, and vol xvii, 1887.

CHAPTER TWO

1 For Sir Samuel Peto, *see* G C Boase, in DNB, vol xv, p 972-4. (Vol 2, p 1649 in Micro ed.)

2 *See* Margaret Richardson, *Architects of the Arts and Crafts Movement*, 1983, p 59. A+P, p 15.

3 Roderick Gradidge, *Dream Houses*, 1980, p 4 *et seq.*

4 E Guy Dawber, 'The late Sir Ernest George RA', *Builder* cxxiii, 1922, p 903. Quoted in Richardson, p 59.

5 Stamp and Amery, p 130.

6 Characteristically, John Ruskin, in *The Seven Lamps of Architecture* wrote: 'Another spirit may be given by another time, and it is then a new building; but the spirit of the dead workman cannot be summoned up, and commanded to direct other hands, and other thoughts...Do not let us talk...of restoration...the thing is a lie from beginning to end.' vi, 18-19. (pp 354-5 in 1880 ed). Did Ruskin in fact mean that destruction in the name of restoration was acceptable? For a superb study of the Queen Anne movement *see* Mark Girouard, *Sweetness and Light: The Queen Anne Movement 1860-1900*.

7 Alastair Service (ed), *Edwardian Architecture and its Origins,* 1975, pp 3-8, gives a fine outline of the period.

8 Lawrence Barton, *A Choice Over our Heads, A Guide to Design since 1830*, pp 55-8 contains a useful summary of these developments. *See* also the works by Girouard, Gradidge and Service cited above, and also Peter Davey, *Arts and Crafts Architecture: The Search for Earthly Paradise*, 1980.

9 Girouard, *Sweetness and Light*, pp 93-5, 173, 224-5.

10 Girouard, *The Victorian Country House*, 1979, p 384.

11 Richardson, *op cit*, p 59.

12 Christopher Hussey, *Life of Sir Edwin Lutyens*, 1950, p 17.

13 Richardson, p 7; A+P, p 17.

14 A+P, p 17.

15 Ibid.

16 Reginald Blomfield, *Memoirs of an Architect*, 1932, p 15; A+P, p 15.

17 A+P, p 17.

18 Ibid.

19 Hussey, p 18.

20 A+P, p 17.

21 A+P, p 19. For an account of architectural education around 1880-90, *see* P Davey 'Profession or art?', AR, July 1989, p 59.

22 A+P, p 19.

23 A+P, p 16; Hussey, *Life*, p 23.

24 A+P, p 16.

25 These drawings are in the Jagger Library, University of Cape Town (JLMA).

26 For brief records of all Thomas Baker's sons at Tonbridge School, *see* Furley, also A+P, p 19.

27 A+P, p 19. For a brief account of fruit exportation, *see* Willem Hefer 'Drakenstein: a valley with a place in history', *Optima*, vol 26, no 2, pp 44-64. *See* too, D J van Zyl in F Smuts, ed, *Stellenbosch Three Centuries*, 1979, pp 201-4; also CRA, pp 60-4.

28 A+P, p 19. *See* Sir Arthur Bryant, *English Saga,* 1940, p 232.

29 A+P, p 19; DAC, p 112. Johnson indicates HB's memory is probably at fault here and the ship was more likely the *Norham Castle*.

CHAPTER THREE

1 A+P, p 20.

2 A+P, p 21.

3 A+P, p 22.

4 A+P, p 23.

5 A+P, p 22.

6 CRA, pp 61-3; Hefer, pp 52-3. According to W J Tijmens, in *Stellenbosch Three Centuries* (ed F Smuts), p 202, Pickstone arrived at the Cape on 15 March 1892.

7 A+P, p 22.

8 A+P, p 23; CRA, p 62.

9 CRA, p 19; A+P, pp 22-3.

10 CRA, p 20; A+P, pp 24, 30. These accounts differ slightly, but significantly, in detail: 'to restore it'; 'to build his house' and 'to rebuild his house' respectively. In CRA, HB says CR was with '...Sauer, another member of the Ministry ...' This was presumably J W Sauer (1850-1903), CR's sometime Colonial Secretary but may have been Dr Hans Sauer, mentioned in CRA, pp 80, 82, *passim*.

11 A+P, p 24.

12 DAC, p 436; A+P, p 25.

13 JLMA; According to DAC, p 66: '...the earliest extant drawing is dated 6 October 1892 and is for a house at Kenilworth.' The Pretoria Observatory predates that by four months.

14 *See* D H Thompson, *The Story of a School (A Short History of Wynberg Boys' High School)*, 1961, pp 73, 93, 107 and plan facing p 91.

15 Plans, JLMA, BC 206; DAC, pp 66, 399; HBSA, p 51.

16 Hopetown House: BC 206, file 51, CCC 1894002166 Claremont; Johnson, *op cit*, p 400. Glion (Sunningdale): BC 206, file 273, DAC, p 400. Roodeboom: CCC 1893002917 Claremont, DAC, p 400.

17 *See* Ronald Lewcock, *Early Nineteenth-Century Architecture in South Africa, A Study of the Interaction of Two Cultures*, 1963, p 30.

18 Barrie Biermann in *Groote Schuur* (ed W J le Roux), p 16. Mary Cook in *Africana Notes and News,* 4 March 1947, pp 37-8.

19 *Groote Schuur* (ed W J le Roux) p 6; CRA, p 25; *see* too, Graham Viney, *Colonial Houses in South Africa*, 1987, p 170.

20 CRA, p 21; A+P, p 24.

21 Biermann, *Groote Schuur* (ed le Roux), p 19.

22 CRA, pp 21-2; *Groote Schuur* (ed le Roux), p 9.

23 CRA, p 9; A+P, p 32.

24 CRA, pp 22-3.

25 Biermann 'The sources of designs for historic buildings at the Cape', in *The Preservation and Restoration of Historic Buildings in South Africa* (eds R F M Immelman and G D Quin), 1968, pp 29-30.

26 R R Langham-Carter, *St Andrew's*, 1977, p 8.

27 A I Little, *History of the City Club, Cape Town 1878-1938*, 1938, pp 23-4, 28.

28 Langham-Carter, *St Andrew's*, p 10. *See* also HBSA, pp 81-3, but note that Dr Greig's term 'Kentish School' (church pattern) cannot be traced in standard English architectural historiography and appears to be of her own invention.

29 Langham-Carter, *St Andrew's*, p 37. *See* HBSA, p 82, for a full-page photo illustration but note incorrect date and implied attribution.

30 Langham-Carter, *St Andrew's*, p 39. *The Thames and Hudson Encyclopaedia of British Art*, p 47, states: 'His gift for two-dimensional design led him to produce models for stained glass, tapestries and other objects...'

31 DAC, pp 400-1; JLMA, BC 206, file 273.

32 DAC, p 400. HBSA, p 50, describes this as '...the first [house] to be designed by Baker at the Cape.'

33 CRA, pp 22, 26.

34 Kolaro: JLMA, BC 206, file 265; also DAC, p 401. Murray Villas: JLMA, BC 206, file 71; DAC, p 402.

35 Garrett and Parker both joined the City Club in 1895.

36 *See* Little, p 28.

37 Surviving drawings show that the design for St Barnabas went through three stages, starting with a Gothic Revival scheme, dated 22 October 1896, followed by a simplified version and the final Arts and Crafts design dated October 1897. *See* also HBSA, p 83.

38 *See* Johnson's biographical notes on Kendall, Masey, *et al*, DAC, pp 376, 379-80.

39 Ibid, pp 408, 93-95; CRA, pp 66-7; and Hefer, p 64.

40 *See Cape Times*, 16 December 1896, for reports and pictures of the fire damage. Also CRA, pp 30-3; A+P, p 31, and J G McDonald, *Rhodes: A Life*, 1927, p 218.

CHAPTER FOUR

1 A+P, p 31; *Groote Schuur* (ed le Roux), p 27.

2 *Groote Schuur* (ed le Roux), p 9.

3 Ibid, p 23; DAC, p 88.

4 *See* HBSA, pp 244, 255.

5 Viney, p 174, remarks: '...the whole is marred by a most ungainly metal plaque in the central gable...an immature mistake and no amount of sophistry on Baker's part about symbolism in architecture can alter this fact.' *See* also HBSA, p 55, and Roderick Gradidge, *Dream Houses: The Edwardian Ideal*, 1980, p 135.

6 James Laver, in DNB, Compact Edition, p 2936.

7 Little, p 29.

8 Ibid.

9 FK to Pearse, 16 January 1946, copy in collection of HSRC, Pretoria.

10 DAC, p 90.

11 Ibid, pp 74-6 and, for notes on Stent, p 113.

12 Invoices for book purchases, JLMA, BC 206. For discussion on these works and their authors *see* David Watkin, *The Rise of Architectural History*, 1980, pp 97-102.

13 DAC, pp 77-8, 403.

14 Ibid.

15 *See* Johnson's chronological list of domestic work by Baker and his partners at the Cape, Appendix F, DAC, pp 456-9.

16 FK, draft of *Appreciation – HB*, attached to letter to Prof Pearse, 9 September 1925, JLMA, BC 206.

17 *See* Eric H Bolsmann, *The Mount Nelson*, 1978, pp 79-82, 86-9.

18 FK, draft of *Appreciation – HB, loc cit.*

19 HB to Archbishop of Cape Town, 28 September 1897, JLMA, BC 206.

20 R R Langham-Carter, *Old St George's*, 1976, p 67.

21 Unidentified quotation from Desirée Picton-Seymour's *Victorian Buildings in South Africa*, 1977, p 88.

22 *See* HBSA, p 88.

23 *Groote Schuur* (ed le Roux), p 9.

24 R R Langham-Carter, *Under the Mountain: The Story of St Saviour's, Claremont*, 1973, p 9.

25 Ibid.

26 DAC, pp 78, 400-1.

CHAPTER FIVE

1 This very architectural depiction hangs in Groote Schuur and is illustrated in *Groote Schuur* (ed le Roux), p 105.

2 HB's design drawing was annotated: '...seen and approved by Rhodes, 16 August 1899.' Illustrated in L Marriott Earle 'The works of Herbert Baker' *Architect and Builder* [SA], vol 17 (Oct 1967, pp 22-7).

3 A+P, p 35; HBSA, pp 61-3; DAC, pp 91-2, 407; CRA, pp 43-4. Plans JLMA, BC 206, file 435.

4 HB 'The origin of old Cape architecture' in A F Trotter, *Old Colonial Houses*, pp 1-7, including a sketch by HB of the hall at Nooitgedacht. *See* also A F Trotter, 'The origin of the Cape Gable' AR, vol 15 (Jan-June) 1904, pp 35-6.

5 DAC, pp 93, 408. HBSA, pp 243-4.

6 HB's Nomination Papers for election to RIBA Fellowship. Application statement, 26 September 1899; elected 30 January 1900. RIBA, London.

7 HBSA, pp 60-1; DAC, pp 92-3, 407.

8 A+P, pp 32-4. *See* Lionel Curtis, *With Milner in South Africa*, 1951, p 249.

9 DAC, pp 437-8.

10 J G Lockhart and C M Woodhouse, *Rhodes*, 1963, pp 437, 439.

11 DAC, p 96.

12 HBSA, p 243 (and 212 for St James).

13 DAC, pp 348-9.

14 CRA, p 55; A+P, p 35.

15 CRA, pp 15 and facsimile of letter following.

16 Lockhart and Woodhouse, *Rhodes*, pp 445-6. They arrived in London on 7 April 1900.

17 CRA, p 52; Answers to 'Pearse's questions' attached to HB to Pearse, 22 November 1925, copy in collection of HSRC. *See also* HBSA, pp 100-5 and A+P, pp 35-6.

18 CRA, pp 18, 52.

19 CRA, p 52; A+P, p 37-9.

20 CRA, p 53.

21 CRA, p 53.

22 FK, *Appreciation – HB*, 9 September 1925, JLMA, BC 206.

23 Indeed it has a decided likeness to Shaw's Alliance Building in St James's Street, London (1882), destroyed in the Second World War but illustrated in Stamp and Amery, *Victorian Buildings*, pp 144-5.

24 HBSA, pp 71-5; Greig, *Guide to Architecture in South Africa*, 1971, p 99.

25 *Cape Times*, 4 October 1902.

26 FK to Pearse, 6 December 1945. Copy in collection of HSRC.

27 A Crawford, *C R Ashbee*, p 119; Extracts from Ashbee's Journal of 7 June 1903, copy in JLMA, BC 318 (Walgate).

28 CRA, pp 44-5; A+P, pp 34-5; DAC, pp 90-1, 407; HBSA, pp 62, 64.

29 Rudyard Kipling, *Something of Myself*, 1937, p 166. *See also* Renée Durbach, *Kipling's South Africa*, 1988, p 61 *et seq.*

30 *See* Picton-Seymour, *Historical Buildings in South Africa*, 1989, p 34. This, however, seems unlikely as the poem was not published until 1910: J M S Tompkins, *The Art of Rudyard Kipling*, p 263. The Kiplings made their last visit to SA in Jan-April 1908.

31 Curtis, *With Milner*, p 250.

32 DAC, pp 79-80, 403.

33 DAC, pp 96, 409; J Rennie, *The Buildings of Central Cape Town*, vol 2: catalogue, pp 300-1. Note that Rennie does not attribute the Secretary's House to HB: 'suspect *c.*1930.'

34 *Cape Times*, 19 August 1901; Greig, *A guide*, p 89.

35 Curtis, *With Milner*, p 248.

36 DAC, pp 96, 409; JLMA, BC 206, file 118.

37 DAC, pp 82-3, 405; JLMA, BC 206, file 49.

38 DAC, pp 81-2, 404; JLMA, BC 206, file 526.

39 DAC, pp 80-1, 404; JLMA, BC 206, file 161.

40 Rennie, *The Buildings of Central Cape Town*, pp 210-12; Picton-Seymour, *Victorian Buildings*, pp 93-5.

41 HBSA, pp 86-8.

42 *See* HB, 'Church building in Africa' *The Builder* (London), vol 166, 1946, pp 274-6, 293-5.

43 *See* DAC, *passim.*

44 'Sir Herbert Baker: in memoriam' SAAR, vol 31, July 1946, pp 168-71.

45 Ibid, p 171.

46 Ibid.

47 Lockhart and Woodhouse, *Rhodes*, p 469 ff.

48 Quoted Ibid, p 478.

49 CRA, 123-4. Also A+P, p 42.

50 *See* Walter Nimocks, *Milner's Young Men: The 'Kindergarten' in Edwardian Imperial affairs*, London, 1968. *See* also A+P, p 49.

51 HB to Pearse, 22 November 1925, answers to 'Pearse's questions' numbers 16 and 17, copy in HSRC collection. A+P, p 48.

52 Ibid.

CHAPTER SIX

1 A+P, p 48.

2 Curtis, *With Milner*, p 329. The remark that 'Baker wants a *pied à terre* when he comes up to Johannesburg' suggests that initially, at least, HB had meant to remain at the Cape whilst conducting his Transvaal practice by means of regular visits and a partner-in-charge.

3 A+P, p 48. Three versions of the name of the house can be found in print, including HBSA and HBDW: The Stone House, Stone House and Stonehouse. HB to Braamfontein Estates, 8 September 1902, clearly states: 'The name by which I wish the property to be called is "Stonehouse."' LB 1: 241.

4 HBDW, Appendix A, pp 19-20.

5 Ibid, p 8.

6 Ibid, p 18; A+P, p 53. Construction began at the end of February 1903.

7 HB to George Farrar, 12 March 1902, LB 1: 12.

8 HB to J Dale Lace, 7 May 1902, LB 1: 13.

9 *See* Dennis Radford, *Ernest Willmott Sloper, The Architects of Parktown*, no A2, The Parktown and Westcliff Heritage Trust, 1987.

10 A+P, p 48.

11 A Crawford, *CR Ashbee*, p 120. Journal, 7 July 1903.

12 'Our patience having become exhausted we are moving into the house today, and must ask you to finish everything immediately.' 16 March 1903, LB 2: 51.

13 HB to Keightley, 26 September 1902, LB 1: 307.

14 *See* Nimocks, *Milner's Young Men.*

15 Curtis, *With Milner*, p 315 *et seq, passim.*

16 A+P, p 50.

17 A+P, p 46.

18 HB to Rand Club, confirming election, 11 March 1902, LB 1: 6.

19 HB to W Sargant, 29 August 1902, LB 1: 217.

20 Curtis, *With Milner*, p 338.

21 Flora Shaw is quoted as saying: 'Johannesburg at present has no politics. It is much too busy with material problems. It is hideous and detestable, luxury without order, sensual enjoyment without art, riches without refinement, display without dignity. Everything in fact which is most foreign to the principles alike of morality and taste by which decent life has been guided in every state of civilisation.' E Moberley Bell, *Flora Shaw*, 1947, p 107.

22 EL to HB, 15 February 1903, BaH/1/1/1-7, RIBA. Quoted by Christopher Hussey, *The Life of Sir Edwin Lutyens*, 1950, pp 121-2.

23 EL to HB, 26 December 1904, BaH/1/1/1-7, RIBA. Quoted by Greig, HBSA, pp 166-7.

24 HBDW, Appendix A, pp 19-20.

25 Ibid, p 19.

26 The letter books enabled copies of handwritten documents, as well as typewritten papers, to be made onto consecutively numbered pages of delicate tissue and stored in volumes.

27 HB to RIBA, 10 July 1902, LB 1: 88.

28 HB to Rev Vyvyan, 28 August 1902, LB 1: 210.

29 HB to Kipling, 29 August 1902, LB 1: 211.

30 HB to Dale Lace, 26 September 1902, LB 1: 304.

31 President of the Military Tribunal.

32 HB to Church, 8 September 1902, LB 1: 236.

33 HB to Standard Bank of SA, 13 November 1902, LB 1: 487.

34 HB to Herbert Nicholson, 27 November 1902, LB 1: 547.

35 HB to Schumacher, 29 October 1902, LB 1. 444.

36 HB to Littlewood, 23 December 1902, LB 1: 666.

37 HB to Littlewood, 2 January 1903, LB 1: 709.

38 HB to DPW, 10 December 1902, LB 1: 606.

39 HB to John Begg, 8 December 1902, LB 1: 593.

40 Begg became Consulting Architect to the Government of India. See Robert Grant Irving, *Indian Summer: Lutyens, Baker and Imperial Delhi*, 1981, pp 92-3, 100.

41 HB to Editor *The Star*, 21 January 1903, LB 1: 818. St Mary's Cathedral, eventually built by Frank Fleming to amended designs.

42 DPW to HB, 29 July 1902, TA PWD, vol 109 and 1102/161.

43 HB to DPW, 30 July 1902, LB 1: 134.

44 HB to Schumacher, 5 August 1902, LB 1: 153.

45 HB to Davidson (Colonial Secretary), 12 August 1902, LB 1: 166.

46 HB to DPW, 27 August 1902, LB 1: 199.

47 HB to DPW, 22 January 1903, LB 1: 823.

48 HB to FM, 7 July 1902, LB 1: 79.

49 HB to Gen Lyttelton, 19 July 1902, LB 1: 103.

50 HB to Lady Lyttelton, 29 November, LB 1: 562.

51 A+P, p 52.

52 HB to Ballantyne (Contractors), 2 February 1903, LB 1: 879.

53 A+P, p 52.

54 HB to Eckstein & Co, 3 October 1902, LB 1: 337.

55 For HB's minehouse projects see three articles by Dennis Radford in *South African Journal of Cultural and Art History*: 1989 3(3); 1990 1(2) and 1990 1(3).

56 DAC, pp 219-20, 405. Plans JLMA, BC 206, file 52. The house was to have been built in Marks Road but no such road is known.

57 A+P, p 55.

58 DAC, pp 227-9, 411-2; SAAB, September 1904, pp 214-7; HBSA, pp 64-7; Picton-Seymour, *Victorian Buildings*, pp 130-1.

59 A+P, p 32.

60 CRA, p 71.

61 A+P, p 33.

62 JLMA, BC 206, file 221.

63 SAAB, September 1904, p 215. HB had the 'great bad fortune' to have missed seeing Ashbee, 'both here, Bloemfontein and Cape Town.' HB to E B Sargant, 16 July 1903, LB 2: 609.

64 Ibid.

65 HB to Sammy Marks, 24 October 1902, LB 1: 431. Letter sent with plans to approve for 'your site in Parliament Street.' Also letters dated 26 November, LB 1: 648, and 18 December, LB 1:654, indicate Baker's close control of the design at the conceptual stage.

66 FK to Pearse, 6 December 1945, copy in HSRC collection.

67 HB to Colonial Secretary, 28 October 1902, LB 1: 433.

68 Ibid.

69 HB to FM, 24 December 1902, LB 1: 679.

70 HB to H W Wilson, 13 June 1903, LB 2: 481.

71 *See* note 67 above.

72 HB to Asst Col Sec Bloemfontein, 28 April 1903, LB 2: 290.

73 HB to Wilson, 24 September 1903, LB 2: 981.

74 HB to G A Wright, 6 May 1903, LB 2: 327.

75 Fred Masey to HB, 1 September 1905, JLMA, BC 206.

76 A+P, p 51.

77 HB to Russell (Asst Dir Ed) , 24 November 1902, LB 1: 523.

78 For Lord Milner's post-war reconstruction policy, *see* John Marlowe, *Milner: Apostle of Empire*, London, 1976, pp 140.

79 Viney, *Colonial Houses*, p 208, 210.

80 HB to Col Byron, 29 December 1903, LB 3: 670.

81 A+P, p 55; HBSA, pp 142-9; Viney, *Colonial Houses*, pp 208-19.

82 Viney, p 214.

83 EWS to HB, 3 November 1904, author's collection.

84 Col Byron to HB, 13 January 1905, author's collection.

85 Ibid, 17 July 1905.

86 HB to E B Hugh-Jones, 18 November 1903, LB 3: 381; 25 November 1903, LB 3: 431.

87 HB to Hugh-Jones, 28 November, LB 3: 464.

88 A+P, p 57.

89 A M Barrett, *Michaelhouse 1896-1968*, 1969, p 17.

90 DAC, p 435. HB to Charles Currey, 'I have an old iron painted chest, more suited to a museum than private house, which I am willing to lend to Groot Constantia...on the understanding that it forms part of the furnishing of the main hall...Though a small gift in itself...' The chest is not in evidence today.

91 DAC, pp 221-2, 420.

92 DAC, pp 221, 409.

93 HB to FM, 4 December 1903, quoted by Viney, *Colonial Houses*, p 214.

CHAPTER SEVEN

1 Baker gave no advance warnings of his departure; the first letter on file to mention it was written the day before he left Johannesburg. 12 January 1904, LB 3: 731.

2 HB to Mrs Dale Lace, 20 January 1904, LB 3: 829.

3 HB to Pearse, 22 November 1925, copy in HSRC collection.

4 A+P, p 56.

5 EWS to Building Inspector, 25 January 1904, LB 3: 839, and to Barrow, LB 3: 848. HBSA, p 256.

6 EWS to Sister Superior, 3 February 1904, LB 3: 891. A sketch for a chapel and altar followed on 19 February 1904, LB 3: 988.

7 EWS to Col Byron, 6 February 1904, LB 3: 917.

8 EWS to Rev A F Newton, 26 February 1904, LB 4: 26. HBSA, pp 258-60.

9 HBSA, pp 119, 122, 214.

10 EWS to J J Kirkness, 4 March 1904, LB 4: 80.

11 EWS to DPW, 5 April 1904, LB 4: 238.

12 EWS to Town Engineer Pretoria, 7 April 1904, LB 4: 241.
13 Several letters on this subject were written in April and May, LB 4.
14 EWS to Rev A Newton, 4 May 1904, LB 4: 377.
15 EWS to Mrs Solomon, 11 June 1904, LB 4: 512.
16 EWS to FK, 6 September 1904, LB 4: 877.
17 EWS to Barrow, 1 July 1904, LB 4: 607.
18 EWS to Editor *The Star*, 27 July 1904, LB 4: 695.
19 EWS to HB, 6 August 1904, LB 4: 740.
20 EWS to Barrow, 9 August 1904, LB 4: 753.
21 FK to FM, 1 December 1904, JLMA, BC 206.
22 EWS to Editor *The Star*, 13 August 1904, LB 4: 765.
23 HB to FF, 16 August 1904, LB 4: 801.
24 HB to Sir George Farrar, 20 August 1904, LB 4: 807; HB to Howard Pim, 29 August 1904, LB 4: 842; HB to Drummond Chaplin, 7 September 1904, LB 4: 880. Farrar's Bedford Court had now been occupied for six months.
25 HB to FF, 12 September 1904, LB 4: 912.
26 HB to Rev Henry Johnson, 11 October 1904, LB 5: 39. St John has since been demolished.
27 Construction started on Marienhof just six days after the receipt of tenders.
28 The firm requested a telephone the next day.
29 HBSA, ch 8, *passim*; Viney, *Colonial Houses*, pp 246-55.
30 HB to Col Fowke, 22 September 1903, LB 2: 966.
31 Ibid.
32 HB to Col C Glyn, 5 December 1904, LB 5: 358.
33 HB to John Ralston, 10 December 1904, LB 5: 385; EWS to HB, 19 December 1904, LB 5: 419.
34 *See* Viney, *Colonial Houses,* p 251 and notes.
35 Viney, pp 246-55 *passim*, takes the view that HB was extravagant, and that 'Perhaps in the end one should just sit back and admire Baker's skill and nerve in manipulating one and all.' However, Viney's contention that: 'At times, Baker's interpretation of allocations and instructions and the firm's withholding of detailed estimates came close to open dishonesty' is, in this writer's view, too far-fetched.
36 Hitchens's Memorandum, 28 February 1906, TA PWD vol 109, 110, 21/161/6. Quoted by Viney, *Colonial Houses,* p 246.
37 A+P, p 51.
38 Ibid.
39 Viney, *Colonial Houses*, p 251.
40 Strangely modernistic in their two-dimensional plane aspect.
41 HBSA, p 129; A+P, p 52-3.
42 Quoted by Viney, *Colonial Houses*, p 223.
43 HB to A Douglas-Pennant, 6 September 1904, LB 4: 869; HB to W Dettlebach, 7 September 1904, LB 4: 882; HB to C L Andersson, 7 September 1904, LB 4: 883; these accounts were paid shortly afterwards.
44 FK to FM, 5 December 1904, JLMA, BC 206.
45 FK to FM, 9 December 1904, JLMA, BC 206.

CHAPTER EIGHT

1 FK to HB, 9 January 1905, author's collection.
2 11 January 1905, '...I was laid up with a bad attack of influenza.' LB 5: 518.
3 HB to Marks, 22 February 1905, LB 6: 25.
4 HB to Marks, 24 March 1905, LB 6: 214.
5 Probably from 1 May. HB to Marks, 26 May 1905, LB 6: 581.
6 Langham-Carter and Rennie, ch 2 of draft manuscript of 'Rhodes Memorial: An Account of the Building of the Memorial'.
7 Ibid.
8 HBSA, p 254.
9 A+P, p 147.
10 *See* Greig, *Guide to Architecture in South Africa*, p 80.
11 Marlowe, *Milner*, p 155.
12 Ibid, pp 152-7.
13 HB to FK, 24 July 1905, LB 7: 43.
14 *Cape Times, circa* late August 1905, cutting in JLMA, BC 206.
15 Fred Masey to Cape Town Office, 25 August 1905, JLMA, BC 206.
16 Ibid.
17 Fred Masey to Cape Town Office, 1 September 1905, JLMA, BC 206.
18 Ibid.
19 Fred Masey to HB, 7 September 1905, JLMA, BC 206.
20 HB to FM, 21 August 1905, LB 7: 258.
21 HB to Col Byron, 21 August 1905, LB 7: 261. *See* note 47 of this chapter.
22 HB to Rev Howell Griffiths, 11 September 1905, LB 7: 384.
23 K C Lawson, *Venture of Faith*, 1968, p 45.
24 Ibid.
25 *See* DNB, *St George's Church, Groot Drakenstein, Cape Province: A Short History of the Church and Parish.*
26 EWS to Arcadia Church Council, 30 October 1905, LB 7: 680.
27 CRA, p131, *The Definitive Edition of Rudyard Kipling's Verse*, 1940, p 210.
28 FM to HB (private), 28 August 1905, author's collection.
29 FM to HB, 23 November 1905, author's collection. Masey added in his own hand: '...upon reading the above my suggestions seem couched in dogmatic terms most unintentionally! Please forgive. FM'
30 FM to HB, 4 December 1905, author's collection.
31 *See* note 29 above.
32 *See* HBSA, pp 111, 113.
33 Quoted in A Wilson, *The Strange Ride of Rudyard Kipling: His Life and Works*, London, 1977, p 224.
34 Langham-Carter and Rennie, 'Rhodes Memorial', ch 5.
35 HB to Col J W Bell, 27 November 1905, LB 7: 900.
36 HB to Col J W Bell, 12 December 1905, LB 8: 42.
37 HB to Archdeacon Hamilton, 19 December 1905, LB 8: 91.
38 HB to C B Johnston, 16 November 1905, LB 7: 800.
39 HB to Harper Bros, 9 December 1905, LB 8: 12.
40 HB to Town Eng (Bye-law submission), 19 December 1905, LB 8: 80.
41 *See* HBSA, pp 256-7.
42 HB to H Spicer, 15 January 1906, LB 8: 271.
43 HB to FM, 25 January 1906, LB 8: 381.
44 Ibid.
45 HB to H Crawford, 22 January 1906, LB 8: 342; and HB to L G Baker, 5 April 1906, LB 8: 673.
46 HB to E Bradshaw, 2 February 1906, LB 8: 411.
47 The arbitration award was made in February. LB 8: 487.
48 HB to Lady Warden of St Anne's, 24 March 1906, LB 8: 638.
49 HB to Arthur Struben, 3 December 1906, LB 10: 40.
50 HBSA, p 270. *See* Willmott's obituary, *Journal of the Association of Transvaal Architects*, vol 3, September 1916.

51 HB to Capt H R Bourne, 16 May 1906, LB 8: 780 and 13 July 1906, LB 9: 34.
52 26 April 1906, LB 8: 734 and 18 May 1906, LB 8: 805 respectively.
53 HB to Lady Warden of St Anne's, 3 July 1906, LB 8: 983.
54 HB to Rev Douglas Ellison, 19 June 1906, LB 8: 906.
55 HB to Lady Warden of St Anne's, 17 May 1906, LB 8: 801.
56 HB to Rev H Hammersley, 30 July 1906, LB 9: 115.
57 HB to Rev H Hammersley, 18 September, 1906, LB 9: 524.
58 Lawson, *Venture of Faith*, p 48.
59 Ibid, p 69.
60 Ibid.
61 HB to Rev A T Hare, 8 August 1906, LB 9: 199; HB to George Hull, 3 September 1906, LB 9: 395; HB to Rev J A Cutter, 3 September 1906, LB 9: 401.
62 HB to Rev A Hankey, 20 August 1906, LB 9: 274; HB to Rev W P G McCormick, LB 9: 493.
63 HB to Archdeacon Furse, 20 September 1906, LB 9: 541.
64 HB to A J Marshall, 18 September 1906, LB 9: 523.
65 HB to A J Marshall, 4 October 1906, LB 9: 648.
66 HB to Furse, 12 October 1906, LB 9: 709; HB to Rev J A Cutter, 23 October 1906, LB 9: 795; FF to HB, 5 November 1906, LB 9: 888.
67 FF to HB, 7 November 1906, LB 9: 902.
68 19 December, LB 9: 180 and 18 December, LB 9: 180.
69 HB to Edmanson and Thomas, 22 December 1906, LB 9: 217.
70 HB to *The Builder* (London), with three-page descriptive report, 24 December 1906, LB 9: 224 and 226.
71 *See* note 69 above.

CHAPTER NINE

1 HB to R H Cooper, 7 January 1907, LB 10: 317.
2 HB to R H Cooper, 4 January 1907, LB 10: 293.
3 HB to Standard Bank, 5 January 1907, LB 10: 310.
4 HB to Exploration House, 16 February 1907, LB 10: 782; and HB to D F Ellis, 4 January 1907, LB 10: 300. By June the work flow had worsened; HB's reference speaks for itself: 'It is with real regret that owing to shortage of work we find it necessary to part with Mr R B Rowley, who has worked with us for more than 12 years...' LB 11: 632. The fact that all the correspondence in August was handwritten suggests the firm was without a typist too. *See* letter books.
5 FM to HB, 15 January 1907, author's collection.
6 HB to Dr C L Samson, 5 January 1907, LB 10: 308.
7 Langham-Carter and Rennie, 'Rhodes Memorial', chs 6 and 9.
8 Ibid, note 5 for ch 9.
9 This was the ninth journey Kipling had made to South Africa and his penultimate. *See* Renée Durbach, *Kipling's South Africa*, for a useful chronology of his visits.
10 HB to Webber and Wentzel, 27 February 1907, LB 10: 908.
11 FF to HB, 4 March 1907, LB 10: 928; and HB to Lady Warden of St Anne's, 6 March 1907, LB 10: 951.
12 HB to Rev Fitzwilliam Carter, 21 March 1907, LB 11: 110.
13 FF to HB, 8 July 1907, LB 11: 678.
14 Ibid.
15 Ibid.
16 HB to Hugh-Jones (from Cape Town), 11 September 1907, LB 11: 863.

17 FF to Hugh-Jones, 27 September 1907, LB 11: 915.
18 FF to Hugh-Jones, 2 October 1907, LB 11: 921.
19 FF to Hugh-Jones, 14 October 1907, LB 11: 953.
20 HB to Hugh-Jones, 17 December 1907, LB 12: 165. HB had arrived back in Johannesburg by 7 November.
21 HB to W K Whittaker, 15 January 1908, LB 12: 266.
22 HB to Mrs Haarhoff, 11 November 1907, LB 12: 43.
23 HB to J A Gutten, 5 December 1907, LB 12: 117.
24 HB to FM, 3 January 1908, JLMA, BC 206.
25 Ibid.
26 HB to FM, 6 January 1908, JLMA, BC 206.
27 HB to FM, 10 January 1908, JLMA, BC 206.
28 HB to FM, 10 February 1908, JLMA, BC 206.
29 Ibid.
30 Ibid.
31 HB to FM, 11 February 1908, JLMA, BC 206.
32 EL to HB, 10 May 1908, RIBA, BaH/1/1/1-7. Quoted in Hussey, *Life of Sir Edwin Lutyens*, p 180.
33 Ibid; and EL to HB, 15 July 1908, *loc cit.*
34 EL to Emily Lutyens, 8 October 1908, *The letters of Edwin Lutyens to his wife Lady Emily,* eds Clayre Percy and Jane Ridley, 1985, pp 163-4.
35 Hussey, *Life*, p 180.
36 February 1909, Ibid. HBSA, p 218. 'Dear, dear Lutyens, the facts [fates?] are intervening...' Greig's parenthesis.
37 HB to FM, 21 January 1908, LB 12: 288.
38 HB to FM, 15 January 1908, LB 12: 259; HB to G E Webber, 25 February 1908, LB 12: 438.
39 HBSA, pp 156, 158-64.
40 HB to Bishop's Chaplain, 13 February 1908, LB 12: 378 and 5 April, LB 12: 612; HBSA, p 160.
41 HB to Canon Farmer, 7 March 1908, LB 12: 489.
42 HBSA, p 164.
43 HB to C W Whall, 5 October 1908, LB 13: 587.
44 HB to Col R Curtis, 10 April 1908, LB 12: 639.
45 HB to Archdeacon Furse, 30 June 1908, LB 13: 40 and 41.
46 HB to Rev W R Gibbons, 15 August 1908, LB 13: 247.
47 HB to Canon Farmer, 28 September 1908, LB 13: 496.
48 *See* Kathleen Cross, *An Open Door: A Brief History of the Parish Church of Saint Michael and All Angels, Sunnyside, Pretoria, 1903-1978*, 1978. This exemplary church history contains HB's own description of the building, p 17.
49 HB to Col Sec, 31 October 1908, LB 13: 799.
50 An arbitration was to be held as 'Your brother has written that there is some evidence putting blame on the electric installation...' HB to FM, 5 November 1908, LB 13: 859.
51 HB to FM, October 1908, LB 13: 814.
52 HB to H Johnstone, 10 November 1908, LB 13: 859. *See* also Radford's articles.
53 HB to Fred Masey, 18 November 1908, LB 13: 997.
54 FF to HB, 26 November 1908, LB 14: 86; FF to General Manager Central South African Railways, LB 14: 105.
55 '...Mr Fleming coming to discuss on the site.' HB to Rev A J Hare, 12 December 1908, LB 14: 205.
56 HB to Church Warden, 24 December 1908, LB 14: 315; HB to Barrow, 17 December 1908, LB 14: 245.
57 HB to E N Ostend, 29 December 1908, LB 14: 332.

CHAPTER TEN

1 HB to Dr Engelenburg, 11 January 1909, LB 14: 457.

2 HB to Dr Engelenburg, 10 February 1909, LB 14: 787.

3 Baker produced the following (undated) memorandum, apparently for his own records, entitled 'Diary of Government Work', covering the year 1909 and set out thus: 'Feb. 11th. First negotiations re Railway Station. 19th. Inspected competition plans. (Railway Station). March (early). Correspondence with Institute of Architects. (R'way Station) 17. Began sketch plan for Railway Station. Apl. 7. Left for Cape Town. May 12. Returned. June 2. Began negotiations re Union Buildings. August 11. Contract plans (Railway Station) taken to Pretoria. Nov. 11. Ill. 24. Final approval of Union Buildings sketches. 27. Went to Muizenberg till December 9th.'

4 HB to Charles Murray, 16 Feb 1909, LB 14: 849.'

5 HB's Memorandum. For HB's letter confirming appointment, and the division of responsibilities see: HB to The Hon R H Brand, 25 March 1909, LB 15: 251.

6 HB's Memorandum.

7 See note 36, ch 9 above.

8 Hussey, *Life of Sir Edwin Lutyens*, pp 180-1.

9 Ibid, p 180.

10 Ibid, p 181.

11 HB to FM, 23 February 1909, LB 14: 927. In HB's letter to A J Marshall, 22 February 1909, LB 14: 906, he writes: 'My proposal...act as half Clerk of Works and half Draughtsman during my absence, working of course under Fleming, whom I have now taken into Junior Partnership...I am also rather more confident about the future than I have been lately...I think you are quite right that the only places where our professions will be prosperous for the next year or so will be here and in Pretoria.'

12 Dorothea Fairbridge, *Gardens of South Africa*, 1924, pp 31-3.

13 A+P, p 53.

14 See HBSA, p 125 and plates 147, 8 and 9.

15 HB to FM, 18 March 1909, LB 15: 180.

16 Ibid.

17 FM to HB, 22 May 1909, author's collection.

18 HB to FM, 23 July 1909, LB 16: 501.

19 HB to FM, 23 July 1909, LB 16: 502. Baker had written an introductory chapter in A F Trotter's *Old Colonial Houses of the Cape of Good Hope* in 1900.

20 Ibid.

21 HB to FM, 14 August 1909, LB 16: 803.

22 A+P, p 57; HBSA, p 172.

23 HB to Hon E P Solomon, 3 June 1909, LB 15: 878.

24 A+P, p 58.

25 Ibid.

26 HB to B P Wall, 9 June 1909, LB 15: 927.

27 Quoted in Marcus Binney 'Attributes of the eternal' CL, 25 February 1982, pp 466-8.

28 Ibid.

29 HB to EL, 24 June 1909, RIBA, LuE/32/27/1.

30 Binney, *loc cit*, p 467.

31 Ibid; Margaret Whinney, *Wren*, 1971, calls the Royal Hospital at Greenwich '...probably the most distinguished group of buildings in England' p 183, and '...the placing of the Hall and Chapel with their domes, and the colonnades running back from them, are the essence of the design', p 190.

32 A+P, p 60. Also, in an undated Memorandum entitled 'Unrealised Designs: Meintjes Kop', he wrote: 'On some first ideas...which I had sketched out, I showed a low dome on the ridge of Meintjes Kop over a hundred feet above them, and on their central axis between the two domed-towers. Some object I felt was wanted there to perfect the design as a whole...' HB papers at Owletts, file S6d, copy in the HSRC collection.

33 A+P, p 61.

34 Ernest George, HB's old employer in London and now President of the RIBA, wrote somewhat belatedly to General Botha in support of HB (15 February 1910): 'Will you allow me to say how thoroughly the action of your Government is appreciated in the appointment of an architect exceptionally gifted for designing of the New Union Buildings at Pretoria...Your Government's action is more likely to result in the production of a dignified and appropriate building than if a competition had been resorted to. A showy drawing is so often selected and afterwards found wanting in essential fitness.' Quoted in HBSA, p 174.

35 See note 27 above.

36 Ibid.

37 Ibid.

38 Ibid.

39 HB to EL, 21 October 1909, RIBA, LuE/32/27/2.

40 HB's handwritten notes of the meeting, with sketches, on a Minute Paper, dated 24 November 1909, author's collection.

41 HB to FM, 2 November 1909, LB 17: 640.

42 Ibid.

43 HB to FM, 8 November 1909, LB 17: 736.

44 HB to EL, 23 December 1909, RIBA, LuE/32/27/4.

45 A+P, p 60.

46 HB to EL, 23 December 1909, RIBA, LuE/32/27/4.

47 For a splendid account of the whole New Delhi saga see Robert Grant Irving, *Indian Summer: Lutyens, Baker and Imperial Delhi* (London: 1981). Hussey's *Life of Sir Edwin Lutyens* is indispensable too, but much prejudiced in Lutyens's favour.

48 EL to HB, 1 February 1910, RIBA, LuE/32/27/5. Quoted by Hussey, *Life*.

49 Dennis Radford makes somewhat more of this point in a useful discussion, 'Baker, Lutyens, and the Union Buildings' SAJCAH, 1988, 2 (1), pp 62-9.

50 See note 27 above.

51 HB himself acknowledges this misnomer, '...concentrated round the "amphitheatre"; it is generally called so, though it is only a semicircular theatre as the Greeks knew it, and not the complete circle or oval which the Romans created for their spectacles.' A+P, p 59.

52 See Michael Keath 'Visions of greatness: Herbert Baker's Imperial Idealism and the Union Buildings' ASA, May/June 1989, pp 35-6; A+P, p 60.

53 Ibid.

54 HB 'The Government offices of Pretoria and the New Delhi', RIBAJ, vol xxxv, no 3, 10 December 1927, p 67.

CHAPTER ELEVEN

1 HB to Walter Reid, 15 December 1909, LB 18: 126.

2 HB returned on 9 December, the day on which the Sunnyside St Michael opened.

3 HB to Maskew Miller, 28 December 1909, LB 18: 214.

4 *See* HB's letter of 19 January 1910, LB 18: 485.

5 HB to FK (in Grahamstown), 'The Zimbabye [*sic*] job alone will take nearly three weeks and there is other work in Rhodesia which he will have to see about.' Kendall was asked to go to help out in Cape town.

6 HB to FM, 8 February 1910, LB 18: 736. *See* also HB to FM, 8 November 1909, LB 17: 736, where HB expresses his delight '...to hear that you have settled the matter of the Parliament House [Cape Town] so quickly and satisfactorily...I do not see how you can do this work and go up there [Rhodesia] at the same time. Therefore, I think you might reconsider your decision about Kendall.'

7 *See* note 34 for ch 10.

8 Quoted in HBSA, p 174

9 'The New Union Government Buildings, Pretoria' *The Architects' and Builders' Journal*, vol 33, 11 January 1911, pp 31-2, with perspective drawing of the west block.

10 Quoted by Marcus Binney, 'Attributes of the eternal' p 468.

11 HB to Sir D P de V Graaf (Minister of Public Works), 26 September 1911, carbon copy in author's collection.

12 Ibid; *see* also HBSA, pp 188-9.

13 HB 'The Government Offices of Pretoria and the New Delhi' *loc cit*, p 66.

14 HBSA, p 188. *See* W Wybergh, *The Building Stones of the Union of South Africa,* 1932, pp 153-62.

15 HB to Charles Murray, 28 June 1911, carbon copy in author's collection.

16 Agreed by the Minister, 5 August 1911, quoted in HBSA, p 187.

17 Quoted in Binney 'Attributes of the eternal' p 468.

18 J M Solomon 'The Union Buildings and their architect' *The State*, July 1910.

19 HB to EWS (in London), 2 September 1910, LB 21: 76.

20 HB to EWS, 10 October 1910, LB 21: 402.

21 Hussey, *Life*, p 200.

22 Ibid, p 203.

23 EL to Emily Lutyens, 13 December 1910; Percy and Ridley, eds, *Letters*, p 208. For other letters from EL to Emily from Johannesburg *see* pp 206-210.

24 Ibid, p 208.

25 Ibid.

26 Ibid, p 209.

27 Ibid.

28 Ibid.

29 Hussey, *Life*, p 391.

30 HBSA, pp 154-6.

31 Ibid, p 156.

32 Peter Jackson, *Historic Buildings of Harare: 1890-1940,* 1986, pp 83-4 'Cathedral of St Mary and All Saints: 1913-1964.' Also HBSA, pp 263-4 and A+P, pp 150-1.

33 HB to FM, 20 March 1911, LB 22: 9[?] 6.

34 HB to E A von Hirschberg, LB 23: 418.

35 Masey's childless marriage to Menne Hellet had been dissolved on 13 May 1910. He died on 3 September 1912.

36 *See* HBSA, pp 260-2. HB to Rev Ponsonby, 11 November 1912, LB 27: 920; print and specification enclosed. A one-sheet set of sketch plans, sections and elevations, dated June 1912, is at JLMA, BC 206, file 524.

37 R F Currey, *Rhodes University 1904-1970,* 1970, p 33.

38 Ibid.

39 Ibid.

40 HB to FK, 14 October 1910, LB 21: 445.

41 HB to FK, 6 February 1911, LB 22: 531.

42 HB to Gordon Leith 1911, 28 February 1911, LB 22, and 13 March, LB 22: 880.

43 J M Solomon 'Reverence in architecture' *The African Architect*, 1 September 1911.

44 HBDW, Appendix A, pp 15-16; HBSA, Appendix B, 241.

45 Ibid, p 7; HBSA, Appendix B, p 241.

46 HBSA, Appendix B, p 240 and HBDW, Appendix A, p 572.

CHAPTER TWELVE

1 EL to HB, 29 February 1912, RIBA, BaH/1/6/1-9. Quoted in Hussey, *Life*, p 246.

2 Hussey, *Life*, p 246.

3 Ibid.

4 Hussey, *Life*, p 247.

5 *See* HBSA, pp 246-8; Greig, *Guide,* p 125; Picton-Seymour, *Victorian Buildings*, p 213; R F Currey, *St Andrew's College Grahamstown 1858-1959,* 1959, pp 106-8.

6 Currey, *St Andrew's College*, p 107.

7 Greig mystifyingly calls this the 'Kentish School' pattern, HBSA, p 246.

8 Currey, *St Andrew's College*, p 108.

9 HB (signed by Marshall) to Prof R A Lehfeldt, 2 July 1912, with prices and estimates, LB 27: 13. HBDW, Appendix A, p 1.

10 HBSA, p 140.

11 A+P, p 55.

12 Langham-Carter and Rennie, 'Rhodes Memorial', ch 11.

13 Ibid.

14 Quoted in Hussey, *Life*, p 270.

15 A+P, p 63.

16 HB 'The problem of style' *The Times* (London), 3 October 1912. Reprinted in A+P, Appendix B, pp 218-22.

17 Hussey, *Life*, p 271.

18 Ibid, p 272.

19 Ibid.

20 A+P, p 64.

21 HB to FK, 23 November 1912, LB 27: 972. 'My cabin no is no 120 so please ask Isaacs to put the chair there, and anything else you have to send.' From Johannesburg, Fleming wrote: 'Mr Baker has left for England for about 3 months', LB 27: 998. Also HB to Bishop of Natal, 7 May 1913, LB 28: 895, 'Mr Fleming is expected to leave here for England on the 26th of this month, sailing from Cape Town on the 28th.'

22 FF to Batsfords (London), 27 December 1912, LB 28: 165. Also ordered was *Gardens for Small Country Houses*, by Gertrude Jekyll and Lawrence Weaver (two copies). Very likely to have been inspired by meeting Jekyll again, and the Lutyens connection.

23 A+P, p 64.

24 Hussey, *Life*, p 285.

25 *See* note 21 above.

26 HBSA, pp 199-201

27 Ibid, p 263.

28 *See* Cecil Graham and Flo Bird, *Sir Herbert Baker,* The Parktown and Westcliff Heritage Trust series no 13, for a reproduction of Alfred Baker's birth certificate, but beware of the numerous minor errors in an otherwise useful pamphlet.

29 EL to HB, 22 August 1913, RIBA, BaH/1/8/1-8. Quoted by Hussey, *Life*, p 296.

30 HB to EL, 26 September 1913, quoted by Hussey, *Life*, p 296.

31 Hussey, *Life*, pp 306, 311.

EPILOGUE

1 Kenneth Clark, *Another Part of the Wood* (London: 1974), p 221 in 1985 edition.

2 *See* Barrie Biermann's review of *Herbert Baker in South Africa*, 1970 by Doreen E Greig, in *Plan*, vol 56, no 10 (October 1971) p 25, for a sympathetic review.

3 John Summerson, Review of *Indian Summer: Lutyens, Baker and Imperial Delhi* (London: 1981) by Robert Grant Irving, in *Architects' Journal*, vol 175 (6 January 1982) p 26.

4 David Watkin, *The Rise of Architectural History*, 1980, p 173.

5 At the Hayward Gallery, London, November 1981 – January 1982[?]

6 *See* note 3 above.

7 *See* Hussey, *Life*, pp 307-8.

8 William Walcot (1874-1943). *See* DNB, 1941-50 and RIBA Library Notes, no 9.

9 Hussey, *Life*, p 323.

10 Ibid.

11 Ibid; LBID, p 149-50.

12 LBID, p 145.

13 Ibid.

14 *See* Mary Lutyens, *Edwin Lutyens: By his Daughter*, 1980, p 126. This author has developed this argument in an unpublished lecture 'Sticks, stones and laurels: Sir Herbert Baker and his critics' given at the Universities of Pretoria, Bloemfontein, Port Elizabeth, Cape Town, Natal and various other institutions, 1987-8.

15 Robert Byron 'The New Delhi' AR, vol 69 (January 1931) pp 1-30.

16 Byron 'New Delhi, 1: The architecture of the Viceroy's House' CL, 6 June 1931; and '5: The architecture of Sir Herbert Baker' 4 July 1931. *See* correspondence between HB and Sir Robert Witt, solicitor, 1931-1945, RIBA, BaH/1/11/1-35.

17 Hussey, *Life*, p 352.

18 Mary Lutyens, *Edwin Lutyens: By his Daughter*, p 189.

19 Nikolaus Pevsner, *The Buildings of England: London, vol 1, the Cities of London and Westminster*, 1957, p 164. *See* also A+P, pp 122-30.

20 HB 'The rebuilding of the Bank of England' *Architects' Journal*, vol 56 (2 August) 1922, p 146. *See* also HB and F W Troup 'The reconstruction of the Bank of England: old features to be retained in rebuilding' *Architects' Journal*, vol 61 (6 May) 1925, pp 706-15.

21 Pevsner, *Buildings of England: London*, p 165n.

22 Sir Charles Wheeler, *High Relief*, 1968, p 55, *passim*.

23 'India House' *Architect and Building News*, vol 123 (25 April) 1930, p 526. *See* Pevsner's views in *London*, p 297.

24 'India House' *Architect and Building News*, vol 119 (16 March) 1928, p 388.

25 A+P, p 134.

26 Arthur Mee (ed), *The King's England, Oxfordshire*, 1942, p 323.

27 Pevsner, *Buildings of England: Oxfordshire* (London: 1974), pp 65, 275-6.

28 Peter Hayworth, *The Oxford Guide to Oxford*, 1981, pp 109, 111.

29 *See* David Howarth 'A home for the spirit' CL, 23 June 1983, pp 1740-3.

30 A+P, p 136.

31 L Cumming-George, ed. *Architecture in South Africa*, vol 2, 1934, p 99.

32 J M Leighton 'South Africa House in the making' *Lantern*, vol 34 (30 April 1985) no 2, p 3.

33 Quotation, ibid, p 8. *See* also A+P, pp 131-3.

34 'South Africa House', *The Architect and Building News*, vol 134 (30 June 1933) p 370. Appended to this article is a list of sub-contractors, suppliers, etc., who built and decorated this building.

35 Pevsner, *London*, p 327.

36 David Atwell, Charles McKean, *et al. The Battle of the Styles: A Guide to Selected Buildings in London of the 1914-39 Period,* 1975, p 69.

37 'The Royal Empire Society new headquarters' *The Architect and Building News*, vol 148 (23 October 1936) pp 68-75.

38 Ibid, p 98.

39 Ibid, caption to illustration.

40 'London House, Guildford St, WC' *Architect and Building News*, 10 December 1937, p 308.

41 Christopher Hussey 'A Hall of Residence for Dominion students in London' CL, vol 97 (22 June 1945) p 1082.

42 Ibid, pp 1082-3.

43 Ibid, p 1083.

44 Pevsner, *London*, p 212.

45 Hugh Honour, *Neo-Classicism*, 1968, p 15. Pevsner disapprovingly describes such buildings as 'almost beyond comprehension', 'incredibly reactionary', 'almost unbelievable for its date', 'almost grotesquely reactionary', 'reactionary beyond belief...inscrutable to a visitor from abroad...', all gathered from Pevsner's *London* and quoted by David Watkin in *Morality and Architecture*, 1977, p 107.

46 'Modernism in architecture'. Report of debate at the RIBA, RIBAJ, vol 35 (9 June 1928) p 521.

GLOSSARY

ABACUS: Uppermost member of a classical capital.

AMPHITHEATRE: Properly, an elliptical or circular space surrounded by tiers of seating, as at the Colosseum in Rome. In South Africa loosely taken to mean any open-air theatre.

ANTLER POSTS: Vertical, timber, structural posts curved to resemble deer antlers. Usually positioned over principal roof timbers.

APEX: Highest point of a roof or gable, usually when these are of triangular shape.

APSE: Semicircular or polygonal end to a building, usually of a church.

ARCADE: A row of arches supported on columns or piers.

ARCHITRAVE: Lowermost member of a classical entablature (qv).

ASHLAR: Freestone (qv) employed in large, smooth, thin slabs as a facing to other materials such as brick.

ATRIUM: Inner court of a (especially Roman) house, open to the sky and surrounded by the roof and often by an arcade.

AXIS: An imaginary straight line on either side of which part of a building, or buildings, is symmetrically balanced.

BARREL VAULT: A continuous arched roof or ceiling over a room, corridor, or building, resembling the curved surface inside a barrel.

BAS-RELIEF: Sculpture or moulding in which carved figures project slightly from their background.

BASTION: Pointed projecting parts of an angled fortification

BOW-TOPPED WINDOW: Having a shallow curved head or top member.

BUTTRESS: A projecting mass of brickwork or masonry built to add strength to a wall by resisting lateral thrust from an arch, roof truss or vault.

CAPITAL: The top section, or head, of a column which spreads to increase its carrying capacity. In classical architecture it carries the entablature (qv).

CATSLIDE: Lower, less steep, part of a roof where a change of slope occurs.

CHANCEL: East part of a church reserved for clergy and choir, where the main altar is situated.

CHEVET: French term for the east end, apse (qv) or chancel (qv) of a church.

CLERESTORY: High level vertical window, or row of windows, occuring between roofs at different levels.

COLONNADE: Row of columns supporting an entablature (qv).

CORBEL: Projecting brick or stone bracket one end of which is built into the wall and the other supporting a beam or roof truss.

CORINTHIAN: Type of column or pilaster (qv). See Orders.

CORNICE: Top, projecting, section of an entablature (qv).

CROSSING: Space at the intersection of nave, chancel and transepts, often surmounted by a tower.

CRUCIFORM: Cross-shaped, usually referring to the plan of a church having a central tower flanked by transepts (qv).

CUPOLA: Small dome or lantern on a circular or polygonal base, crowning a larger dome, roof or turret.

CUSP: Projecting points at the meeting of the foils in Gothic tracery (qv).

DADO: Part of wall below waist height, usually panelled or painted differently from the upper part of the wall.

DENTILS: In classical architecture a series of small square blocks set in the cornice (qv).

DORMER WINDOW: Window with vertical front and sides projecting from a sloping roof and having a roof of its own.

DRUM: Circle of walling on which a dome rests.

ENTABLATURE: In classical architecture, the collective name for the horizontal elements which span between the supporting columns below.

FLECHE: Slender spire, usually of wood, rising from the ridge of a roof.

FREESTONE: Stone that cuts well in all directions, especially a fine-grained limestone or sandstone.

GABLE; GABLE WALL: The wall which fills the triangular area beneath a pitched roof, or rises above the roof to form a decorative outline terminating a building or a projection, such as an entrance.

GROIN VAULT: Junction of two intersecting barrel vaults (qv).

HIPPED-ROOF: Roof with sloping ends instead of vertical (gabled) ends.

ITALIANATE: Of Italian style or appearance.

JOISTS: Horizontal timbers laid parallel to each other to carry floor boards or other platforms.

LANCET WINDOW: Slender, pointed-arched, Gothic window.

LEAN-TO ROOF: Single slope roof, the upper part of which is supported by leaning against a higher vertical wall.

LYCH GATE: Covered wooden gateway at entrance to churchyard, providing a resting place for a coffin.

MANSARD ROOF: A roof having two pitches, the lower being steeper than the upper, containing attic accommodation with dormer windows.

MODILLIONS: A series of ornamental brackets, usually with scrolled ends, which give symbolic support to a cornice, especially in the Corinthian Order.

MULLION: A slender, vertical, element of stone, wood or other material which divides a window into smaller sections and gives strength to the whole.

NARTHEX: Enclosed vestibule or covered porch, often arcaded, at the main entrance to a church, leading into the nave (qv).

NAVE: Main body of a church west of the crossing or chancel (qv) often flanked by aisles.

ORDERS: In classical architecture, a system of design comprising a column with base, shaft, and capital supporting an entablature, following one of the established modes of decoration and proportion: Doric, Tuscan, Ionic, Corinthian, or Composite.

ORIEL: Bay window built off projecting brackets or corbels rather than based on ground foundations.

PALLADIAN: Architectural style following the examples and writings of Andrea Palladio (1508-80).

PARAPET: A low wall at the edge of a roof, bridge or sudden drop, providing safety, to conceal drainage gutters and – where decoratively shaped – an ornamental outline against the sky.

PEDIMENT: In classical architecture, a low-pitched gable above a portico, doors, windows, etc.

PENDENTIVES: The concave walling which fills the space between the base of a dome and the curves of supporting arches, as in '... a dome on pendentives'.

PILASTER: Flat column set against a wall projecting not more than one third of its width.

PLINTH: The base of a wall or pedestal, usually projecting slightly but, especially in the twentieth century, often recessed.

PORTICO: Roofed structure supported by columns to form an entrance feature.

QUEEN-POSTS: Pair of vertical posts placed symmetrically on a tie-beam (qv), connecting it with the rafters above.

QUOINS: Dressed stones at the corner of a building, sometimes imitated in brick contrasting with plastered walling.

REREDOS: A decorated screen or wall behind an altar, usually carved in stone or wood, but often a painting and, rarely, a tapestry.

REVEAL: Surface of wall lying between the frame of a window (or door) and the outer, or inner, wall face. If cut diagonally it is called a Splayed reveal.

RUSTICATED: Masonry cut in massive blocks with chamfered V-joints, or square section channelling, exaggerated to emphasize the lower portion of a classical building and give an impression of strength.

SASH WINDOW: One made of glass in two wooden frames, sliding vertically in a surround containing counterweights for ease of operation.

SPANDREL: Triangular space between arch and rectangular surround.

STOEP: Dutch and Afrikaans term for open or covered veranda.

STRING-COURSE: Horizontal moulding used for punctuation or for linking features together.

TETRASTYLE: Of a portico with four columns.

TIE-BEAM: A transverse horizontal beam connecting the lower ends of rafters and counteracting outward thrust.

TRACERY: Ornamental stone window divisions, or ribwork of various types, such as leaf-shaped foils, vertical mullions, arches and circles. Often filled with stained glass in Gothic architecture.

TRANSEPT: The transverse arm of a cruciform church forming spaces of equal height to the nave.

TRANSOM: A horizontal member over a door separating it from a fanlight; any horizontal dividing a large window into smaller sections, as a mullion does vertically.

TREFOIL: Three arcs arranged in a circle forming part of a Gothic window.

TUSCAN COLUMNS: A sturdy, simplified form of Roman Doric column, having a smooth shaft and a base, unlike the Greek Doric.

VAULT: Arched roof or ceiling of brick or stone or their imitation in wood or plaster.

VENETIAN WINDOW: Window or archway in three parts, the centre section arched and wider than the flat-topped side openings. Also known as the Palladian or Serlio's motif.

SELECT BIBLIOGRAPHY

UNPUBLISHED SOURCES

1. Herbert Baker and Frank Fleming: The firm's correspondence, engagement diaries and an account book, 1902-1954, presented by Mrs L H Fleming. 114 volumes. Housed in the Strange Collection of the Africana Museum, Johannesburg Public Library. S Store 72(68).

2. The Kendall and Earle gift, presented by Mr L Marriott Earle to the University of Cape Town Library, containing the business records of the chain of architects starting with Herbert Baker in 1892, finishing with Kendall and Earle in the late 1960s, the link throughout being F K Kendall. Housed in the Jagger Library, BC 206. Also in the Jagger Library are the papers of several of Baker's associates and contemporaries relevant to this study.

3. The Sir Herbert Baker Papers. Correspondence and memoranda, mainly concerning New Delhi, India, and including letters by Sir Edwin Lutyens, 1901-1945. Housed in the British Architectural Library, Royal Institute of British Architects, London. Two boxes. BaH/1-2.

4. The author's collection of original Herbert Baker papers and sketches; photocopies of original documents; photographs; slides; the author's notebooks, published cuttings, journals and books.

UNPUBLISHED DISSERTATIONS, THESES AND WORKS IN PROGRESS

GREIG, Doreen E. 'The Domestic Work of Sir Herbert Baker'. M Arch Thesis, University of the Witwatersrand, 1958. Mimeographed.

JOHNSON, B A. 'Domestic architecture at the Cape 1892-1912: Herbert Baker, his associates and his contemporaries'. Unpublished D Litt et Phil thesis, Unisa, 1987.

LANGHAM-CARTER, R R and RENNIE, John W L. 'Rhodes Memorial: An Account of the Building of the Memorial'. Cape Town: unpublished mimeographed, 1983.

BOOKS AND PAMPHLETS

AGAR-HAMILTON, J A I. *A Transvaal Jubilee*. London: SPCK, 1928.

ANDERSON, Dean. 'Architecture in Cape Town' in *City of Good Hope*, edited by A H Honikman. Cape Town: Timmins, 1966.

ASLET, Clive. *The Last Country Houses*. London: Yale University Press, 1982.

ASPINAL, John. *Port Lympne Wildlife Sanctuary and Gardens, Hythe, Kent.* (Guide). nd. (*c*1977.)

ATWELL, David and MCKEAN, Charles, *et al. Battle of the Styles: A Guide to Selected Buildings in London of the 1914-39 Period.* London: Royal Institute of British Architects, 1975.

AVERY ARCHITECTURAL LIBRARY, *An Index to Architectural Periodicals.* Boston (Mass), vol [?], pp 102-105.

BAKER, Arthur and BAKER, Herbert. *Plas Mawr, Conway, N Wales.* London: Farmer and Sons, 1888.

BAKER, Henry Edmeades. *Exhibition: The Athenaeum, Nov 1971, Sir Herbert Baker 1862-1946.* Mimeographed.

BAKER, Henry Edmeades. *Owletts.* London: The National Trust, 1969 (rev 1975).

BAKER, Herbert and TROTTER, Alys Fane. *Old Colonial Houses of the Cape of Good Hope.* London: Batsford, 1900. *See* also A F Trotter.

BAKER, Herbert. *Architecture and Personalities.* London: *Country Life,* 1944.

BAKER, Herbert. *Cecil Rhodes by his Architect.* Oxford: OUP, 1934.

BAKER, Herbert. 'Herbert Baker' in *T E Lawrence By His Friends.* Edited by A W Lawrence. London: Jonathan Cape, 1937. pp 248-256.

BAKER, Herbert. *The Church House: Its Art and Symbolism.* London: Church House, 1940.

BARRETT, A M. *Michaelhouse 1896-1968.* Balgowan: Michaelhouse Old Boys Club, 1969.

BARRY, Margaret and LAW, Nimmo. *Magnates and Mansions, Johannesburg 1886-1914.* Johannesburg: Lowry, 1985.

BIERMANN, B E. *Boukuns in Suid-Afrika.* Cape Town: Balkema, 1955.

BLOMFIELD, Reginald. *Memoirs of an Architect.* London: Macmillan, 1932.

BOLSMANN, Eric H. *The Mount Nelson.* Pretoria: Haum Publishers, 1978.

BURTON, Lawrence. *A Choice Over Their Heads: A Guide to Architecture and Design Since 1830.* London: Talisman Books, 1978.

COLE, David. *The Work of Sir Gilbert Scott.* London: Architectural Press, 1980.

CRAWFORD, Alan. *C R Ashbee: Architect, Designer and Romantic Socialist.* London: Yale University Press, 1985.

CROSS, Kathleen. *An Open Door: A Brief History of the Parish Church of Saint Michael and All Angels, Sunnyside, Pretoria, 1903-1978.* Pretoria: St Michael and All Angels Church, 1978.

CULLEN, Gordon. *The Concise Townscape.* London: Architectural Press, 1971.

CUMMING-GEORGE, L (Editor). *Architecture in South Africa.* Cape Town: Specialty Press, 1933, vol 1.

CUMMING-GEORGE, L (Editor). *Architecture in South Africa.* Cape Town: Specialty Press, 1934, vol 2.

CURREY, R F. *Rhodes University 1904-1970: A Chronicle.* Grahamstown: [The University], 1970.

CURREY, R F. *St Andrew's College, Grahamstown, 1858-1959.* Oxford: Blackwell, 1959

CURTIS, Lionel. *With Milner in South Africa.* Oxford: Blackwell, 1951.

DAVEY, Peter. *Arts and Crafts Architecture: The Search for Earthly Paradise.* London: Architectural Press, 1980.

DAY E H. *The Cathedral Church of St George.* London and Cape Town: South African Church Institute, 1939.

DE BOSDARI, C. *Cape Dutch Houses and Farms: Their Architecture and History, together with a note on the role of Cecil John Rhodes in their preservation.* Cape Town: Balkema, 1953.

DILET, Marc. 'Herbert Baker' in McMillan's *Directory of Architects.* London, 1983. pp 131-132.

DILKE, Christopher. *Dr Moberly's Mint-mark: A Study of Winchester College.* London: Heinemann, 1965.

FRANSEN, Hans. *Three Centuries of South African Art.* Johannesburg: Ad Donker, 1982.

FRANSEN, Hans and COOK, Mary Alexander. *The Old Buildings of the Cape.* Cape Town: Balkema, 1980. A survey and description of old buildings in the Western Province extending from Cape Town to Calvinia in the north and to Graaff-Reinet, Colesberg and Uitenhage in the east covering substantially the 18th and 19th century styles: Cape Dutch, Cape Regency, Georgian and Victorian.

FURLEY, H D (Editor). *The Register of Tonbridge School from 1861-1945 with a list of headmasters and second masters from the foundation of the school.* London: Rivingtons, 1951.

GIROUARD, Mark. *Sweetness and Light: The Queen Anne Movement 1860-1900.* Oxford: OUP, 1977.

GIROUARD, Mark. *The Victorian Country House.* London: Yale University Press, 1979.

GRADIDGE, Roderick. *Dream Houses: The Edwardian Ideal.* London: Constable, 1980.

GRAHAM, Cecil and BIRD, Flo. *Introducing Sir Herbert Baker.* Johannesburg: The Parktown and Westcliff Heritage Trust (Series no 13) nd. [c1986.]

GREIG, Doreen E. 'Baker, Sir Herbert' in *Dictionary of South African Biography.* Cape Town: Tafelberg Publishers for Human Sciences Research Council, 1968 – .

GREIG, Doreen E. *Herbert Baker in South Africa.* Cape Town: Purnell, 1970.

GREIG, Doreen E. *A Guide to Architecture in South Africa.* Cape Town: Howard Timmins, 1971.

GREIG, Doreen E. 'Baker, Sir Herbert' in *Contemporary Architects*, edited by Muriel Emanuel. London: Macmillan, 1980.

HARTDEGEN, Paddy. *Our Building Heritage: An Illustrated History.* Halfway House: Ryll's Publishing Company [for the National Development Fund for the building industry], 1988.

HERBERT, Gilbert. *Martienssen and the International Style: The Modern Movement in South African Architecture.* Cape Town: Balkema, 1975.

HEYWORTH, Peter. *The Oxford Guide to Oxford.* Oxford: OUP, 1981.

HITCHCOCK, Henry Russell. *Architecture: Nineteenth and Twentieth Centuries.* Harmondsworth: Penguin Books, 1968.

HOWIE, Duncan. *Contemporary Architecture in South Africa.* Fact paper 52. Pretoria: State Information Office, Feb 1958.

HUXLEY, Elspeth. *White Man's Country: Lord Delamere and the Making of Kenya.* London: Macmillan, 1935, vol 2 (1914-1931).

IRVING, Robert Grant. *Indian Summer: Lutyens, Baker and Imperial Delhi.* London: Yale University Press, 1981.

JACKSON, P. *The Historic Buildings of Harare: 1890-1940.* Harare: 1986.

JAY, Fay. *They Came to South Africa.* Cape Town: Howard Timmins, 1963. Chapter on Herbert Baker, pp 98-107.

JOURDAN, Philip. *Cecil Rhodes: His Private Life by His Private Secretary.* London: John Lane, The Bodley Head, 1911.

LANGHAM-CARTER, R R. *Old St George's: The Story of Cape Town's First Cathedral.* Cape Town: Balkema, 1977.

LANGHAM-CARTER, R R. *St Andrew's in the Oaks: A Hundred and Twenty Years.* Cape Town: np, 1977.

LANGHAM-CARTER, R R. *Under the Mountain: The Story of St Saviour's Claremont.* Cape Town: np, 1973.

LAWSON, K C. *Venture of Faith: The Story of St John's College, Johannesburg, 1898-1968.* Johannesburg: Council of St John's College, 1968.

LE ROUX, W J (Editor). *Groote Schuur: Residence of South Africa's Prime Minister.* Pretoria: Department of Information, 1970.

LITTLE, A I. *History of the City Club, Cape Town 1878-1938.* Cape Town: City Club, 1938.

LUTYENS, Mary. *Edwin Lutyens: By his Daughter.* London: John Murray 1980.

MACLEOD, Robert. *Style and Society: Architectural Ideology in Britain, 1835-1914.* London: RIBA Publications, 1971.

MACNAB, Roy. *The Story of South Africa House in Britain – The Changing Pattern.* Johannesburg: Jonathan Ball, 1983.

MALAN, Marais. *In Quest of Health: The South African Institute for Medical Research 1912-1973.* Johannesburg: Lowry Publishers, 1988.

MALCOLM, Dougal. 'Baker, Sir Herbert (1862-1946)' in *Dictionary of National Biography.* Oxford: OUP, vol 1941-1950, pp 41-43.

McINTIRE, Donald. *A Century of 'Bishops'.* Cape Town: Juta and Co. Ltd., 1950.

MEE, Arthur (Editor). *The King's England: Oxfordshire.* London: Hodder and Stoughton, 1942.

MEIRING, Hannes. *Pretoria 125.* Cape Town: Human and Rousseau, 1980.

MIDDLETON, G A T. *Modern Buildings, Their Planning, Construction and Equipment*. London: Caxton, 1910, vol 6.

MORRIS, Jan. *Stones of Empire: The Buildings of the Raj*. Oxford: OUP, 1983.

OBERHOLSTER, J J. *The Historical Monuments of South Africa*. Cape Town: National Monuments Council, 1972.

PARKTOWN and Westcliff Urban Walk, The. Johannesburg: City Council, 1982.

PERCY, Clayre and RIDLEY, Jane (Editors). *The letters of Edwin Lutyens to his wife Lady Emily*. London: Collins, 1985.

PEVSNER, Nikolaus (Founding editor). *The Buildings of England*. Harmondsworth: Penguin Books, 1951 – Series of 45 vols. Work of Herbert Baker included in County volumes for: Berkshire, Cambridgeshire, Essex, Hampshire and the Isle of Wight, Hertfordshire, West Kent and the Weald, North East and East Kent, Middlesex, Northumberland, Oxfordshire, Surrey, Worcestershire, Yorkshire, West Riding.

PICTON-SEYMOUR, Desirée. *Victorian Buildings in South Africa including Edwardian and Transvaal Republican Styles, 1850-1910*. Cape Town: Balkema, 1977. A survey of houses, churches, schools, public and commercial buildings with notes on the materials used, the architects concerned, the use of prefabricated ironmongery and the influence of European style.

PICTON-SEYMOUR, Desirée. *Historical Buildings in South Africa*. Cape Town: Struikhof, 1989.

PLOEGER, Jan. *Over-Vaal: The History of an Official Residence*. Pretoria: Transvaal Provincial Administration, 1963.

RADFORD, Dennis. *Villa Arcadia*. Johannesburg: The Parktown and Westcliff Heritage Trust (Series no 7) nd. (c 1986.)

REILLY, C H. *Representative British Architects of the Present Day*. London: Batsford, 1931. Sir Herbert Baker, pp 40-53.

RENCKEN, C R E. *Union Buildings: The First 75 Years*. Pretoria: Bureau for Information. 1989.

RENNIE, John. *The Buildings of Central Cape Town*, vol 2: catalogue. Cape Town: Cape Provincial Institute of Architects, 1978.

RENNIE, John W L and Langham-Carter, R R. *See* LANGHAM-CARTER.

RICHARDSON, Margaret. *Architects of the Arts and Crafts Movement*. London: Trefoil Books, 1983.

RIBA Drawings Collection.

SAW, Reginald. *The Bank of England 1694-1944*. London: Harrap, 1944.

SERVICE, Alastair. *The Architects of London and their Buildings from 1066 to the Present Day*. London: Architectural Press, 1979.

SHAW, Gerald. *Small Beginnings: The Cape Times 1876-1912*. Cape Town: Oxford University Press, 1975.

SIMONS, Phillida Brooke. *Cape Dutch Houses: A Concise Guide*. Cape Town: Struik, 1987.

STAMP, Gavin. *Silent Cities. Catalogue of an Exhibition of the Memorial and Cemetery Architecture of the Great War*. London: Royal Institute of British Architects, London, 1977.

STAMP, Gavin and AMERY, Colin. *Victorian Buildings of London 1837-1887: An Illustrated Guide*. London: Architectural Press, 1980.

ST PAUL'S Church, Woldingham (Surrey): A Guide for Visitors. nd.

TROTTER, Alys Fane. *Old Colonial Houses of the Cape of Good Hope*. With a chapter on 'The origin of old Cape architecture' by Herbert Baker, RIBA. London: Batsford, 1900.

VAN DER WAAL, Gerhard Mark. *From Mining Camp to Metropolis: The Buildings of Johannesburg 1886-1940*. Pretoria: Chris van Rensburg Publications, 1987.

VINEY, Graham. *Colonial Houses in South Africa*. Cape Town: Struik-Winchester, 1987.

WALLIS, J P R. *Fitz: The Story of Sir Percy Fitzpatrick*. London: Macmillan, 1955.

WHEELER, Sir Charles. *The Autobiography of Sir Charles Wheeler, Sculptor*. Feltham: Country Life Books, 1968.

WHITTICK, Arnold. *European Architecture in the Twentieth Century*. Aylesbury: Leonard Hill, 1974.

WHITTICK, Arnold. *War Memorials*. London: Country Life, 1946.

WRIGHT, Harrison M (Editor). *Sir James Rose Innes Selected Correspondence 1884-1902*. Cape Town: Van Riebeeck Society, 1972.

WYBERGH, W. *The Building Stones of the Union of South Africa*. Pretoria: The Government Printer, 1932.

ARTICLES IN PERIODICALS

ADAMS, A M. 'A South African Country House: Arcadia, Johannesburg'. *Country Life*, vol 51 (Jan 21) 1922. pp 93-94.

'Allied Societies: the Cape Institute of Architects'. *Journal of the Royal Institute of British Architects*, vol 18 (Oct) 1911. p 776. Exhibition of designs submitted by Herbert Baker Scholarship candidates, Cape Town, 25 Sept 1911.

ALWIN, G Maxwell. 'An imperial architect'. (Review of *Architecture and Personalities) The Builder*, vol 167 (Nov 17) 1944. p 307.

ANDREWS, Martin. 'Port Lympne, near Hythe, Kent'. *Landscape Design*, no 143, June 1983. pp 31-33.

'Annual Banquet: presentation of the Royal Gold Medal to Sir Herbert Baker, ARA, The'. *Journal of the Royal Institute of British Architects*, vol 34 (July 16) 1927. pp 591-599.

'Architectural and building interests in South Africa'. Obituary of Francis Masey. *Architects' and Builders' Journal*, vol 36 (Nov 20) 1912. p 557.

'Architecture at the Royal Academy'. *Architect and Building News*, vol 121 (May 3) 1929. p 573. Illus of Chiswick Bridge; *see* also pp 574, 576.

ARMITAGE, Edward. 'Joseph Armitage, craftsman: 1880-1945'. *Thirties Society Journal*, no 3, 1982. pp 25-30.

ARNOLD, G M and BAKER, H. 'The old rectory, Northfleet'. *Archaeologia Cantiana*, vol 20, 1893. pp 71-75.

ATKINSON, G Anthony. 'British architects in the tropics'. *Architectural Association Journal*, vol [?] (May) 1953. pp [?].

BAGENAL, Hope, 'The acoustics of the new legislative chamber at Delhi'. *Architect and Building News*, vol 121 (June 28) 1929. pp 851-853. 'African studies'. *Architectural Association Journal*, vol [?] (April) 1954. pp [?].

'Baker the butcher?'. Report of talk by Roderick Gradidge at the Architectural Association on 26 Jan 1978. *Building Design*. 17 Feb 1978. p 42.

'Baker and Masey are architects of Rhodes Building'. *Architectural Review*, vol 14 (July-Dec) 1903. pp 128-131.

'Baker and Masey are architects of Rust en Vrede, Muizenberg, Cape'. *Architectural Review*, vol 17 (May) 1905. pp 214-221.

BAKER, Herbert. 'The artistic side of Mr Rhodes'. A letter in *The Times* (Cape Town), 7 Oct 1902. 'New colonial architecture'. *The Star* (Johannesburg) 6 May 1905. A paper read to Transvaal Institute of Architects on 2 May 1905. 'The architectural needs of South Africa'. *The State* (Johannesburg) 1 May 1909. pp 512-524. 'Plea for English Gothic'. A letter in *African Architect*, vol 1 (July) 1911. p 36. 'The problem of style'. Letter. *The Times* (London), 3 Oct 1912. Reprinted in *Architecture and Personalities*, 1944. 'The New London'. Letter. *The Times* (London), 17 Nov 1916. Also Leader article. Reprinted in *Architects' Journal*, vol 44 (Nov 29) 1916. p 251. 'The New Delhi'. *Journal of the Royal Society of Arts*, vol 74 (July) 1926. pp 772-793. 'The Government Offices of Pretoria and the New Delhi'. *Journal of the Royal Institute of British Architects*, vol 35 (Dec) 1927. pp 63-77. 'Architectural design: symbolism in stone and marble'. *The Times* (London) 'India Number' 18 Feb 1930. 'Notes on my American visit'. *South African Architectural Record*, vol [?] (June) 1930. pp [?]. 'History of the English house'. Letter on houses in Kent and reference to Nathanial Lloyd's letter. *Journal of the Royal Institute of British Architects*, vol 39 (Feb 6) 1932. p 274. 'Modernism by evolution'. Letter. *Journal of the Royal Institute of British Architects*, vol 40 (Nov 11) 1933. p 87. 'Symbolic constellation of the Empire'. *United Empire* (London), 28 (Oct) 1937. pp 561-564. 'Architecture and town planning: a lecture by Herbert Baker delivered on July 11, 1911, in the hall of the Normal College, Pretoria'. *South African Architectural Record*, vol 24 (March) 1939. pp 92-105. 'The story of the Union Buildings'. *South Africa* (London) no 207 (Aug 23) 1941. pp 122-123. 'Church building in Africa'. *Builder*, vol 166 (April 7) 1944. pp 274-276 and (April 24) pp 293-295.

'Bank of England. The plan before and after the alterations, The'. *Journal of the Royal Institute of British Architects*, vol 39 1931-32. p 603.

'Barclay's Bank, Cape Town'. *Builder*, vol 136 (May 5) 1929. p 809.

BIERMANN, B E. Review of *Herbert Baker in South Africa* by Doreen Greig. *Plan*, vol 56 (Oct) 1971. pp 25, 43.

BINNEY, Marcus. 'Attributes of the eternal: Sir Herbert Baker's Union Buildings, Pretoria'. *Country Life*, vol 171, no 4410, (Feb 25) 1982. pp 466-468.

'Bishop Jacob Memorial Church, Ilford, The'. *Architectural Review*, vol 62 (July) 1927. p 8.

'Bishop Jacob Memorial Church, Ilford, The'. *Architects' Journal*, vol 60 (Nov 12) 1924. pp 718-727, 736-737.

BRAITHWAITE, J S. 'Christian Science Churches: their plan requirements as exemplified in the latest London building'. *Architects' Journal*, vol 74 (16 Dec) 1931. pp 806-809.

'British architects' conference, London, 20-25 June 1927: the Annual Banquet, Presentation of the Royal Gold Medal to Sir Herbert Baker, ARA '. *Journal of the Royal Institute of British Architects*, vol 34 (July) 1927. pp 591-600.

'Buildings at Cape Town'. *Architectural Review*, vol 30 (July-Dec) 1911. pp 217-221. National Mutual Life Association of Australia and the Marks Building. Also pp 220-221 'A house in Cape Town' by Francis Masey.

BURDETT, Osbert. 'Harrow school War Memorial'. *Architects' Journal*, vol 64 (July 21) 1926. pp 74-75.

BYRON, Robert. 'New Delhi'. *Architectural Review*, vol 69 (Jan) 1931. pp 1-30. 'New Delhi, V: The architecture of Sir Herbert Baker'. *Country Life*, vol 70 (July 4) 1931. pp 12-19.

'Cape Town and South African architecture'. *Architects' and Builders' Journal*, vol 35 (June 26) 1912. South African export supplement, pp 21-26.

'Chatham House, St James's Square, SW: the lecture hall'. *Builder,* vol 138 (Feb 28) 1930. p 432.

'Chiswick Bridge'. *Architect and Building News*, vol 121 (May 3) 1929. p 373.

CHIPKIN, Clive M. 'New Delhi'. *South African Architectural Record*, vol 43 (Nov) 1958. pp 21-28.

'Church House, Westminster, SW1, designed by Sir Herbert Baker and A T Scott'. *Architects' Journal*, vol 92 (July 4) 1940. pp 7-13.

COLLINGWOOD, Frances. 'Sir Herbert Baker: a centenary tribute'. *Builder*, vol 202 (June 8) 1962. pp 1181-1182.

'Cubley Village, Penistone, Yorkshire'. *Architectural Review*, vol 51, (Jan-June) 1922. pp 39-42.

DAVEY, Peter. 'Profession or art?'. *Architectural Review*, vol [?] (July) 1989, pp 59-66.

DAWBER, Guy. 'The late Sir Ernest George RA'. *The Builder*, vol 123, 1922. p 903.

'Delhi'. *Town Planning Review*, vol 3 (Oct) 1912. pp 167-168.

DELLATOLA, Lesley. 'Westminster Estate'. *South African Panorama*, vol [?], (Feb) 1973. pp 28-31.

DENNISON, Baird. 'Architecture at the Royal Academy'. *Architects' Journal*, vol 75 (May 4) 1932. pp 583-586.

'Downing College, Cambridge'. *Builder*, vol 138 (May 9) 1930. p 901.

'Downing College, Cambridge. Sir Herbert Baker, ARA, Architect'. *Architects' Journal*, vol 71 (May 21) 1930. p 801.

EARLE, L Marriott. 'The works of Herbert Baker'. *Architect and Builder* (South Africa), vol 17 (Oct) 1967. pp 22-27.

EMANUEL, Frank L. 'British and Dutch architecture in South Africa'. *Architectural Review*, vol 7 (Jan-June) 1900. Part 1: Cape Town and Kimberley, pp 2-8. Part 2: Johannesburg, Heidelburg, Pietermaritzburg, Durban, East London, Port Elizabeth. pp 50-58.

E.R. Review of *Old Colonial Houses of the Cape of Good Hope* by Alys Fane Trotter and Herbert Baker. *Architectural Review*, vol 7 (Jan-June) 1900. pp 142-44.

GARDINER, Nancy. 'A stately home'. *South African Garden and Home*, vol [?] , pp 44-50.

'Glyn Mills Bank'. *Architects' Journal*, vol 79 (Jan 11) 1934. pp 81-86.

'Government offices of Pretoria and New Delhi, The'. *Builder*, vol 133 (Nov 25) 1927. pp 809-810, 813-816.

GREIG, Doreen E. 'Symbol of unity'. *South African Panorama*. Feb 1971. 'Herbert Baker: Union Buildings, Pretoria (1910)' and 'A biographical history: Sir Herbert Baker'. *UIA International Architect*, no 8, 1985. pp 6-7, 58.

'Groote Schuur'. *Architectural Review*, vol 30 (Sept) 1911. pp 112-116.

'Harrow School Memorial Buildings'. *Architect and Building News*, vol 116 (Aug 20) 1926. pp 211-215.

HARVEY, William. 'Some minor problems of a great building: Imperial Delhi Secretariats'. *Builder*, vol 122 (Jan 6) 1922. pp 43-44.

'Herbert Baker and his work'. *Architect Builder and Engineer* (South Africa), vol [?] (August) 1918. pp 12-19.

'Herbert Baker elected ARA'. *Builder*, vol [?] (Dec 8) 1922. p 860.

'The Herbert Baker Scholarship'. *Journal of the Royal Institute of British Architects*, vol 18 (Oct) 1911. pp 773-774.

'House in California'. *Builder*, vol 136 (June 21) 1929. p 1117.

'House in California'. *Architect and Building News*, vol 121 (June 28) 1929. p 897.

HOWARTH, David. 'A home for the spirit'. *Country Life*, vol 173 (June 23) 1983. pp 1740-1741, 1743.

HUSSEY, Christopher. 'London House, a hall of residence for dominion students in London'. *Country Life*, vol 97 (June 22) 1945. pp 1080-1083.

'India House'. *Architect and Building News*, vol 119 (March 16) 1928. pp 385-388.

'India House, Aldwych'. *Architect and Building News*, vol 119 (May 18) p 728.

'India House'. *Architect and Building News*, vol 123 (April 25) 1930. pp 522-523, 526-533.

'India House, Aldwych'. *Architects' Journal*, vol 71 (May 7) 1930. p 727.

'India House, Aldwych'. *Architectural Review*, vol 68 (Sept) 1930. pp 127-129. Also p 26, designs for marble floor, India House.

'India House, Aldwych'. *Builder*, vol 138 (May 9) 1930. p 900.

'India House, Aldwych, W.C.'. *Builder*, vol 139 (Oct 31) 1930. pp 728, 737-742.

'Johannesburg'. *Architect, Builder and Engineer* (South Africa), vol [?] (Aug) 1918. pp 16-19.

KEATH, Michael. 'Visions of greatness: Herbert Baker's imperial idealism and the Union Buildings'. *Architecture South Africa*, (May-June) 1989, pp 35-36.

KNAPP-FISHER, A B. 'Sir Herbert Baker'. *Architects' Journal*, vol 65 (Feb 16) 1927. pp 251-262. Review of *Architecture and Personalities* by Herbert Baker. *Journal of the Royal Institute of British Architects*, vol 5 [?] (Jan) 1945. p 83.

LANCHESTER, H V. 'Architecture and architects in India'. Lecture with discussion. *Journal of the Royal Institute of British Architects*, vol 30 (March 24) 1923. pp 293-308.

'Late Sir Ernest George, RA, The'. *Builder*, vol [?] (Dec 15) 1922, p 903.

'Late Sir Herbert Baker, RA, The'. *Architect and Building News*, vol 185 (Feb 15) 1946. p 95.

LEIGHTON, J M. 'South Africa House in the making'. *Lantern* (Pretoria), vol 34, (April) 1984. pp 3 [?].

'London House, Guildford St, W.C.'. *Architect and Building News*, vol 152 (Dec 10) 1937. pp 308-312.

'Martins Bank, Lombard Street, E.C., designed by Sir Herbert Baker'. *Architects' Journal*, vol 73 (March 11) 1931. pp 373-377.

'Martins Bank, Lombard Street, London'. *Architect and Building News*, vol 124 (Nov 28) 1930. pp 715-721.

McWILLIAMS, H H. 'Architecture at the Cape'. *Architectural Review*, vol 68 (July) 1930. Part 1: 'In the Country' pp 4-8; Part 2: 'In the Towns' pp 107-112.

'Memories of Sir Edwin Lutyens: nostalgia at the AA'. *Builder*, vol 116 (Feb 13) 1959. pp 318-319. Reminiscences by J Brandon-Jones, C Hussey, H Bagenal, R F Jordan, H Farquharson, O P Milne, N Hannen, Sir H Worthington, W C Green, A G Shoosmith, H A N Medd, H A Hall, and A S G Butler.

'Merchant Taylors Hall, Threadneedle Street, EC: the Cloister'. *Builder*, vol 138 (Feb 28) 1930. p 431.

'Messrs Glyn Mills Bank new headquarters, London'. *Architect and Building News*, vol 135 (Sept 22) 1933. pp 325-329.

'Modernism in architecture'. *Journal of the Royal Institute of British Architects*, vol 35 (June 9) 1928. Contribution by Sir Herbert Baker. pp 521-522.

MORTLOCK, C B. 'The new Church House, Westminster'. *Country Life*, vol 88 (July 13) 1940. pp 30-33.

'Mr Abe Bailey's house at Muizenberg: Rust en Vrede'. *South African Architect and Builder*, vol 1 (Sept) 1904. pp 214-217.

'Mr Herbert Baker's architectural scholarship for South African architects'. *Journal of the Royal Institute of British Architects*, vol 18 (Jan) 1911. pp 212-213.

'New buildings at Downing College, Cambridge'. *Architect and Building News*, vol 130 (June 24) 1932. pp 424-427.

'The New Church House, Westminster'. *Architect and Building News*, vol 137 (Jan 26) 1934. p 119.

'The New Delhi'. *Architect and Building News*, vol 115 (May 21) 1926. pp 464-470.

'The New Delhi'. *Builder*, vol 103 (Oct 18) 1912. p 429.

'The New Delhi. Sir Herbert Baker, architect'. *Architects' Journal*, vol 73 (Jan 21) 1931. p 21. Also (Feb 11) p 232.

'The New Delhi: the work of Sir Edwin Lutyens and Sir Herbert Baker'. *Architectural Review*, vol 60 (Dec) 1926. pp 216-225.

'New Government Buildings, Delhi'. *Builder*, vol 107 (Sept 25) 1914. p 296.

'The new Grey College: architects grumble'. *The Times* (Cape Town) late [?] Aug 1905. Anonymous complaint regarding competition for work.

'The new South Africa House'. *Architect and Building News*, vol 125 (Jan 2) 1931. pp 4-5.

'New terrace and terrace approach at Harrow School'. *Architect and Building News*, vol 122 (Sept 6) 1929. p 302.

'The new Union Government Buildings, Pretoria'. *Architects' and Builders' Journal*, vol 33 (Jan 11) 1911. pp 31-32.

'Ninth Church of Christ Scientist'. *Architect and Building News*, vol 123 (March 21) 1930. pp 372, 377-381.

'Ninth Church of Christ Scientist, Westminster'. *Builder*, vol 138 (March 14) 1930. pp 512, 522-528.

'Ninth Church of Christ Scientist, London'. *Builder*, vol 138 (May 9) 1930. p 899.

'The Ninth Church of Christ Scientist, Westminster, Sir Herbert Baker, architect'. *Architects' Journal*, vol 73 (Jan 14) 1931. p 61.

'Obituary: Arthur Baker'. *Journal of the Royal Institute of British Architects*, vol 4, series 3, 1897. p 360.

'Port Lympne-1, Kent: the residence of Sir Philip Sassoon'. *Country Life*, vol 53 (May 19) 1923. pp 678-684.

'Proposal for reconstruction of the Bank of England'. *Architect*, vol 108 (July 28) 1922. p 69.

RADFORD, D. 'Baker, Lutyens and the Union Buildings'. *South African Journal of Cultural and Art History*, vol 2, no 1 (Jan), 1988. pp 62-69. 'Baker and the mining houses – an initial investigation into this aspect of his architecture'. *South African Journal of Cultural and Art History*, vol 3, no 3 (July), 1989. pp 257-267.

'The rebuilding of the Bank of England'. *Architects' Journal*, vol 56 (Aug 2) 1922. pp 146-151.

'Recent domestic architecture: Port Lympne: Sir Philip Sassoon's house at Port Lympne'. *Architectural Review*, vol 52 (July-Dec) 1922. pp 90-95.

'The reconstruction of the Bank of England: old features to be retained in rebuilding'. *Architects' Journal*, vol 61 (May 6) 1925. pp 706-715.

'Reconstruction of the Bank of England'. *Architect*, vol 113

(May 15) 1925. pp 60, 353-357.

'Reminiscences on Sir Edwin Lutyens'. *Architectural Association Journal*, vol 74 (March) 1959. pp 226-236. Reminiscences by J Brandon-Jones, C Hussey, H Bagenal, R F Jordan, H Farquharson, O P Milne, N Hannen, Sir H Worthington, W C Green, A G Shoosmith, H A N Medd, H A Hall, and A S G Butler.

'The Rhodes Building: a grand structure'. *The Star* (Johannesburg) 4 Oct 1902.

'Rhodes House, Oxford'. *Architect and Building News*, vol 121 (May 10) 1929. pp 605-611.

'Rhodes House, Oxford'. *Builder*, vol 136 (May 17) 1929. pp 908, 911.

'Rhodes Memorial, Cape Town, South Africa'. *Architect*, vol 102 (Nov 28) 1919. p 322.

'Rhodes' University College, Grahamstown: the accepted design'. *African Architect*, vol 1 (Sept 1) 1911. pp 79-81. Fine perspective views.

RICHARDSON, A E. 'Obituary: Sir Herbert Baker'. *Journal of the Royal Institute of British Architects*, vol 53 (March) 1946. pp 189-190.

'Royal Academy, The' (The Hall, Rhodes House, Oxford). *Architect and Building News*, vol 119 (May 11) 1928. pp 682-683.

'Royal Academy Summer Exhibition' (Gairdner Memorial Church, Cairo). *Architect and Building News*, vol 134 (May 5) 1933. p 128.

'Royal Empire Society New Headquarters, The'. *Architect and Building News*, vol 148 (Oct 23) 1936. pp 98-105.

'Rust en Vrede, Muizenberg'. *Architectural Review*, vol 17 (Jan-June) 1905. p 215.

'Secretariats, New Delhi'. *Architectural Review*, vol 52 (July-Dec) 1922. pp 19-27.

'Sir Herbert Baker, ARA'. *Architect and Building News*, vol 117, (Feb 18) 1927. p 305. RIBA Gold Medal for 1927.

'Sir Herbert Baker: a memoir by a friend'. *Builder*, vol 170 (Feb 15) 1946. pp 158-159.

'Sir Herbert Baker in memoriam 1862-1945'. *South African Architectural Record*, vol 31 (July) 1946. pp 161-183.

'Sir Philip Sassoon's house at Lympne'. *Architectural Review*, vol 52 (Oct) 1922. pp 90-95.

SOLOMON, J M. 'The Union Buildings and their Architect'. *The State*, vol [?] (July) 1910. pp [?]. 'Reverence in architecture'. *African Architect*, vol 1 (Sept) 1911. pp 90-91. Prize essay for Herbert Baker Scholarship.

'South Africa House: a neighbourly building'. *The Times* (London) 22 June 1933. Article by architectural correspondent on day of opening by the King, with discussion on its symbolism.

'South Africa House'. *Architect and Building News*, vol 134 (June 30) 1933. pp 369-372.

'South Africa House, London'. *Architects' Journal*, vol 77 (June 29) 1933. pp 861-863 and supplement.

'South African College'. *The Star* (Johannesburg) 6 Oct 1902. Report on Commemoration Day; Future of the College; Great scheme of expansion; an appeal to the public; interesting addresses.

'South African College extension: the Engineering School'. *Cape Argus*, 10 April 1903.

'South African National Memorial, Delville Wood'. *Architect and Building News*, vol 116 (Oct 15) 1926. p 436.

'South African War Memorial, Delville Wood'. *Architect*, vol 111 (May 2) 1924. pp 319-320.

'South African Reserve Bank, Pretoria'. *Builder*, vol 134 (May 18) 1928. p 849.

'South African Reserve Bank, Pretoria'. *Architect and Building News*, vol 119 (May 11) 1928. p 682.

'St Andrew's Church, Ilford'. *Builder*, vol 132 (April 29) 1927. p 685.

'St Mary's Cathedral, Johannesburg'. *Architectural Review*, vol 68 (July) 1930. pp 21-23.

TROTTER, Alys Fane, 'The origin of the Cape gable'. *Architectural Review*, vol 15 (Jan-June) 1904. pp 35-36.

'Two banks in Lombard Street, London' (Martins Bank and Glyn Mills Bank). *Architects' Journal*, vol 75 (May 4) 1932. p 586.

'Union Buildings, Pretoria'. *Architect*, vol 112, plates following: July 25, p 58; Oct 10, p 224; Oct 31, p 276; Nov 28, p 340; Dec 12, p 372. 1924.

'Union Buildings, Pretoria'. *Builder*, vol 133 (July 1) 1927. pp 14-18.

'Union Buildings, Pretoria'. *Architect*, vol 108 (Dec 22) 1922. p 450.

'Union Buildings, Pretoria, South Africa'. *Architectural Review*, vol 55 (June) 1924. pp 246-7.

PICTURE ACKNOWLEDGEMENTS

Union Buildings, Pretoria, construction scaffolding on dome. Author's collection, origin unknown. Page vi.

Charles H Thompson's portrait of Sir Herbert Baker. Permanent Collection, South African National Gallery, Cape Town. Frontispiece.

Owletts, Cobham, Kent. Watercolour sketch by Baker. Jagger Library Manuscripts Archive, University of Cape Town Libraries (JLMA). Page 2.

Pulpit and details. Drawings by Baker. JLMA. Page 5.

Llanidlow church. Drawing of roof details by Baker. JLMA. Page 6.

Cross in Derwen churchyard, Denbighshire, North Wales. Pencil drawing by Herbert Baker, 1884. Staircase in Restoration House, Rochester. Drawing by Baker. Chimney piece, Plas Mawr, Conway, North Wales, by Robert Wynne, 1588. Ink drawing by Herbert Baker, 1887. JLMA. Page 7.

Church of St Padarn, Llanberis, Caernarvonshire, North Wales. Ink drawing by Herbert Baker, circa 1886. JLMA. Page 8.

The young Herbert Baker. Author's Collection. Page 9.

House for Sir Henry Cunningham, Edwin Lutyens, sepia ink and wash drawing by Herbert Baker. Cross at Rochester. Drawing by Baker. Design for a house at Southend, Herbert Baker, circa 1890. JLMA. Page 13.

Groote Schuur, Rondebosch. Watercolour by unknown artist as it looked in 1838. Courtesy of the State President, Mr F W de Klerk. The painting hangs in Groote Schuur. *Groote Schuur today, view of rear.* Author. Page 20.

Observatory to be erected on the Government Building, Pretoria. Herbert Baker, June 1892. The earliest known drawing by Baker in South Africa. JLMA. Page 22.

House for J B Moffat, Kenilworth, 1892. Demolished. JLMA. Page 24.

Hopetown House for Alex Bell. JLMA. Page 25.

Groote Schuur, Rondebosch, for the Rt Hon C J Rhodes. Elevations, circa 1897. Drawing Collection, Department of Architecture, University of the Witwatersrand (DCDA). Page 26.

Groote Schuur, Rondebosch, kitchen gable details. November 1897. DCDA. Page 28.

Groote Schuur, Rondebosch, ground floor plan. DCDA. Page 29.

Church of St Andrew, Newlands (St Andrew's in the Oaks). Plan, after Greig. Author. Page 31.

Church of St Andrew, Newlands, 1894. East-end gables. Author. Page 32.

Church of St Andrew, Newlands. West gable. Author. Page 33.

Church of St Andrew, Newlands. Nave interior. Author. Page 34.

Karatara. House for J Rose Innes, Kenilworth, 1894. Author. Page 35.

Church of St Barnabas, Tamboerskloof. Drawing of first design, 22 October 1896. JLMA. Page 36.

Church of St Barnabas, Tamboerskloof. Entrance elevation facing Kloof Road. Author. Page 37.

Church of St Barnabas, Tamboerskloof. Elevations, October 1897. JLMA. Page 38.

St Barnabas, drawing of church as built, October 1897, stamped 'approved' by the City Engineer of Cape Town, 29 January 1898. JLMA. Page 39.

Languedoc, rectory. Languedoc village, workers' housing, recently restored. Author. Page 40.

Languedoc, church-cum-schoolhouse, circa 1898. Author. Page 41.

Church of St Barnabas, Tamboerskloof, ground plan, working drawing. Approved 29 January 1898. JLMA. Page 43.

Languedoc, church-cum-schoolhouse, gable end, circa 1898. Author. Page 44.

City Club, facing Queen Victoria Street, Cape Town. Peter van Niekerk. Page 45.

Groote Schuur, Rondebosch, end gable. Author. Page 48.

Groote Schuur, Rondebosch, gargoyle detail. Kelvin Grove, Newlands, main entrance. Author. Page 49.

City Club, Queen Victoria Street, Cape Town. Gable detail. Author. Page 50.

Trovato, Wynberg, side front. Author. Page 52.

Cathedral of St George, Cape Town, the apse as built. Author. *St George, first design, north elevation.* JLMA. *St George, perspective view from the north-east.* JLMA. Page 55.

Cathedral of St George, Cape Town, the nave. Peter van Niekerk. Page 56.

Cathedral of St George, Cape Town, foundation stone, 22 August 1901. Author. Page 57.

Cathedral of St George, Cape Town, final ground plan. JLMA. Page 58.

National Mutual Life of Australasia, Church Square, Cape Town, elevation. JLMA. Page 59.

Church of St Philip, Chapel Street, Woodstock, apse end. Author. Page 60.

Church of St Philip, Chapel Street, Woodstock, interior. Author. Page 61.

Church of St Saviour, Claremont, first design. Shown are the elevations, roof plan, ground plan and cross-sections. JLMA. Page 63.

National Mutual Life of Australasia, Church Square, Cape Town, drawings by Baker and Masey. DCDA. Page 64.

Church of St Saviour, Claremont, interior of Baker's side chapel. Peter van Niekerk. Page 65.

237

INDEX

246